Russia and the Classics

I0593009

CLASSICAL DIASPORA

Russia and the Classics

POETRY'S FOREIGN MUSE

Zara Martirosova Torlone

Duckworth

First published in 2009 by
Gerald Duckworth & Co. Ltd.
90-93 Cowcross Street, London EC1M 6BF
Tel: 020 7490 7300
Fax: 020 7490 0080
info@duckworth-publishers.co.uk
www.ducknet.co.uk

© 2009 by Zara Martirosova Torlone

All rights reserved. No part of this publication
may be reproduced, stored in a retrieval system, or
transmitted, in any form or by any means, electronic,
mechanical, photocopying, recording or otherwise,
without the prior permission of the publisher.

A catalogue record for this book is available
from the British Library

ISBN 978 0 7156 3717 3

Typeset by Ray Davies

Contents

Preface and Acknowledgements   vii
Note on Translation and Transliteration   ix
Introduction   1

1. 'Russian Antiquity'   7
    Classical tradition or reception studies: where does Russia   8
    fit?
    East or West?   10
    From Byzantium to the 'Third Rome'   13
    Peter the Great and the classics   14
2. From Russian Classicism to Alexander Pushkin   23
    Antiokh Kantemir and Vasilii Trediakovskii   24
    Mikhailo Lomonosov and Alexander Sumarokov   26
    Gavriil Derzhavin   34
    Alexander Sergeevich Pushkin: the *vates*   36
3. *Poetae Docti* and their Discontents   55
    The twentieth century   55
    Innokentii Annenskii: a singer of sorrow   58
    Viacheslav Ivanov: between two worlds   61
    Russian neoclassical tragedy and the 'Slavonic Renaissance'   74
4. Marina Tsvetaeva's Tragic Heroines   92
    'Theseus': trilogy interrupted   96
5. Osip Mandelshtam: 'Yearning for World Culture'   118
    Greek dreams   121
    'I was born in Rome and Rome returned to me'   132
6. Joseph Brodsky: 'The Uncommon Visage'   153
    The anxiety of influence   153
    Mythological inversions   156
    Wrestling with Empire   174
    Epilogue to *Exegi monumentum*   186

Post Aetatem Nostram: A Brief Postscript and a Very Short   197
    Introduction
Notes   199
Bibliography   235
Index   250

book; my brother Sergei who shared with me the angst of growing up in the Soviet Union: 'slava Bogu, chto ia na zemle bez otchizny ostalsia'; my sister-in-law Lisa Koch for her ability to brighten my most difficult days. And finally and most importantly I am thankful to my daughter Christina for the infinite joy and meaning she has given my life.

Preface and Acknowledgements

This book is what the Greeks referred to as *nostos* and the Russians call a 'vozvrashchenie na krugi svoia': a homecoming. In 1985, when I started my journey on the road of classics at Moscow University, I would not have thought that a book like this could ever be published. Classics at that time in Russia was an esoteric and strictly philological discipline with little connection to the poetry of the modern age. Poetry, however, was everywhere: in the much circulated and crudely bound volumes of the *samizdat*, in private diaries, in the hushed late-night conversations in crowded kitchens. This book is homage to two guiding lights that brightened my way in those uncertain but memorable years.

Numerous people helped me to bring this project to fruition. I owe a debt of gratitude to them all: to James Zetzel for showing me what it means to be a true scholar and teacher; to Susanna Zetzel for her unfailing support and encouragement; to Michael Wachtel for his astute criticism and generosity at every stage of this project; to Sarah Brown, the editor of the series *Classical Diaspora*, for her numerous careful readings of the whole manuscript; to my colleagues at Miami University, Vitaly Chernetsky, Judith de Luce, Denise McCoskey, Stephen Nimis, Stephen Norris, Peter Rose, Steven Tuck, for their open-mindedness and unceasing help; to the kind and thorough readers of the earlier versions, Pamela Davidson, Sibelan Forrester, Craig Kallendorf, Lev Loseff, and Margaret Ziolkowski; to Karen Dawisha, the director of the Havighurst Center for Russian and Post-Soviet Studies at Miami University, whose friendship and kind support of many years inspired and facilitated this study; to Carol Hershenson for her tireless efforts to make my prose sound more English; to Paul Christesen for his advice and friendship; to Deborah Blake at Duckworth for her help and professionalism; to my students at Miami University whose interest in Russian reception of the classics has helped this book along its way. I also want to thank the Office for the Advancement of Research and Scholarship at Miami University, which provided me with two summer fellowships to complete this project, and Loeb Classical Library Foundation at Harvard University for their generous grant that helped to prepare this manuscript for publication.

On a more personal note I want to thank my husband Mark Torlone – always my first, and best, reader – for his love, patience, and unmatched sense of humour: *tu mihi curarum requies*; my parents, Dr Sergey Martirosov and Samvelina Pogosova, who are the main inspiration behind this

for
MY PARENTS

and
DIS MANIBUS OF JOSEPH BRODSKY

I chasovoi na fone neba
vpolne napominaet Feba.
Kuda zabrel ty, Apollon!

And sentry seen against the sky
Resembles Phoebus well enough.
Where have you wandered to, Apollo!

Joseph Brodsky, 24.5.65 KPZ

Note on Translation and Transliteration

Unless otherwise noted, all translations in this book are mine. The translations that are not my own are reprinted with permission and full acknowledgement of the source. For most of the poetic texts I cite both the Russian original and the English translation since I have written this study for both types of readers: those who know Russian and those who do not. For the convenience and satisfaction of the readers who can read the original I cite Russian even when I do not directly analyze the Russian text. However, in a few cases I cite only the English version when I believe that it is easier to follow the argument without the lengthy Russian quotation.

In transliterating Russian texts, I have used the Library of Congress system without diacritics and ligatures and with some modifications. Although for the most part I used -*skii* in proper names, some well-known proper names are given in their most commonly used forms; e.g. Brodsky, not Brodskii. The same applies to Mandelshtam, not Mandel'shtam. The spelling Mandel'shtam is used, however, in book and article titles transliterated from the Russian in the bibliography. Some Russian names in the text modify the system further by using standard English forms: i.e. Alexander, not Aleksandr, and Peter, not Petr. In citing bibliographical works in English I have retained the spelling and transliteration as it appeared in print.

Introduction

No one absorbs the past as thoroughly as a poet, if only out of fear of inventing the already invented. (This is why, by the way, a poet is often regarded as being 'ahead of his time', which keeps itself busy rehashing clichés). So no matter what a poet may plan to say, at the moment of speech he always knows that he inherits the subject.

Joseph Brodsky[1]

In the fall of 2006, when I was looking for a publisher for this manuscript, I approached an editor at the American Association for the Advancement of Slavic Studies convention, who was very candid in his scepticism about a book on poetry. He told me that he was not sure which sells worse: books of poetry or books about it. I had by then lived and taught in the United States for more than fifteen years, so this statement did not come as a cultural shock. In his 1998 book on Alexander Pushkin, David Bethea stated that 'poetry as we know it, is dying'.[2] While I agree with him overall, especially when I try to rekindle the interest of students in poetic expression, this truth is hard to accept for anyone who grew up in the Soviet Union. To persist, then, in writing about poetry, despite depressing if realistic predictions of its demise, calls for what the poets of Roman antiquity referred to as a *recusatio*: a sort of disclaimer.

'Poetry places language in a state of emergence', stated Gaston Bachelard,[3] and if one is interested in the role of classical tradition in the formation of Russian literary identity, poetry is not *a* place but *the* place to start. In Russia poetry, at least before the collapse of the USSR, has never been merely poetry. Since 1730 (the year Antioch Kantemir's verse began to circulate widely) the most influential forms in Russian literature have been poetic ones.[4] Poetry on Russian soil was (and to a small portion of the population probably still is) more important and informative than the daily news is in the West: it encompasses social struggles, political debates and cultural awakenings. It reflects and responds, in Simon Schama's words, to every 'cultural craving and cultural framing'. Poetry is in short an exact mirror of national concerns and cultural evolution. Poets in Russia were seen more as secular saints than artists. In what other country were poets continuously persecuted and prosecuted, jailed, exiled and even killed – for writing poetry?[5] If John Hollander is correct that poetry of real power depends upon a police state, then the importance of the poetic word in Russia comes into sharp focus throughout all of Russian literary history and acquires a special poignancy in the twentieth century.[6] For the two hundred and fifty-odd years of its existence, Russian poetry, as Lev Loseff points out, 'has been constantly under the thumb of state censorship'.[7] In these circumstances *vita* becomes *brevis* while *ars* must remain *longa* regardless of the price. In this respect Osip Mandelshtam's statement that 'poetry is power' was not an insecurity-ridden justification of some frivolous occupation, as it was, for example, for the Roman elegists. Russian poets have continually found themselves in the peculiar position of being the voices of freedom, the heralds of sorrow, the outlets for the anguished soul, and the artistic martyrs on the guillotine of the persecuting state that always regarded literature as a serious threatening enterprise. Poetry placed its creator at times in a position of mortal peril since the Russian, and much more so the Soviet State, saw in it a rival authority. Mandelshtam himself proved to be a victim of that peril.

In one of her poems the great Anna Akhmatova ruefully exclaims: 'If only you knew from what kind of trash poetry shamelessly grows' ('Kogda b vy znali iz kakogo sora rastut stikhi ne vedaia styda'). This unsentimental observation came from a poet who wrote both the most refined and delicate of love poems and lyrics full of anguish and pain. She recognized the roots of poetry as 'trash' ('sor'), a term that clearly belongs to the realm of *unpoetische Wörter*. As a poet Akhmatova was perhaps aware that poetry is not always inspired by lofty feelings or sublime experiences. The Russian historical and cultural context, especially the one in which the beauty and intensity of Akhmatova's own verse was born, proved her statement true. And yet there is also another, equally significant source of poetic inspiration. We can interpret and understand the poetry of love, sorrow, anguish and exile in the immediate circumstances of the poets' lives, but we must also take into consideration the literary poetic memory and their 'wrestling' with predecessors as the poets attempt to assert their own place within the world both inside and outside their immediate cultural context.

This book explores a poetic memory that might seem foreign to Russian literary self-identity. What was so natural to many European poets became on Russian soil a purposefully defined and targeted quest. Russian poets themselves always perceived the classical tradition as formative for their own self-positioning in the literary family of European nations. Russian poetry, as it attempted to 'catch up' with the Western literary legacy, throve on the classical heritage. But in Russia the perpetuation of the Greco-Roman classics also owes a debt to poetry, especially since poets were martyred by the rulers there while they were cherished by the entire literate urban milieu and sometimes (like Pushkin) by the whole nation. The relationship of Russian poets to the West was never that of a humble pupil to an accomplished teacher. Geography looms large in that respect. For a country that spanned two continents and was as much an heir to the Byzantine Empire as to the legacy of Genghis Khan's hordes, Western influence was not always a natural path – at times it was a forcible and contrived implantation. Since Greco-Roman roots were at the basis of that implantation, the Russian response to the classical tradition was unavoidably idiosyncratic. Even when Russian writers, in their pursuit of a European identity, strove to imitate European classicism, in the end they created a classical tradition unlike any other: they came late to the 'table' of that tradition and their response, as one might expect, encompassed not only their direct reception of the classics but also the European reception. Russian monarchs as well as men of letters became interested in Greece and Rome, spurred on by a fierce desire to 'catch up' with Europe and its culture and eventually, as Peter the Great somewhat unpoetically phrased it, to 'show their ass to the West'.[8] In the earlier part of the twentieth century Lev Pumpianskii observed that during Peter's time 'Russia entered into a circle of nations which had already (and, what's more, recently) acquired antiquity. Perhaps it was Russia that received the classical ideal through the greatest number of refractions.'[9] If the Greeks and Romans were formative for European national literatures, they *had to* become formative for Russian literature as well if Russia were to emulate the Western literary canon. But the 'refractions', which were at the time a part of the European classical reception, became absorbed into the Russian reception of antiquity as an integral part of it.

I cannot pretend to be able to unravel all the intertextual allusions, means of acculturation, and levels of influence that link the classical tradition with Russian poetry. An inquiry of such breadth can make no claims to exhaustiveness. My task in this book is to gain partial insight into the role of the classics in Russian poetry by limiting this study to a few particularly significant or indicative poets, genres and themes. This book is an attempt to identify and explain the principles behind these particular poets' interest in specific aspects of the classical legacy.

While many scholars both in Russia and in the West have offered profound insights into the poetic texts discussed in this study, there is no comprehensive monograph on classical reception in Russian poetry or even one that addresses the question of 'reception studies' in Russia. This book aims to look at the texts of several Russian poets from the perspective of classical reception by combining both theoretical and historical approaches with the traditional study of allusions and influences in the poetic texts. The choice of the poets for discussion owes as much to subjective taste in poetry as it does to the commonality of 'classical' themes in the texts of these poets.

I shall focus especially on the heightened Russian literary response to the classics during the twentieth century. That issue, however, cannot be addressed on its own – a certain amount of historical, chronological and cultural background is needed to illuminate the role and meaning of classical reception in twentieth-century Russian poetry. Furthermore, each poet discussed in this study is viewed not only diachronically, as an heir to the prior tradition, but also synchronically, in the context of his or her own epoch. In that respect this book follows the principles outlined by Mikhail Bakhtin, who observed that 'literature is an inseparable part of culture and cannot be understood outside of the whole context of the culture of the given epoch'.[10] To unearth the complex classical context of the poetic texts of the last century one must delve both into the archaeology of the national poetic memory as it is reflected in actual poetic practices and into the individual experience and cultural poetics of each poet.

Chapter 1, **'Russian Antiquity'**, explains my approach to classical reception and tries to explicate why the question of the classics in Russia is always fraught with tormenting issues of self-identity, inferiority complexes and feelings of indebtedness and belatedness that persist in poetic texts until as late as Joseph Brodsky's. The chapter also offers a brief chronology of Russian interest in the classics and the contributive effect on Russian classical reception of Christianity, the Petrine reforms and military conquests in the Crimea.

Chapter 2, **From Russian Classicism to Alexander Pushkin**, focuses on the poetic chronology, the history of the Russian development of classical poetic genres and the role played in the formation of a national literary language by translations from Greek and Latin. All the poets of the decades following 1730 became greatly concerned with developing a Russian poetic language and prosody. By laying the foundations for a synthesis between classical and national tendencies, they led to the rise of the 'sun' of Russian poetry, Alexander Pushkin. Pushkin's 'classical' texts offer some clues to a better grasp of classical reception in the twentieth century as related to themes of poetic legacy, the alienation of the poet in society and Ovidian themes of exile and nostalgia.

Chapter 3, ***Poetae Docti* and their Discontents**, introduces the historical and cultural contexts of twentieth-century Russian poetry and explains my choice of poets and themes for discussion. The analysis then moves to the phenomenon of the *poetae docti* ('learned poets') in Russian literature, best represented by Innokentii Annenskii and Viacheslav Ivanov. While I offer a glimpse of classical reception in their poetry as a whole, I focus mainly on their mythological tragedies and on the literature and philosophy that influenced them. What also comes into sharper focus in this chapter is the theme of Rome, which originated in the time of Russian classicism and was perpetuated in the twentieth century by Viacheslav Ivanov, Osip Mandelshtam and Joseph Brodsky. *Poetae docti*, regardless of the long debated quality of their poetry, were crucial in influencing two trends discussed in later chapters: the 'modernizing' of classical myth and the themes of Rome and Empire.

Chapter 4, **Marina Tsvetaeva's Tragic Heroines**, continues the focus on mythological tragedy, this time represented by one of the two most influential women poets of Russia, Marina Tsvetaeva (the other being Anna Akhmatova). The *poetae docti* and their use of mythological tragedy are a perfect foil to Tsvetaeva's tragedies and contrast strongly in their poetic philosophy with Tsvetaeva's interest in female self-expression and the artistic potential in the treatment of familiar tragic plots and protagonists. Tsvetaeva's tragedies *Phaedra* and *Ariadne* as well as the poetic cycles with the same names are viewed both in their cultural and biographical contexts and in light of the influence of Tsvetaeva's identity as a 'woman-poet' on her poetic choices.

Chapter 5, **Osip Mandelshtam: 'Yearning for World Culture'**, returns to the theme of Rome discussed in the poetry of Viacheslav Ivanov. While Mandelshtam's 'Greek' poems possess a more dreamlike quality and can be understood better in the context of his Acmeist philosophy and overall cosmopolitanism, the city of Rome in his poetry has much more defined features and relates strongly to Mandelshtam's treatment of his own city of St Petersburg and the historical changes it was undergoing. I look at Mandelshtam's 'Roman' and by extension 'Ovidian' poems in connection with the evolution of his 'St Petersburg text' from a city of classical grandeur and a Third Rome to a city of death.

Chapter 6, **Joseph Brodsky: The 'Uncommon Visage'**, the last and longest chapter of the book, is concerned with classical reception in the poetry of the Russian poet who is perhaps the most famous in the West. Brodsky's poetry provides closure to many of the themes discussed in the previous pages. This poet's interest in the classics manifests itself ubiquitously both in poetry and prose; his claim to a rightful place within the poetic tradition is usually contemplated in the context of both his Russian and his ancient predecessors. Having looked at the beginnings and the evolution of the classics in Russian poetry, the reader can fully appreciate Brodsky's complete reinvention of the poet as the mouthpiece of the Muses in the modern age. In Brodsky the familiar classical myths are altered beyond recognition and the subjects of heroic achievement turn into laments of defeat. His Roman and Ovidian ruminations acquire even greater poignancy once he is banished from St Petersburg and Russia but refuses to cultivate the mournful image of an exile. Brodsky's antiquity is carefully and thoughtfully sculpted, developing a peculiar kind of final intimacy with Greece and Rome and thus presenting a challenge to the new poets of Russia to continue the poetic *belle époque* of classics in Russian poetry.

1

'Russian Antiquity'

We Russians have two motherlands: our Rus' and Europe ... a great deal, a
very great deal of what we have taken from Europe and transplanted to our
country has not just been copied by us ... but has been grafted into our
organism, into our flesh and blood; ... I maintain and repeat that every
European poet, thinker and philanthropist is always most fully and inti-
mately understood and accepted in Russia, out of all the countries of the
world apart from his own ... This Russian attitude to world literature is a
phenomenon which is almost unparalleled to the same degree among other
nations throughout world history ... every poet-innovator of Europe, everyone who appears there with a new idea and a new source of strength, cannot
fail to immediately become a Russian poet as well, cannot bypass Russian
thought, cannot fail to become an almost Russian force.

Fedor Dostoevskii[1]

There is a great sense of pride in these words of Dostoevskii's, pride not of
a mere inheritor of some greater and more ancient culture but of one with
a strong self-confidence of its own. From the standpoint of Russian literary
history, 'Europeanization' was initiated in Russia by Peter the Great and
continued under Catherine the Great. But in a country like Russia, with a
passionate propensity for doing away with the past and starting again
with a clean slate, absorbing and internalizing an historical culture based
on a completely foreign legacy (Greece and Rome) was a complicated and
intricate process. This involved process is elucidated by Peter Viazemskii's
witty observation: 'Many things in our past can be explained by the fact
that a Russian, Peter the Great, sought to make us Germans, while a
German, Catherine the Great, wanted to make us Russians.'[2] This illuminates Russian 'Europeanization' and by extension Russian reception of
antiquity. Peter wanted Russians to imitate and eventually surpass
Europe. While the great tsar-reformer understood keenly how different his
country was from any European nation, for him the European (and specifically German) way was the only road to political, economic and cultural
progress. Although Catherine continued his reforms, she simultaneously
embraced Russian geographic, political and cultural peculiarities. She was
not interested in ruling a servile shadow of the more splendid European
courts; she now wanted Europe to envy Russia, for its vastness, for its
wealth, for its uniqueness, and for its untamable and unprecedented
talent. With respect to these attitudes to Europe, the legacy of Greece and
Rome proved crucial for the Russian literary imagination.

7

There are two sets of issues I would like to explore in this chapter in order to clarify my interpretations of the poetic texts analyzed in the following pages. First, a brief word is required regarding Russia's place in reception studies and the methodology used to analyze the Russian poetic texts in the context of reception. Secondly, classical reception in Russia was not perceived and absorbed by itself, in the historical context of Greece and Rome, but always in the context of European culture, complicated by the context and tradition of baroque and neoclassical reception in Germany, France and Italy. Hence a concise chronology of Russia's self-construction as a European nation is offered with particular attention to the role played by the legacy of Greece and Rome in the formation of a national poetry.

Classical tradition or reception studies: where does Russia fit?

As reception studies of European literature become prominent in classical scholarship, the nature of 'Russian antiquity', in the words of Georgii Knabe, remains somewhat problematic. The study of the *Nachleben* (afterlife) of classical culture, texts and ideas is most certainly not new in relation to Russia. However, it belongs more to the strand of classical scholarship that may be termed 'the classical tradition'. This studies the transmission and dissemination of classical culture and includes terms such as 'legacy', 'influence'[3] and 'literary canon'.[4] While the legacy and canon created by the ancient writers has been acknowledged as a cornerstone of western humanism, the significance of Russia's participation in the reception of antiquity remains for the most part a vast uncharted territory. In a recent 407-page *Companion to Classical Tradition*, the whole of Central/Eastern Europe occupies only 23 pages, and Russia is covered in a few paragraphs.[5] The authors of these pages, Jerzy Axer and Katarzyna Tomaszuk, share the previously expressed view[6] 'that even the last European wave of Latinization (the Enlightenment) was never accepted there [in Russia], and that pagan Latin writers were included in Russian culture only in the nineteenth century, as school reading under the strictly educational reform of Nicholas I'.[7] While I agree with this view of the Enlightenment in Russia, I will demonstrate in the following pages that the interest in pagan authors started long before Nicholas' educational reform.

Axer and Tomaszuk further assert that in the case of European culture the concept of 'ancient heritage' was used to indicate an accepted cultural canon and that 'passing it on ensured the proper upbringing of future generations'.[8] In modern studies of the classical tradition in Europe, the concept of a canon has been decisively replaced by the concept of 'reception', and even that term is seen by some recent critics as too passive for the dynamics involved in the appropriation of and resistance to the classical tradition. In recent Russian scholarship the study of classical tradition as the 'affirmation of cultural heritage without memory of its meaning' is juxtaposed with the reception of antiquity, not in a canonical sense but as an elective undertaking in search of antiquity's real meaning and its application to the interpretation of national history.[9] The canon, as Axer and Tomaszuk point out, has become a 'nonoperational concept and is unattractive to the contemporary consumer of culture; resistance, transformation and non-canonical consumption are now perceived in a positive light'.[10] Although 'reception' reflects the complexity of the relationships between ancient and modern cultures better than 'tradition' and 'heritage', it is still insufficient in its acknowledgement of the role played by the receivers of antiquity in any subsequent European cultural tradition. The term *Rezeptionsästhetik* (sometimes translated as 'the poetics of reception') was coined in 1967 by Hans Robert Jauss and has subsequently been applied frequently in discussions of the European reception of antiquity. This term not only acknowledges the historicity of the texts, but also allows the aesthetic responses of readers in the present to be a part of the study of the reception of the past.[11]

The application of this term to Russian literature is not without its difficulties as a result of the idiosyncratic way in which reception of the classics occurred in Russia.[12] The archaeological and linguistic heritage that tied Western Europe to Greek and Roman antiquity helped to produce a certain consistency and continuity in regard to reception, while the absence of any such heritage in Russia led to a notably higher degree of heterogeneity and intermittence in classical reception. While the precepts of classicism were the basis for a widely accepted system of education in Europe, in Russia there was considerably less unanimity about the importance of the classical heritage for contemporary life even after Peter's forceful reforms. Russians did not view themselves as belonging to any historical continuum at the beginning of which stood the Greeks and the Romans. The isolation of the Russian literary canon from the Greco-Roman heritage was further promoted by the use of Old Slavonic rather than Greek or Latin as an ecclesiastical language.[13] The result of this isolation was that the influence of Greco-Roman antiquity was only intermittently significant and manifested itself intensely in certain periods of the country's spiritual and intellectual development. During those times Russians responded to classical antiquity in a variety of ways which, taken together, constitute a comprehensive reaction to the legacy of Greece and Rome, particularly when viewed against the overall history of Russian literature after the foundation of the city of St Petersburg in 1703.

The discussion of classical reception in Russian poetry is additionally complicated by the fact that it lacked consistency and a commonality of sources. On the one hand, some poetic works, like Ozerov's classical dramas and some Russian classicizing poetry, display an imitation of French classicism that has little or nothing to do with the Greek and Latin originals. Trediakovskii, for example, was less of a classicist than some

9

interpretations indicate, and more reliant on his French sources. As will be demonstrated in the following pages, even Pushkin's 'classics' are indebted more to the French tradition than to his direct familiarity with the ancient sources, although Pushkin no doubt had more contact with classical originals (at least in Latin) than did Ozerov. On the other hand, in the approach to the twentieth century, the humanistic school system of eighteenth- and especially nineteenth-century Russia produced a number of classical scholars who were also good poets (Annenskii and Ivanov), and poets who were also classical scholars (Fet and Briusov). And finally there are poets, like Mandelshtam, Tsvetaeva and Brodsky, whose interest in Greek and Roman themes hardly falls into any literary movement or group but is nonetheless inseparable from their poetics.[14]

A few words are needed here to explain how these very different texts will be analyzed in the following pages. My approach to poetic works in this book is not limited to specific terms such as 'tradition', 'reception', 'acculturation', 'refiguration' or 'adaptation', because the texts in question combine most of the above approaches to Greek and Roman literature and culture.[15] My interest in the relationship between Russian poetry and the classics is framed by two key assumptions. The first is that the cultural context of the receiving culture must be examined closely in order to explain the use of an ancient source. Secondly, as concisely phrased by Lorna Hardwick, 'reception of classical material is an index of cultural continuity and change and therefore has a value beyond its role in classical studies'.[16] This cultural continuity is especially difficult to follow in the case of Russian reception since it is often complicated by the need to decipher the palimpsestic nature of Russian cultural and literary identity. The construction of that identity in poetry, which started with Russian classicism, did not move in a linear direction in terms of its unconditional acculturation of classical culture into a Russian context.[17] Russian feeling was always ambivalent towards the West, and by extension towards the Greco-Roman literary canon. On the one hand, there was (especially after the foundation of St Petersburg) a growing interest in Greece and Rome as the entrée to a European identification. On the other hand, geographically, spiritually and culturally many Russian intellectuals saw themselves as different from their Western European counterparts. There was considerable uncertainty whether Russia indeed belonged to the West, or should in fact pursue its Eastern roots, which are so evident in Russian early arts and folklore. Thus emerged one of the eternal Russian questions –

East or West?

In 1836 Pushkin wrote in his letter to Peter Chaadaev:

Of course the schism separated us from the rest of Europe and we took no part in any of the great events that stirred her; but we have had our own mission. It was Russia who contained the Mongol conquest with her vast expanses ... The Tatar invasion is a sad and impressive history ... Do you not discern something imposing in the situation of Russia, something that will strike future historians? Do you think they will put us outside Europe? ... I do not by any means admire all that I see around me ... but I swear to you that not for anything in the world would I change my country for another, nor have any history other than that of our ancestors, such as it has been given us by God.[18]

As Orlando Figes observed, Pushkin was almost unique among Russian intellectuals of the time in embracing wholeheartedly the dual nature of the legacy handed to Russia: East and West intertwined. It is also important to consider the addressee of this letter: the Russian Europhile Peter Chaadaev would hardly find the Mongol legacy impressive – indeed he probably considered it abhorrent. Chaadaev was an example of a Russian intellectual who (at least earlier in his life) embraced Western influences on Russian culture at the expense of Eastern.

In 1836 Chaadaev published the first of his *Filosofskie Pis'ma* (*Philosophical Letters*), which, in Alexander Herzen's words, had 'the effect of a pistol shot in the dead of night'. The anger provoked by this letter reached as high as Nicholas I, who felt that Chaadaev had insulted Russia and the emperor himself. Even a short excerpt from the letter demonstrates why there was such a violent reaction from the Russian public:

> We do not belong to any of the great families of the human race; we are neither of the West nor of the East, and we have not the traditions of either. Placed, as it were, outside time, we have not been touched by the universal education of the human race ... What is the life of man, says Cicero, if memory of earlier events does not relate the present to the past? But we [Russians], who have come into the world like illegitimate children, without a heritage, without any ties binding us to the men who came before us on this earth, carry in our hearts none of the lessons preceding our own existence ...[19]

Chaadaev is often cited as an example of Russian cultural consciousness and even insecurity in the face of European intellectual achievement.[20] After the publication of this letter, morbidly signed 'Necropolis, 1829, December 1', Chaadaev was declared insane and put under house arrest. Even though he composed eight other letters between 1827 and 1831 (not printed in his lifetime) in which he predominantly contemplated religious questions, the first letter delineated sharply the complexity of Russia's relationship with the West. It is clear from Chaadaev's somewhat bitter and perhaps not altogether fair dismissal of Russian heritage, that, like most Russian intellectuals, he wanted Russia to have ties to the Western tradition, which he saw as a progressive movement of ideas. He characterized these Western ideas as ones 'of duty, justice, right and order' and juxtaposed them to the 'frivolity' of even the most enlightened Russian minds.[21]

It is also noteworthy that Chaadaev started his discussion of Russia's relationship with the West with a quotation from Cicero, citing the Roman author almost as a sage whose single opinion could outweigh years of national history. If Russia were not connected to that past to which Cicero was referring (to Greek and early Roman history), then Russia would need to change its ways. Chaadaev then went on to lament that 'fundamentally, we Russians have nothing in common with Homer, the Greeks, the Romans and the Germans; all that is completely foreign to us'.[22] In 1837 Chaadaev was to write a 'palinode' to his unfair assessment of Russia's place in the family of nations. In his 'Apologie d'un fou' ('Apology of a Madman') he still lamented and assertively stated that Russia's topographic location to the east of Europe does not mean that it has 'ever been part of the East'.[23] In the same work Chaadaev also declared a deep love of his country and praised Russia's ability to 'perfect most of the ideas which have come up in the old societies', warning at the same time against the blind patriotism which led to such a violent reaction to his first letter.[24]

There was, however, an inherent flaw in Chaadaev's reasoning, which, it seems, Pushkin tried to 'correct'. Chaadaev analyzed Russia under the assumption that for Russians, just as for the European nations, West is the 'centre' and East the 'periphery'.[25] Hence Chaadaev's narrative ignored 'complicating factors including the ancient Greek trading colonies around the Black Sea that the Romans perpetuated, or more significantly, the established relations between Kievan Rus' and the Byzantine Empire during the tenth and eleventh centuries'.[26] It is also interesting that Chaadaev's critique was eagerly and unexpectedly appropriated by Slavophiles, who wanted to embrace Russia's lack of historical consciousness as a sign of superior and mystical Russian spirituality, a mark of a chosen nation.[27]

There is certainly an explanation for the one-sided view of the classical tradition displayed by Russian intellectuals such as Chaadaev: the phenomenon David Bethea termed 'belatedness'.[28] Russia never had a Renaissance or a Reformation, two cultural periods of which the first brought the classical period to the fore and the second contributed to affirmation and self-identification with the cultural heritage of Western Europe. Chaadaev's concern was that Russia did not so much need to *re-discover* the Western heritage but simply to *discover* it and integrate it.[29] From the time of her early years as a state, Russia faced the complex and uneasy question of her own identity in the family of nations. In this respect Russia was similar to the rest of 'younger Europe', to use Kloszowski's expression.[30] The basis of this problem, which revealed itself fully between the Middle Ages and Humanism, was a self-definition of one's place in European history and then translation of that definition 'into renaissance anthropological language, which used signs of classical tradition'.[31] In the case of Russia, that self-definition and the choice between East and West also involved the Russian path into and then within the Christian community. Bethea observes that 'many of the turning points in [Russia's] history and many (if not most) of its cultural monuments have centred on the issue of whether this increasingly vast and diverse country and its people are "Western," "Eastern," or some significant, new combination of the two'.[32] This controversy was not resolved with Peter's reforms, and the foundation of the city of St Petersburg in 1703 only exacerbated the division between the Westernizers and the Slavophiles who could not forget the Eastern half of the Roman Empire, from which the Russian alphabet and religion had emerged, and which in turn set Russia apart from the West.

To understand better the complexity of Russia's simultaneous acceptance of and resistance to the classical heritage, a few words are needed on the chronology of Russian interest in the classical tradition, especially as it relates to the development of national poetic forms and language.

From Byzantium to the 'Third Rome'

There are two distinct trends that characterize Russia's cultural development; both are of foreign provenance, and both concern Russia's self-perception as a part of Europe.[33] From the ninth to the fifteenth century, the culture of Rus' underwent Christianization and Byzantinization, while from the sixteenth century to the present, secularization and Westernization were the most formative factors in the cultural history of Russia.

The fate of the classical legacy on Russian soil was intertwined with Russia's Christian identity from the beginning.[34] Perhaps the best known example of a Russian claim to classical credentials is the 'Third Rome' doctrine. This had its origins in the early sixteenth century, when a Pskovian monk, Filofei, explicitly stated the sequence of 'Romes': Rome, Constantinople, Moscow.[35] Until the Petrine reforms Europeans refused to recognize Russia as an equal and the result of that rejection was the development of Filofei's view that Moscow was the last remaining Rome, the new core of Christendom after the Byzantines were conquered by the Moslem Turks in 1453:

> The Church of old Rome fell for its heresy; the gates of the second Rome, Constantinople, were hewn down by the axes of the infidel Turks; but the Church of Moscow, the Church of the new Rome, shines brighter than the sun in the whole universe ... Two Romes have fallen, but the third stands fast; a fourth there cannot be.[36]

This long-standing connection of Rus' with Byzantium played a significant role in the reception of antiquity as a part of the Christian legacy and manifested itself especially strongly at the end of the nineteenth and beginning of the twentieth century in the writings of the philosopher Vladimir Solov'ev and the Russian Symbolists whom he influenced.

E.D. Frolov traced the historical roots of Russian interest in classical antiquity as far back as the eleventh century and the culture of the Kievan Rus'.[37] G.S. Knabe and D.S. Likhachev discussed the Byzantine sources of Russian intellectual thought and literary development at length. There was an especially pronounced interest in the classical tradition in Russia during the fourteenth and fifteenth centuries, which were characterized by continuous contact with Byzantium; this interest resulted in numerous visits from representatives of Russian Orthodoxy who copied some of the texts kept in the Byzantine monasteries.[38] In 1472 Ivan III married Zoe Paleologue, niece of the last Byzantine emperor, and (following the Latin Caesar) coined the title 'tsar', adding the two-headed eagle of Byzantium to the symbols of Russian monarchy.[39] There were also several Russian orthodox monasteries established in Constantinople, which helped to copy, translate into Russian and disseminate some ancient texts. These texts, however, were mainly from late antiquity and helped to further the Christian cause rather than educating Russian intellectuals in classical antiquity.

Certain linguistic factors also appear to have contributed to the manner in which the Greek and Roman heritage was introduced into Russian literary development and to the nature of its influence thereafter. When Christianity became the dominant religion in Russia during the tenth century, neither Latin nor Greek was used by the Russian clergy. Instead the Church used Old Slavonic, partly based on the Greek from which most of its literature derived.[40] Although Church Slavonic in Russia played the same role as Latin did in parts of Europe, unlike Latin it did not offer Russians any pre-Christian past with highly sophisticated literary forms. Boris Uspenskii convincingly characterized the linguistic situation in Russia until the seventeenth century as 'diglossia';[41] until as late as the Petrine reforms Russian and Church Slavonic fulfilled functionally completely different roles within what was perceived as a single language. While Church Slavonic was assigned to the sphere of the Divine, Russian was used mainly for practical purposes, as a language of laws, official correspondence and decrees. The 'diglossia' created a certain difficulty for the development of a Russian literary language, which became a hybrid of normalized spoken Russian (with the inclusion of folk and dialect norms), Church Slavonic influences, and eventually Western European imports. As the literature developed, however, that Chimera of a language, in fairy-tale manner, shed its original awkwardness and blossomed into an extraordinarily textured swan of literary forms.

Peter the Great and the classics

A consistent and at times forceful introduction of the classical legacy first intruded into Russian culture with the reforms of Peter the Great. Peter saw his city as the New (and eventually Third) Rome, the centre of a burgeoning and powerful empire. He adopted the title *Imperator*, in which

14

frame he united both the conception of his absolute autocracy and his predilection for a Roman and thus Western frame of reference. As he urged the Russians to embrace the ways of the modern West, he also wholeheartedly understood the need for classical education as the first step to encouraging and implementing Western technological and cultural achievements. From the very first years of Peter's rule, imagery (in both art and literature) was frequently connected with Greco-Roman mythology. Peter also reinforced the genealogy of the Russian royal house promulgated by Ivan the Terrible, who had declared the Russian monarchs to be the direct descendants of Rurik who in turn claimed to be related to Octavian Augustus through the latter's mythical brother Prus. The Romanov family to which Peter belonged not only accepted this genealogy but in addition made classical heroic allusions central to the symbols and imagery propagating the power of their ruling house. Peter himself, for example, liked to be depicted as Ulysses, Perseus and Heracles. Peter also realized that in order to be seen as a European power Russia needed Rome more than it needed Greece.[42] Richard S. Wortman wrote that already in the late fifteenth century, Russian tsars were claiming the status of Western rulers by asserting Roman traits. Classical symbols were appropriated as signs of Russia's own Western character.[43] In addition to the title *Imperator*, Peter adopted those of *Pater Patriae* ('Otets Otechestva') and *Magnus* ('Velikii') and celebrated his military victories with Roman triumphal pomp. His new city naturally had to follow the model of Rome and with the establishment of the St Petersburg Academy of Sciences in 1724 Russian scholars began to study the classical tradition seriously.

However, antiquity, even after Peter's reforms, continued to be viewed in the context of Christianity. In the love poetry of Peter's time (as well as in the so-called school dramas) biblical characters coexist with ancient gods.[44] Most of the best known writers during Peter's reign were churchmen like Dmitrii Tuptalo, bishop of Rostov, who composed sermons as well as dramas, and the monk Simeon Polotskii, a chief representative of Ukrainian humanism in Moscow. The latter, as Okenfuss observed, 'represented a distinctive "southwestern Russian ideology" for which it was perfectly acceptable to mix the Christian God with pagan gods, and to merge Christian heaven with Olympus'.[45] Knabe cited an example of a drama contemporary with Peter, *The Liberation of Livonia and Ingermanlandia*, in which Jupiter and Phoebus Apollo watch over a fight between the 'two-headed eagle' of Russia and the lion representing Sweden; this fight is also likened to the struggle of Moses with the Pharaoh. Antiquity in early Russian literature was not viewed as a cultural entity in itself but always as a parallel to Christianity. The gods and the heroes of literature were deprived of any claim to accuracy in accordance with the ancient sources. They aimed to give the new Westernized Russia, and especially the imperial family, an aura of antiquity, magnificence, and political and cultural continuity, and to make them players on the stage of European, not merely Russian, history. From this point of view Russia did not have a dynamic and authentic view of antiquity, but only a cultural and historical reflection of it. The ancient and pseudo-ancient images were part of the new culture imposed by Peter the Great. With time that culture became an inextricable part of Russian reality and reflected, along with its initially stereotyped and mediated classical components, the character and spirit of the new reforms. The wide use of ancient images and mythological plots in Russian literature subsequent to Peter's reforms was the result of what might be called 'the revolution from above'.

Despite his own mediocre education, a vital part of Peter's insistence on reforms was his acute and early understanding of education as the only means to unleash Russian intellectual potential, for the sake of which wounded national insecurity and pride had to be swept aside. Although Peter, as Lindsey Hughes observed, 'inherited little on which to base his educational programme', he already had two institutions within his realm that facilitated education in classics: the Slavonic-Greek-Latin Academy in Moscow, established in 1687, and the Kiev Academy, established in the 1630s, on which the former was modelled.[46] Since he was setting out to establish educational curricula, he complemented his efforts in Russia by sending some of his subjects abroad to receive proper training so that they could then return to Russia and apply their acquired knowledge. By the end of his reign Peter, although still driven mainly by practical goals, had come to appreciate the appeal of a well-rounded education, and as 'a crowning glory' of his educational programme he established the St Petersburg Academy of Sciences in 1724.[47]

The Petrine reforms of the seventeenth and early eighteenth century were emphatically directed toward rearing a new generation that would serve the newly industrialized and culturally advanced Russian state.[48] The development of printing, the publication of the first Russian newspaper, the establishment of the new secular schools and lyceums, and finally the foundation of the new Academy of Sciences – all this served one single-minded purpose: to overcome Russia's strongly felt insecurity in the face of European nations.[49]

Peter dabbled in many arts, including architecture, garden design and ship building, but literature was not one of his hobbies. In the words of one writer: 'Peter and poetry is a completely contradictory concept.'[50] However, despite his 'utilitarian' approach to the humanities, he understood the necessity of developing a Russian literary identity. Peter's literary interest in classical antiquity manifested itself mainly in his encouragement of translations from Greek and Latin, the importance of which is hard to overestimate. Translations had a broader reach than education as instruments of the cultural transmission of classical texts.[51] Furthermore, as Lorna Hardwick observed in the case of European reception, 'translating classical texts became a sign of linguistic vigour and independence, with the receiving language gaining additional dignity and authority by dem-

16

onstrating its role in the transmission of classical learning'.[52] We owe some of the first editions of ancient texts in Russian to the work of Il'ia Kopievskii, who not only published Aesop's fables in Russian but in 1700 also compiled a Latin grammar for Russian readers, *Latina grammatica in usum scholiarum celeberrimmae gentis slavonico-rosseanae adornata.* There is no doubt that Peter's choice of books for translation and publication was once again driven by practical considerations. Peter was interested in educating mathematicians, architects, doctors and military officers. Such works as *Ovidian Figures in 226 Depictions* (*Ovidievy figury v 226 izobrazheniiakh*), published in 1722, were chosen not for Ovidian poetic genius but because the Russian student, in order to acquire a well-rounded education, needed to become acquainted with classical mythology, for which the mythological stories taken from the *Metamorphoses* were judged to be an appropriate didactic medium. The book offered visual but not textual renditions of classical myths.

Literary culture was secularized significantly under Peter, and the publication of books was transferred from the Church to the government.[53] Ancient translations also increased appreciably under Peter's rule. Peter realized that the Western Renaissance was conditioned by the availability of translations of Greek and Roman texts and that Russia had missed out on that first wave of translations, the print revolution and the classical revival. Russia, as Max Okenfuss pithily observed 'could never reproduce or relive the culture of Western Europe'.[54] It is thus important to consider the extent to which Peter made ancient authors available in Russia and which translations were first undertaken. During Peter's reign such translations were relatively few and targeted primarily the reading habits of the court. They included Aesop's *Fables*, a free rendition of Quintus Curtius' *Life of Alexander the Great*, some excerpts from Caesar's *Gallic Wars* and stories from the mythographer Apollodorus. An additional significant 'classical' publication was the tri-lingual Slavic-Greek-Latin primer issued by Fedor Polikarpovich Polikarpov-Orlov in Moscow in 1701, which contained reading texts by Gregory of Nazianzus, Basil the Great, John Chrysostom and the *Stoslov*-catechism of Gennadius of Constantinople.[55] This illustrates that Orthodox morality still played a more important role in the selection of texts for reading than their literary quality. Ovid and Vergil remained 'cursed' pagan authors in Russia for some time after the reign of Peter the Great. The Latin prose authors essential for Western humanism – Cicero, Lucian, Lucretius, Seneca and Tacitus – were mostly translated and published in Russia during Catherine's reign (1762-1796) or shortly before.[56] However, even these meagre drops of the Greco-Roman canon into Russian intellectual culture helped to hone Russian literary language and provide it with texture and richness.

For the purposes of this study the work of Feofan Prokopovich (1681-1736) is of special interest, although Prokopovich was a Ukrainian rather than Russian humanist.[57] A professor and then the Rector of the Kiev

Academy before studying at L'viv and at the Athanasian College in Rome, upon his arrival in Russia in 1709 Prokopovich became a loyal supporter of Peter's reforms and the most erudite scholar of his time. His 3,000-volume library reflected his main interests as a teacher of Latin grammar, poetics and rhetoric. This library, even if mediocre by European standards of the day, contained the writings of over 75 Latin and Greek authors of antiquity with special attention to Roman authors from Plautus to Claudianus. Prokopovich may have been the first person in Moscow and even in Russia to own the works of Roman poets such as Catullus, Propertius and Tibullus, which he had studied in Rome but were previously completely unknown in Russia. An especially interesting facet of Prokopovich's library collection is that, unlike those of nineteenth-century Russian intellectuals, it contained very few French or English authors such as Molière, Racine, Corneille, or even Shakespeare and Hobbes, staples in the collection of any Western European humanist. His familiarity with the ancients was therefore direct and unmediated by the European reception. He was a very influential figure in the dissemination of the classics in Russia, but he was not interested in a secular Enlightenment in the manner of Western Europe. He was a writer, an orator, a dramatist, and also a poet. His treatises on the theory of literature, *Poetics* and *Rhetoric*, are full of references to ancient poets, especially Roman ones – Horace, Ovid and Vergil – whom he quoted often and at length. His activity directly and indirectly influenced the interest of Russian society in ancient literature. A typical example of his poetry is his 'Epinikion' (1709) in praise of Peter's victory over Charles XII of Sweden at Poltava, which includes a somewhat misguided allusion to the Trojan War and references to Peter as the 'Russian Mars'. Prokopovich should perhaps be seen as the main source and 'ancestor' of Russian classicism.

After Peter's death in 1725 more classical texts and translations appeared in print. An edition of Aesop was published in 1747 as well as Quintus Curtius' *Alexander of Macedonia* in a new translation by Krashennikov in 1750. Out of Cornelius Nepos' *De Viris Illustribus (On Illustrious Men)* the *Life of Generals* was translated by the Academy of Sciences in 1748 and the students of the gymnasium of Moscow University received a Latin version of other *vitae* for reading.[58] However, while ancient prose writers such as Epictetus, Eutropius, Marcus Aurelius and finally Aristotle made their entrance into Russian literary culture, ancient poetry did not receive the same attention except for Kantemir's lonely translation of Horace's *Ars Poetica* in 1744.[59]

It is only under Catherine the Great and Alexander I that ancient texts gained a firmer foothold in Russia and began to be disseminated consistently. At the beginning of her reign Catherine especially encouraged Latin learning. In the 1760s and 1770s several youths completed their studies at Oxford and Cambridge in order to become teachers of Latin in Russia. Catherine also took further steps to ensure the dissemination of classical texts and authors, and in 1768 she funded the Society Striving for the Translation of Foreign Books. Among the Society's publications were the first renderings of some ancient poetic texts: the *Iliad* prose translation by Peter Ekimov, Koznitskii's prose translation of Ovid's *Metamorphoses*, some of Terence's comedies, and the only edition of Claudius Claudianus.[60] Despite the Society's hard work, Russian readers proved uninterested in serious reading, preferring a more frivolous type of writing or the narratives of fantastic journeys, such as *Candide* and *Gulliver's Travels* respectively. The Society produced, but did not publish, only a few more poetic translations: selections from Lucan's *Pharsalia* and the *Odyssey* by Peter Ekimov.[61] After scrutiny by E.R. Dashkova, Catherine's close friend, the activities of the Society in translating the pagan classics came to an end in 1783. Dashkova's vision had moved away from the pagan classics and towards a native Russian literary revival.

The intertwining of the classical and Christian legacies, which had been so prominent in Peter's promotion of antiquity, was continued by Catherine. Judith Kalb observed that 'mastering territory that had once been part of the eastern Roman Empire could be seen as a first step en route to the restoration of Orthodox domination of Constantinople'.[62] As Russia expanded its territory, Rome came to be seen as the model empire, poignantly expressed in Stephen L. Baehr's words: 'the glory-that-was Rome iconographically signified the glory-that-was-to-be Russia'.[63] The *translatio imperii* was completed when Russia acquired the Crimea under Catherine in 1783 and then annexed parts of Georgia under Alexander I. These two additions to Russia's Empire finally added the missing element to Russia's claim to a classical heritage: the geographic connection. The southern coast of the Crimea was the site of the ancient Greek trading colony of Chersonesus, which had also been used later by the Romans to ensure their grain supply.[64] The cities of the Crimea were thus given magniloquent Greek names like Sevastopol' and Simpheropol'. Catherine's then-favourite Grigorii Potemkin, who had been assigned the development of the new lands, became Prince Potemkin of Tauride in honour of the ancient Greek name for the Crimea.[65] Catherine made a triumphant tour of her new lands, her routes adorned with triumphal arches bearing the words 'the path to Constantinople', echoing Filofei's ambitious vision of uniting the Second and Third Rome under Russian auspices. Georgia and the rest of the Caucasus (added in the nineteenth century), including territories such as Armenia (once a colony of the Romans), added even more legitimacy to 'Russian antiquity'.[66] The 'myth' of the Caucasus, but especially the Crimea, as will be demonstrated later, would become inextricably connected in Russian poetry with the classical Mediterranean world and its myths.

Catherine wanted to be seen as an enlightened European monarch and she dedicated the 'Bronze Horseman', a statue of Peter the Great, in both Russian and Latin; its inscription ('*Petro Primo Catharina Secunda*') speaks eloquently of the eagerness of Russian royalty to make Latin at least superficially familiar to the masses and to establish their claim to be seen as European monarchs. It would be a mistake to think, however, that Catherine's Public School Reform aimed at making Latin widely available for study; it was in fact regarded as a special skill and acquired by only a selected group of students. Furthermore, in its remaining activities the Translation Society rejected the pagan classics and favoured religious texts. Between 1786 and 1795 the reading public was presented with seven editions of St Augustine's various works, the *Ecclesiastical History* of Eusebius, the *Divine Institutions* by Lactantius, Boethius' *Consolations*, and the writings of the second-century Christian Justinus.[67] Ancient poetry at that time was all but forgotten as Catherine's age ended its 'early modern flirtation with the Classics'.[68] Nevertheless, it was during Catherine's reign that V.P. Petrov undertook his translation of Vergil's *Aeneid*, which appeared in print between 1772 and 1786, an undertaking that provoked much controversy and parody rather than the poetic laurels Petrov had expected.[69]

It was not until the nineteenth century that the educational policy of the Russian governing elite again became concerned with assimilating the classical languages and heritage. This era saw the flourishing of classical gymnasia ('gimnazii') in Russia, and under Sergei Uvarov, Minister of Education from 1833-49, a special emphasis was put on Latin and Greek. Uvarov himself was considered an erudite scholar of classical antiquity despite his sometimes careless and unacknowledged use in his research of works published abroad. His most important contribution to Russian educational policy was his conviction that mastery of the classics in Russia had the potential to impart a common culture with Europe. The forceful 'implantation' of Latin and Greek in the gymnasia occasionally backfired; so much emphasis was placed on mechanical memorization of Greek and Latin paradigms that understanding of the cultural significance of antiquity seems to have disappeared.[70] A playful poem by Alexander Pushkin, written in 1814 when he was only fifteen and addressed to his friend Baron Anton Del'vig (in 'Piruiushchie Studenty' – 'Feasting Students') reflects the boredom inflicted on young men of privilege by their classical education:

Dai ruku, Del'vig, chto ty spish',
Prosnis' lenivets sonnyi,
Ty ne pod kafedroi sidish',
Latyn'iu usyplennyi.[71]

Give me your hand, Del'vig,
Why are you asleep, wake up,
My sleepy lazy-bones.
You are not sitting under the lectern
Lulled to sleep by Latin.

1. 'Russian Antiquity'

Despite such impediments, which resulted from the forceful 'implantation' ('nasazhdenie') of the classics, 'Russian antiquity' came into its own in the nineteenth century and started to be assimilated into the poetic language. At that time Russian men of letters began to work on smoothing the rough edges that had resulted from the contrived nature of Peter's forceful introduction of classical and European heritage into Russia.

Europe had taken several centuries to absorb classical literary genres and integrate them harmoniously into its national literatures. Russia, on the other hand, compressed those centuries into fifty years, during which 'the neoclassical canon, as it had been elaborated in Europe, was tested against Russians' increasing sense of cultural distinction'.[72] The beginnings of the classical 'revolution from above' were not without ridiculous moments, especially for a cynical Western European observer convinced of Russian inferiority. Marinus Wes cited the reaction of Casanova walking through the Summer Garden in St Petersburg in 1765: 'I marvelled at the statuary it contained, all the statues being made of the worst stone and executed in the worst possible taste ... A weeping statue was Democritus, an old woman, Avicenna; another, with grinning mouth, Heraclitus ...'[73] While this testifies to the initial crudeness of Russian familiarity with antiquity, which was shaky at best, the Russian tsars also possessed wealth sufficient to enable them eventually to overcome the lack of material components and purchase original ancient artifacts for their collection in order to refine the reception of the classical tradition in the years to come. When ancient images and mythological characters timidly entered Russian literature in the eighteenth century and the first years of the nineteenth century, they planted the seeds of two very important phases of Russian classical culture, periods which Knabe defined as the 'peterburgsko-imperatorskii' (connected with St Petersburg and Peter's appellation as Emperor) and 'pushkinsko-dekabristskii' (connected with Alexander Pushkin and the Decembrist Uprising of 1825).[74]

In the first period there was still a need for significant acculturation and assimilation of the classics. However, in the poetry of Pushkin and his *pleiad* the abundance of classical images seems not forced but convincingly integrated. As we will see in the next chapter, the traces of 'implantation' of the classical tradition in literature are more palpable in the poetry of Lomonosov or Derzhavin, where the names of the gods and heroes sometimes seem out of place. But as Russia started to adopt classical literary genres, it used them to convey a sense of national experience rather than adhering strictly to classical themes. The Russian attitude towards Europe was still ambivalent and fraught with a sense of inferiority. When Russian writers initially tried to introduce classical forms into their national literature, it was usually in a cautious attempt to find the fine line between homage to and innovative emulation of classical predecessors.

Despite the half-hearted and even failed attempts of their sovereigns to bring the classics to Russia, the most prominent literary figures of the eighteenth and the nineteenth centuries made a significant contribution to their dissemination and rejected the servile imitation of ancient genres and forms. As we will see in the following pages, the reforms in poetic language, metre and diction carried out by Kantemir, Lomonosov and Trediakovskii, and the original poetry of Sumarokov and Derzhavin, enabled the rise of a unique and authentic Russian poetry and its most prominent genius, Alexander Sergeevich Pushkin.

2

From Russian Classicism to
Alexander Pushkin

Muza vchera mne, pevets, prinesla zakotsitnuiu novost';
  V temnyi nedavno Aides ten' slavianina prishla
Tam, okruzhennyi sonmom tenei liubopytnykh, propela
  (Slushal i drevnii Omer) pesn' Iliady tvoei.
Starets nash, k persiam vozhatogo-iunoshi sladko priniknuv,
  Vskriknul: 'Vot slava moia, vot chego veki ia zhdal!'

Singer! The muse just brought me some news from the realm of the shadows:
  Down into Hades so dark, recently entered a Slav;
There in a circle of curious shadows this Slav then recited
  Iliad's Russianized song; Homer was listening too –
Nestling up to the newcomer's bosom our old man, rejoicing, cried loudly:
  'Waiting of epochs is past! This is true glory for me!'[1]

This poem, written in 1821-2 by Baron Anton Del'vig, Pushkin's dear friend, shows, as Michael Wachtel has observed, Del'vig's conception of the Russians as the heirs of the classical tradition.[2] The poem (with tongue in cheek) narrates the story of a Slav, who in the manner of the legendary Orpheus, descends into the Underworld to bedazzle Homer with a much-awaited Russian translation of his masterpiece. But the poem is only half ironic. Nikolai Gnedich's translation of the *Iliad* into Russian hexameters showed that the Russian poetic language had finally come into its own, employing classical metaphors and forms as freely as any other European tradition. The road to that newly acquired confidence had been breathtakingly short and owed much to Gnedich's and Del'vig's predecessors.

The representatives of Russian classicism introduced into the Russian literary and poetic vernacular a wide array of classical allusions and a system of versification based on regular alternations of stressed and unstressed syllables, traditionally referred to by Russian scholars as the 'syllabo-tonic' system.[3] Despite the fact that Russian literature was already familiar with the Greco-Roman world, it was not until the advent of Russian classicism that the classics became a ubiquitous presence in poetic texts. A national culture can absorb and develop the traditions of an ancient and highly evolved foreign culture only when the receiving culture has achieved a certain degree of evolution itself. Furthermore, the absorption of meaning, character and spirit of the past foreign culture can happen only if the receiving culture has achieved what Georgii Knabe refers to as 'consonance' ('sozvuchnost' ') with the culture being received. Knabe refers to it as 'entelechy of culture' ('entelekhiia kul'tury').[4] Such 'entelechy' and fruitful symbiosis of two previously unrelated cultures become possible when the receiving culture finds the answers to its own aesthetic and ideological inquiries in the earlier culture.[5] Russia in the eighteenth century was ready to absorb the traditions of previous civilizations in order to refuel and to a degree reshape its national identity. As the Russian nation was finding its place in the international family of European nations, there arose a great need for a national literature that would not only use the firmly established traditions of old Russian literature, but also the literary experience of the classical and European traditions.

The classicist movement turned to antiquity in search of a cultural continuity that would legitimize Russian claims to partake in the classical heritage. For the Russian literary elite the classical world became the most important point of literary reference. The classical heritage provided a practically limitless source of genres, plots, images and poetic devices for the representatives of Russian classicism. This enabled them to move away from a strictly Russian context, and classical images gave their poetry the power to address universal issues rather than isolated Russian experiences. Russian eighteenth-century men of letters were presented with a challenging task similar to that faced by their European counterparts since the Renaissance: they had to decide the degree of importance that could be assigned to the Greco-Roman legacy without underestimating the cultural contribution of later national sources. The famous 'Quarrel of the Ancients and Moderns', as it was known in France, centred, in Pierre Hart's words, on the issue of 'an absolute standard of cultural achievement, inherited from antiquity, which could be approximated but never surpassed'.[6] The division between Westernizers and Slavophiles centred on the same issue, amplified by the vexed question whether Russia's future lay with the West or with an indigenous culture now jeopardized by Peter's reforms.

There were five equally important figures in the Russian literary landscape whose contribution to Russian letters ensured its strength and unique voice. The representatives of Russian classicism,[7] Kantemir, Trediakovskii and Lomonosov, and the first truly national poets, Sumarokov and especially Derzhavin, played a significant role in the Russian reform of versification, enabling the rise of Russian national poetry to new heights of refinement in the nineteenth century.[8]

Antiokh Kantemir and Vasilii Trediakovskii

Antiokh Dmitrievich Kantemir (1709-1744), the son of Dumitru Kantemir, the Rumanian Governor of Moldavia, was well educated in ancient languages, history and literature. He may have been (though not for long) a student in the Slavonic-Greek-Latin Academy in Moscow. He then became a pupil of the German Gottfried Siegfried Bayer (1695-1738), Professor of Archaeology at the Academy of Sciences, and during his long stay in France was a personal friend of Montesquieu. Kantemir was also close to Feofan Prokopovich and, like Prokopovich, was an avid supporter of the Petrine educational reforms. Kantemir's political ideals were thus closely intertwined with his idealization of a monarch as an enlightened civilizer of the people.

As a writer Kantemir is mostly famous for his satires composed in imitation of Horace, Persius and Juvenal. His interest in antiquity is reflected in a number of translations that comprise a significant part of his literary legacy. Kantemir was drawn to translation partly because he felt that it was not only a means of educating Russian readers but a way to renew and enrich Russian poetic language. The most important feature of his translations was that they were translated directly from the original. In 1744 Kantemir translated Horace's *Ars Poetica,* although, as I indicated in Chapter 1, this was a rather lonely effort on his part to bring pagan poetry to the Russian reader and underscored further the divide between him and Russian society.[9] His translations of the rest of Horace's *Epistles* and also of Anacreon's 55 poems (dated 1742 and 1736 respectively) are important because in addition to being the first translations of these poets into Russian, they are also translated in the metre of the original and without rhyme, which, Kantemir was aware, a Russian reader might find strange and difficult to digest.[10] In his 'Letter of Khariton Makentin',[11] in which he expounded the main rules of Russian versification, Kantemir explained his choice by dividing Russian verse into three kinds. The verse lines composed in imitation of Greek or Latin he titled 'measured verse'. 'It is true', he wrote, 'that no one among our poets has practised this kind of verse; but notwithstanding, I do not see why such lines should not have their place in Russian versification. The differences between the Russian and Greek languages in grammatical constitution are not so great ... To those curious to test their powers in this type of verse I recommend it, and I would not advise despising anything simply because it has not hitherto been put to use. Once it is put to use, perhaps it will prove agreeable'.[12] Kantemir's translations and examples of such 'measured verse' contributed as much to the polishing of Russian poetic language as the poetic reforms and innovations carried out by Vasilii Trediakovskii and Mikhailo Lomonosov.

Vasilii Trediakovskii (1703-1769) was a fledgling of Moscow's Slavonic-Greek-Latin Academy, after which he continued his education in Europe. Trediakovskii's literary activity was all connected with antiquity. Especially relevant to this book is his work on poetic translations linked with the 'purification' of Russian literary language and the creation of a new system of poetic metres. Trediakovskii approached the work of a translator seriously, considering it as valuable as the original work of the author. With unprecedented zeal he applied himself as translator to several ancient authors, translating 51 of Aesop's fables, Terence's *Eunuch*, an excerpt from Seneca's *Thyestes*, and, in prose, Horace's *Ars Poetica*.

He also rendered into Russian a novel by the French novelist Fénelon, *Télémaque*, under the title *Telemakhida*, which became one of the most remarkable literary achievements of the eighteenth century, although it has frequently been derided for its awkward diction and wording.[13] The remarkable feature of Trediakovskii's translation was that it was rendered in Russian as a 'heroic poem' and written from beginning to end in dactylic hexameter.[14] It is important to emphasize the role Trediakovskii's *Telemakhida* played in the development of classicism as a distinct poetic movement. For the first time the Russian reader was introduced to the realm of imagery borrowed directly from ancient mythology. Furthermore, the use of dactylic hexameter prepared the Russian public for subsequent translations of the *Iliad* and the *Odyssey* by Nikolai Gnedich and Vasilii Zhukovskii respectively, in which Trediakovskii's rules of 'heroic verse' were used to full effect.

Trediakovskii's treatise on Russian versification, *New and Brief Method for Composing Russian Verse*, was published in 1735 and offered a number of poems written by the poet to demonstrate examples of various metres and genres. In the treatise he also explained the rules of 'heroic verse' in Russian and how they differ from those in Greek and Latin. He criticized the slavish imitation of Greek and Latin prosody in the work of Meletii Smotritskii, in which the rules on quantitative Russian versification were elaborated but which defied the nature of Russian grammar in an attempt to compose verse similar to Greek and Latin poetry. Trediakovskii observed that 'the terms, "length" and "brevity" of syllables, as they are used in this new Russian versification, are not the same as those the Greeks and Romans used. They are tonic, that is consisting of voice stress (*udarenie golosa*) alone.'[15] Since Russian vowels, unlike those in Greek and Latin, could not be divided into longs and shorts, the most important feature of the versification should be the stress on the syllable.[16] Trediakovskii also emphasized the advantages of the Russian system: 'Thus, whereas the Greek and Latin quantity of syllables is recognized with great difficulty, ours can be known to every Great Russian easily, readily, without any difficulty and, finally from general usage alone; in this lies the whole strength of our versification'.[17] With Trediakovskii's and Kantemir's treatises the main foundations and rules of Russian versification were clearly and consistently explained and established.

Mikhailo Lomonosov and Alexander Sumarokov

The great literary critic Vissarion Belinskii characterized Mikhailo Vasil'evich Lomonosov (1711-1765) as 'the Peter the Great of Russian literature', since he took Russian literary language in the direction of advanced refinement. The son of a peasant and fisherman from Kholmogory on the

White Sea, he was encouraged in his early years by Feofan Prokopovich himself to get a sound classical education and then study abroad in Marburg on the Lahn, where in 1736-9 he became a student of Johann Christoph Gottsched.[18] In 1739, while still studying in Germany, Lomonosov sent to the Russian Academy *The Ode on the Siege of Khotin* written in iambics, accompanied by *A Letter On the Rules of Russian Versification*. This missive was essentially an attack on Trediakovskii's *New and Brief Method for Composing Russian Verse*. In contrast to Trediakovskii, Lomonosov approached the problems of Russian versification not as a theoretician but as a practitioner.[19] From Trediakovskii's teachings he accepted only one: that any versification must rely on the natural elements of the language, and in the Russian case on the juxtaposition between stressed and unstressed vowels. But, unlike Trediakovskii, he did not altogether reject the preceding national tradition of versification present in folk songs. Lomonosov believed that by combining the new versification intended for the 'high' poetic genres with folk poetry, the new Russian verse would not become an alien entity relying solely on classical, French, or German versification patterns but would have the elements of a national tradition.[20]

In 1748 Lomonosov published *A Brief Manual on Eloquence*, usually known as Lomonosov's *Ritorika* (*Rhetoric*). Both *A Letter* and *A Brief Manual* were strongly indebted to ancient precepts on poetics and rhetoric. In the first work Lomonosov followed the main rules established by Trediakovskii for writing 'syllabo-tonic' verse according to the stress, not the quantity, of the syllables. That work also reveals the influence of his teacher Gottsched, who criticized attempts to force German versification into Greek and Latin moulds.[21] Lomonosov's *Rhetoric* was the first text of this kind written in Russian rather than Latin. This made it easily accessible to broader circles of Russian readers, and introduced them to lengthy translations from Demosthenes, Cicero, Vergil and Ovid. Lomonosov's work as a translator is remarkable because he, like Trediakovskii, showed significant attention to poetic figures and prosody in an attempt to continue the refinement of Russian poetic language.[22] One of the most important achievements of Kantemir's, Trediakovskii's and Lomonosov's unceasing dedication to the classical tradition is that it was finally separated from Christian doctrine and could stand on its own in literature and education.[23]

Alexander Pushkin, who is hailed as the first Russian poet with *Naturgenie*, did not have a very high opinion of Lomonosov's poetic talent, although he acknowledged his significance for Russian letters by calling him, not without a touch of irony 'the first Russian university'. In the realm of poetry Pushkin viewed Lomonosov as a craftsman rather than a poet endowed with divine inspiration: 'For him poetic composition was a pastime, or, more often, an exercise undertaken out of a stern sense of duty ... In our first poet we would look in vain for flaming bursts of feeling or imagination'.[24] These observations about Lomonosov's poetic talent are hardly flattering or even fair, but they are also complicated by Pushkin's perception of his own place in the Russian poetic tradition. Great poets such as Pushkin, however, do not appear out of nowhere, but are preceded by a tradition that enables their growth and creates what might be called a 'poetogenic' situation. What Ennius did for Catullus, Lomonosov did for Pushkin, and his role in initiating the reforms leading to the creation of truly national Russian poetry should not be underestimated. Nikolai Gogol', although not a poet, gave Lomonosov his due by admitting that 'Lomonosov precedes all our poets as an introduction precedes the rest of the book'.[25]

Lomonosov was a driving force behind one of the most crucial and long standing tasks in Russian literary development: he started the creation of a new Russian poetic language, basing it not on Old Slavonic but rather on classical languages. Such an approach was conditioned not only by the cultural and historical changes of Peter's era but by Lomonosov's own education, which was based on Latin rhetoric at the Slavonic-Greek-Latin Academy. He tried to transfer the construction of Latin and Greek syntax to Russian grammatical constructions, as is evident in the text of the panegyric written for the empress Elizabeth.[26]

For Lomonosov ancient poetry, especially that of Homer and Pindar, was an object of imitation. The qualities that attracted Lomonosov most in the works of these two ancient poets were their pathos and attention to the heroic. In his cycle of poems entitled *Conversations with Anacreon*, Lomonosov argued with the Greek poet of love and banquets by pointing out that he preferred a heroic theme and by juxtaposing the 'singer of love' with his own stance as a 'poet-citizen':

Mne struny ponevole
Zvuchat geroiskii shum.
Ne vozmushchaite bole,
Liubovny mysli, um,
Khot' nezhnosti serdechnoi
V liubvi ia ne lishen,
Geroev slavoi vechnoi
Ia bol'she voskhishchen.[27]

The strings unwillingly
play for me the heroic sounds.
Do not excite much longer
amorous thoughts; although
my mind is not deprived
of tenderness in love,
I am more in awe
of eternal and heroic glory.

In the following poem Lomonosov opposed the Roman Cato, who committed suicide as he struggled to preserve the Republic, to Anacreon absorbed with sensual pleasures.[28] If Anacreon asked a painter to paint a portrait of his beloved, Lomonosov requested the portrait of his homeland, thus emphasizing that poetry has a political and not purely entertaining goal:

O master v zhivopiststve pervoi
Ty pervoi v nashei storone
Dostoin byt' rozhden Minervoi
Izobrazi Rossiiu mne.[29]

Oh, Master first in the painting,
You first should be deemed worthy
to be born by Minerva in our country:
depict Russia for me.

In his ode written in 1742 on the occasion of the coronation of Empress Elizabeth, Lomonosov enjoined his Muse to fly high aloft:

Vzleti prevyshe molnii, muza,
Kak Pindar bystryi tvoi orel ...
Sladchaishii nektar lei s Nazonom;
Prevys' Parnas vysokim tonom,
S Gomerom, kak reka, shumi,
I, kak Orfei, s soboi vedi ...[30]

Muse, fly above the lightning,
Like Pindar, your fast eagle ...
Pour the sweet nectar with Naso;
Over Parnassus with your high tone,
Resound, like a river, along with Homer,
And like Orpheus, lead me with you.

The choice of poets in these lines, which may initially appear random, is not coincidental. Homer and Pindar were inseparable from the heroic tradition in classical poetry and were considered by Lomonosov the highest style of verse and the ultimate model for imitation. Orpheus attracted Lomonosov mainly because he was connected with the scientific tradition in poetry; Lomonosov's contribution to Russian science far exceeded his poetic talents. Ovid was singled out for his mellifluous verse, reflecting Lomonosov's preoccupation with proper poetic diction and rhetorical devices. None of the poets (including Ovid) to whom Lomonosov alluded in these lines interested him as the singers of mundane or sensual experiences. The poet chose his classical allusions carefully and aimed for grandiose figures both in poetry and in classical mythology. In his celebratory odes Zeus, Pluto, Neptune, Atlas, Mars and Olympus appear frequently. Lomonosov can be considered to a certain degree a court poet although his preference for 'loud' classical allusions was not solely directed towards extolling the imperial family but rather his homeland, Russia, her might and wealth, and the talent of her people. For example in his 'Ode to Elizabeth' (1742) he used a classical metaphor to praise not only the empress but also an ordinary Russian:

> ... Kvirity, Mark vash zhiv
> Vo vsiakom rosse, chto bez strakhu
> Chrez ogn' i rvy techet s razmakhu.[31]

> ... Quirites, your Marcus is alive
> In any Russian, who without any fear
> Goes through fire and trenches zealously.

The allusion here is to Marcus Curtius, a legendary Roman hero and patriot who 'in obedience to an oracle, to save his country, leaped armed and on horse-back into the chasm which suddenly opened in the Forum'.[32]

The purpose of Lomonosov's classical allusions is especially manifest in his didactic poem with Lucretian overtones, 'Epistle on the Usefulness of Glass' ('Pis'mo o pol'ze stekla', 1752) in which the scientific side of Lomonosov's interests emerges clearly.[33] Lomonosov employed here the myth of Prometheus. However, while paraphrasing the myth, he added one significant change to the traditional mythological story: in his version Prometheus did not steal the fire from the gods but

> Pokhitil s solntsa ogn' i smertnym otdal v ruki.[34]

> He stole the fire from the sun and gave it to mortals.

Lomonosov, the scientist, is manifest in this change. The traditional mythological conflict, which depicted Prometheus as a rebel against the Olympian gods, did not interest him; he was concerned rather with an 'imitation of Prometheus', as it were ('we receive the fire of sun with Glass, and that is how we imitate Prometheus'), and the consequences of scientific pursuit inherent in Prometheus' plight:

> I tol'ko lish' o tom my dumaem zhaleia,
> Ne svergla l' v pagubu nauka Prometeia?[35]

> And we only think with pity about one thing:
> Didn't science bring Prometheus to utter destruction?

Along with Prometheus he introduced a historical example: he recalled Aristarchus, the Greek philosopher and astronomer of third century BCE, who boldly proposed that the earth revolved around the sun and was accused and persecuted for sacrilege. Aristarchus was presented by Lomonosov as a martyr for enlightenment and progress, an image very dear to Lomonosov, who against all opposition introduced numerous innovative ideas to advance the progress of Russian science.[36]

While developing the idea of the superiority of knowledge and wisdom over persecution in his translation of Jean Batiste Russo's ode, Lomonosov used both historical and mythological exempla. He opposed Socrates to Sulla, Hannibal and Alexander the Great. He also underscored two aspects of the reign of Octavian Augustus:

Naprasno Rima povelitel'
Octavii, sveta pobeditel',
Navel v ego predely strakh;
On Avgustom by ne nareksia,
Kogda by v krotkost' ne obleksia
I strakha ne skonchal v serdtsakh.[37]

It was in vain, that the lord of Rome,
Octavius, the conqueror of the world,
brought fear into the city;
he would have never been called Augustus,
if he were not clad in humility
and had ended fear in everybody's heart.

This stanza (its somewhat contradictory take on Roman history notwithstanding) can also be seen as a warning to Russian emperors wanting to model themselves on the Roman imperial family and reflects the didactic leanings of Lomonosov's poetry.[38] However, it is also apparent that Lomonosov was not actually interested in the facts of Augustus' reign but rather in an idealized, mythologized version of it. Andrew Kahn argued that after Lomonosov 'pronounced judgment on Russia's relationship to antiquity, the image of the ancient world tended to be confined to Rome'.[39] Russia, in truth, had rather more similarity to Rome than to Greece, but Lomonosov's tendency to identify with Rome is closely connected with his desire to bridge the discontinuity that he felt between the ancients and the Russians. Rome for Russia was undoubtedly a more natural choice in terms of both pleasing the rulers and weakening the intimidating pre-eminence of European influence.[40] It is especially remarkable that while Lomonosov 'cast Russia in the role of new Rome, Rome's afterlife had gone into decline throughout the donor-cultures of Europe, nowhere more strikingly than Italy itself'.[41] Andrew Kahn pointed out that 'when the French revolutionaries swept away the *ancien regime* they exploited the republican symbolism of Greece with only a courteous nod to Roman exemplary figures. In England around the close of the eighteenth century, scholars not only re-interpreted the classical universe but sharply shifted their field of interest from Rome to Greece'.[42] But the Russian polymath did not choose to move in the same direction as European cultures. Roman imperial legacy was used by Lomonosov as a means to analyze and praise

31

Russia's imperial attitudes and its monarchs. His unfinished attempt at Russian national epic, *Peter the Great*, echoed Vergilian text in its most patriotic interpretation. Despite Lomonosov's mostly one-sided approach to the most influential of Roman texts, he paved the way for future Russian poets to focus on Rome and self-identification with the Romans. They singled out Roman political and cultural legacy as the most formative for their own classical universe.

While Lomonosov's poetry displays a breadth of knowledge of ancient mythology and history, it lacks the generic diversity characteristic of the poetry of his contemporary, Alexander Sumarokov. Epigrams or satires or any kind of invective poetry occupy a small part of Lomonosov's writings.[43] His attempt at writing drama is illustrated by his 1752 tragedy *Demofont*, which conveyed Lomonosov's admiration for Greek culture but was hardly influential. When Lomonosov alluded to mythological plots and characters he very rarely satirized or ironized them. In his choice of poetic genres Lomonosov remained extremely conservative and limited them primarily to poetry of 'high style' ('vysokii shtil'') like odes, court poetry ('nadpisi') written on festive occasions, didactic poems, and some attempts at epic poetry.[44] He is known to have written only a few love poems, although it is possible that there were more; he did not deem them appropriate to publish under his own name, because he wanted to be considered a 'serious poet' with a didactic mission.

Alexander Sumarokov (1718-1777), however, experimented more widely with poetic genres and as a result achieved more freedom in the use of the classics. An imitator of Trediakovskii and a pupil of Lomonosov in his youth, he later parted company with each of them, both in theory and in practice, in his advocacy of the principle of stylistic and thematic simplicity for most poetic genres. Unlike Trediakovksii and Lomonosov, Sumarokov did not adhere to a lofty or elitist view of poetry, although he himself came from the hereditary gentry: 'Leisure, idleness and love are the main sources of poetic composition ... Even if not all human minds are enlightened, in their feelings everyone is equal'.[45] Sumarokov acquired fame within Russian society during the 1740s for his love songs which were set to music and sung at gatherings of the gentry.[46] The main principle of Sumarokov's approach to classical mythology was similar to his attitude to the sources of poetic inspiration, as explained by P.I. Berkov in his introduction to Sumarokov's poems: '... for the classicist Sumarokov mythology was beautiful and valuable because it allowed the introduction of the base, mundane, and ordinary into art as sublime, abstract and detached from the local accidental features'.[47] The majority of Sumarokov's poetic output was in drama. Appointed the first director of the first permanent theatre in St Petersburg, he found himself in an advantageous position to bring culture to the masses through the staging of his tragedies. Six of Sumarokov's best known tragedies were set in the Kievan era, sometime between the tenth and twelfth century.[48] They presented stultified versions of classical tragedies with heroes and rulers chosen from the nobility and lacked any realistic details of everyday life. These tragedies were primarily indebted to the European tradition of classical tragedy in structure and themes, in particular Racine and Voltaire.[49] For Russian society, however, these tragedies were new and astounding because of the system of ethical principles they offered. Although, in imitation of classical drama, the action was set in a pagan era dominated by the forces of fate and destiny, Sumarokov removed the participation of gods from the development of the plot. Kievan Rus was depicted as a heroic era, a Russian equivalent of the Trojan cycle, a society in which the concept of honour rather than passion was the focus of ethical values and drove the action.

While Sumarokov was mainly noted by his contemporaries for his tragedies and his fables, based on Aesop and Phaedrus and loaded with social commentary, his lyrics attracted much less attention. Nevertheless, in his use of prosody and genre Sumarokov far surpassed both Trediakovskii and Lomonosov in originality. There was hardly a single poetic genre that Sumarokov left untouched; he composed odes, elegies, epistles, love lyrics, idylls, eclogues, fables, tragedies and comedies. He inventively exploited the possibilities of Russian 'syllabo-tonic' verse by composing in every sort of metre from classical strophic forms to 'dol'niki' (accentual verse), which would not become widely popular in Russian poetry until the twentieth century. Most of all, however, he favoured invective poetry, especially satires and epigrams. Sumarokov's imitation of the ancients was on the whole of a formal nature. He was less interested in the ideas than in the metre and formal characteristics of each genre, although he himself believed that he followed the 'sklad' and 'dukh' (form and spirit) of his models.[50]

Sumarokov used both mythological and historical material in his poetry without any differentiation. In addition, his odes dedicated to the empresses Elizabeth and Catherine the Great reveal unequivocally that he was a court poet, since he used the names and attributes of ancient goddesses to extol the virtues of his sovereigns. He likened Elizabeth to Diana and Catherine to Minerva when he praised them as the followers of Peter's reforms. This limited use of ancient mythology also extended to Sumarokov's use of the names of ancient historical figures, which he introduced largely for didactic purposes, as examples of positive or negative role models. In his epistle to the Emperor Paul (Pavel), which was emphatically didactic, he named Caligula and Nero as examples that should be avoided by any aspiring monarch, and Titus as a positive role model.

Random overuse of ancient images is noticeable in Sumarokov's poetry, rather than conscious choices that make a point. Sometimes he deliberately overused classical allusions for the sake of parody, as in his 'nonsense odes' ('vzdornye ody'), in which he parodied Lomonosov's panegyrics and odes.

Sumarokov was especially fond of mythological characters associated with poetic inspiration. He often used the names of Parnassus, Helicon, Pegasus and the Muses. In his Epistle II he listed all the Greek and Roman poets that he considered role models for an aspiring poet. The epithets he attached to some of the poets are especially reflective of the way Russian poets-classicists perceived and interpreted ancient poets. He called Pindar bedazzling, Ovid sweet, Vergil unrivalled, and placed Vergil above Homer because he found him more 'rational' than the Greek poet.[51]

One of the highest aspirations that Sumarokov expressed in his poetry was to see the 'Russian Parnassus' one day ('Ode to E.V. Kheraskova'):

Sovershenstvo tshchusia videt'
Drevnikh grekov i u nas,
I podobnyi ikh Parnassu,
V Petrovoi oblasti Parnass.

I strive to see perfection
Of the ancient Greeks amongst us
And Parnassus in Peter's region
Similar to the one they had.[52]

Sumarokov realized that aspiration in his attempt to give every classical genre its legitimate place in Russian literature. The most important result of Sumarokov's efforts was that Russian classicism after him was 'complete'. Classical metaphor no longer seemed a rarefied exercise in imitation but had become a naturalized component of poetic expression. At the same time it became clear with Sumarokov that this phase of Russian classical movement had fulfilled its role as the harbinger of classical tradition in Russian poetry. There was a distinct need for a confident assertion of the uniqueness of the Russian poetic voice.

Gavriil Derzhavin

Despite Lomonosov's and Sumarokov's merits, the first writer who deserved acknowledgment as a truly original Russian poet, in the opinion of subsequent generations of poets, was Gavriil Derzhavin (1743-1816). Grigorii Gukovskii pointed out that 'the poetic system of classicism was radically destroyed by Derzhavin'.[53] Derzhavin was the first realist in Russian poetry; 'in Derzhavin literature entered life, and life entered literature'.[54] Il'ia Sherman noted that in the late 1770s 'Derzhavin destroyed the solemn ode's taboo on the personal and the biographical. He appears in his odes addressed to tsars not only as a poet, a singer of grandeur and beauty, but also as a person, a government bureaucrat, a family man, a victim of the persecutions of high officials who dislike him, a fighter for truth and justice both social and individual.'[55] It is easy to see from that description why Derzhavin became Pushkin's most frequently

34

acknowledged precursor. In Derzhavin's work the use of ancient material also lost the elevated register that had been so important to his predecessors. He was not trying to detach himself from the concrete reality of life by employing ancient images; nor did he try to elevate everyday events to the rank of the sublime. For Derzhavin antiquity constituted something else: a limitless wealth of poetic innovations, associations and forms of diction. He used all of them to create his own realm of images inseparable from his private thoughts and feelings.

For Derzhavin, as for Lomonosov, the ancient Greek and Roman poets remained the role models that should be imitated. He especially singled out Pindar, Anacreon and Horace, but he was not as interested in their genre canons and differences as in the themes of their poetry. He favoured Pindar for heroic themes but in Horace he was especially attracted to the poems related to the ideal of private life. He, however, unlike Lomonosov, was fond of Anacreon and Sappho because they extolled the sensual pleasures of life and the poet's love for life. He teasingly and admiringly referred to Anacreon as 'tender, tender suitor, a singer of love and pleasure' ('Nezhnyi, nezhnyi vozdykhatel',/ O pevets liubvi i negi').[56] It is especially interesting, however, that Derzhavin's imitation of Anacreon and Sappho was built on concrete, Russian and even autobiographical material.[57]

Derzhavin did not shy away from listing himself among the greatest of ancient poets, showing thus, perhaps not in an altogether humble way, that he, tossing away the classicizing convention of idealizing antiquity, was able to see Russian poets as the heirs to the tradition. In his famous poem 'Evgeniiu. Zhizn' Zvanskaia' ('To Evgenii. Life at Zvanka') he stated:

> Ottuda prikhozhu v sviatilishche ia muz
> I s Flakkom, Pindarom, bogov vossedshi v pire,
> K tsariam, k druz'iam moim il' k nebu voznoshus'
>   Il' slavliu sel'sku zhizn' na lire.[58]

> I enter the shrine of the Muses,
> With Flaccus, Pindar, partaking in the banquets of the gods,
> I ascend to the tsars, to my friends, or to the heavens
>   Or I praise the country life on my lyre.

This poem, rather remarkable in the context of lyric poetry of the eighteenth century, praises, in the manner of Horace's musings about his Sabine country (*Odes* 1.22), an idyllic life of a landowner in the country and describes all the details of everyday life, shunned previously by the representatives of classicism. The poem depicts the 'works and days' of Derzhavin in Zvanka: his hunting, walks, occupations and entertainment. Nevertheless, amid this mundane narration, Derzhavin claimed his place in the shrine of the Muses among his favourite ancient poets. The high style and the evocation of antiquity become for the first time intertwined

35

with everyday events of Russian life, a combination that contradicted the aesthetic norms of classicism. In his 'Monument' ('Pamiatnik'), written in imitation of Horace, he prided himself on his ability to talk about the sublime with 'playful verse' ('zabavnyi slog') and still to claim his place in the poetic tradition after the solemnity of classicism.[59]

Despite Derzhavin's populist leanings and the new poetic themes he introduced, it is hard not to agree with Sergei Averintsev who pointed out that Derzhavin's poetry is full of 'incorrigibly upper-class snobbishness' ('nepopravimo barskoe'), conditioned by decades of Catherine's rule.[60] His poem about life in Zvanka contains phrases such as 'it is noon, the slaves are running to serve the table', a detail of life in the Russian countryside that Derzhavin in 1807 saw much in the same way as ancient poets viewed their slaves: as a fact of life with no ethical ramifications. Derzhavin was a convinced follower and supporter of the enlightened but absolute Russian monarchy complete with serfdom – a system which less than twenty years later would be seen by Pushkin and his Decembrist friends as backward and repulsive. It is clear, however, why Pushkin found Derzhavin important if not influential for his own poetic coming of age.[61] Derzhavin was the first Russian poet in the true meaning of the word. While Trediakovskii, Lomonosov and Sumarokov created and applied the rules and principles for nascent Russian poetry, Derzhavin polished these rules to a degree that allowed Pushkin's talent to grow on fertile ground.

Alexander Sergeevich Pushkin: the *vates*

Pushkin dutifully if grudgingly acknowledged his debt to his predecessors by filling his works with references to Russia's eighteenth-century poets, especially Lomonosov and Derzhavin. After all, it was the latter who had noticed the young man at a poetry recital in Tsarskoe Selo, when Pushkin's declamation of his own poem 'Remembrances at Tsarskoe Selo' induced, according to Pushkin himself, the elderly Derzhavin to hail Pushkin as his successor.[62] Pushkin, however, considered himself and no one else the first truly Russian poet. David Bethea pointed out Pushkin's 'urge to be first' ('stremlenie pervenstvovat'') as one of the 'psychological dominanta of Pushkin's personality'.[63] That is perhaps why his evocation of classical antiquity was very different from that of his precursors, displaying more subtlety and thematic coherence. It is noteworthy that Iurii Lotman in his biography of the poet compared Pushkin to the mythological King Midas because Pushkin turned 'everything he touched into creative work [tvorchestvo], into art'.[64]

For anyone who has not read Pushkin in Russian it is hard to explain why any discussion of Russian poetry must inevitably involve him. As Donald Davie has suggested in his critical study of Pushkin, non-Russian speakers have to take Pushkin's achievement on trust.[65] In 1838 Vissarion Belinskii, called by his contemporaries 'raving Vissarion' ('neistovyi Vissarion') declared: 'Every educated Russian must have a complete Pushkin, otherwise he has no right to be considered either educated or Russian'.[66] This view was also supported by Fedor Dostoevskii, who with equal ardour stated: 'It is not only his poetry that matters ... If it weren't for Pushkin, we would have never acquired with such a decisive force ... the faith in our Russian independence, a conscious by now belief in our national strength, and after that also the faith in our future independent mission in the family of the European nations ...'.[67] As categorical and sweeping as these statements might seem, they reflect the way Russians felt and still feel about Pushkin. His importance for Russian poetic evolution is hard to overestimate. If the development of Russian poetry is compared with that of the Romans, Pushkin is for the Russian literary tradition simultaneously Catullus and Vergil: Catullus, because he took Russian poetic language in a completely different direction not anticipated even by Trediakovskii and Lomonosov who started the language reform; and Vergil, because he became for every subsequent Russian poet a genius par excellence, or what the Romans referred to as *vates*, a poet-prophet inspired by divine grace.

Pushkin himself keenly and unabashedly understood his unique importance in the Russian literary landscape. It is with Pushkin that poetry in Russia unequivocally took on the burden of cultural leadership. At the heart of that leadership was the dissatisfaction of Pushkin and his contemporaries with merely 'catching-up' with the West, and their desire that the Russian literary tradition rival that of France, Germany and England. Pushkin may have seen himself as a harbinger of that tradition, and he also understood, as he noted in his letter to Chaadaev, that Russia's peculiar position in relation to the West need not result in cultural insecurity but could be used to Russia's advantage as a nation occupying a unique position between the East and the West.

It is noteworthy that Pushkin was the Russian poet who combined both Western and Russian predecessors naturally in his writings. The impression gained from reading Pushkin's poetry is that the sense of inferiority had significantly decreased and had been replaced by a strongly defined feeling of national history and national destiny. Pushkin was extremely well read and thus keenly aware of the European literary legacy. The study in his apartment at No. 12 on the Moika in St Petersburg contained one of Russia's best private libraries.[68] His erudition led him to expand the boundaries of genre in Russian literature, composing lyric poems/elegies, verse narrative, novel-in-verse, prose fiction, historiography – a variety that earned Pushkin the title of the 'Russian Proteus'. But that alone would not have been enough to make him the prophetic figure of the early modern period in Russian literature. As David Bethea pointed out, 'Pushkin gave nineteenth-century Russian poetry one of its defining (if not always popular) attributes: a primarily aesthetic/ private/ meditative character as opposed to one that was ideological or social activist.'[69] In addition Pushkin completed the revolution in Russian poetic language started by his predecessors. Following the lead of Trediakovskii, Lomonosov, Sumarokov and Derzhavin (as well as the example of his contemporaries Del'vig and Gnedich) Pushkin further and more definitively demonstrated that Russian is indisputably suitable to be a language of poetry and can adapt to traditional classical metres.

Pushkin's relationship to classical heritage is much more subtle than that of the representatives of Russian classicism or even Derzhavin. A sense of both caution and confidence in its appropriate use underlies Pushkin's employment of classical motifs. His use of these was not at all random and he clearly differentiated between mythological and historical allusions, which had often been combined by the representatives of classicism. In the following pages I choose to dwell on those selections of Pushkin's 'classical' poetry that I consider the 'milestones' of his poetic journey and that proved to be influential for the poets of the twentieth century.

Pushkin's antiquity: the milestones

I

Dovol'no. S plech doloi obuza!
Ia klassitsizmu otdal chest':
Khot' pozdno, a vstuplen'e est'.[70]

Enough. The load is off my shoulders!
To classicism I've paid my due:
it may be late, but it is an entry.

A.S. Pushkin, *Evgenii Onegin* VII.55.

In order to understand better the role of classical references in Pushkin's poetry, a few words must be said about the influences that Pushkin encountered as he emerged on the literary scene. Aleksei Nikolaevich Olenin (1763-1843), whose salon Pushkin frequented and whose daughter was once the object of his serious affection,[71] enjoyed both tremendous wealth and the role of a Russian Maecenas. He was especially proud of two of his appointments: he was President of Academy of Arts and Director of the Imperial Public Library. While the salon welcomed all kinds of literary tastes, there was one particular trend that defined it: classical antiquity was understood and interpreted in the tradition of Winckelmann and Lessing and worshipped as a paragon of cultural achievement.[72] One of Olenin's librarians was Nikolai Gnedich (1784-1833), who undertook a translation of the *Iliad* into Russian hexameters which has remained unsurpassed since its publication in 1829.[73] Gnedich undoubtedly had some influence on Pushkin although Pushkin did not always treat Gnedich's poetic achievement with respect:

Kriv byl Gnedich poet, prelozhitel' slepogo Gomera,
Bokom odnim s obraztsom skhozh i ego perevod.[74]

Gnedich, the poet, blind Homer's translator, had one eye only,
And his translation itself, mirrors no more than one side.[75]

These lines, like most of the acerbic quips Pushkin made regarding his poetic predecessors (and contemporaries) must, however, be recognized for what they reflect: Pushkin's reluctance to acknowledge any indebtedness to anyone as a poet. It is also interesting, however, that Pushkin later regretted these lines and crossed them out in his notebooks so aggressively that they were published only in the twentieth century after thorough textological recovery.[76] In general Pushkin spoke extremely highly of Gnedich's work, as his poem of 1821 'Iz Pis'ma k Gnedichu' ('From a Letter to Gnedich') and his note of 1830 'Iliada Gomerova' ('Homer's *Iliad*') about Gnedich's translation of the poem both testify. Furthermore, Pushkin would have had only vague (if any) familiarity with the Greek original. The poem of 1832 'To Gnedich' ('Gnedichu') displays both Pushkin's insecurity about his knowledge of Homer and his gratitude to Gnedich for the latter's monumental accomplishment in bringing the *Iliad* to the Russian readers.[77] In another poem 'Na perevod Iliady' ('On the Translation of the *Iliad*') written also in 1830, he even endowed Gnedich's translation with the ability to bring alive the spirit of the Greek language and the shadow of Homer himself:

Slyshu umolknuvshii zvuk bozhestvennoi ellinskoi rechi,
Startsa velikogo ten' chuiu smushchennoi dushoi.[78]

I hear the silenced sound of divine Hellenic speech,
With my confused soul I feel the presence of the great old sage.

Therefore Pushkin's first comment must be taken with a grain of salt; one can only assume that to his highly attuned poetic ear the translation might have sounded contrived and alien. The acerbic lines, nonetheless, written in imitation of ancient elegiac distich (first line hexameter, second – pentameter), also testify to the emulous character of Pushkin's ridicule: he attempted to beat Gnedich at his own game of imitating an ancient metre.

Two other contemporary figures might also have contributed to Pushkin's interest in antiquity: Konstantin Batiushkov (1787-1855) and Vasilii Zhukovskii (1783-1852). Batiushkov, who was also an assistant custodian in Olenin's library, produced literary works full of Greek mythological references and translated Horace and some poetry believed at that time to be by Tibullus.[79] The beginning of Pushkin's *Mednyi Vsadnik* (*The Bronze Horseman*) refers to Batiushkov's famous essay of 1814, 'Progulka v Akademiiu Khudozhestv' ('A Walk to the Academy of Arts'), in which Batiushkov expressed his aesthetic viewpoint, taking as his touchstone the culture of antiquity. Zhukovskii, who produced the finest extant translation of the *Odyssey* into Russian, significantly extended the semantic boundaries of Russian poetic vocabulary, the influence of which facilitated Pushkin's revolution in Russian poetic language.[80]

In 1811-17 Pushkin was admitted in the first elite group, thirty in number, to a new Lycée of Tsarskoe Selo (Imperatorskii Tsarskosel'skii Litsei), near St Petersburg. Nikolai Koshanskii, the professor of ancient languages, seems to have made a strong impression on the young poet although he did not find Latin or Koshanskii's method of teaching it particularly exciting.[81] Koshanskii, on the other hand, appreciated his young charge's energy and talent, though he stated in the official report that Pushkin 'has more ability for comprehension than memory, more taste for refinement than industry for mastering the fundamentals ... His success in Latin is good, but in Russian it is not so much solid as it is brilliant'.[82] Pushkin's phlegmatic friend Baron Anton Del'vig was, by all accounts, a much better classicist whose poetry Nabokov concisely characterized as 'half amphora half samovar'.[83] Although Pushkin never attained fluency in Latin (and Greek was never even in question), altogether to deny Koshanskii's imprint on Pushkin's knowledge of classical antiquity would be unfair. Pushkin may have found Koshanskii's method extremely pedantic and his views reactionary, but Koshanskii knew and loved antiquity and tried his best to convey that appreciation to his young charges.[84] This early influence would also explain Pushkin's interest in the poet-classicist Batiushkov and his life-long adherence to classical metres and aesthetics.[85] As Boris Tomashevskii persuasively argued, Pushkin, who admired Lord Byron, was impressed by Batisuhkov's lyric hero with his persistent contemplation of a romanticized escape from life and his melancholy. However, Pushkin was influenced more by the historical and mythological reminiscences of Batiushkov, whom Pushkin called the 'Russian Parni'[86] and whose treatment of antiquity in such elegies as 'Moi Penaty' ('My Penates'), 'Na razvalinakh zamka v Shvetsii' ('On the Ruins of a Castle in Sweden'), and 'K Zhukovskomu' ('To Zhukovskii') influenced Pushkin's own.[87] In imitation of Batiushkov's poetry, Pushkin's early poems display a remarkable interest in mythology. For example, in his poem 'Torzhestvo Vakkha' ('Bacchus' Triumph') Pushkin clearly alluded to Batiushkov's 'Vakkhanki' ('The Bacchae') by reproducing in his poem not only the visual imagery of the Maenads' divinely inspired frenzy but also the sounds they utter ('Euhoi!').

There is no doubt even in Pushkin's early poetry that he was familiar (most likely in French translations) not just with Homer and Pindar, Plato and the tragedians, but even with authors much less prominent in the school curriculum, such as Anacreon, Theocritus, Moschus, Hedylus and Xenophanes of Colophon. The last two he probably read in their citations in Athenaeus' *Deipnosophists* which Pushkin owned in a lavishly illustrated French edition and which inspired two short poems of 1832, 'From

Xenophanes of Colophon ('Iz Ksenofana Kolofonskogo') and 'From Athenaeus' ('Iz Afenia').[88] Latin authors he knew much better, starting with Catullus, Horace, Vergil and the elegists, and also including Tacitus, Apuleius, Petronius and even Aurelius Victor. It remains unclear how well Pushkin knew any of these authors in the original. In his essay on the influence of Tacitus' portrayal of Tiberius on Pushkin's character of Boris Godunov, Glen Bowersock demonstrated that 'there is little room for doubt that Pushkin read the *Annals* in Latin'.[89] Bowersock acknowledged that Pushkin found his way through the Latin text by using the French translation on the right-hand page of his edition. However, Bowersock maintained that at points of particular interest to Pushkin he worked out the meaning of the Latin directly on his own. He also tried to show in the case of *comparatio deterrima* that Pushkin clearly rendered the Latin original and not the French version.[90] This argument is persuasive, especially taking into consideration how many people find their way around ancient authors by perusing the Loeb English translations, and, even if their Latin or Greek is minimal, endeavour to determine the meaning directly.

However, some other instances of Pushkin's display of familiarity with Latin originals cause me to doubt Pushkin's ability to read the Latin text with complete comprehension. One such instance is his rendition of Catullus 27, entitled 'Mal'chiku' ('To a Boy') with a subtitle 'Iz Katulla' ('From Catullus').[91] Pushkin's epigraph to the poem is *'minister vetuli puer'* after which quotation he put a decisive period, thus rendering incomprehensible the beginning of Catullus' poem. It is not merely that Pushkin did not bother to quote the second line of the poem *'inger mi calices amariores'* without which the genitive case of *Falerni,* not to mention *vetuli,* cannot be construed; he also altered the punctuation of the original text causing anyone with even remote knowledge of Latin grammar to question his knowledge of it. Furthermore, while Pushkin's poem itself is wonderful, it is by no means a precise translation of the Latin original (he omitted some challenging constructions and the fourth line: *'ebrioso acino ebriosioris'*), which leads me to believe that he was not so much intending to stay true to the Catullan original as simply to convey (and successfully so) the spirit of the poem.[92] If Pushkin could not get through a short poem of Catullus without stumbling, his facility with the far more complex text of Tacitus must necessarily be questioned.[93]

Some early versions of *Evgenii Onegin* also testify to Pushkin's ambivalence about reading Latin authors in the original. For example, in the first chapter strophes VI and VII had the following variants when Pushkin described his hero's classical education: 'ne mog on Tatsita <poniat'>' ('he could not understand Tacitus'), 'ne mog on Liviia <poniat'>' ('he could not understand Livy') and even 'ne mog on *tabula* spriagat'' ('he could not conjugate [*sic!*] *tabula*').[94] Latin was for Onegin (and one might assume for Pushkin as well) nothing more than a dull chore, which any young man would happily abandon for more pleasurable activities:

Po krovle on v okoshko lazil
I zabyval latinskii klass
Dlia alykh ust i chernykh glaz.[95]

He climbed into a window from the roof
And forgot his Latin class
For the crimson lips and black eyes.

Nevertheless, Pushkin undoubtedly read a fair number of Latin authors
even if he did so mostly in French translations and frequently expressed a
dislike of the language. This could have been due to the influence of
Koshanskii and even more to his temporary replacement (from May 1814
to June 1815), Alexander Galich (1783-1848) who was not a Latinist but a
philosopher and one of the first Russian followers of Schelling.[96] Koshanskii also introduced Pushkin to Ossian whom the young poet preferred
even to Homer. Some passages from *Evgenii Onegin* testify to the influence
of those years under Koshanskii's and Galich's tutelage. It is quite easy to
discern a certain autobiographical component in Pushkin's description of
the hero of the poem (*EO* I.6):[97]

Latyn' iz mody vyshla nyne:
Tak esli pravdu vam skazat',
On znal dovol'no po-latyni,
Chtob epigraphy razbirat',
Potolkovat' o Iuvenale,
V kontse pis'ma postavit' *vale*,
Da pomnil, khot' ne bez grekha,
Iz Eneidy dva stikha.

Latin has now gone out of fashion.
Well, if the truth needs to be told,
He barely knew enough of Latin
In order to decipher some epigraphs,
To chat of Juvenal on occasion,
And write '*vale*' at letter's ending,
And he remembered, albeit with some error,
Two whole verses from the *Aeneid*.

In the next stanza there is further ironic reference to the classical education of his hero (and by extension Pushkin himself) (*EO* 1.7):

Branil Gomera, Feokrita;
Zato chital Adama Smita
I byl glubokii ekonom.

He cursed Theocritus and Homer
But read instead Adam Smith
And was a deep economist.

Pushkin himself became proficient in economics while at the Lycée and enjoyed reading most of the classics in French translation (rather than struggling through them in Latin), for which preference he was nicknamed 'Frantsuz' ('the Frenchman'). Despite this rather ambivalent attitude towards his classical education, Pushkin emerged from the experience of the Lycée with some grounding, if only superficial, in Greco-Roman classics. More important, however, was his experimentation with different poetic genres during his student years, which helped him find his own unique voice. His epigrams, madrigals and philosophical tales akin to Aesop's fables, as well as the adaptations of Anacreontica and epicurean themes in his poetry, reveal as early as the Lycée years what Zhukovskii recognized in his letter to Viazemskii 'as the hope of our literature'.[98]

II

Puskin's deep engagement with ancient motifs did not begin until 1820-4, the time of his exile to Bessarabia (Moldova).[99] During the exile years Pushkin turned his attention to that 'archetypal' exile of all times, Ovid, and alluded to him several times, starting with a letter dated 24 March 1821 to Nikolai Gnedich,[100] which also contained a poem:

V strane, gde Iuliei venchannyi
I khitrym Avgustom izgnannyi
Ovidii mrachny dni vlachil,
Gde elegicheskuiu liru
Glukhomu svoemu kumiru
On malodushno posviatil:
Daleche severnoi stolitsy
Zabyl ia vechnyi vash tuman ...
Vse tot zhe ia, kak byl i prezhde,
S poklonom ne khozhu k nevezhde,
S Orlovym sporiu, malo p'iu,
Oktaviiu, v slepoi nadezhde,
Molebnov lesti ne poiu ...[101]

In the country where, crowned by Julia
and exiled by cunning Augustus,
Ovid dragged out his gloomy days
and in his weakness devoted his elegiac lyre
to his deaf idol. Away from the northern capital-city
I forgot your eternal fog ...
I am just the same as I was before,
I don't pay homage to an ignoramus,
I argue with Orlov, drink a little,
And I don't, blinded by hope,
Sing to Octavius my plights of flattery.

At the beginning of the poem the juxtaposition between 'crowned by Julia' and 'exiled by cunning Augustus' shows Pushkin's thorough familiarity with the historical circumstances of Ovid's exile. Julia Minor, Augustus' granddaughter exiled for adultery by the *princeps*, acquired, according to several testimonies, a particular fondness for Ovid's poetry, especially the unfortunate *Ars Amatoria*.[102] Furthermore, Pushkin found Ovid's exilic poetry unsettling in its attempt to recant previous mistakes and attain the good graces of Augustus. That attitude would remain constant, as we will see, in Pushkin's treatment of the Ovidian theme.

In these lines, as well as in his second epistle 'To Chaadaev', and in the poems 'To Baratynskii, from Bessarabia' and 'To Ovid', the place of the Roman poet's exile is identified by Pushkin as exactly the same as his own. Even in his narrative poem 'The Gypsies' ('Tsygane') the old gypsy tells Aleko a legend about Ovid in Bessarabia.[103] Pushkin seems to have cherished this theme, for he returned to it repeatedly.[104] It is impossible to assume that Pushkin was so geographically confused as to believe that Ovid had ever been to Bessarabia.[105] Nevertheless, Tomi (modern Constanza) was close enough and, like Moldova, was also near the Black Sea, so Pushkin kept insisting that the place of his exile was still full of the memory of the great Roman who had suffered a similar fate. The facts of Pushkin's life at that time can provide an explanation for this geographic 'confusion;' Pushkin was interested in literary not actual geography. He was exiled to Bessarabia by the Emperor Alexander and it was quite natural that the analogy with Ovid's fate would occur to Pushkin in his own exile. But the mere similarity of two poets' fates would hardly have been a sufficient reason for Pushkin's persistent return to the Ovidian theme.[106] The preoccupation with the theme of Ovid's exile suggests another, perhaps deeper and more substantial level of Pushkin's poetics, namely the poet's contemplation at that time of his own legacy and poetic mission. In his poem 'To Ovid' Pushkin explicitly compared Ovid's exile to his own and offered another 'poem of sorrow' that can be seen as an *oppositio in imitando* ('criticizing while imitating').

Pushkin began his poem by recalling Ovid's sad plight, his pleading with Augustus for return, and his death away from his beloved Rome.[107] 'A magnificent citizen of golden Italy' Pushkin called Ovid as he lamented Roman poet's fate of exile and his unceasing nostalgia. There are several aspects in the poem that deserve special consideration. At the centre of 'To Ovid' is 'an act of ventriloquism',[108] in which Pushkin, speaking in an Ovidian voice, expresses what the exilic plight might have felt like to his Roman predecessor:

Ty v tiazhkoi goresti dalekoi druzhbe pishesh':
'O vozvratite mne sviashchennyi grad ottsov
I teni mirnye nasledstvennykh sadov!
O drugi, Avgustu mol'by moi nesite!

44

Karaiushchuiu dlan' slezami otklonite!
No esli gnevnyi bog dosel' neumolim
I vek mne ne vidat' tebia, velikii Rim, -
Posledneiu mol'boi smiagchaia rok uzhasnyi,
Priblizh'te khot' moi grob k Italii prekrasnoi!'

You write, in your heavy sorrow, to your far away friends:
'O return to me the holy city of my fathers
And the peaceful shades of the family gardens!
O friends, carry my prayers to Augustus!
With your tears turn away the punishing hand!
But if the wrathful god is still inexorable,
And I will not ever see you again, great Rome,
With this last prayer soften this terrible fate,
Bring at least my coffin close to beautiful Italy!'

This recollection is in tune with Ovid's own sorrow expressed in his *Tristia* and *Epistolae ex Ponto*, and it lasts until line 48 of Pushkin's poem. The homage of sorrow ends with line 49, when Pushkin asks what seems at first to be a set of rhetorical questions:

Ch'e serdtse khladnoe, prezrevshee kharit,
Tvoe unynie i slezy ukorit?
Kto v gruboi gordosti prochtet bez umilen'ia
Sii elegii, poslednie tvoren'ia,
Gde ty svoi tshchetnyi ston potomstvu peredal?

Whose cold heart, despising the Graces,
Can reproach your despair and your tears?
Who can in his crude pride read and not be touched
By these elegies, your last creations,
Where you bequeathed your last groan to the descendants?

The answer to these questions, one would expect, is that nobody could remain unresponsive to Ovid's sorrowful plight of exile. Ovid's exile was and would surely continue to be a sad page of Roman history. But Pushkin is not a poet of clichés. The very next section of the poem starts with a peculiar line:

Surovyi slavianin, ia slez ne prolival,
No ponimaiu ikh; ...

A stern Slav, I never shed tears.
But I understand them; ...

Understanding, however, is not the same as complete, unconditional empathy. Thus Pushkin has almost confessed that *he* is in fact that man with the 'cold heart' who comes to Ovid's plight from a different cultural and geographical perspective. As Stephanie Sandler pointed out, 'what is south to Pushkin, therefore comparatively warm and inviting, is north to Ovid'.[109] In Ovid's poetry of exile, the country of the Getae, the land of his banishment, is a barren terrain deprived of trees and the joy of bountiful nature.[110] That different understanding and perception of the landscape also led Pushkin to juxtapose his solemn and severe Slav soul to Ovid's vulnerable Mediterranean temper, pointing out that his own exile had not driven him to tears and that he even found Ovid's exile enabling in terms of poetic legacy.

Thus the 're-writing' of Ovid's exile commenced. When Pushkin travelled to the terrain described by Ovid as cold, gloomy and generally unsuitable for human habitation, he was rather taken by the beauty of the landscape. He in fact juxtaposed the mildness of the winter there to its early arrival and fierceness in Russia. Unlike Ovid, Pushkin was mesmerized by the beauty of nature in his place of exile. He then moved to the poem's even more unexpected finale: 'Utesh'sia;', he said addressing the famously inconsolable Roman poet, 'ne uvial Ovidiev venets' ('Be consoled, the Ovidian wreath has not withered'). The sentence is almost condescending in its conviction that poetic immortality was worth the suffering of exile. If a descendant of mine, Pushkin continued, should come to this remote country searching for the traces of my ashes, I would rejoice in the mere fact of that. 'So why don't you, Ovid?' is the implicit message.

One line of the poem (98) 'it is not in fame but in lot that we are equals' provides the contrast that Pushkin drew between himself and his great predecessor. At the time of his exile to Tomi, Ovid had already written his most famous poetic works (one of which, the *Ars Amatoria*, was allegedly a cause of his exile); in contrast, Pushkin was conscious while writing 'To Ovid' that he was at the beginning of his poetic career. The 51-year-old Ovid did not earn much pity from the 22-year-old Russian poet who refused to see Ovid's plight as pitiful considering the immortality of Ovid's poetic reputation. This line (98) was followed in Pushkin's final version by the following two lines, which were excised upon publication by the tsar's censors: [111]

No ne unizil vvek izmenoi bezzakonnoi
Ni gordoi sovesti, ni liry nepreklonnoi.

But I never degraded by a lawless betrayal
Neither my proud conscience nor my untameable lyre.

Are we to infer from this 'but' that follows line 98 that in Pushkin's opinion Ovid had compromised his poetic integrity, for which Pushkin berated him? Can the exilic poems of Ovid be those compromises? That view is also clear in the poem included in the letter to Gnedich cited above, written on 24 March 1821, in which Pushkin suggested that 'Ovid in his weakness devoted his elegiac lyre to his deaf idol' and juxtaposed to that his own refusal to flatter the sovereign in hope of return: 'and I don't, blinded by hope, sing to Octavius my plights of flattery'.

Furthermore, it appears that Pushkin 're-wrote' Ovid's exile, contradicting the ancient poet himself in his view of exile as a poetic death. Pushkin saw it almost as a resurrection, a cleansing moment, an opportunity for a new beginning but more importantly for the assertion of his freedom, a theme that later in the poems written after 14 December 1825 acquired a special poignancy.

For Pushkin the evocation of the Roman poet led to a joyous celebration of the power of poetry to transcend imperial decrees.[112] Exile was enabling rather than incapacitating. Pushkin's preoccupation with Ovid's fate must thus be considered in the context of a larger theme in Pushkin's poetry, one concerned with the place of a poet in society and his role as a defender of liberty – themes in which he had a genuine interest from his schooldays to his death and to which he continually returned.[113]

III

During Puskin's years in Mikhailovskoe (1824-6) his poetic mode began to change. Lyric poetry gave way to more dramatic and solemn poetry. His obsession with Byron was replaced by an increased interest in Shakespeare, while his interest in antiquity shifted from Ovid to Tacitus and Greek poetry and myth. In 1827 he wrote a poem called 'Arion':

> Nas bylo mnogo na chelne;
> Inye parus napriagali,
> Drugie druzhno upirali
> V glub' moshchny vesly. V tishine
> Na rul' sklonias', nash kormshchik umnyi
> V molchan'i pravil gruznyi cheln;
> A ia – bespechnoi very poln,
> Plovtsam ia pel ... Vdrug lono voln
> Izmial s naletu vikhor' shumnyi ...
> Pogib i kormshchik i plovets!...
> Lish' ia, tainstvennyi pevets,
> Na bereg vybroshen grozoiu
> Ia gimny prezhnie poiu,
> I rizu vlazhnuiu moiu
> Sushu na solntse pod skaloiu.[114]

> We have been many on the ship:
> some helped to stretch the sail tight,
> others, all in unison,
> dug mighty oars into the depth. Our clever
> helmsman in silence led our weighty craft
> leaning on the steering wheel.
> while I sang, full of carefree faith,

to the oarsmen ... Then all of a sudden
a raging whirlwind ripped through the waves,
The helmsman and oarsman – all gone! –
But I, the enigmatic bard,
was cast up on the shore by the storm.
I am singing the former hymns again,
and drying off my soaked cloak
in the sunshine beneath the cliff.

The poem was written in fifteen iambic tetrameters and was immediately recognized as an allegory of the brutally suppressed Decembrist conspiracy of 1825 in which Pushkin was emotionally invested but from which he was physically absent since he was not in St Petersburg at the time. The Decembrist rebellion was perhaps the most formative event for the gentry of Pushkin's generation. From his days in Tsarskoe Selo Pushkin had been extremely close to many of the Decembrists, such as Pushchin and Kukhel'beker, who ended up in Siberian exile.

The classical allusion in this poem is remarkably interesting, and it differs significantly from the ancient legend. The story of Arion was told by Herodotus in *Histories* 1.23, where the Greek historian told the story of the famous musician connected with the invention of the dithyramb. When Arion was returning by ship to the court of Periander in Corinth, the sailors plotted to kill him and steal the considerable wealth he had earned on his singing tour of Sicily and Italy. Given a choice between being murdered by them on the ship (and attaining a burial ashore) or jumping overboard, Arion persuaded the sailors to permit him a last song, at the end of which he threw himself into the sea and was rescued and carried to the shore by a dolphin attracted by the beauty of his music. Arriving in Corinth before the sailors, Arion exposed their plot to Periander.

It is interesting to see how Pushkin used this story in his poem; he omitted the plot and violence altogether. Arion (narrating in the first person singular) is depicted as a carefree singer whose activity is opposed to the mundane tasks performed by the crew. The crew on the ship, however, are not pirates ready to strip Arion of his riches but silent and diligent sailors who want to ensure a safe voyage. The only vocal part in the poem is given to the poet, who does not contribute physically to sailing the ship but is the only one rescued from the 'raging storm', a detail not present in the traditional story about Arion. The poet is called an 'enigmatic bard' who apparently knows how to charm nature into helping him. For Pushkin, that unique power of the poetic word was the most fascinating element of the story of Arion. He omitted the rescue by a dolphin and other dramatic elements of Herodotus' account and kept only Arion's power as a singer that enabled him to survive a storm in which everybody else died. Pushkin also used the Church Slavonic word 'riza' ('cloak'), emphasizing the sacerdotal vestment worn by the poet and giving him a

Statue of Alexander Pushkin in
Pushkin Square, Moscow.
Sculptor: Alexander Opekushin.
Photo by Sergio Sanabria

mystical and divine power.[115] Apart from historical specificities, this poem reflects Pushkin's conviction that a poet's highest purpose is to be a singer of liberty.

This concern and interest in the power of poetry eventually found its way into Pushkin's most remarkable and final contemplation of his poetic legacy in the context of antiquity in one of his last poems, which, although Pushkin never used that title, later came to be known as 'Pamiatnik' ('Monument'). Pushkin's 'Pamiatnik' is the third in a line of Russian imitations of Horace's poem. Lomonosov, the first Russian poet to translate it, stayed faithful to the original but focussed poetic attention on this particular ode as he tried to establish an affinity between the ancients (especially the Romans) and the Russians. Derzhavin was the first poet on Russian soil to apply a certain poetic licence to the poem. His first seven lines are an exact translation from Horace, followed by a specifically Russian context in which the poet introduces Russian temporal ('Until the universe will honour the race of Slavs ...') and spatial ('From the White Sea's waters all the way to the Black')[116] boundaries for his future fame. The list of poetic merits also differs significantly:

> I was the first who dared in the playful Russian verse
> To sing the virtues of Felitsa,[117]
> To talk of God with heartfelt simplicity,
> And tell the truth to the tsars.

Derzhavin's self-perception in relation to the mighty of the world and the emphasis on his own integrity are significant in these lines; especially noteworthy is the last line, which undoubtedly was the most influential for Pushkin's own claim to greatness.

Before turning to the text of Pushkin's 'Pamiatnik', it is helpful to look briefly at one of his earlier poems in which he contemplated his poetic inspiration and legacy. That poem is 'The Muse' ('Muza'), written in 1821 in which Pushkin without a hint of modesty presented himself as a poet favoured by the Muse from early infancy ('V mladenchestve moem ona menia liubila' –'In my infancy she loved me'). Even more, he saw himself, in the manner of Hesiod and Callimachus, as inspired by a divine visitation and guided by his benevolent and charming Muse.

The poet of 'The Muse' was only 22 years old; in contrast, Pushkin wrote 'Pamiatnik' as an unintentional testament of sorts, a few weeks before his tragic death. The latter poem by Pushkin is further personalized, and is in every sense far superior as poetry to Lomonosov's or Derzhavin's versions. For facility of the discussion I quote Horace and Pushkin one after the other.

Odes 3.30

I have erected a monument outlasting bronze
And higher than the regal structure of pyramids,
which the gnawing rain and raging North Wind
cannot destroy, nor can the chain
of countless years and the flight of time.
Not all of me shall die; a great part of me
will evade the death goddess; I will grow
with future praise still youthful, as long as the priest
climbs the Capitoline hill together with the silent Vestal.
I will be talked about as someone who from humble origins
had the power to be the first to bring Aeolian songs
to Italian measures in a land where raging Aufidius roars
and where Daunus poor in water ruled
over his rustic people.
Melpomene, grant me the pride
sought because of my merits and willingly
crown my hair with Delphic laurel.

['Pamiatnik']

Ia pamiatnik sebe vozdvig nerukotvornyi.
K nemu ne zarastet narodnaia tropa,
Voznessia vyshe on glavoiu nepokornoi
    Aleksandriiskogo stolpa.

Net, ves' ia ne umru – dusha v zavetnoi lire
Moi prakh perezhivet i tlen'ia ubezhit –

I slaven budu ia, dokol' v podlunnom mire
  Zhiv budet khot' odin piit.

Slukh obo mne proidet po vsei Rusi velikoi,
I nazovet menia vsiak sushchii v nei iazyk,
I gordyi vnuk slavian, i finn, i nyne dikoi
  Tunguz, i drug stepei kalmyk.

I dolgo budu tem liubezen ia narodu,
Chto chuvstva dobrye ia liroi probuzhdal,
Chto v moi zhestokii vek vosslavil ia svobodu
  I milost' k padshim prizyval.

Velen'iu bozhiiu, o muza, bud' poslushna,
Obidy ne strashas', ne trebuia ventsa,
Khvalu i klevetu priemli ravnodushno,
  I ne osporivai gluptsa.

I have built myself a monument, but not with hands I made it;
The people's path to it shall not overgrow with grass.
With an unruly head it soared, and in its height
  Alexander's Column it surpassed.

Not all of me shall die! My soul, in sacred lyre,
Will yet survive my dust and even fly decay.
And I shall be renowned until in the moonlit world
  Even a single bard shall live.

My fame will travel through all of Russia mighty,
And every living tongue in her my name shall tell;
Proud Slav's grandson, and Finn, and now still wild,
  Tungus, and Kalmyk, the friend of steppe.

And many years to come I will be loved by the people,
For with my lyre I stirred up kind feelings,
And in my ruthless age I extolled Freedom,
  And asked clemency for those who fell.

Heed to the Lord's command, my Muse, nor disobeying;
Fear not offence nor demand the crown of bay,
Indifferent to praise and slander, and never
  Argue with the fool, but let him have his say. [118]

Horace's approach to his poetic legacy is consistent with his overall understanding of the meaning of poetry in a society that was obsessed with
military glory and the erection of material memorabilia for outstanding
achievement. Gordon Williams observed that the impression of immortality created in the long opening sentence 'with a great series of pictures
beginning with bronze tablets or statues, then the Pyramids, then the

destructive forces of nature' presented 'the common idiom for human immortality' rather than a specifically Roman or even Greek idea of it. In the second sentence, however, the vision of perpetual fame became 'completely Roman in sentiment and outlook'.[119] Horace's perception of his own immortality was also inextricably linked with the immortality of the Roman Empire and her achievements. The impressive portrait of the Capitol was linked with state ceremonial led by the *pontifex maximus* and the Vestal Virgins. In addition, Horace was proud of his poetic achievement as someone who had introduced Greek metres into Latin poetry. His address to the Muse may even seem somewhat arrogant since he claimed 'pride' (expressed by a multilayered Latin word, *superbia*, in line 14) as his due. In the last lines of the poem he asked Melpomene for the Delphic laurel both as a herald of the poetic gift granted by Apollo and as a prophet since Delphi was a place of Apollo's oracle. Thus Horace did not just claim for himself poetic glory but implicitly asserted his immortality as a *vates*, a word he usually preferred to *poeta*.

The similarities of Pushkin's poem to Horace's are numerous, and the divergences are illuminating. The first line of the poem contains the word *pamiatnik*, which is derived from the Russian word 'pamiat'' ('memory'), as the Latin word *monumentum* is derived from *memini*. 'Pamiatnik' thus, like *monumentum*, is a reminder of someone's achievement. However, in Russian the word is more often used to signify a material rather than metaphorical trigger for memory and usually refers to a statue, a visual aid to assist the process of remembering. Another peculiarity is the word 'nerukotvornyi' ('not made by hands') applied to the monument. The word is taken from Church Slavonic and is a calque of Greek *acheiropoietos*.[120] It replaces two words used by Derzhavin in his poem: 'chudesnyi, vechnyi' ('wondrous, eternal'). I am inclined to disagree with Kelly who observed: 'Pushkin's poem ... is teasingly insubstantial: 'a monument not made by human hands' is from some points of view not a monument at all'.[121] The adjective 'nerukotvornyi' has a far more important connotation than simply 'not made by human hands'; it takes the reader into the realm of the divine. Thus Pushkin elevated the idea of his legacy from the world of the mundane to the world of the immortal. Furthermore, the adjective illuminates and sums up Pushkin's obsession with sculptural themes throughout his poetry.[122] The comparison of his poetic legacy to Alexander's Column is especially notable in this light.[123] Alexander's Column is one of the most prominent and impressive landmarks of St Petersburg, located in Palace Square. Pushkin, however, had an aversion to it; at the end of August 1834 he left St Petersburg for Boldino in order to avoid the unveiling of the column. The victory over Napoleon that the column celebrates, Pushkin deemed in his poem a lesser achievement than his own accomplishments as a poet.[124] According to Pushkin's 'Pamiatnik', the poetic *logos* (the word) soars over the *eidôlon* (the idol) and, more importantly, the idolatry.[125] Moreover, Alexander's victory immortalized by the material commemoration is dwarfed by Pushkin's divine one. This statement would become even more poignant near the end of the poem.

There is unquestionably a certain patriotic pride in the poem similar to that of Horace. Pushkin spanned the vast geography of Russian land asserting that even the wildest of her nations would pronounce his name with reverence.[126] But that was not Pushkin's main claim to glory, nor was the fact that he would live as long as there is poetry in the world. Pushkin aimed for a much more personal and deep understanding of his own importance. This becomes clear in the last two stanzas, which are not borrowed from Horace. 'In my ruthless age I extolled Freedom' is not an abstract poetic statement. It is, in fact, again a very clear and painful allusion to the Decembrist rebellion of 1825 in which many of his closest friends had participated and after which they were brutally punished. Pushkin's sense of guilt for not being on the Senate Square on that fateful day abated in this poem. Here, in a summary of his own legacy, he finally found peace with himself by saying that his poetry at least was a part of the liberation movement and, even after his friends had fallen, he never ceased to call for clemency. This stanza also explains that the statement in the first stanza was aimed obliquely at tarnishing the reputation of the Romanov tsars, one of whom, Nicolas, so cruelly suppressed the 1825 uprising. The reputation of a poet, on the other hand, is not subject to aging and the elements because it is a part of a spiritual, not material, memory. In that light Pushkin comes very close to Horace, who also opposes his 'monument' to bronze and the pyramids.

Pushkin's address to the Muse at the end of the poem, however, differs significantly from Horace's. Humility and pride in the poem go hand in hand. Pushkin encouraged his Muse to stay indifferent to praise or slander and, in fact, rejected the 'crown of bay'[127] whereas Horace actively sought one. The last stanza has an aura of resignation that again suggests that this poem is more than just a final summary by the poet of his own poetic achievement. The poem was written in 1836, a short time before his fatal duel, when Pushkin was especially tormented by financial worries, the struggle to publish, and most importantly by the false rumours of his beloved wife Natal'ia's infidelity with Georges D'Anthès, a Russian counterpart to Antonio Salieri, an evil murderer of the national genius.[128] Pushkin eventually challenged the dashing Frenchman, the darling of the Russian court, to a duel in which Pushkin met his end. 'Pamiatnik' can thus be considered a kind of 'poetic suicide note', which raises the question (not easily answered) whether Pushkin, in fact, planned and foresaw his own death.[129] It is clear, however, that Pushkin felt compelled to create some kind of poetic testament in a year during which he felt especially overwhelmed. Turning to Horace's *Exegi monumentum* as a model was surely at this point a part of the poetic tradition; Pushkin's Russian predecessors had imitated the poem, albeit in a less innovative manner. For Pushkin, however, Horace was only a departure point for a text replete with national context and personal feeling. The poem's comfortable familiarity is thus only a first impression; 'Pamiatnik' is as much Pushkin's as *Exegi monumentum* is Horace's.

Pushkin represents a decisive and confident departure in Russian poetry from contrived and sometimes misplaced classical allusion to deeper individualization and personalization of the ancient models. Following the versification reforms and classical themes introduced by Russian classicism and developed by Derzhavin, Pushkin's Foreign Muse began to acquire distinctly Russian features as she entered the twentieth century, fortified by contemplation of the poet's place in society, and wrestling with Empire and the poetics of physical and existential exile.

Several poets (omitted in this study) who followed Pushkin in the later part of the nineteenth century continued the pursuit of classical themes in their poetry. Such major figures in the Russian poetic landscape as Afanasii Fet (1820-1892) and Fedor Tiutchev (1803-1873) were much influenced in their poetics by the precepts of classicism and wrote several poems on classical themes.[130] Their rise to poetic eminence, however, coincided with the zenith of realistic prose, which started to overtake poetic forms in Russian literature after 1855.[131] Most of the latter part of the nineteenth century was dominated by prose, but growth in poetry again became palpable in 1883 when Fet published his first original verse collection in twenty years, *Evening Lights* (*Vechernie Ogni*), which later influenced the symbolist movement. In addition to Tiutchev and Fet, a lesser poet of that time, Iakov Polonskii (1819-1898), demonstrated that classical themes remained very much alive in Russian poetry. In his two poems 'Prometheus' and 'Cassandra' he contemplated the meaning of love, joy, and suffering – themes more conducive to the affirmation of lyric poetry – after several decades of literature that aimed to study social problems and deliver civic messages.

With the onset of the twentieth century a new brilliant *pleiad* of poets gave the Russian poetic landscape a fresh and vigorous creative impetus by combining the wisdom of the classics inherited from the previous centuries with a new meaning for classical idiom as it entered an era of cataclysmic changes and unprecedented losses.

Poetae Docti and their Discontents

The twentieth century

Vek moi, zver' moi, kto sumeet zaglianut' v tvoi zrachki
I svoeiu krov'iu skleit dvukh stoletii pozvonki?[1]

My age, my beast, who can look into your pupils
and glue with his own blood the vertebrae of the two centuries?

Osip Mandelshtam, 'Vek' ('Century')

The 'Silver Age' ('serebrianyi vek') of Russian poetry, whose beginning has traditionally been dated to the beginning of the twentieth century, grew out of the 'Golden Age' of the nineteenth century, at the centre of which loomed the figure of Alexander Pushkin. Although Pushkin's influence on subsequent generations of Russian poets is hard to overestimate, the term 'Silver Age' is something of a misnomer since this period is generally considered a time of spiritual and poetic renewal comparable to the European Renaissance. The first use of the term has traditionally been ascribed to a philosopher, Nikolai Berdiaev, and it was established in the critical vernacular with the publication in 1933 of Nikolai Otsup's essay ' "Silver Age" of Russian Poetry' and in 1962 of Sergei Makovskii's book *On Parnassus of the Silver Age*.[2] In a recent study Omry Ronen traced the origins of the term and argued against ascribing it to Berdiaev since the latter in fact never used it or made any references to a 'Silver Age' in the Hesiodic-Ovidian sense of a gradual deterioration of ages.[3] Otsup's understanding of the term implied the presence of hard labour and significant creative effort, features that brought him somewhat closer to the ancient classification of the ages, especially that of Hesiod's *Works and Days* where the 'silver generation' was characterized as lacking the effortlessness of the Golden Age.[4] However, in Otsup's description the artists of the Silver Age were no less gifted than those of the Golden, since their talent remained the same.[5] It is in this light that the 'Silver Age' of Russian poetry must be seen: not as inferior to its predecessor but as its equal and its emulator.[6]

Although the date for the beginning of the 'Silver Age' is not usually disputed (most scholars place it in the early 1890s), its end is somewhat more controversial. Innokentii Annenskii died in 1909, while Viacheslav Ivanov and Ivan Bunin lived until 1949 and 1953 respectively. All three poets, however, are usually discussed in the context of 'Silver Age' poetry.

It would perhaps be appropriate to say that all three came out of the 'Silver Age' and its poetic movements but that the poets who lived past the October Revolution of 1917 reconfigured the poetic fascinations of their youth. As the map of the country was redrawn, so also was the map of the poetic landscape.

The poets of the Russian nation that emerged from the havoc of 1917 had to question their purpose within the new Bolshevik state. While the 'Golden Age' of Russian poetry had been characterized by a romantic preoccupation with liberty and national identity, the 'Silver Age' vied with European traditions in its search for new forms. Furthermore, the literature of the 'Golden Age' had been aimed at acquiring an equal footing with European traditions and had honed classical forms and genres in the context of national poetry, whereas the 'Silver Age' turned to mysticism, emphasized a crisis of faith and spirituality, and acquired an eschatological bent. An apocalyptic mood of impending disaster entered Russian literature during the later nineteenth and early twentieth centuries, exemplified by the writings of Vladimir Solov'ev. As some poetic movements of that time, including the Symbolist, Futurist, and Acmeist – there were many more – emerged from the Russian experience of war and revolutions, the sense of *fin-de-siècle* deepened in their writings.

After the Revolution there was, at least briefly, a certain alliance between the literary artistic milieu and the Communist vanguard. It could not have been otherwise. For many members of the Russian intelligentsia the Russian revolution harked back to the myths of the French Revolution in its most idealized narrative. In a spirit of intoxicated euphoria, Alexander Blok, one of the 'younger' Russian Symbolists, chastised the intelligentsia for its inability to see in the October Revolution the beginning of a long-awaited dream.[7] For most poets the euphoria was short-lived, although some persisted in it amid the deprivations, persecutions, executions and social unrest. Poetry of 'the generation that squandered its poets'[8] generally conveys an apocalyptic tendency, evident even in the most ardent supporters of the Revolution.

In the rapidly changing political and cultural landscape of Russia during the period of the October Revolution, what was the use and purpose of the classical idiom for poets who had to reconfigure their place in the new culture? In the following pages I discuss precisely that question in relationship to very different poetic texts. The twentieth-century poets I have chosen for discussion include Viacheslav Ivanov, Innokentii Annenskii, Osip Mandelshtam, Marina Tsvetaeva and Joseph Brodsky; I have mentioned only in passing many other poets (such as Alexander Blok, Valerii Briusov, Andrei Belyi and Fedor Sologub, as well as other poets of Russian Symbolism), whose 'classical' poetry warrants an equally thorough analysis. I have limited my analysis to two examples of *poetae docti* from the twentieth-century Symbolist movement (Viacheslav Ivanov and Innokentii Annenskii) because for them alone the classics provided the most formative influence on their poetics and philosophical views. Neither of them, in the apt if acerbic observation of Sergei Averintsev, 'could accidentally confuse hermetics with hermeneutics like Alexander Blok, or ascribe the French epicurean of the XVII century Gassendi to *Arabic* scholars, like Andrei Belyi, or could conflate Latin *lugere* ('to weep') with German *lügen* ('to lie'), as Valerii Briusov (proud of his gymnasium Latin) once did, when he translated Catullus' *"Lugete, o Veneres Cupidinesque ..."* as "You are lying, Cupids and Venuses".[9] While all these poets undoubtedly were extremely important in the Russian poetic landscape, only Annenskii and Ivanov deserve the title of poet-scholars.

My choice of the texts for the following discussion is also based on the commonality of certain important themes and genres shared by the Symbolist *poetae docti* and the poets discussed later in this study. Therefore, although Ivanov's lyric poetry, unlike Annenskii's, was extremely influential for the transmission of the poetic tradition of classicism, only a small fraction of it is addressed in this chapter, focused on his treatment of the Roman themes. The majority of my discussion is devoted to Ivanov and Annenskii as salient examples of Russian experimentation with mythological drama.

By the time Russian poetry entered the twentieth century, 'Russian antiquity' had found its place both in the educational system and in the poetic discourse. Classics was taught at Moscow and Petersburg Universities by renowned scholars like Faddei (Tadeusz) Frantsevich Zelinskii, who, as discussed below, undoubtedly influenced the Russian mythological tragedies analyzed in this chapter. Zelinskii was of Polish origin but had been educated in Russia and Germany. He was a professor of classical philology at St Petersburg University from 1885 to 1921. Zelinskii also enriched the library of Russian translations from classical authors by publishing Sophocles' complete plays in 1914 accompanied by eleven essays about the tragedies.[10]

The system of classical education in both capitals mainly continued to follow the old Germanic model of strict philological training, which produced generations of scholars engaged in meticulous textual criticism and interpretation but not necessarily in broader theoretical or historical scholarly pursuits.[11] While in Europe 'classicizing' the past for contemporary life was becoming a way of disseminating the classical legacy, in pre-revolutionary and even more in Soviet Russia, classics remained the lot of a chosen few, viewed as an elitist, esoteric education and line of study, and in the later years of the regime as a perfect mode of escapism.[12]

In periods of catastrophic changes, the continuous appeal by Russian poets to the classical past and its assimilation sought to unite Eastern-based spirituality and Western secular imperialism.[13] Greece and Rome were no longer seen as a part of the same 'classical' tradition; Greece was always more connected with a democratic ideal and spiritual quest while Rome was used as a well-articulated parallel to the Russian and then the

Soviet Empire. The roots of that approach, as has been demonstrated, went all the way back to Lomonosov in the eighteenth century who identified Rome as the most appropriate classical model for Russia. Greece, however, still exerted a strong attraction on the poet-scholars who were, like Ivanov and Annenskii, preoccupied with Attic drama and wanted to use it to revitalize the Russian theatre.

As the following pages illustrate, in Ivanov's poetics both Greece and Rome found their reflections, while Annenskii's devotion to Euripidean drama resulted in a more pronounced interest in the legacy of Greece.[14] My analysis discusses first the classical education and career of each poet along with some of his lyric poetry; the classical tragedies of each author are subsequently analyzed in greater detail in the context of the 'Slavonic Renaissance'.[15]

Innokentii Annenskii: a singer of sorrow

Poetic fame came late to Innokentii Annenskii. While Viacheslav Ivanov was acknowledged both as a poet and as a scholar during his lifetime, few of Annenskii's contemporaries acknowledged his importance as a poet.[16] One of them, Nikolai Punin, suggested that Annenskii was perhaps ahead not only of his own times but even of his own poetic impulses and that this explains both his amazing vitality and his relative obscurity.[17]

Although he cannot be considered a classical scholar of the same calibre as Ivanov, Annenskii received a thorough training in comparative, classical and Slavonic philology at St Petersburg University. Annenskii, like Ivanov, also had knowledge and command of quite esoteric subjects of classical philology. For example, in 1897 he published an essay entitled *From Observations on the Language of Lycophron*, in which he discussed the alliterations in the *Alexandra* of Lycophron (285-247 BCE). The essay was primarily concerned with phonetic patterns of alliteration and it helps to explain why Annenskii was so attuned to form and sound in his translations and original poetry.

Annenskii started writing poems early in life but, according to his own admission, he completely abandoned his poetic attempts during his university education and 'fell in love with philology'.[18] Upon completing his studies at the university he began his teaching career as an instructor of Greek and Latin in the private *gimnaziia* of F.F. Bychkov (later Ia.G. Gurevich), at that time one of the most progressive schools in St Petersburg. In 1891 his pedagogical career took him to Kiev where he began his life's work of translating and supplying commentary for Euripides' tragedies.[19] In 1896, after a short teaching appointment in St Petersburg, he became the director of the *gimnaziia* for men in Tsarskoe Selo where he acquired popularity as a teacher. There is a testimony from that time that Annenskii in his Greek grammar classes was able to dissipate with 'his Hellenism the miasma of boredom. From Greek grammar he made a

3. Poetae Docti *and their Discontents*

Innokentii Annenskii.
Nineteenth-century
photograph.

poem ...'.[20] In Tsarskoe Selo Annenskii continued his work on Euripides and at the same time began writing his own 'classical' tragedies. Mikhail Gasparov aptly observed that Annenskii's deep involvement with Euripides should not be taken lightly and that it plays an important role in understanding Annenskii's own poetry, especially, as will be demonstrated, his classical tragedies.[21] According to Aristotle, Sophocles said that he portrayed humans as they ought to be, while Euripides portrayed them as they were.[22] In that respect Annenskii's choice of Euripides is especially significant. Annenskii, the translator, lyric poet and dramatist, was interested in the existential struggles of the modern man. Metaphysical questions and religious mysticism interested him very little and his main objective was to provide psychological and aesthetic commentary on life. In Annenskii's translations Euripides was not only elegant and poetic; he was also reflective and at times even full of hopelessness and despair, in a manner not found in the original Greek.[23]

While all of Ivanov's poetic output is imbued with the spirit of classical antiquity, Annenskii's lyrical poetry bears almost no influence from his scholarly pursuits.[24] Most of the famous poets of his generation published their first poetic books under titles laden with lofty metaphor – some even in Latin: Briusov published *Me Eum Esse*, *Tertia Vigilia* and *Urbi et Orbi*; Konstantin Bal'mont titled his collections *Burning Buildings*, *Let's Be Like the Sun* and *Only Love*; Viacheslav Ivanov's first books of lyric were *Kormchie zvezdy* (*Pilot Stars*) and *Cor Ardens*. Annenskii gave the reading public *Tikhie pesni* (*Quiet Songs*), a collection marked by an appealing blend of emotional intensity and delicate melancholy lyricism.[25] Vladislav Khodasevich, another Russian poet, defined the focus of Annenskii's lyric

59

poetry in the following, perhaps slightly exaggerated way: 'Death is the central theme of his poetry, always explicitly repeated and always more or less palpable.'[26] Nancy Pollak identified the recurrent theme of his poetry as 'toska' ('anguish'), which was both Annenskii's inspiration and his Muse.[27] Unlike Ivanov's lyric voice, Annenskii's was not dedicated to a spiritual or religious quest derived from his intricate affinity with and knowledge of classical antiquity. In his obituary essay on Annenskii, Ivanov characterized his poetry as 'a self-enclosed utterance, a poetry that does not lead to a higher stage of enlightenment'.[28] Indeed, his lyrical voice was subdued, immersed in nature and in sad contemplation. His lyric protagonist was an alienated Everyman who lacked romantic demons and did not exult in artistic genius or erudition. The epigraph to his first 1904 collection *Quiet Songs*,[29] which combined Annenskii's original poems with his translations from Latin, French and German poetry, reveals the poet's own perception of his poetic undertaking:

Iz zavetnogo fiala
V eti pesni prolita
No uvy! ne krasota.
Tol'ko muka ideala.[30]

From the cherished phial
Into these songs has been spilled
Alas! not beauty.
Only the torment of the ideal.

This epigraph reveals Annenskii's aesthetic 'anxiety for the beautiful', an awareness of the constant threat that the ideal Beauty faces from 'real' life. Annenskii, in Setchkarev's fitting observation, was not a poet with 'a hope'.[31] His poetry is completely devoid of any life-affirming tendencies. Mikhail Gasparov described Annenskii as 'unacceptably pessimistic' and that is perhaps also a precise characterization of his poetry.[32]

Annenskii published his first poetic book under the *nom de plume* 'Nik. T---o' which in Russian means 'nobody'. The classical allusion to Odysseus' crafty concealment of his identity from Polyphemus is hard to miss but the pseudonym also shows Annenskii's reluctance to declare his identity as a poet; his second collection, *Kiparisovyi Larets* (*Cypress Chest*), was only printed posthumously in 1910. Therefore his original 'classical' tragedies acquire a special importance within the context of his poetry. For Annenskii these tragedies combined his passion for philology and Attic drama with his aspirations as an original poet. They also exerted a noticeable influence on the treatment of mythological themes by subsequent poets.

Viacheslav Ivanov.
Portrait by Konstantin
Somov, 1906.

Viacheslav Ivanov – between two worlds

Studying classical philology was not simply training, but more than that, a
means to re-create life.

Nikolai Bakhtin[33]

Unlike Alexander Pushkin, Viacheslav Ivanov is not a poet for a broad
audience. His poetry is often obfuscated by its 'uchenost'' ('learnedness')
and his diction can sometimes be overwhelming, appropriate more for a
masterful translator of Bacchylides, Pindar and the *Oresteia* than for a
Russian poet in his own right. The incomprehensibility of his poetry was
censured by Ivanov's fellow-poets, such as Briusov and Blok, as well as by
contemporary literary critics.[34] Even the great Vladimir Solov'ev (1853-
1900), who first noticed and appreciated Ivanov, and whose considerable
influence on Russian Symbolism is also reflected in Ivanov's poetry, observed that 'content in it overwhelms the form'.[35] Osip Mandelshtam, an
admirer of Ivanov's writing, in a letter addressed to him summed up
concisely (if unintentionally) the main difficulty with Ivanov as a poet:
'Every true poet, if he were able to write books on the basis of the exact and
immutable laws of his own art – would write like you'.[36] Mandelshtam's
poetry, as will become clear in the next chapter, would not follow any
'immutable laws'; the poet might have found those in Ivanov's poetry of
that time too coherent and constricting for his own poetic impulses and
tastes.[37] The rigidity and difficulty of Ivanov's poetry are to some degree a

61

product of his thorough classical training and his tendency to incorporate his scholarly interests into his poetic writings. On a much deeper level, however, as a lifelong scholar of the Dionysiac religion, Ivanov might consciously have chosen to write 'difficult' poetry deepened and enriched by his consummate scholarship. That choice can be explained as a deliberate technique to promote the role of poetry and the reader's response as a path of initiation.[38]

Although Ivanov began writing poetry in his childhood, during his youth he was more preoccupied by scholarly investigations into classical antiquity, first at the Faculty of History and Philology at Moscow University (1884-6) and then in Germany under the tutelage of Otto Hirschfeld (1843-1922) and Theodor Mommsen (1817-1903).[39] He never formally completed his degree; his dissertation on the Roman system of taxation was completed in 1895, but was published only fifteen years later.[40] The conclusions of his dissertation ran counter to Mommsen's methodology but to the latter's credit he bestowed high praise on his student, acknowledging great merits in his work.[41] The respect was mutual and Mommsen may have provided the model for Ivanov's conception of the scholar-poet.[42] Ivanov could perhaps have pursued an academic career in Germany, but his interests at that time exceeded strictly scholarly activities.

His disenchantment with Roman history may have stemmed from his inability to 'identify himself with the Roman spirit' because he was 'indifferent to the imperial ideal, so crucial in Roman experience'.[43] However, as the examination of his 'Roman' poems reveals, the significance of Roman antiquity in Ivanov's poetry remained unwavering. His poetry abounds in Latin quotations, inscriptions, and titles. On two occasions he heard voices reciting poetry in Latin to him, an experience that he interpreted in his 1946 essay 'Ein Echo' ('An Echo') as divine initiation and inspiration reminiscent of those experienced by Hesiod and Callimachus visited by the Muses.[44] The cycle of poems dedicated to his fellow poet Valerii Briusov, with whom he occasionally communicated in Latin, bore the name *Carmen Saeculare* and made use of numerous Latin allusions.[45] Even in the last years of his life Ivanov retained a special fondness for the language; he chose Latin elegiac distich to compose a letter to C.M. Bowra in order to initiate a dialogue between two poet-scholars 'belonging to a common humanist tradition'.[46]

However, Ivanov's most intense scholarly and spiritual interest was in Dionysiac religion, which, according to his fundamental belief, had an organic connection with Christianity. His study of Dionysus, by his own account, was initially aimed at 'overcoming Nietzsche in the sphere of questions of religious consciousness' ('preodolet' Nitsshe v sfere voprosov religioznogo soznaniia').[47] In contrast to Nietzsche, who in *The Birth of Tragedy out of the Spirit of Music* saw in Dionysus a 'phenomenon of primarily psychological and esthetic character, an impersonal element, spontaneous and chaotic',[48] the antithesis of Christ, Ivanov believed that

Dionysus first and foremost was a suffering deity, a yet incomplete embodiment of the idea of Christ, the truly suffering god; on that basis, Ivanov sought to find a syncretism of paganism and Christian faith, perceiving in Christianity, unlike Nietzsche, not an anti-Dionysiac phenomenon, but a religious improvement of the Dionysiac idea.[49] Ivanov, nevertheless, should not be understood as a neo-pagan trying to combine paganism and Christianity as equivalent belief systems; rather, he emphasized mystical, psychological and ecstatic aspects of Christianity, which he found important, by drawing parallels with the Dionysiac cult.[50]

There is little doubt that Ivanov occupies an important place in the Russian poetic landscape of the twentieth century as a result of his extraordinary learning and his prolific poetic and scholarly writings. My purpose here, however, is not to rehearse the most famous issues that have repeatedly vexed Ivanov's readers and critics. An exploration of all of Ivanov's complex ideas about antiquity would require several monographs.[51] In this study I address a selection of these ideas, focusing primarily on his most indicative 'Roman' poems and his mythological tragedies. Furthermore, at the end of this chapter I discuss briefly the 'judgment of taste' concerning Ivanov's experimentation with the tragic genre. Did his profound knowledge of ancient languages and texts negatively affect the composition and diction of his own drama and its reception by the audience?

In order to understand and appreciate Ivanov's poetic output the long span of his life must be measured against the historical and literary events of his age as well as his personal tragedies. In 1866, the year in which he was born, Dostoevskii published *Crime and Punishment* in the *Russian Herald (Russkii Vestnik)*. In 1949, the year of his death, Jorge Luis Borges published his *El Aleph* in Argentina.[52] Ivanov spent 47 years in Russia and 46 in Europe, witnessed the havoc of the October Revolution and of two World Wars, outlived three wives and a baby daughter, and underwent major spiritual and creative changes. His life journey was indeed much longer than that of any other Russian poet. It also displayed, in Pamela Davidson's apt words, 'a remarkable discontinuity of both time and space', juxtaposed to an even more remarkable inner coherence and unity in his writings.[53]

Ivanov's poetry is usually discussed in the context of Symbolism, a poetic movement whose two main ideological branches, according to the poet himself, were primarily preoccupied with aesthetics and religion respectively.[54] The former produced such writers as Valerii Briusov, Fedor Sologub and Konstantin Bal'mont, who stressed the autonomy of art as a valid form of human existence. For representatives of the latter, such as Zinaida Gippius and a slightly younger 'second generation' that included Alexander Blok, Innokentii Annenskii, Andrei Belyi and Viacheslav Ivanov, art was not so much an end in itself as part of a religious, mystical and generally spiritual quest. While the representatives of the 'older' symbolists recognized their indebtedness to Baudelaire, Verlaine and Mallarmé, the later 'younger' generation claimed complete independence from French models.[55] It is certainly a misnomer to categorize Viacheslav Ivanov as a 'younger' symbolist. The first mentions of Viacheslav Velik-olepnyi ('Viacheslav the Magnificent'), as Lev Shestov somewhat sarcastically labelled him,[56] and his famous 'Tower' (Bashnia), the apart-ment on Tavricheskaia 25 (now 35) on the seventh floor opposite Tavricheskii Garden in St Petersburg, were in 1905 when Ivanov was almost 40 years old, a mature, highly educated Russian intellectual. His most formative years had been spent abroad where the German revival of classical antiquity in Berlin had left an indelible imprint on him. During the famous Wednesday gatherings at the 'Tower' Ivanov and his wife Lydia Zinov'eva-Annibal tried to create an atmosphere reminiscent of Platonic symposia, aimed at reviving the spirit of classical antiquity in life itself ('zhiznetvorchestvo').[57] Ivanov's poetic debut had occurred two years earlier with *Kormchie zvezdy* (*Pilot Stars* 1903), which followed two decades of serious pursuit of classical languages and scholarship. This first collection is saturated with the forms and themes of ancient poetry and displays a complete immersion in the classics.

That immersion also produced impressive translations of Greek poetry, which show profound understanding of the intricacies of the ancient languages. Davidson rightly noted that 'Ivanov saw translation and poetry as two closely related forms of creativity and used both as a powerful tool for the assimilation of classical antiquity into Russian literature' and that 'according to Ivanov's understanding and own experience, the activities of scholarship and translation are rooted in the poetic impulse, represented as an act of religious theurgy'.[58] His translations from Pindar, Alcaeus, Sappho and Bacchylides display his extensive interest in reviving Greek poetic forms in Russian and in experimenting with the possibilities of the Russian language, an interest apparent also in his original verse.[59] His first published translation, Pindar's *Pythian I*, exemplifies Ivanov's intro-duction of 'church and old folk elements' into the Russian text and includes a defence of that practice in the preface.[60]

This first collection of Ivanov's poems was praised highly by Vladimir Solov'ev, who according to Ivanov himself was 'patron' ('pokrovitel') of his Muse: this collection also reflects Ivanov's intense involvement with Hel-lenism.[61] *Pilot Stars*, a title enthusiastically approved by Solov'ev himself, included several sections on ancient Greek themes ('To Dionysus', 'The Hesperides', 'Thalassia', 'Oreades'). Some of the poems were accompanied by epigraphs in ancient Greek. The poetic collections that followed this one – *Prozrachnost'* (*Transparency*, 1904), *Eros* (1907), *Cor Ardens* or *Plame-neiushchee serdtse* (*The Heart Ablaze*, 1911-12), and *Nezhnaia taina* (*The Tender Mystery*, 1912) – continued to display Ivanov's impressive knowl-edge of and unbreakable connection with classics. The last collection concluded with a cycle of poems in Greek and Latin, entitled '*Humaniorum*

studiorum cultoribus' ('To the cultivators of humanist studies') and contained some poems addressed to Ivanov's fellow classicists Mikhail
Rostovtsev and Faddei Zelinskii.

Ivanov settled in Moscow in the autumn of 1913 after his marriage to
Vera Shvarsalon (a daughter of Lydia from her first marriage) and not long
before, in Fedor Tiutchev's much quoted words, the 'fateful moments'
('minuty rokovye') of Russian history. The key to appreciating the learned
'classical' writings of Ivanov lies perhaps in a better understanding of his
reserved response to the October Revolution of 1917. Ivanov had little
reason to regret the demise of Russian monarchy, but his reaction to the
events of 1917 was very different from that of most of his contemporary
poets. In Averintsev's observation, it contributed at that time 'a very
unusual note into the polyphony of Russian poetry. First of all it was the
very mature voice of a man for whom history did not start today or even
yesterday'.[62] His somewhat detached calmness in the face of all the cataclysmic events of that time differed drastically both from the unbridled
euphoria of Alexander Blok and Andrei Belyi and from the apocalyptic
predictions and attacks of Dmitrii Merezhkovskii, Zinaida Gippius and
Ivan Bunin. That is not to say that Ivanov was not eager to contribute to
the new regime, albeit on his own terms; in fact he tried to recycle his old
ideas on theatre in the context of the new epoch. However, he lived, to
borrow the terminology of Mikhail Bakhtin, within the 'great time'
('bol'shoe vremia'), sifting all the immediate and topical events of life
through a larger cultural prism.[63] Russia for him was neither closer nor
more distant than Athens or Rome, for example. Specific events and
specific times had very little value in Ivanov's poetic and scholarly pursuits
since his essential quest in both was the accumulation of spirituality *sub
specie aeternitatis*.[64] On the one hand, this detachment provoked much
criticism of Ivanov's poetry, but on the other, it helped him maintain till
the end his stance as an original and continually evolving poet. Some of his
most wonderful and moving poetry was written in the twilight of his life in
the last collection of verse, *Svet Vechernii* (*Vespertine Light*).[65] The learnedness for which Ivanov was repeatedly criticized may have helped clarify his
vision for the larger picture, allowing him to see the troubles of the present in
the broad contexts of the births and deaths of great civilizations.

Ivanov was unquestionably very conscious of Russian history but found
the events of 1917 uninspiring. Having spent his entire life in search of a
perfect reconciliation of paganism and Christianity, he could not have
found the atheistic nature of the new propaganda at all appealing. But
there was more: Bolshevism for Ivanov was without any doubt a wave of
barbarity to which he juxtaposed his 'Hellenic' calmness. In his article of
1918, 'Our language', written immediately after the revolution for the
forbidden anthology *De Profundis*, he described the new regime as an
epidemic of 'raving blindness, obsession and oblivion'.[66] The last word is
especially important for understanding Ivanov's lifelong views of culture

65

in general and of classical culture in particular; for Ivanov the most important feature of culture, indeed its essence, was 'the cult of memory', the opposite of which was oblivion leading into barbarity.[67] In that respect the classical heritage acquired a special significance. 'There is no culture in Europe', according to Ivanov, 'except it be the Hellenic one'; 'the classical antiquity that rises every morning virgin and young anew, like the celestial spouse of supreme Jove, continues to ennoble, refine, and stimulate the mind of posterity, but only insofar as our soul, as Livy puts it *"fit antiquior"* '.[68]

In this light Ivanov's move to Rome in 1924 is understandable.[69] He might happily have moved to Germany (in the first years after the Revolution Berlin was an important centre for Russian emigration), the place of his student years, but Italy proved more feasible. Furthermore, Rome and *Latinitas* existed for him as an embodiment of what he termed the 'Hellenic Principle' (*ellinstvo*) identified with Mediterranean and European culture and rooted in 'the blood and language of the Latin tribes'.[70] Rome was also a natural setting for a poet whose main philosophical and spiritual preoccupations were classical antiquity and Christianity. Ivanov's quest to integrate those two worlds – classical scholarship and poetry on the one hand and devotion to Christianity on the other – permeates all his writings. That quest continued also after his move to Rome and his conversion to Catholicism in 1926. Rome for Ivanov was a perfect locale that embodied two of his spiritual passions, not as a utopian fantasy, but as a geographical city in which pagan shrines and the Hellenic spirit existed side by side with Christian churches, and the pagan past was neither disturbed nor annihilated by the advent of a new religion. On a personal level, he was also returning to the place of his great love, where in the summer of 1893 he had met Lydia Zinov'eva-Annibal, his second and much beloved wife.[71]

Admiratio Romae

Although Ivanov became disenchanted with his study of Roman history, his nine most touching sonnets, 'Rimskie sonety', dedicated to the city of Rome and written upon his arrival in Rome from the Soviet Union in 1924, show his unceasing, almost Ovidian delight at the spectacle of Rome, combined this time with the exultation of a Christian in the holy city.[72] Some three decades earlier, in 1892, he had come to Rome for the first time when his interest in that city was shaped by his studies with Mommsen.[73] In his poem 'Laeta' ('Joys'), written during his first sojourn in Rome (1892, *Pilot Stars*) he wrote with exhilaration: 'Having reached my sacred goal, I, a pilgrim, have attained bliss'.[74] Ivanov declared Rome 'a new homeland', the place where finally the 'homeless traveller' could 'establish the altar for his Penates'. The poem, 156 lines of elegiac distichs (in imitation of the ancient elegiac metre), was written in response to Ovidian exilic poetry. It juxtaposes Ovid's *Tristia* with the title of the poem, 'Laeta', in order to emphasize Ivanov's exhilaration at being in Rome.[75] Ivanov began his poem by explicitly stressing the difference between Ovid and himself:

V Rim svoi 'Tristia' slal s beregov Pontiiskikh Ovidii:
  K Pontu iz Rima ia shliu - 'Laeta': ...[76]

From the shores of Pontus to his Rome Ovid sent his *Tristia*
  To Pontus from Rome I am sending – *Laeta*: ...

The addressee of the poem, Aleksei M. Dmitrievskii, Ivanov's then brother-in-law and beloved friend, was residing at the time in the Crimea, which Ivanov used in the poem as a metaphor for the Ovidian Tomi. Two Latin epigraphs precede the poem: one is from Propertius 4.1.67: *Roma, fave, tibi surgit opus* ('Rome, be favourable, for you a [poetic] toil is rising'). The second epigraph is appropriately from Ovid: *Tristia miscentur laetis* ('Sad things are mixed with joyous'), not from his exilic poetry but from the *Fasti* 6.463. Ivanov may have seen his poem as an homage to Rome and her history in the manner of Propertius' aetiological fourth book of elegies and Ovid's own unfinished attempt on Roman aetiology. Although his exulting acceptance of Rome as the final, most desired destination is unconditional:

Kak ty mne dorog moi Rim! Vechnyi, velikii, sviatoi![77]

How dear you are to me, my Rome, eternal, magnificent, sacred,

Ivanov followed Ovid's example of mixing sad and happy thoughts. Along with joy that the sight of Rome caused him, the poet allowed himself to doubt his present happy state:

Veselo mne! ... No ne chasto li, drug, chto vysoko i divno,
  My prevosznosim i chtim, serdtsem inoe liubia?[78]

I am joyous! . . But don't we often, my friend, extol
  What is lofty and magnificent, but love something else in our hearts?

Ivanov did not offer an answer to this question nor an elaboration on what he meant by loving 'something else' amid Rome's alluring magnificence. He immediately returned in the poem to the *admiratio Romae* as if afraid to break the magical spell that the city had on him.

Apart from his personal experiences that were so inextricably connected to Rome, Rome is central to Ivanov's poetics as the focus of the world culture in which the Russian artist could assert his place. Influenced by the writings of Vladimir Solov'ev, Ivanov saw the task of a Russian artist as two-fold: on the one hand a Russian poet living in the First Rome had a duty to contemplate thoroughly and to understand Russia's role as the Third Rome and her 'selfless ability to synthesize East and West'.[79] On the other hand, the merging of East and West would be fully realized by joining in the creation of a Kingdom of God, in which the Eastern and Western churches could enter the long-awaited union.[80] Cultural unity would lead to a religious one, human culture would merge with religious faith, and the Christian *Civitas Domini* could be understood through Rome's ancient past as the *Caput Mundi*. Thus Ivanov claimed kinship in his vision of Rome not only with Vergil and Aeneas but also with Augustine of the *Confessions* and Dante of the *Divine Comedy*.[81]

By 1924, the year of his final move to Rome, Ivanov had lived through the deaths of his two beloved wives, Lydia Zinov'eva-Annibal and Vera Shvarsalon, and the havoc of the first post-revolutionary years in Moscow and Baku.[82] He found in Rome at last his promised land and expressed his exultation in the *Roman Sonnets* yet again in the manner of his earlier poem 'Laeta'. The first sonnet, written a few days after his arrival, related Ivanov's feelings of Phoenix-like rebirth, a resurrection from the cleansing fire:[83]

Vnov', arok drevnikh vernyi piligrim,
V moi pozdnii chas vechernim 'Ave Roma'
Privetstvuiu kak svod rodnogo doma,
tebia, skitanii pristan', vechnyi Rim.

My Troiu predkov plameni darim;
Drobiatsia osi kolesnits mezh groma
I furii mirovogo ippodroma;
Ty, tsar' putei, gliadish' kak my gorim.

I ty pylal i vosstaval iz pepla,
I pamiatlivaia golubizna
Tvoikh nebes glubokikh ne oslepla.

I pomnit v laske zolotogo sna,
Tvoi vratar' kiparis, kak Troia krepla,
Kogda lezhala Troia sozhzhena.[84]

Again, true pilgrim of your vaulted past,
I greet you, as my own ancestral home,
With evening 'Ave Roma' at the last,
You, wanderer's retreat, eternal Rome.

The Troy of your forebears we give to fire;
The chariot's axles crack from furious churning
In this hippodrome of the world entire:
You, king of roads,[85] see how we are burning.

And you went down in flames and rose from embers;
The mindful blueness did not grow blind[86]
With space in your unfathomable skies.

Your cypress, standing sentinel, remembers
In the caress of golden dream
How strong grew Troy as she lay burned in ashes.[87]

Ivanov's lyric protagonist greets his beloved city in Latin: 'Ave, Roma'. 'The introduction of Latin, as Judith Kalb observed, 'into an otherwise Cyrillic text semantically links Russia to the Western world, thus echoing the poet's own journey from Russia to Rome'.[88] Just as Troy had metamorphosed into Rome, so the poet felt that he had been granted another life and raised from the ashes, as he emerged from Russia in turmoil into the sun-lit piazzas of the eternal city. The poem brings to mind Aeneas' address to his comrades amid the devastating shipwreck (*Aen.* 1.202-7):

... revocate animos maestumque timorem
mittite; forsan et haec olim meminisse iuvabit.
Per varios casus, per tota discrimina rerum
tendimus in Latium, sedes ubi fata quietas
ostendunt; illic fas regna resurgere Troiae.
Durate, et vosmet rebus servate secundis.

Restore your spirits, and let go of the sad fear; perhaps some day it will be pleasing to remember even this. Through various trials, through so many misfortunes we strive to reach Latium, where the fates portend peaceful dwellings; there it is permitted for Troy to rise again. Endure and save yourselves for happy events.

In contrast to Aeneas, who was terrified by the storm and uncertain of his future when he delivered these words (ll. 208-9: *talia voce refert curisque ingentibus aeger/ spem vultu simulat,* 'he says these words aloud but vexed with great sorrows he feigns hope on his face'), Ivanov's triumph over fear and trying fate was unreserved. The identification with the Trojan hero en-route to his new home was not new to Ivanov's poetry. In his first collection, *Pilot Stars*, the poem 'Kumy' ('Cumae')[89] referred to Aeneas' plight again through the prophecy of the Cumaean Sibyl given to the hero during his descent to the Underworld in Book 6 of the *Aeneid*.[90] That descent had been necessary for the hero to abandon his past as a vanquished Trojan and prepare for his future as a victorious if ruthless Roman. Without the descent into the Underworld the rebirth of Aeneas from the Trojan *Flammentod* would have been impossible.

In the *Roman Sonnets* Ivanov identified himself even more with Aeneas who had to undergo the transformation from a Trojan into a Roman. The poet envisioned the rise of the new city in the Trojan fire and of life out of the destroyed civilization. The hope was not feigned; it was confident and exhilarating. The cypress tree, in Roman poetry a traditional symbol of death, became a symbol of resurrection, a new beginning that the poet anticipated in Rome, his new abode. Resurrection from the annihilating fire as a spiritual rebirth was one of Ivanov's persistent themes, which was

69

especially prominent in his *Cor Ardens* collection (1911) and was even reflected in the title. Zelinskii explained Ivanov's interest in the theme of rebirth by means of fire with reference to the suffering and resurrected god Dionysus, Ivanov's main scholarly interest.[91] The poem not only evoked the burned Troy but also the rebirth of Rome herself: 'i ty pylal i vosstaval iz pepla' ('and you burned and rose from the ashes'). Ivanov might have been alluding here to the numerous resurrections of the city: from destruction by the Gauls, from the great fire of Nero, from the barbarian attacks. Rome in a cyclical motion soars over time and the sky of the city is 'mindful' ('pamiatlivaia') of all its history. The word in Russian is derived from 'pamiat" ('memory'). The idea of memory was reiterated again in relation to the cypress tree, to which the ability to remember was also attributed.[92] Here Ivanov was following in the footsteps of his beloved Greeks for whom loss of memory signified death: Lethe, the river of oblivion, was located in Hades; as long as memory persisted, however, resurrection was inevitable and death was kept at bay.

The second sonnet devoted to the Dioscuri twins and their role in the battle of Lake Regellus in 496 BCE as protectors of the Roman *quirites*, added to the general feeling in the *Roman Sonnets* of exultation and triumph over suffering, death and despair. The poet started his triumphal walk on the Appian Way and ended on the Monte Pincio, from which he could see the dome of St Peter's. The idealization of the city is unmistakable and at times it is rather unsettling how the city is portrayed as a perfect symbiosis of all cultures, in defiance of any strife. In that respect Vergil's significance to Ivanov's Roman 'poetics' is especially emotional. The greatest names of Latin literature – Catullus, Propertius, Seneca, Tacitus, Juvenal – hardly ever entered Ivanov's poetics, whose focus on all things Greek remained unwavering.[93] The only exception was Vergil.[94] In his 1931 article 'Vergils Historiosophie' (765-7)[95] Ivanov argued, as Judith Kalb observed, 'that through his use of the older gods of Rome and popular legend to ordain Aeneas' mission, and correspondingly, Rome's Empire, Vergil had in fact demonstrated the long-standing religious intent inherent in Rome's sway over much of the then known world'.[96] In Ivanov's perception of Rome, the *Aeneid* was interpreted as a narrative of a far-reaching triumph brought about by divine guidance and destined to promote world unity. There was no mention of fratricide, rape or violence troubling the foundations of a universal and divinely sanctioned state.[97] The distress was ignored, and the triumph was complete. In the end the Russian Ivanov was more Roman than the Trojan Aeneas or even the Roman Vergil. Rome for Ivanov acquired a universalism in which the Eastern Trojan Aeneas was transformed into the founder of the Western Roman nation and the Russian poet into a harbinger of a renewed Christian ideal. For Ivanov, furthermore, Vergil (especially in the Fourth Eclogue) stood on the threshold of a new world bridging the gap between the pagan past and the Christian present and future.[98] Therefore even

Vergil's own doubts about the brutalizing price of building Rome did not enter Ivanov's perception of Rome and his interpretation of Rome's greatest poet. This curious detail, however, in Ivanov's treatment of the Vergilian text is consistent with his overall philosophical views. In his essay 'Legion i Sobornost" ('Legion and Communality') Ivanov juxtaposed the two terms: 'legion' represented the power of the community against which any individual within that community is powerless; 'sobornost" ('communality') was the Orthodox concept of a unity of believers in the Church through Christ within which any individual is respected and valued.[99] That concept, in Olga Deschartes' words, 'unifies the living with the living and the living with the dead, it springs from *Memoria Aeterna* and creates the *Communio Sanctorum*'.[100] While Ivanov associated ancient Rome and the new communist Russia with the concept of the 'legion', 'sobornost" for him was a uniquely old Slavic concept, which was closely linked both to Ivanov's 'metatemporal, or "panchronic" interpretation and representation of culture' and to his belief that Russia and the Russians had a 'Roman' unifying mission in the history of Christendom.[101]

In this light Vergil's work was not treated by Ivanov as a text of the emerging Roman Empire conquering the world with its imperial collective enforced by legions but as a religious text transfigured in the epiphanic light of unifying 'sobornost". Ivanov, the new Aeneas, walked from the ancient gates of Rome to the citadel of the Christian fate. This journey in the *Roman Sonnets* also showed Ivanov's move from the classics to Christ; like Dante he chose Vergil to be his guide and then abandoned him at the gates of St Peter's because as a pagan even Vergil must be barred from the Kingdom of God.

That spiritual journey through Rome also fitted into Ivanov's perception of Russia as a 'Third Rome', which, unlike her Roman predecessor, would have different priorities. Ivanov thought of the Russian Revolution as he was writing his sixth sonnet 'Fontana delle Tartarughe'.[102] The entry in his diary dated 3 December 1924 reads: 'The entire time I've been abroad, I've been maintaining, 'Hannibal *ad portas*'.[103] By interpreting communism as Russia's Hannibal, and thus her undoing, Ivanov linked together Russian and Roman history.[104] While Russia, with Hannibal-communism at her gates, was temporarily unable to fulfil her Christian mission, Ivanov, like a Russian Aeneas, took upon himself the task of representing the 'Third Rome' in the First until Hannibal could be defeated.

In this respect Russia's designation as the spiritual Third Rome (although temporarily hindered in its mission) becomes particularly poignant. In his essay 'On the Russian Idea' ('O Russkoi Idee') Ivanov revealed his expectations: 'You, Russian, must remember one thing: universal truth is your truth and if you want to preserve your soul, do not be afraid to lose it'.[105] Here Vergil's importance for Ivanov was disclosed by the author himself through his citation of the famous Vergilian lines in *Aeneid* 6.788-853 alongside his injunction to Russians. When Aeneas descended into the Underworld in Book 6 to hear the prophecy from his father Anchises about his destiny, Anchises showed him the 'Roman parade' populated by the future great figures of Roman history; following Augustus were the souls of heroes from earlier times – the kings of Rome, then the great men of the republic, ending with the two Scipios who had defeated the Carthaginians and Quintus Fabius Maximus Cunctator who had saved Italy from Hannibal. Anchises broke off this pageant to prophesy Rome's mission (*Aeneid* 6.851-3):

tu regere imperio populos, Romane, memento,
(hae tibi erunt artes), pacique imponere morem,
parcere subiectis et debellare superbos.

Roman, remember to rule the nations under your sway (these will be your arts), and to impose the custom of peace, to spare the vanquished and to bring down the haughty.

Ivanov construed these Vergilian lines not as an expression of 'national selfishness but the providential will and idea of sovereign Rome in the process of becoming the world'.[106] Subsequently, he borrowed the didactic tone for his message to his compatriots, but the imperial pride was gone, replaced by a spiritual quest. In this essay Ivanov made it clear that Rome represented for him not just an image of Empire but a spiritual entity with a spiritual mission, thus again linking classical antiquity to Christian values on the common basis of faith. Russia's loss of itself would culminate in a resurrection of the spirit just as Troy in the *Roman Sonnets* rose from ashes to become Rome. By understating Roman imperial aspirations and linking them with Russia's spiritual role in the world Ivanov moved even further away from the world of classical antiquity into the world of Christian faith.

Three years after the *Roman Sonnets* Ivanov wrote a poem that unequivocally manifested that move away from classics. 'Palinodiia' (the 'Palinode'), written in 1927, was almost Augustinian in its recanting of love for classical antiquity.

I tvoi gimetskii med uzhel' menia presytil?
Iz roshchi mirtovoi kto tvoi kumir pokhitil?
Il' v veshchem uzhase ia sam ego razbil?
Uzheli ia tebia, Ellada, razliubil?
No, dukhom obnishchav, tvoei ne znal ia laski,
I zhutki stali mne dushi nedvizhnoi maski,
I tel nadmennykh svet, i dum Evklidov stroi.
Kogda zh, podzemnykh fleit razymchivoi igroi
V urochnyi chas ozhiv, lichiny poloi ochi
Miatezhnoiu toskoi neukrotimoi Nochi,
Kak vstar' ispolnilis', – ia slyshal neba zov:
'pokin', sluzhitel', khram ukrashennyi besov'.
I ia bezhal, i em v predgor'iakh Fivaidy
Molchan'ia dikii med i zhestkie akridy.[107]

Have I really become sated with your honey from Hymettus?
Who carried off your idol from the grove of myrtles?
Or did I break it myself in prophetic terror?
Have I really, Hellas, stopped loving you?
Yet, impoverished in spirit, I no longer knew your caresses,
And began to find awesome the masks of your immutable soul,
And the light of lofty bodies and the Euclidean structure of thoughts.
When the eyes of the hollow mask, having revived at the fated hour
Filled once more, as in olden times,
With the restless longing of indomitable Night, – I heard a call from the heavens:
'Abandon, devotee, the ornate temple of demons'.
And I fled, and eat in the foothills of the Thebaid
The wild honey of silence and tough locusts.[108]

The title of the poem evokes a famous story about Stesichorus of Himera who related the conventional account of Helen's adultery in his now lost poem *Helen*. According to the legend narrated in Plato's *Phaedrus* (243a) Stesichorus was blinded because of this poem until he recanted in his second poem, the *Palinode*, in which he rejected the story of Helen's abandonment of Menelaus and travel to Troy (Fr. 192), for which he blamed Homer and Hesiod (Fr. 193).[109] In the same spirit Ivanov's *Palinode* is a 'recanting' of his love affair with Hellenism. Vasilii Rudich believed that these discords between antiquity and Christianity in Ivanov's writing 'were never profound or serious'.[110] The poem, however, testifies to a distinct if fleeting tension in Ivanov's spirituality.[111] It most certainly should not be interpreted as a decisive rejection of Hellenism by Ivanov; it is more in tune with the contemplation of the early Christian philosophers about the nature of the relationship between antiquity and Christianity. Davidson pointed out that 'Ivanov was consciously emulating the spirit of the early Church fathers, particularly St Jerome and St Augustine'.[112] Additionally, the 'Palinode' provides an insight into Ivanov's own creative path in the context of his spiritual development; his conversion to Catholicism in 1926 represented a new departure in his religious quest, still intended to be revitalized by Hellenism.[113] For example in his poetic collection entitled *Roman Diary of 1944* (*Rimskii Dnevnik 1944 goda*) Ivanov asserted the link between antiquity and biblical revelation:

Komu rech' Ellinov temna,
Uslysh'te v simvolakh bibleiskikh
Tu vest', chto Muzoi vnushena
razdum'iu strun pifagoreiskikh.[114]

Those who find the speech of the Greeks obscure,
Hear in the biblical symbols
That message, by which the Muses
Inspired the contemplation of the Pythagorean strains.

'Palinode', as well as this poem, shows Ivanov's desire to see paganism and Christianity not as two philosophically and spiritually opposed entities but as a syncretic cultural and religious whole.

As Ivanov established firmer connections between antiquity and Christianity, his focus as an artist shifted 'from philological to ontological, from culture to religion'.[115] Christianity was viewed by him then not as a structure at odds with pagan values, but as an integral part of the classical world, which only reinforced Christian faith and its creative potential.

Russian neoclassical tragedy and the 'Slavonic Renaissance'

Western Europe had begun to rediscover Greek tragedy in the second half of the fourteenth century, though neither Dante nor Chaucer recognized it as a dramatic genre different from narrative forms.[116] The Renaissance saw the recovery of the Greek dramatic structure and plot in original plays (e.g. Politian's *Orpheus* in 1471), although Attic tragedy was not translated into the vernacular until the sixteenth century.[117] For the Russians of the eighteenth century, neoclassical French tragedy of the seventeenth century exemplified by the works of Pierre Corneille (1606-1684) and Jean Racine (1639-1699) proved the most formative influence.

The genre of tragedy in imitation of classical drama entered Russian literature in the middle of the eighteenth century and was popularized by Alexander Sumarokov and Iakov Kniazhnin.[118] It reached its culmination in the plays of Vladislav Ozerov (1769-1816), the last Russian author of classical tragedies to write in alexandrines.[119] Ozerov wrote five tragedies in, to use Vladimir Nabokov's words, 'the stilted and sentimental manner of the Frenchified era'.[120] He recited his tragedy *Oedipus in Athens* in 1804 in the salon of Aleksei Olenin, who later (in 1817) became the new president of the Academy of Arts in St Petersburg – the same individual whose salon was frequented by Pushkin. Ozerov's tragedies enjoyed tremendous popularity as a result of their mellifluous diction and saccharine sweetness infused into classical forms. The best example of the genre was Ozerov's last play *Polyxena*, which is considered the finest sentimental tragedy in the Russian language, 'genuinely evocative of the atmosphere of the *Iliad*' and also following French classical models.[121] The genre and Ozerov himself were obliterated after Pushkin labelled his tragedies as mediocre and his friend V.K. Kukhel'beker wrote a choric tragedy, *The Argives,* in which he attempted to revive Greek drama by rejecting the influence of French classicists. With the Symbolist generation, however, the interest in neoclassical drama was revived once again and this time acquired a serious ideological base.

Catriona Kelly observed that, despite Annenskii's and Ivanov's thorough classical training and ability to read Greek, these two authors did not write their tragedies 'to appeal to other scholars' but for the general public in an attempt to popularize classical literature. Both Ivanov and Annen-skii were associated with the so-called 'Slavonic Renaissance', 'one of the most remarkable, if one of the most eccentric, literary phenomena of the early twentieth century'.[122] It is rather paradoxical that these scholar-poets revived classical themes as a means to invigorate and proselytize national literature. Faddei Zelinskii, who was the most energetic proponent of the 'Slavonic Renaissance', viewed it as a harmonious synthesis of Greek and true Slavonic and national culture.[123] Zelinskii believed that 'Slavs were particularly receptive to the Dionysiac emotions' and hence the 'Slavic world was especially suited to the revival of classical culture'.[124] Like Ivanov, Zelinskii also believed that classical antiquity could serve as an 'antidote to the impending new period of barbarism he feared was menacing Europe'.[125] To that barbarism he juxtaposed Dionysiac ritual barbarity as a vigorous revitalizing force, which would enable the young Slav nations to be the ideal carriers for a renaissance of classical, especially Greek culture.[126] His eagerness to popularize Greek culture led Zelinskii to become a zealous translator of Sophocles. Zelinskii's approach to the past in an attempt to interpret and influence the present was typical of Russian intellectuals at the turn of the century. It was, as Judith Kalb observed, 'a backlash against historicism', an attempt to put emphasis on the historian's duty 'to resurrect the spirit of a vanished era not only through painstaking research, but through active imagination'.[127] This approach is evident in A. Piotrovskii's introduction to the Russian translation of Aristophanes' *Acharnians*:

> Sophocles and Aristophanes cannot have any 'historical' value: they are either completely dead, or alive and like our contemporaries, challenged, revered, and slandered. Therefore it would be faulty and foolish to extract Aristophanes' theatre from the two thousand year old past, to translate it, stage and watch it, unless we are sure that our perception of him is different from our forefathers', and it is the only true and undeceiving perception. After the ethical revelations of the Renaissance and the aesthetic fantasies of Winckelmann, underneath the sentimental, humanistic trash of nineteenth century philology, our generation was given a chance to see a simple and majestic antiquity, our antiquity resting in its blood and its pedigree on the social and religious foundations of Athenian art.[128]

It is clear from these lines that the study of antiquity during the years of revolutionary chaos and its aftermath was not seen as a form of escapism but as an active shaping of contemporary literary tastes and perhaps even historical events. While the most important milestones of the European classics (Renaissance, Winckelmann, nineteenth-century philology) were given their due, they were at the same time deemed outdated whereas classical authors were not. Furthermore, participation in the revival of antiquity and the pursuit of classics were sometimes described as a form of conspiracy. That can be seen in Nikolai Bakhtin's recollection of the gatherings of the self-proclaimed 'Union of the Third Renaissance' ('Soiuz tret'ego Vozrozhdeniia') at Zelinskii's apartment during the revolutionary years:[129]

> Studying classical philology was not simply training, but more than that, a means to re-create life. The study of the Greek language was like participation in a dangerous and exciting conspiracy against the very foundations of modern society in the name of the Greek ideal.[130]

Although the 'Slavonic Renaissance' probably cannot be termed a 'movement' in any political sense or a 'school' in any culturally influential respect, a passion for Greek culture and a desire to share it with others energized Annenskii's and Ivanov's experimentation with the tragic genre.[131] This period was further marked by Ivanov's closeness to the famous theatre director, Vsevolod Meierkhol'd, who also frequented the 'Tower' and who, together with the renowned actress Vera Komissarzhevskaia, brought about a brief flowering of the Symbolist Theatre in Russia.[132] In 1905 Meierkhol'd was attempting to open a new experimental Theatre-Studio in Moscow. He was interested in the participation of Ivanov and his wife Lydia in the attempts to find and establish a new repertoire for the theatre and even planned to stage Ivanov's *Tantalus* there.[133] Nor were Ivanov and Annenskii the only poets interested in 'mythological' tragedy. Valerii Briusov and Fedor Sologub penned *Protesilai Umershii* (*Protesilaus Dead*, 1912) and *Dar Mudrykh Pchel* (*The Gift of Wise Bees*, 1907) respectively. The declared objective of this increased interest in drama based on Greek myth was populist: to take the privilege of participation in literary activity from an elite to a mass audience.[134] Ivanov and Annenskii best exemplified this turn to classical drama because for them it stemmed from a broad, lifelong preoccupation with ancient Greece and presented an opportunity to bring their passion for Greece and Rome to a wider audience and to the theatrical stage.

The discussion of Ivanov's and Annenskii's tragedies offered below in no way constitutes the comprehensive exploration that these dramas deserve. While each tragedy would benefit from a separate detailed analysis, they have so far received little individual attention, with the exception of a study of the metrics of *Tantalus* by A. Hetzer and Donata Mureddu's article on *Prometheus*.[135] The focus of the following pages is limited to two issues: the analysis of the dramatists' classical sources and influences, and an inquiry into their success at exploring the concerns of the present through the myths of the past in the context of the 'Slavonic Renaissance'.[136]

While both Annenskii and Ivanov used classical myth for the creation of their dramas, to term their tragedies merely 'classical' would be superficial since they held significantly different (if not diametrically opposed) views of Greek culture. These two poets, also the most erudite Greek scholars in the history of Russian poetry, were both driven by the intent to revive Greek tragedy but the undercurrent and the effect of their dramas is quite different.

One basis for that difference lies in the ideological division between Ivanov and Annenskii. Ivanov held an abstract and broad perspective of the nature of Greek tragedy to which he devoted several critical essays. A lifelong scholar of the Dionysiac religion, Ivanov, as Kelly observed, 'believed that tragedy was universal because it was a Dionysiac mystery. When the Dionysiac principle was ignored, tragedy was no longer possible'.[137] Annenskii's views on tragedy were not religious or ritualistic in nature. His interest in classical tragedy was primarily aesthetic and Dionysus attracted him not as the ritualistic beginning of tragedy but as a suitable character of drama.[138]

The main differences between Ivanov and Annenskii also lie in their adherence to different Attic tragedians. Ivanov's predilection for Aeschylus and for the choric spirit was a further extension of his interest in the Dionysiac principle, whose spirit was most eloquently represented, in Ivanov's opinion, by Aeschylean tragedy.[139] Ivanov more than any of his contemporaries was 'inspired by the sense of myth', but his understanding of myth bore a significantly Aeschylean influence.[140] Both tragedies by Ivanov belong to an unfinished trilogy (in the sense that the *Oresteia* is a trilogy), intended to consist of *Tantalus* (1904), *Niobe* and *Prometheus* (1914);[141] *Niobe*, however, was never finished.[142] *Prometheus* and *Tantalus* are similar in their exploration of titanism and theomachy.[143] The tragedies are also concerned with the notion of *hybris*: all three of them feature protagonists who push the boundaries of the human and interfere with the divine.

Annenskii, on the other hand, viewed Euripides as the true representative of the Attic tragic spirit. A lifelong translator of Euripidean tragedies into Russian, Annenskii favoured Euripides' realism and 'modernity'.[144] While Ivanov's loyalty to Aeschylus allied his views with Weimar classicism, affinity with Euripides made Annenskii an heir to the French tradition, more specifically Leconte de Lisle and his play *L'Apollonide* based on Euripides' *Ion*.[145] These theoretical differences between Annenskii and Ivanov manifest themselves in the treatment of their tragic characters.

Tantalus and Prometheus – 'bogobortsy' (god-defiers)

Both *Tantalus* and *Prometheus* are works that display the impressive and intimidating erudition of their author. While *Tantalus* with all its semantic and rhythmic complexity is an attempt to reproduce Greek tragedy, *Prometheus* must be regarded as a dramatic poem like Shelley's *Prometheus Unbound* or the second part of Goethe's *Faust* rather than a neoclassical drama.[146] I therefore offer a brief review of the ancient (and some modern) sources for both tragedies in order to understand Ivanov's interest in these particular myths, then to analyze how Ivanov's treatment of the Prometheus myth differs from those of his influences in light of his overall philosophy and poetics, and finally to analyze *Tantalus* in greater detail.

The ancient mythological sources for Ivanov's *Tantalus* are many and they vary in their rendition of the myth. The main Tantalus myths concern his crime and punishment. Most of the accounts agree that Tantalus abused the munificence of the gods by serving them his own slaughtered son, Pelops, at a banquet and then by plotting to steal nectar and ambrosia from them.[147] Tantalus, however, was separated from the human condition by his immortality and thus also by his punishment, which had to be everlasting because he could not be killed.[148] In Homer's *Odyssey* (11.582-92) his punishment was to be hungry and thirsty while tempted by the proximity of ripe fruit and water. Pindar narrated in *Olympian* I.57-61 that Tantalus was punished by perpetual fear of a stone hanging over his head. Euripides (*Orestes* 4-7) followed this account but contrary to other versions put Tantalus up in the air rather than in Tartarus. Ivanov freely mixed the accounts from Homer and Pindar with Apollodorus' and Pausanias' mythographies, thereby recreating 'the experience of the Greek tragedians'.[149] In addition to these accounts of *hybris* and its consequences Ivanov seems to have combined the same type of story about Ixion and Sisyphus, the other two ill-famed 'bogobortsy', who became projections of Tantalus' character.

Ivanov's ancient sources for the Prometheus myth are less complicated, and Aeschylus' *Prometheus Bound* is perhaps the most important of them. The nucleus of the Aeschylean plot can be summarized as follows: Prometheus, a wise and clairvoyant Titan, created mankind and gave them a gift of fire stolen from Zeus. In retaliation Zeus ordered Hephaestus to chain Prometheus to a rocky mountain in the Caucasus until he accepted the rule of Zeus and stopped helping mankind. Prometheus refused and mentioned that he held a secret about Zeus' fate and that Zeus' punishment would also come. When Io, tortured by a gadfly, entered, Prometheus found a grateful listener since Io was also a victim of Zeus, forced to endure prolonged wandering and suffering. Prometheus revealed to her that Zeus would choose a mate who would eventually topple him and that Io's descendant would one day liberate him from Zeus' tyranny. Hermes then entered and demanded that Prometheus reveal the identity of Zeus' future son. After the Titan refused he was sent into Tartarus to emerge only when Zeus' eagle arrived to eat his liver every day. Aeschylus' tragedy focused on Prometheus' punishment. The play closed as Prometheus, surrounded by thunder and shaking of the earth, called on the elements to witness his suffering. The tragedy (and from what we know the whole intended trilogy) of Aeschylus did not offer any certain resolution, however: Prometheus was not condemned and Zeus' triumph was not clearly declared.

While Ivanov's mythogenesis owed much to this Aeschylean plot, the interest of English and German Romanticism in titanism also contributed to Ivanov's re-elaboration of the original story. Hölderlin, for example, saw in titanism the original primeval elements of Mother Earth, which turned its wild nature into a 'Holy Nature'.[150] Ivanov, influenced by that transformation through martyrdom, made his Prometheus a symbol of the spiritual redemption of mankind. Mureddu observed that in so doing Ivanov came closer to August Wilhelm Schlegel, for whom the centre of the Aeschylean theatre lay precisely in the rebellion of the Titans against the new gods.[151] Ivanov's focus, unlike that of Aeschylus, was not on the punishment and subsequent release of Prometheus by Heracles but on Prometheus, the benefactor of an ungrateful mankind, who was martyred for his selfless gifts.

In the European tradition of the original myth three solutions, already present in Aeschylus, dominated modern poetic revisions: eternal torment, the defeat of Zeus and final reconciliation between the Titans and the Olympian order. The first was chosen by Rousseau and A.W. Schlegel, the second by Herder's and Shelley's works on Prometheus, and the third by Friedrich Schlegel and Hölderlin.[152] Ivanov's treatment of Prometheus pursued yet another path, exploring 'a metaphysical solution to the problem of titanism through hints at the Dionysiac aspects of the myth'.[153] In this Ivanov followed Nietzsche for whom Prometheus was Dionysus' 'closest mask'.[154] For Ivanov, however, unlike Nietzsche, art did not belong solely to the realm of an elitist circle, but carried a burden of social and moral responsibility. Nietzsche saw Prometheus' revolt against the Olympian gods as Dionysian, but not his quest for justice. Contrary to Nietzsche, Ivanov 'sees justice (Themis) as an element of the primordial heritage of female monotheism that Prometheus seeks to restore' as the true cosmic order.[155] In that respect Ivanov's innovative mythogenesis is noteworthy. He replaced Aeschylus' Io with Pandora, who represented the feminine double of Prometheus and was equally defiant of Zeus' order. In the Hesiodic tradition Pandora was Prometheus' antagonist, the feminine force hostile to and destructive of humanity. In Ivanov's rendition she, like Prometheus, was the continuation of Themis.

For Ivanov, Dionysus' and by extension Prometheus' martyrdom for mankind transcended the limits of paganism and had Christ-like features. In his essay 'On Act and Ritual' ('O deistvii i deistve'), Ivanov emphasized these features: 'As he [Prometheus] summons the human race to being he knows that he will be betrayed and crucified by it, but still he believes that it will save him too'.[156] In the same essay, however, Ivanov noted that the identification of Prometheus with Christ was only partial and that Prometheus 'embarks on his feat not as a Lamb of God but as a seditious Titan, in sin and in arrogant hope'.[157] Furthermore, a prominent Russian classicist and philosopher Aleksei F. Losev, in a study tracing the images of Prometheus in world literature, saw Ivanov's Prometheus as a symbol of the defeat of absolute individualism.[158] This last aspect in *Prometheus* was a continuation of the main tragic conflict of the first drama of intended trilogy, *Tantalus*.

Close study of *Prometheus* and *Tantalus* reveals many similarities at the base of which was Ivanov's interest in titanism. The son of Zeus and the nymph Pluto, Tantalus descended both from heaven and earth, which made him also a Titan, although not pre-Olympian like Prometheus.[159] According to Ivanov's conception of titanism, Titans were the carriers of the principle of individuation resolved only by violence and by the attempt to dominate others in the process of self-affirmation. 'The negative self-definition of each titanic creature', wrote Ivanov, 'turns his life-affirmation into the desire to devour someone else, other than himself, turns into a constant, unquenchable hunger ....'[160] In that sense Tantalus' character was more representative of titanism than Prometheus'. Toporov observed that neither Tantalus nor Prometheus were 'ordinary' Titans. They were the primordial god-defiers (*bogobortsy*), the 'founders', so to speak, of the 'original' sins, atonement for which was impossible because Zeus' order (Aeschylus *Prometheus Bound* 553: *Dios harmonia*) had been irrevocably disrupted by them.[161] These original sins were similar in both tragedies: theft or violation of the divine gift(s) in the name of individual self-affirmation. Tantalus somewhat tautologically proclaimed 'I am; I am within myself. To me – my own. But mine is me myself' ('Ia esm'; v sebe ia. Mne moe; moe zh ia sam').[162] That self-affirmation expressed his quest to define himself against his Olympian father. That principle of individuation as a means of self-definition was also present even in the 'altruistic' Titan Prometheus. By his own confession at the end of the tragedy he stole the divine fire not so much for the benefit of mankind as to plant 'the seed of a feud' with Zeus ('ne mir mne nadoben, no semia raspri').[163]

The story of Tantalus is one of the best-known tales in Greek mythology. Tantalus, who engendered the ill-fated House of Atreus, was portrayed in the mythological tradition as the 'original sinner', the ancestor whose sins had to be expiated by all his descendants down to the last of them, Orestes. Ivanov's tragedy began with a dialogue between Tantalus and the chorus; Tantalus expressed his dissatisfaction with his life, which to an observer might seem perfect and replete with divine gifts. As the gods showered Tantalus with different kinds of favours, Tantalus was bored by the lack of strife in his life. In a state close to despair he exclaimed:

Bessmertnym ia sodruzhnik. I kakoi by dar
izmyslil mne Kronion? Nebozhitelei
blazhennei, devy, Tantal ... i pechal'nee![164]

I am the peer of the gods. What other gift
Can son of Cronus invent for me? More blessed,
maidens, is Tantalus than a deity ... and more sorrowful!

He felt that his status as the invariable recipient of divine blessings deprived him of his creative powers. Addressed by the chorus over and over as 'Sun' ('Solntse'), 'Son of bounty' ('Izobil'ia syn'), 'Tantalus-tsar', 'lord' ('vladyka'), 'Man-God' ('chelovekobog'), he nonetheless identified more with the plight of mankind than with his divinely bestowed privilege. He continuously used the word 'alkat' – 'to yearn, to strive' – and he felt that the gods had taken away his human right to yearn by their unceasing gifts. It is not coincidental that in the pivotal moments of the tragedy he repeated the same phrase taught to him by his divine wife Adrasteia: 'Learn not to deem Man's power boundless' ('Uchis' ne mnit' bezmernoi cheloveka moshch").[165] Tantalus, however, himself remained excessive and scornful of human limitations. He was also completely self-absorbed, which was why, as he stated at the beginning of the tragedy, he was 'divinely lonely' ('odinok bozhestvenno').

Unlike his ancient archetype, Ivanov's Tantalus was also tormented by the idea of mortality inherent in human nature:

Neizmennym byt' –
nezakatnykh bogov udel;
a cheloveku sud –
solntsezrachnykh dostich' vershin
i niskhodit' v sumrak.[166]

To be unchangeable is the lot of never-setting gods; while the final judgment for a man is to reach the sun-lit heights and to descend into darkness.

His acts of rebellion against the gods, first stealing the ambrosia with the help of Sisyphus and Ixion, and then sacrificing Pelops, were motivated by his desire to transcend human limitations: 'The world is too small for my yearnings' ('No tesen mir moim alkaniiam').[167] The tragic results of these 'yearnings' followed. First, his mortal son Broteas, overcome by jealousy and conceit, drank the divine ambrosia and was struck by lightning. His death signified the death of Tantalus' human, base side. But Tantalus also 'sacrificed' his best, his divine nature by 'offering' to the gods Pelops, his half-divine son from a goddess Adrasteia. The gods rejected Tantalus' 'offering' because it was given to them as a gift of conceit when Tantalus decided that, since he could not be like the gods, he would at least be free of them. Tantalus' rebellion against the gods was thus pointedly different from Prometheus'. His god-defying was selfish and did not consider the consequences for anyone else, including his own progeny. However, Tantalus' feat of 'bogoborstvo' was not cast in a solely negative light by Ivanov but can be construed initially as 'an almost existential-like affirmation of the dignity of man's individualism'.[168] Vladimir Toporov interpreted the conflict in *Tantalus* as a tragedy of freedom (understood as an arbitrary existential concept) and individual loneliness. Tantalus should not be seen only as a *hybristês* who trampled the inviolable divine laws.[169] At the end

81

of the play Adrasteia, the divine mother of Pelops, did not condemn Tantalus, although he fought against everything she represented (fate, necessity, the divine), and she acknowledged the daring nature of his acts. The myth of Tantalus, transcending its ancient sources, was translated into the tragedy of modern man, tormented by the fear of death and his own faulty and insecure individuality. There emerged a positive side in the tragic depths of mortal man's transitory existence. Tantalus realized that his defiance of the gods grew out of his ignorance of his own nature. His words addressed to his divine wife, 'Adrasteia, Adrasteia! Reveal to me myself' ('mne menia iavi, povedai'), were an appeal for the belated self-knowledge fortified with which he could have avoided the pitfalls of his tragic human flaw. Tantalus' final atonement in Ivanov's tragedy may perhaps lie in this final realization of his ignorance. He willingly entered his state of perpetual martyrdom, acquiring, like Prometheus, the aspect of a suffering deity although he was but a mere mortal.

The tragedy is undoubtedly anthropocentric and the gods are marginal to the action. Ivanov did not even grant the gods the power of speech in the play; they were silent except for Adrasteia and for one brief moment at the end when Hermes summed up Tantalus' crime and punishment.[170] There is little doubt that the author expected the play to elicit, in Aristotelian fashion, pity and fear combined with sympathy for the suffering hero. However, even the quest to defy man's limitations was eventually found in the play to be inadequate and wrought with failure. Tantalus' plight was portrayed as that of an isolated individualist powerless to benefit his kind. Although both Tantalus and Prometheus were initially depicted as harbingers of freedom and self-affirmation, in the end both protagonists fell victim to the Aeschylean forces of necessity. Prometheus' god-fighting led to the loss of his freedom and Tantalus was deprived of the gifts of divine munificence.

Annenskii the tragedian

Between 1900 and 1906 Annenskii wrote four neo-classical tragedies, *Melanippa-Filosof* (*Melanippe the Philosopher*, 1901), *Tsar' Iksion* (*King Ixion*, 1902), *Laodamiia* (*Laodamia*, finished 1902, first published 1906), *Famira-Kifared* (*Thamyris Cytharoede*, finished 1906, first published 1913).[171] These tragedies are deeply lyrical and replete with events and emotions. Ivanov contrasted his ideas on tragedy with those of Annenskii in his essay on his fellow tragedian: 'He wrote his classical dramas not because he wanted to substantiate some aesthetic thesis, but because classical myth was close to him'.[172] While Ivanov, following Nietzsche, viewed Aeschylus as the grandest of the three great Greek tragedians, Annenskii's adherence to Euripidean principles of tragic composition manifested itself in several aspects of his dramatic 'mythopoeia'. Ivanov's characters were dominated by divine necessity, but Annenskii emphasized the remoteness of the gods and the centrality of the human presence. Annenskii interpreted the classical concept of fate not as a mystical divine predeterminism but as an irrational concept that impeded the way to happiness and that also beset modern man. His gods were jealous – even ruthless – and humans, although suffering, strove to overcome the predetermined nature of their destiny. Annenskii's great interest in formal directives for the staging of his tragedies and the elaborate explanation with which he preceded every play significantly differentiates his dramatic approach from Ivanov's.

While Ivanov's tragedies have always been seen as closely connected with his lyric poetry, Annenskii's plays have often been perceived as disconnected from the hero of his lyric poetry. However, there is much that connects his lyric hero with his tragic protagonists. First and foremost is Annenskii's permanent preoccupation with the loneliness of man in the world and his inability to connect with his surroundings due either to unrequited love, outstanding talent, or the impossibility of overcoming an unhappy destiny. In this respect there are two pivotal points of reference for Annenskii's poetics: one is Euripides, but the other is Fedor Dostoevskii, the suffering of whose heroes becomes a form of rebellion, of doubt about the righteousness of the existing world order.

Ivanov the scholar manifested himself explicitly both in his tragedies and in his lyric poetry; Annenskii's plays, like his lyric poetry, demonstrated outstandingly their author's humanity. Annenskii himself in his essay 'On Modern Lyricism' ('O sovremennom lirizme') asserted that Ivanov appeared in his tragedies 'as if boasting that he can distance himself from his characters as much as he wants'. He then continued: 'Try to find for example Viach. Ivanov in *Tantalus*. No, do not even try, he has never even been *there*.'[173] Even in the subjective realm of poetry, it is clear upon reading the plays of Annenskii and Ivanov that Anneskii's mythological protagonists are more 'modernized' and speak a simpler language. They are, simply put, a much lighter reading experience.[174] The plays to a certain degree reflect Annenskii's approach to his translations of Euripides in which Annenskii also introduced some modernization of the text by inserting authorial remarks absent from the original, which clarify the visual aspects of the performance and the psychological conditions of the protagonists. Annenskii was criticized especially because he also made use of rhyme, which is completely foreign to ancient drama but is expected as a natural form of poetry by a modern Russian reader. In his original tragedies the poet went even further; rhyme became ubiquitous not only in the monologues and dialogues of the characters, but even in parts of the chorus. Annenskii introduced highly colloquial Russian expressions and exclamations taken from Russian folklore, aesthetically unimaginable for Ivanov.[175] All this 'modernization' of the diction contributed to the main characteristic of Annenskii's tragedies, their non-scholarly and lively approach to antiquity.

The sources of Annenskii's 'mythopoetics' are complex. As Annenskii informed readers in his detailed introduction to *Melanippe the Philosopher*, the title of the tragedy was borrowed from a lost play by Euripides (*Wise Melanippe*). Euripides wrote another tragedy, *Captive Melanippe*, based on the same myth but also lost. The Euripidean *Wise Melanippe* was based on a myth that has been preserved by Dionysius of Halicarnassus and Gregory of Corinth, as Annenskii himself pointed out again in his introduction to the tragedy.[176] Annenskii combined both Euripidean versions and became, as he noted, not only a dramatist but also a 'mythurgos' in the creation of this tragedy.[177] He embraced the latter role also in *Tsar' Iksion, Laodamia* and *Famira-Kifared*, perhaps choosing these less familiar myths for his plots in order to avoid 'competition' with Euripides. Annenskii expressed the main reason for his selection of these tragic plots, which gave him room for imaginative 'reconstruction' of the myth, in his introductory remarks to *Melanippe the Philosopher*: 'The author interpreted the myth following the ancient models, but his play mirrors the soul of the modern man.'[178]

At the centre of each of Annenskii's tragedies is a Hero, a human who in some of his/her characteristics surpasses everyone around. The explanation for that segregation of the Hero from the rest of the humanity can be found in one of Annenskii's articles in which he divided the whole of humanity into two distinct types: dreamers ('mechtateli') and the chosen ones ('izbranniki'). 'A dreamer', he wrote, 'is afraid of life ... a dreamer is naïve, sentimental, and kind in a somewhat weak way. But for every myriad of dreamy worms and withered moths life sometimes fondly selects a single chosen one. Life fondly selects him only if it sees that he is not some puppet king of dream, but its madman, its martyr.'[179] That second type attracted Annenskii as he was creating the characters for his dramas, since he saw them as unique individuals entering into an unequal and always tragic combat with life. All Annenskii's tragic protagonists are united by common characteristics: they are all young and wholesome beings driven by and loyal to their callings, who carry in themselves a creative spirit that clashes with the base matter of life, and for a fleeting moment they each subjugate that matter and become triumphant. Melanippe believed that her maternal love was the ultimate truth to which everything else must be sacrificed, and to that end she endured blindness, humiliation and imprisonment; Ixion served his pride and love for Hera, which are not seen solely as shortcomings and an attempt at blasphemy but as an aspiration for higher truth; Laodamia was consumed by her mourning for the slain Protesilaus. All their passions are human and, unlike Ivanov's, Annenskii's protagonists are very little concerned with immortality or 'bogoborstvo' unless, as in the case of Ixion, it is a direct result of their passions. All of the characters depicted as 'izbranniki' ('the chosen ones') are united by the same display of bravery in the face of adversity and divine irrationality.

3. Poetae Docti *and their Discontents*

In *Melanippe the Philosopher*, the heroine differs from everyone who surrounds her in her rational reason and the strength of her love for her children. The myth itself provided ample opportunity to create an intellectual character. Melanippe, the daughter of king Aeolus, conceived from Poseidon two boys out of wedlock. Upon the god's order they were exposed on the meadow where a cow suckled them. The twins were found by shepherds who then delivered them to the king. Aeolus, interpreting their appearance as a bad omen, decided to sacrifice them on a pyre to please the gods. Melanippe tried to rescue her babies and to reason with her father in an attempt to prove that he was wrong about interpreting the foundlings as a bad omen. When her reasoning failed, she confessed that she was the mother. The boys were exposed again, and Melanippe was blinded for having lost her chastity.

In his interpretation of the myth Annenskii followed Euripides closely; in the latter's tragedy *Wise Melanippe*, the heroine, according to some testimonies, was a mouthpiece for the concepts of Anaxagoras' philosophy.[180] Already the first words of Melanippe in Annenskii's play indicated her ability to question the traditional divine order: 'Whoever you are, o Zeus, in heaven of aether − god or reason, enlivened night vision or a haughty dream ....'[181] However, her perception of Zeus as an idea was in conflict with Melanippe's own tryst with a god in the flesh, Poseidon;[182] hence there was a contradiction between her reflections on the world order and her actual existence in the world. This conflict reached its climax in Melanippe's philosophical debate with her father as she tried to save her children. While the long defence speech of Melanippe in the third act reflected the system of Anaxagoras, it was far from being merely a 'didactic exposition of philosophic theory';[183] it was full of fear and anxiety. It also remained completely ineffective. The wise maiden, who at night talked to the stars and who understood the teachings of the ancient sages, tried to disprove the prophecy of her grandfather Hellenus, who mistook the omen sent by Poseidon for confirmation that the twin boys were the offspring of evil. Melanippe, in a protracted speech explained logically to her father the vagueness and double nature of prophecies in general, and offered him different possible interpretations for this particular omen. She painted a rational picture of the world order, where gods appeared not as active participants in human affairs but 'as steps of fiery spirit'. The philosophical thought spread its wings in her monologue but just as it was about to achieve its culmination of reasoning it became fruitless because Melanippe fell victim to her own destiny as a woman when faced with her real children. This contradiction between her real love for Poseidon in his anthropomorphic state and her detached conceptualization of the Olympian gods formed the basis of Melanippe's tragic martyrdom.

Aeolus, captivated briefly by his daughter's philosophical eloquence, still had to decide the destiny of the foundlings: were they real children or omens of evil? Melanippe, having failed in her abstract philosophical

85

argument, had to make her case on the basis of concrete facts, appealing to parental feelings in Aeolus and to his piety as she named Poseidon, the unresponsive father of her children. But this invocation of the god angered Aeolus, who then began to see his daughter's philosophical testimony as nothing more than an attempt to cover up her sin. He sentenced her to blinding. Even the appearance of a *deus ex machina,* the ghost of her dead mother Hippe, who promised to return her sight to her and to rescue her children, did not affect the role of Melanippe as an ultimate martyr since she refused the alleviation of her suffering and declined the return of her sight. That refusal of a better human destiny contributes to Annenskii's attempt to depict his heroine as connected directly with the sublime and thus impervious to any human suffering: indeed suffering only helps her to achieve the ultimate philosophical truth.[184] The end of the tragedy is attuned to the general tenor of Annenskii's lyric poetry: in the war between reason and passion there are no winners. Humans must suffer regardless, and the only redeeming power is the power of belated repentance (as illustrated by Aeolus).

In his second tragedy, *King Ixion,* Annenskii tried again to resolve the problem of the alienation of an individual from the laws of mundane existence that prevent him from achieving his spiritual prime. In the introduction to the play Annenskii revealed that he intended to interpret the myth of Ixion as a story about a 'superman'.[185] Here, as in *Melanippe,* Annenskii again embraced the role of a mythographer; tragedies by Aeschylus, Sophocles and Euripides on the same theme have been lost.[186] King Ixion committed a horrible crime by killing his wife's father. He was, however, absolved by Zeus and even invited to the gods' banquet where he tasted the nectar of immortality. Welcomed on Mount Olympus and loved by the gods, Ixion however could not overcome his hybristic nature and offended Zeus a second time by falling in love with Hera. Zeus then punished him again by crucifying him on a fiery wheel moving around the heavens.

Ixion appeared in Annenskii's tragedy one year after his first crime, wandering around the world rejected by everyone. His only companion was the goddess of madness with whom he spent many sleepless nights. These sufferings, however, were only a prelude to the destiny that awaited him. Although exculpated by Zeus for his murder, Ixion could not cease from challenging the laws established by Zeus. Drinking the nectar of immortality was not enough for him; he attempted to prove that he was in fact one of the immortals by wooing Hera. The goddess granted him a 'golden dream' by sending her phantom of cloud shaped by the dexterous hands of Apate (the goddess of deceit) to his bed during one night. Ixion spent that night in the sweet belief that Hera responded in kind to his passion and consummated it with him. As his senses reached their summit of pleasure, the truth was revealed to him and he realized that he was but a mere mortal and that the divine realm was closed to him once and for all.

In *Ixion* Annenskii tried to decide one of the persistent questions contemplated by Dostoevskii in *Crime and Punishment*: is everything permitted if there is no God? God did not exist for Ixion as a symbol of moral law; his *hybris* was justified because his feelings and his suffering put him above the divine. In that sense Ixion was not perceived by Annenskii as a *hybristês* at all. In characterizing Annenskii's plays, Viacheslav Ivanov noted that 'suffering is the sign of human dignity before the gods, perhaps even of human advantage. Gods cannot love: they are blissful.'[187] As Ixion exited the stage on the way to his final punishment and eternal suffering, he was full of tragic calmness:

> You are expecting my curses ... They say,
> That when a man is on his way to execution or torture,
> He either bids good-bye or curses. No,
> All anger has departed from my chest.
> Yes, I fear suffering ... but only god ...
> Let's go while my feet are willing to carry me.
> And you, o nymphs, will blossom. My 'good bye'
> Do not forget to pass to ... Hera.[188]

Ixion persisted in his *hybris* and his suffering only confirmed, as it did for Melanippe, his complete isolation from everyone who surrounded and judged him. The 'superhumanity' of Ixion was doomed to a tragic demise not because it was a hybristic trampling of the boundaries that separate the human from the divine but because he strove to break out of the confines of human existence. Ixion's restless spirit sought an outlet in a world where no harmony between individual aspiration and established moral laws could be achieved.

That conflict between life's imperatives and individual happiness was developed even further in *Laodamia*, which signalled a turn to a new type of a tragic hero significantly different from the previous two. The myth of Laodamia appeared in Greek literature as early as Homer (*Iliad* 2.695-710). Iolaus (Protesilaus is his surname), the king of Phylace, was the first Greek killed on landing on Trojan soil. Homer also stated that 'his wife was left mourning and his house half-finished' indicating his newly married status.[189] Based on this a legend developed that has been preserved almost exclusively in Latin authors: Catullus 68.73ff., Ovid's *Heroides* 13 and *Remedia Amoris* 723-4, and Hyginus' *Fabulae* 103ff. According to these accounts Protesilaus' young wife Laodamia remained violently in love with her husband and was granted three hours to consummate her love. After that tryst she committed suicide to be with Protesilaus forever. One important addition to this basic outline of the story was the waxen statue of Protesilaus, with which Laodamia slept during his absence. Hyginus mentioned it in his *Fabulae* (104) and Ovid discussed it in *Remedia Amoris*. Despite this attractive plot, of the Greeks only Euripides wrote a tragedy based on the myth, called *Protesilaus*, of which brief fragments are preserved.

   In Russia the myth of Laodamia was developed by several dramatists in addition to Annenskii; shortly after the appearance of Annenskii's play, Fedor Sologub wrote his *Dar Mudrykh Pchel* (*The Gift of Wise Bees*, 1907) and later in 1912 Valerii Briusov wrote *Protesilai Umershii* (*Protesilaus Dead*). While Sologub's heroine was a lusty Bacchant and Briusov's a powerful and mature queen, Annenskii's Laodamia was merely a very young girl on the brink of adulthood whose lover was taken from her on her wedding day and who was left to spend her days with his wax image. Annenskii was certainly aware of all the important ancient sources. He · listed them in his foreword to the play and took the epigraph from Ovid's *Heroides* 13.108: 'Dum careo veris, gaudia falsa iuvant' ('While I lack the truth, the false joys please me').

   Laodamia's delusional and childlike love for Protesilaus at first prevented her from grasping fully the news of his death, and her songs and dances resembled those of a mad Ophelia more than an ancient Maenad in the grip of divine inspiration. Annenskii's Laodamia was, however, given a certain intuitive hypersensitivity in her perception of the world, the demands and suffering of which prevented her from even attempting to come into full contact with life. Laodamia was like Melanippe and Ixion in her inability to adjust her inner world to reality and in the intense nature of her feelings. The substantial difference, however, lay in Laodamia's ultimate powerlessness to analyze and articulate her feelings consciously; her process of reasoning proved completely incapable of interpreting and coping with the concrete events of life and with her collapsed hopes and dreams. If Melanippe's and Ixion's behaviour inspired some admiration for their strength even though it was hybristically expressed, the demise of Laodamia provoked nothing but pity, which can be felt only for someone equal and familiar but not a superhuman. What interested Annenskii in Laodamia was no longer the break into ultimate freedom but the actual fall from the flight. That interest manifested itself especially in Annenskii's last play.

   Famira Kifared (*Thamyris Cytharoede*) has to be considered separately from Annenskii's other three classical tragedies. The author himself expressed uncertainty about this play, subtitling it a 'Bacchic drama', not a tragedy. Ironically, it was the only play by Annenskii that was ever actually staged; in 1916 it opened under the direction of Alexander Tairov at the Kamernyi Teatr in Moscow, where it ran until February 1917.[190]

   The story of Famira (Thamyris) was derived mainly from *Iliad* 2.594-5; it may also have been the subject of a lost play by Sophocles.[191] Here again Annenskii became a mythographer by combining different distinct variants and adding a number of invented elements. Famira is also a complicated psychological play, which lacks the definitive endings of the three previous tragedies. It seems best to include here a brief summary of the play's plot since its hero is more obscure than Ixion, Laodamia or even Melanippe. Famira was a bard par excellence who chose a solitary existence and isolated himself in a hut with his old nurse. The son of the

Thracian king Philamon, he rejected his royal lineage and responsibilities and was expelled by his father from the kingdom. His mother Agriope (and here Annenskii has invented freely) was a nymph who had been lost to him for twenty years during which a stinging wasp had tormented her because she had rejected Zeus' amorous advances. The play began with the return of Agriope looking for Famira in Thrace, where she was confronted by a chorus of Maenads, whose song aroused in her a desire (not altogether motherly) for her son. With the help of an old Satyr she arranged a musical contest between Euterpe and Famira but then, overcome by jealousy of the Muse's ability to share her son's musical passion, she asked Zeus to grant victory to the Muse in the contest so that Famira would favour her exclusively. Famira lost the contest and as a punishment for challenging the Muse he also lost his hearing and talent. Finally he blinded himself in despair and was forced to live as a beggar with a tablet around his neck inscribed 'Here is the rival of the Muses'. Agriope was changed into a bird.

Famira is united as a tragic protagonist with his counterparts in Annenskii's other plays by his single-minded devotion – in this case his obsession with music. The drama, however, contains some modernized elements that do not transcend *fin-de-siècle* Symbolist clichés: the characters are isolated in their neurotic behaviour and self-doubt, the *deus ex machina*, Hermes, seems cynical, and the Satyrs offer sarcastic remarks as the bard describes the sound of Euterpe's song. Kelly aptly observed that 'the irony of *Famira-kifared* is that the chorus mocks the hero at a time when he is a figure of genuine pathos'.[192] Famira's singing genius was undermined in a comical way that is suggestive of a parody of classical tragedy. He often appeared as an anti-hero and a degenerate version of a tragic protagonist.[193] He was utterly and pathetically disconnected from reality and went to the extreme of depriving himself of sight so that he would not be distracted from retaining in his memory the divine melodies he heard. He rendered himself irretrievably detached from the experience of life and love and wanted to experience only spiritual joys. Although *Famira* appears to have been Annenskii's most experimental mythological piece, at the same time its protagonist was perhaps the closest to the poet. His creative concentration, the haughty isolation of his inner world – these characteristics so treasured by Annenskii in an artist – are the mark of Famira. In *Famira* the chorus also received a larger role as the ideological antagonist of the hero. The high style exemplified by Famira was juxtaposed with a sometimes prosaic chorus of satyrs reminiscent not of tragedy but of satyr-drama, the comic relief from the tragic performance.[194] The fluctuation of the play's style and diction also contributed to the perception of Famira as a hero incapable of any kind of real competition in the context of either love and life or even of his beloved music. He voluntarily refused to enter into the competition with the Muse, thus acknowledging his utter defeat without any resistance. The consequence of his passivity and weakness was the inability to sustain his divine musical gift. Although some aspects of Famira were dear to Annenskii, one can sense the poet's disapproval of his own hero's complete failure to live up to his gift, which united him with the hero of Annenskii's lyric poetry but failed to provoke Aristotelian pity or fear.

The play is also best understood in the larger context of the Symbolist theatre, characterized, according to Vsevolod Meierkhold, by the artist's ability 'to thrust the spectator from a plane he has only just succeeded in comprehending to another for which he is completely unprepared'.[195] In *Famira* the Apollonian world of the high arts, represented by the protagonist, exists side by side with the world of grotesque Satyrs and Maenads. A sense of mystification, unease and ambiguity runs through the whole play, creating a dualistic vision of the new theatre's projected appeal.

While some plays of the Russian Symbolist theatre, such as Alexander Blok's *The Puppet Show*, Leonid Andreev's *The Life of a Man*, and Fedor Sologub's *The Triumph of Death* enjoyed, albeit briefly, great theatrical success, the same cannot be said about Ivanov's and Annenskii's plays. In Ivanov's case this can be explained by the poet's ambitious goal of writing dramas intended to enact a transforming religious epiphany. *Tantalus* represents a failure in the equation of drama with ritual in the absence of an emotional undercurrent. Ivanov's plays are intellectually challenging works in which the known mythic stories are internalized and psychologized to a degree that at times is difficult for a spectator or even a reader to follow. In his style of writing Ivanov also remained true to his 'learned Muse'. There is a challenging and distracting rhythm to the verse in the plays (especially *Tantalus*) ranging from rhetorical pronouncements by the protagonists to lyrical passages of the chorus and explosively rapid exchanges among the characters. The lexicon of the plays only strengthens the distancing nature of the main *dramatis personae*. The repetition and number of church-slavonicisms like 'strastoterpets' ('martyr'), 'dshcher" ('daughter'), 'dlan" ('hand') and of outdated bookish words like 'svetoch' ('light'), 'vyia' ('neck'), 'mnit" ('to think'), 'zertsalo' ('mirror') were perhaps intended to bring the Russian reader closer to the text of classical tragedy, but the effect is exactly the opposite. Ivanov also tried to recreate, as Joanna Kot noted, Greek quantitative verse in Russian, and by recreating the Greek syntactical structures rendered the Russian ones equally hard on the ears and eyes.[196]

Annenskii's plays, although less challenging and at times superb poetry, also remained in the realm of philosophical and abstract reflections in tune with Annenskii's 'anguished Muse'[197] vexed by existential sorrows. Furthermore, despite Annenskii's and Ivanov's different ideological interpretations of classical drama, their main characters have more in common than one might imagine. They are not really three-dimensional realistic characters to whom a modern reader can relate. They are typified, generalized, and sometimes entirely alienated from the public by the self-absorption of their inner struggles.

Conceived in the context of the 'Slavonic Renaissance', Russian neoclas-

sical drama wanted to move away from the elitist view of artistic produc-
tion and assume an ambitious duty to transform its recipients
spiritually.[198] For the *poetae docti* the main appeal of classical myth was in
its universalizing nature, which enables an archetypal approach to life's
problems and human strife, since myth is, in Ivanov's own words, 'a
hieroglyph of the ultimate truth'.[199] The classical tragedies of Ivanov and
Annenskii were intended to revive interest in antiquity and extend its
appeal to a broader public. It is probably fair to say that this goal was not
fully achieved. The reasons for that partial failure (or only partial success)
are perhaps not solely literary. As Nikolai Bakhtin bitterly observed, 'in
those years Russia was clearly on her way towards something entirely
different from the Greek Renaissance'.[200]

A few words, however, are required here about the way the failure of the
'Slavonic Renaissance' was perceived and interpreted by another of its
theoreticians. Lev Pumpianskii, a devoted student of Zelinksii, criticized
the ardent belief of his teacher in the revival of antiquity as early as 1921
(just before Zelinskii's emigration). He did so, however, as Nina Braginskaia argued, in an elegant gesture of rendering the 'Slavonic Renaissance'
as *vaticinatio ex eventu*;[201] he saw the 'Slavonic Renaissance' as an event of
the *past* not the future. According to Pumpianskii's conception, the 'Slavonic Renaissance' had actually existed throughout the whole history of
Russian literature from Peter's reforms through to the works of Zelinskii,
Ivanov and Annenskii. Russian literature then, starting with Lomonosov,
must be understood as an inherently 'classical' literature because it carried
a sustained reception of classical antiquity. What Zelinskii and Ivanov
viewed as the beginning of a new classical Renaissance, Pumpianskii
interpreted as a tragic epilogue of ancient civilization on the Russian soil.

It is perhaps in the light of this insight that the effectiveness of Annenskii's and Ivanov's mythological tragedies should be assessed. On the one
hand, these dramatic experiments, apart from being superb manifestations of each poet's ideological and philosophical preoccupations, neither
lent themselves readily to a stage performance nor were easily digested as
poetry. If anything, they might reinforce the belief that Classics is an
esoteric and detached discipline and classical drama is unable to represent
emotive action. On the other hand, these classical tragedies had an un-
doubted influence simply by virtue of the fact that they reminded their
readers of the ancient heritage, were published, read, reviewed and discussed.[202] The classical Renaissance was perhaps defunct, but a new
literary epoch was rising to reshape and reconfigure the classical idiom yet
again. These classical dramas of the Symbolist theatre, although unable
to adapt to modernity and its demands, were the precursors of Marina
Tsvetaeva's experimentation with dramaturgy, which offered the Russian
reader examples of mythological tragedy that were brilliantly modernized
and innovative, both in style and in content.

4

Marina Tsvetaeva's Tragic Heroines

Je ne crois pas à l'inconscience d'êtres pensants, encore moins – d'êtres pensants écrivants, point du tout – à l'inconscience écrivaine feminine.

I don't believe in the unintentionality of thinking beings, even less of writing thinking beings, and not at all in the unintentionality of feminine writing.
Marina Tsvetaeva, Lettre à l'Amazone[1]

After Heinrich Schliemann's discovery of the site that he identified as Homer's Troy, archaeologists of Russia followed their European colleagues in the eager pursuit of classical material remains. Russia's Imperial Archaeological Commission, created in 1859, supported the excavations in Southern Russia and the Crimea, especially the Chersonesus.[2] Among the participants and planners of these expeditions were prominent scholars such as Ivan Zabelin, Vasilli Kliuchevskii and Ivan Tsvetaev, the father of Marina.

Marina Tsvetaeva always downplayed her direct knowledge of antiquity. Nevertheless, it is not easy to forget that she grew up in the household of Professor Ivan Tsvetaev, who had begun his career by writing a dissertation about the Oscans for which he had travelled extensively around Italy, copying and deciphering numerous inscriptions.[3] After he published his findings, he pursued an academic career in which his major success was the foundation of the Museum of Fine Arts, today known as the Pushkin State Museum of Fine Arts. The Museum testifies to his unwavering commitment to popularizing the art and culture of the ancient world. Through her childhood Marina Tsvetaeva kept hearing of the Museum as her 'gigantic younger brother'.[4] A consideration of Tsvetaeva's classical dramas must take into account the cultural atmosphere in which she was raised, which was imbued with her father's professional involvement with Greece and Rome. Unlike Ivanov and Annenskii, however, Marina Tsveateva was not herself a scholar of classical antiquity; she did not receive an uninterrupted formal education, although her education would have been considered more than satisfactory for a woman of her times and during the peregrinations of her childhood she attended several schools that emphasized classical education both in Russia and abroad.

Tsvetaeva's interest in classical myth was evident from her first collections of poems. Her use of classical references matured especially in *Remeslo* (*Craft* 1922) and in her collection *Posle Rossii* (*After Russia* 1923);

Marina Tsvetaeva.
Prague, 1920.

the characters taken from classical mythology were chosen not at random but in connection with the central preoccupations of Tsvetaeva's poetic system. It comes therefore as no surprise that in the same year (1923) Tsvetaeva began working on her classical dramas.[5]

Her interest in classical drama stemmed from different concerns from those of Ivanov or Annenskii. First of all, Tsvetaeva had a long-standing interest in playwriting as 'a new ... means of expressing human interrelations, conflicts, characters and passions'.[6] In 1918 she grew increasingly close to a group of actors in the Third Studio of the Moscow Art Theatre and wrote her six 'romantic' plays with several of the actors in mind (especially Iurii Zavadskii and Sonechka Holliday, for both of whom Tsvetaeva had romantic feelings).[7] These dramas, with themes ranging from the adventures of Casanova to the love affairs of the French Duke of Lauzun, were written more with the hand of an imitator of Edmond Rostand than by the mature poet evident in Tsvetaeva's classical plays. None of these plays, which were completed in 1918-19, was ever performed during her lifetime and, although her interest in drama continued, Tsvetaeva articulated rather vocally her dislike for the theatre. She included her opinion on theatre in the preface to her play *Konets Kazanovy* (*The End of Casanova*) published in 1922, stating categorically:

I do not respect Theatre, I am not attracted to Theatre, and I do not reckon with Theatre ... But the essence of the Poet – is to believe in the word! ...

93

Theatre I always feel as a violence.
Theatre is the destruction of my solitude with the Hero, solitude with the poet, solitude with the Dream – the third player at a love rendezvous ...
'And yet you write plays!' – This is not a play, this is a *poèma* – simply love: Casanova's thousand and first declaration of love. This is [just as much] theatre, as I – am an actress. Anyone who knows me will smile.[8]

Tsvetaeva directed the reader to interpret her classical plays, then, in the same vein as the *End of Casanova*, not as dramas intended for a stage or as part of a literary movement but as a continuation of the main preoccupations of her poetics. Furthermore, all Tsvetaeva's poetry was inextricably connected with her biography and her binary perception of the world. One of the most important binary oppositions in Tsvetaeva's poetry was that of masculine and feminine.[9] This opposition is obvious in her lyric poetry and in her longer poems based on Russian folk tales, such as *Tsar'-Devitsa* (*The Tsar-Maiden*), which told the story of a lecherous old Tsar, his beautiful second wife, and her desire for her stepson. The struggle between masculine and feminine, the unavailable object of passion, and the theme of *eros-nosos* ('love-sickness') reappeared in Tsvetaeva's tragedies, fuelled by the sweeping strength of personal emotion rather than as a reflection of ideological and philosophical views as in Annenskii and Ivanov.

While Russian Symbolist poets were the most erudite classical scholars of Russian culture, Tsvetaeva's use of classical sources in the creation of her classical dramas was limited, by her own assertion, to the didactic moralizing adaptation of Greek myths by Gustav Schwab, *Die schönsten Sagen des klassischen Altertums*, published in 1837-9, which targeted German children of the Victorian era.[10] Although most scholars agree that this bowdlerized adaptation of Greek myths was the main source of Tsvetaeva's mythics, her denial of any knowledge of ancient sources must be taken with a grain of salt. She may have been unwilling to admit that she had read and absorbed (albeit in translation) Euripides' and perhaps Catullus' and Seneca's renditions of the myth of Theseus as a result of her conscious desire to set herself apart from her Russian predecessors in mythological tragedy. Tsvetaeva's interest in Greek myth and tragedy was not scholarly; it was, as will be demonstrated, personal, strongly related to the circumstances of her life, and intertwined with the rest of her poetics.

Another reason for Tsvetaeva's self-professed predilection for German sources was her lifelong fondness for German Romanticism. An avid reader of the German Romantics – Heine, Novalis, Bettina von Arnim, and Goethe –, she may have absorbed some of her classical mythology through these authors as well as through the German anthologies of Schwab and Stoll.[11] Olga Hasty argued that Tsvetaeva's 'uneasy configuration of eros, poetry, and death', which influenced both her perception of the Orpheus myth and the *Theseus* trilogy, was shaped by her immersion in the works of German romantics.[12] In her 1919 essay 'O Germanii' ('On Germany') Tsvetaeva wrote:

> I might be saying something bizarre, but for me Germany is Greece continued, ancient, and youthful. The Germans are the heirs. And not knowing Greek, I will not accept from anybody's lips but the German that nectar, that ambrosia.[13]

Considering this interest in the German reception of antiquity, it is understandable that, in writing her classical tragedies, Tsvetaeva was interested in Nietzsche's *The Birth of Tragedy*, which probably influenced her conception of Bacchus in *Ariadne*.[14]

Annenskii and Ivanov, of course, provided the immediate Russian context for Tsvetaeva's interest in classical drama, although she can by no means be considered their follower in experimenting with the genre. Tsvetaeva would certainly have been familiar with the works of Annenskii and Ivanov, but her plays offered a significant departure from the works of her Russian predecessors. First of all, her choice of plots was a refreshing change from Ivanov's and especially Anneskii's obsessive interest in the *arcana* of classical mythology and in assuming the role of a mythographer. Furthermore, as Michael Makin observed, 'her source-based works frequently alluded – implicitly or explicitly – to familiar, traditional treatments of canonical material'.[15] While Ivanov and Annenskii strove to display the confidence and knowledge of classical scholars in their classical dramas, Tsvetaeva portrayed herself as someone with only a superficial if any knowledge of her classical sources.[16] One must justifiably question Tsvetaeva's own flippant admittance of ignorance. As the daughter of Ivan Tsvetaev and as a close friend of the classical philologist Vladimir Nilender, who published his translation of Heraclitus in 1910 (the year Marina met him), she most likely had more than a passing acquaintance with classical tragedy (Nilender later also translated Aeschylus and Sophocles). In her letters to Alexander Bakhrakh in 1923 she admitted that she was avidly reading the Greeks ('I cannot read anyone except the Greeks') and asked him for a copy of Nietzsche's *Birth of Tragedy*.[17] Tsvetaeva's disingenuousness in asserting her independence from any sources is also evident in her letter to Iurii Ivask in which she also denied any indebtedness to Ivanov: 'I have never been under the influence of V. Ivanov – nor of anyone at all').[18] In one of her letters Tsvetaeva even went so far as to call Ivanov 'a pseudoclassicist', an attack that demonstrated her insistence on emulation rather than imitation of any source.[19] Tsvetaeva's anxiety of influence manifested itself in such strong declarations. In addition to her denial of any 'literary paternity', Tsvetaeva, as Maria Stadter Fox suggested, 'through her belligerently unscholarly approach ... demystifies the power ascribed to the Greek myths and texts'.[20]

Tsvetaeva discovered her dramatic voice even earlier than many of the European writers who were also breathing fresh life into Greek tragedy. Jean Cocteau wrote *Antigone* in 1922 and *Orphée* in 1926, while Jean Giraudoux's *Amphitryon* did not appear until 1929, and Jean Anouilh's *Antigone* and Jean-Paul Sartre's *Les mouches* until 1942 and 1943 respectively. W.B. Yeats wrote his *Sophocles' King Oedipus* in 1928 and *Sophocles' Oedipus at Colonus* in 1934, while T.S. Eliot began his use of Greek plots for a modern audience only in 1939. Tsvetaeva was decisively one of the pioneers in creating original neoclassical tragedies with a pronounced and explicitly articulated twentieth-century sensibility, which centred on the exploration of a dialectic between the main generative oppositions in her poetics: male and female.

'Theseus': trilogy interrupted[21]

'In the creation of a contemporary work on a mythological theme,' wrote Tomas Venclova in his discussion of Russian mythological tragedy, 'a double transition takes place: from the language of myth into the language of art and from the language of an ancient (classical or other) culture into the language of modern culture. It is rather difficult in practice to distinguish these processes.'[22] While Ivanov and Annenskii tried to rethink Greek tragedy in modern terms, each following his chosen Greek model, Tsvetaeva was doing the same in *personal* terms applicable to the rest of her poetics at that time. Svetlana Boym has emphasized a 'structure of love' that organized Tsvetaeva's writing, and Joseph Brodsky discussed Tsvetaeva's 'emotional' poetic form.[23] Both of these characteristics can also be applied to Tsvetaeva's innovative attitude in her 'modernization' of the familiar myths.

In 1923 during her first year as an emigrant in Czechoslovakia Tsvetaeva turned her attention to classical mythology. In the summer of 1923 she started to conceive the dramatic trilogy 'The Wrath of Aphrodite', later renamed 'Theseus'.[24] The theme she aimed to explore in the trilogy was the fatal and doomed but true passion of love. According to Tsvetaeva's original intention, the three plays of the trilogy were supposed to be named after three women whom Theseus loved and lost: Ariadne, Phaedra and Helen. In a letter to Anna Tesková on 28 November 1927 Tsvetaeva explained the plan for her trilogy: 'Did you know that all women, once and for all, were the destiny of Theseus – Ariadne (the soul), Antiope (the Amazon), Phaedra (passion), Helen (beauty) ... So many loves and *all of them* unhappy.'[25] This letter to some extent explains Tsvetaeva's choice of the Theseus cycle. Her life, which was full of breathtaking passions and painful break-ups that fuelled her poetic talent and caused her great suffering as a woman, found its expression in all her poetry; her classical dramas could not have been any different. Tsvetaeva's uncanny penchant for selecting unavailable and sometimes unworthy lovers was translated into Theseus' passion for Ariadne, Ariadne's for Theseus, and Phaedra's for Hippolytus. In that respect Tsvetaeva was not much different from her ancient predecessors at least in Latin poetry, who found the myths about Cretan women especially attractive because of 'the voicing of feminine passion'.[26]

Ariadne: *abandoned or conceded?*

Ariadne (*Ariadna*) was intended as the first play of the unfinished trilogy 'Theseus'.[27] The play consisted of five scenes (tableaux) that retold the familiar myth about how Ariadne helped Theseus and her subsequent abandonment by him on the island of Naxos. The play opened in the Palace Square at Athens as a herald announced that the customary Athenian sacrifice to Minos was due. A mysterious Foreigner, who later revealed himself to be Poseidon, urged the masses to force King Aegeus to include his own son Theseus among the seven youths. Theseus voluntarily offered himself, not convinced by the entreaties of his father to stay behind and assume his kingly responsibilities as the only heir to the throne. The curtain rose on the second scene to reveal Ariadne playing with a ball in the throne room of her father Minos' palace and singing a hymn to her patron Aphrodite. This was followed by her encounter with Minos, who chastised his daughter for her mindless play and lack of sincere mourning for her murdered brother. She answered that although Androgeus was dead, she was alive and would be her father's consolation in his old age, to which Minos responded:

> Doch' – ne syn.
> Doch' – uvy! – khorosha zamena! –
> Vmesto syna. Oplot – na penu
> Promeniat'? V etom more slez
> Pena – deva, a syn – utes.[28]

> A daughter is not a son,
> A daughter, alas! – what a poor substitute! –
> For a son. To exchange a stronghold
> For foam? In this sea of tears
> A daughter is foam, a son – a rock.

Shortly afterwards Theseus entered, and at the sight of him Minos, struck by Theseus' resemblance to his late son Androgeus, had second thoughts about sending him into the Labyrinth and offered to accept him as his son-in-law. Theseus hotheadedly refused and reminded Minos of the latter's duty. While Theseus lamented his pending unheroic death because he would have to face the Minotaur unarmed, Ariadne entered to convince him that despite his promise to Minos he must accept arms as the gifts of Aphrodite and fight the Minotaur. Theseus then, in a proleptic moment,

97

exclaimed that there is no power superior to a god's. The entrance to the Labyrinth was the setting for the third scene, where Ariadne was waiting for Theseus. She heard the sounds of his struggle with the Minotaur and then welcomed him after his victory. After a long resistance, Ariadne finally agreed to accompany Theseus to Athens but with heavy premonitions. The scene ended with Theseus' somewhat ironic inquiry: 'Maiden, what is your name?' to which she replied 'Ariadne'. The fourth scene, set on the island of Naxos, began with Theseus' monologue over the sleeping Ariadne reflecting on the strength of his passion. His musings were interrupted by a voice declaring that Ariadne was destined for Bacchus and that he [Theseus] must surrender her. A debate (to which I will return later) ensued between the god and Theseus and was resolved while Ariadne remained asleep. In the final scene, set again in Athens, Aegeus anxiously awaited the return of his son, peering out to sea and hoping for the white sails. A herald entered and announced that the ship had been sighted bearing black sails, at which point Aegeus threw himself in despair off the cliffs. Theseus upon his arrival blamed his forgetfulness on the loss of Ariadne and provided the last words of the play: 'Uznaiu tebia, Afrodita!' ('I recognize you, Aphrodite!').

It is clear from Tsvetaeva's treatment of the characters that she could not have been solely dependent on Schwab since in that source Theseus was presented as the epitome of heroic behaviour, a role model for the young. Tsvetaeva's Theseus was irrational, often foolish in his single-minded desire for heroic glory and yearning for combat. He rejected Minos' invitation to forget the feud and take the place of his son, he initially refused to accept arms from Ariadne, and he barely seemed to hear anything she had to say (which was not all that much) throughout the play. His thoughts before entering the Labyrinth were not of the loss of young life or of his old father but the self-absorbed musings of an immature youth; they were not, however, altogether incongruous with his ambition to be remembered as a great hero:

> Plakal'shchikom smezhu
> Ochi, – bez boia bit!
> Imeni net semu
> Gnevu – inogo: styd.[29]

> I will shut my eyes
> Mournfully crying, defeated without battle,
> There is no name for this
> Outrage except – shame.

Tsvetaeva also emphasized his legendary forgetfulness but cast it in a different light. Her Theseus, then, was far removed from Schwab's Victorian paragon of heroic valour. Most importantly, Tsvetaeva's Theseus underwent an evolution as the play progressed: immature at first, he eventually came of age, forced to part with his love and to make a choice in which neither alternative was unambiguously positive.

By the same token Tsvetaeva's Ariadne was also much more complex than her bowdlerized version in Schwab. Her decision to sail with Theseus was burdened with proleptic premonitions bordering on divine vision.[30] She even asked Theseus if he was ready to compete with a god for her love: 'Will you, mere ashes, dare to compete with a god?' ('... osmelish'sia li, prakh,/ S nebozhitelem tiagat'sia?').[31] While this question was prophetic in light of Theseus' later confrontation with Bacchus, it was also Ariadne's attempt to explain to Theseus that his earthly love might be powerless to overcome her own connection with the divine (first Aphrodite and then Bacchus). Since her only meaningful earthly relationship with Minos was one of insecurity and uncertainty because he longed for a son, she anticipated Theseus' weakness in the realm of emotions as well. While Ariadne, for the most part, fulfilled the expectation of the traditional demure female (at least in comparison with her sister Phaedra), she also understood the consequences of her choice when she decided to follow Theseus away from her homeland. Not yet fully developed into a tragic heroine (as Phaedra would be) she nonetheless reflected Tsvetaeva's main preoccupation in the trilogy: unhappy love. It was, however, the *agôn* between Bacchus and Theseus that recalled ancient tragedy most strikingly and formed the culmination of the play.

It seems appropriate at this point to survey briefly which ancient sources contributed to Tsvetaeva's version of the story. At the centre of this inquiry is Theseus' abandonment of Ariadne since this seems to be of pivotal interest for Tsvetaeva's dramatic action and 'modernization' of the play.[32] The most famous recounting of Ariadne's abandonment is Catullus 64.52-75, where the *ecphrasis* on the coverlet for the marriage bed of Peleus and Thetis depicted Ariadne engulfed in rage and grief, cursing Theseus as she watched his sail disappearing at sea.[33] The entry in the *Oxford Classical Dictionary* has based an assumption of magically induced forgetfulness by Theseus on a fragment from Theocritus.[34] Neither of these versions, however, contributed much to Schwab's. Rather, it was the less familiar rendering of Diodorus Siculus that provided most of Schwab's version of the story.[35] Schwab borrowed from Siculus the episode of the dream in which Bacchus appeared to Theseus and scared him into abandoning Ariadne. In that version fear was the primary reason for Theseus' treacherous conduct, which even Schwab acknowledged to be lacking in heroic honour.[36] Tsvetaeva, however, altered significantly the confrontation between Bacchus and Theseus over the body of the sleeping Ariadne and turned it into the *agôn* at the core of the tragic conflict. The *agôn* between god and mortal was as much a struggle between two rival lovers as it was a matter of general and social import. Tsvetaeva explicated the confrontation between Bacchus and Theseus in the outline in her notebook from November 1923 as follows:

Dialogue between Dionysus and Theseus. To *understand* Dionysus: does he want merely Ariadne or immortality for her? Who is more magnanimous: Theseus or the god? Dialogue over her sleeping. Theseus' doubts: but maybe earth is worth the sky? – Yes, especially when these cheeks become earth! I cannot become a man, you become a god. (I cannot become less, you become – more!)[37]

These preliminary notes found their reflection in more detail in the culminating scene with one added feature reflected in the final line of her notes of August 1924:

It is nothing to slay the Minotaur, but there is a monster most horrible: your own greedy heart: slay that![38]

The final version of the confrontation settled for this interpretation of Theseus' act of abandonment. Theseus, unlike his ancient counterparts, was at first reluctant to give Ariadne up and was fearless when faced with the divine presence. Furthermore, he juxtaposed the intensity of his mortal passion to the ephemeral promise of the god's affection:

Tezei:
Ot alchby moei zhadnoi
Ei vovek ne ochnut'sia!
Vakkh:
U *moei*[39] Ariadny
Budut novye chuvstva ...
Tezei:
Muzha znavshaia riadom
Bozhestva ne voskhochet!
Vakkh:
U *moei* Ariadny
Budet novaia oshchup'![40]

Theseus:
From my yearning desire
She will never recover.
Bacchus:
But *my* Ariadne will have
New feelings ...
Theseus:
A woman who knew a mortal man
Would not desire a deity.
Bacchus:
But *my* Ariadne
Shall acquire a new sense of touch.

Although Theseus' arguments sounded persuasive, Bacchus (who remained only heard but unseen throughout the entire exchange) prevailed not because his love for Ariadne proved stronger, but because Theseus

100

came to realize that he could not give Ariadne one thing Bacchus could: immortality.

> *Tezei:*
> Ne v predele muzhskom!
> Vyshe sil chelovech'ikh -
> Podvig!
> *Vakkh*:
> Stan' bozhestvom.[41]

> *Theseus*:
> It is not in man's power!
> And above human strength –
> This feat!
> *Bacchus*:
> Become a god.

The metrics of this exchange are highly curt and the remarks of both protagonists have a staccato rhythm, increasing the intensity of their confrontation. The undercurrent of antagonism in this *agôn* might be patterned after Euripides' *Bacchae*, especially the confrontation between King Pentheus and the captive Dionysus, which also forms the turning point of that play.[42] Both *agones* are concerned with the theme of initiation into the divine. Like Tsvetaeva's Theseus, Pentheus challenged Dionysus' assumption of supremacy over his own position as a king of Thebes. Like Tsvetaeva's Bacchus to Theseus, Dionysus offered advice to young Pentheus:

> *Dionysus*:
> If I were you,
> I would offer him [Dionysus] a sacrifice, not rage
> and kick against necessity, a man defying god.[43]

Here too the juxtaposition between human powers and divine necessity was represented explicitly, as it was in Tsvetaeva's dialogue between the man and the god. Like Pentheus, Tsvetaeva's Theseus was initially a sceptical challenger of the god. But unlike Pentheus, who rashly refused to follow the advice of Bacchus and brought upon himself a gruesome demise, Theseus in the end acknowledged his powerlessness and his *hybris* in face of the divine and admitted the fleeting nature of the happiness he could offer to Ariadne. Although Theseus started off in the play as a hero embarking on a concrete and earthly adventure, a saviour of the Athenian youths and maidens, after his encounter with Bacchus he began to see beyond the trappings of mortal glory. The abandonment of Ariadne, which was represented in most versions of the legend as an act of betrayal (to some degree even in Schwab, Tsvetaeva's alleged source), became in Tsvetaeva's rendering a heroic endeavour, a rational and even selfless choice signifying the maturity of the hero.[44] Theseus' subsequent forgetfulness and guilt in the death of his own father were explained as the result of his grief over the loss of Ariadne rather than as another moral failure to fulfil his promises.

The most astonishing feature of Tsvetaeva's tragic plot in *Ariadne*, however, was the absence of Ariadne's voice after her abandonment. While Catullus allowed a central figure in the *ecphrasis* of his poem to express her rage in bitter words, Tsvetaeva decided her fate in the play through the debate of two male protagonists over her sleeping body. It was only in the lyric cycle *Ariadne*, written in 1923 (before the play was finished) and included in her 1928 collection *After Russia* (*Posle Rossii*) that Ariadne received the right of final complaint so conspicuously missing in the play:

Ostavlennoi byt' – eto vtravlennoi byt'
V grud' – siniaia tatuirovka matrosov!
Ostavlennoi byt' – eto iavlennoi byt'
Semi okeanam ... Ne valom li byt'
Deviatym, chto s paluby snosit?

Ustuplennoi byt' – eto kuplennoi byt'
Zadorogo: nochi i nochi i nochi
Umoisstuplen'ia!!! O, v truby trubit' –
Ustuplennoi byt'! – Eto dlit'sia i slyt'
Kak guby i truby prorochestv.[45]

To be abandoned – is to be with a blue tattoo
Of sailors etched right into the chest!
To be abandoned is to be thrown
To the seven seas ... Isn't it to be the ninth
Wave that sweeps you off the deck?

To be surrendered is to be bought
Expensively: nights, nights, and nights
Of mind's ecstasy! O, to blow the trumpets –
To be conceded! It's to be continued and to be renowned
Like the lips and the trumpets of oracles.

In these lines Ariadne compared her pain to that of engraving a tattoo on a chest, which would also leave an unsightly, indelible mark. At the same time she still could not decide whether she had been 'abandoned' ('ostavlennoi') or 'conceded' ('ustuplennoi'). While these two stanzas were merely a lament of the embittered Ariadne who did not explicitly blame Theseus, the last stanza of the poem, which was omitted from the final publication, suggested that Tsvetaeva might have been familiar with the Catullan version of Ariadne's abandonment (Catullus 64.52-163).[46] In Catullus' poem Theseus was not justified in forsaking Ariadne. The beautiful cover on the marriage bed of Peleus and Thetis represented in detail

102

Ariadne's agony after Theseus had left her on the island of Naxos where Bacchus would come to her. Catullus' description, however, was mostly concerned with Ariadne's state of mind, and the deeds of Theseus were understood only from her point of view. She was seduced only to be abandoned. She looked toward the horizon where the diminishing sail of Theseus' ship could still be seen. Theseus' disregard for Ariadne and her plight was punished with the suicide of his father, for in his oblivion of her Theseus also forgot to exchange the black sails of mourning for the white ones announcing the happy news of his return (247-8):

> Morte ferox Theseus, qualem Minoidi luctum
> Obtulerat mente immemori, talem ipse recepit.

> Theseus cruel with death, the same sorrow that he brought to the daughter of Minos because of his forgetful mind, the same sorrow he himself received.

Tsvetaeva's last stanza of the poem (but not the tragedy) is replete with the same sense of bitterness:

> Tezei! Ty ostavil! Tezei, ty kak vor
> Ostavil i guby, i zuby, i busy ...
> (Velen'iu Dionisovu rasproster
> Podrugu!) – Gremi zhe, bessmertnyi pozor
> Tezeia – bessmertnogo trusa![47]

> O Theseus! You abandoned her. O Theseus, like a thief,
> You left both the lips, and the teeth, and the beads ...
> (You prostrated your lover to Bacchus' orders!) –
> Resound then, immortal disgrace of Theseus, the immortal coward.

Catullus' Ariadne addressed Theseus as *perfide* ('a traitor', 64.132) and *immemor* ('forgetful', 64.135) while she recounted how she had rescued him from the Minotaur and the maze of the Labyrinth. In Catullus' rendition the blame lay solely with him, while Ariadne was portrayed as a victim (still lovely in her disarray and anguish) of his treachery, who cursed Theseus even as the procession of the Bacchants was heard from afar, coming to claim her as their god's bride.

The second poem of Tsvetaeva's *Ariadne* cycle continued to depict the maiden in despair, but the physical imagery changed to figures from nature:

> – O vsemi golosami rakovin
> Ty pel ei ...
> – Travkoi kazhdoiu.
> – Ona tomilas' laskoi Vakkhovoi.
> – Leteiskikh makov zhazhdala ...
> – No kak by te moria ni solony,

Tot mchalsia ...
  – Steny padali.
– I kudri vyryvala polnymy
Gorstiami ...
  – V penu padali ...[48]

'Oh, with all the voices of shells
You have sung for her ...'
  'With every blade of grass'.
'She languished for Bacchus' caress'.
'She yearned for the poppies of Lethe ...'
'No matter how salty the taste of the sea
He was rushing on ...'
  'The walls were falling'.
'And she tore out her curls in full
Handfuls ...'
  'They fell into the foam'.[49]

The preliminary title that Tsvetaeva herself gave the poem in her letter to Boris Pasternak was 'Antifon'.[50] This title, not retained in the final edition, might indicate that Tsvetaeva wrote this poem having in mind alternating lines for a chorus, each expressing an opinion about the events transpiring. This poem shows that while writing her lyric cycle Tsvetaeva was already thinking in the form of the tragedies which would follow the cycle.

In the tragedy, however, Tsvetaeva deprived Ariadne of the Catullan rage, despair and curses originally granted to the heroine of her lyric cycle. Furthermore, the chorus of Athenian youths and maidens who accompanied Theseus on his journey was not given any lines to comment on the most important event of the play. Like Ariadne, the chorus was muted. The reasons for this might be connected (but not completely equated) with several aspects of Tsvetaeva's biography and one of the core themes of her poetics. It has been pointed out that *Ariadne* was influenced to a certain degree by the end of Tsvetaeva's affair with the 'unworthy', by most accounts, Konstantin Rodzevich.[51] Other critics suggested that the planning of the trilogy and the beginning of *Ariadne* chronologically overlapped with the writing of the poems occasioned by the departure from Berlin of Boris Pasternak, with whom Tsvetaeva had maintained a long and passionate correspondence in the preceding years.[52] Tsvetaeva may have projected both romantic disappointments into Ariadne's lack of choice over her destiny. The heroine received her final apotheosis without desiring it although she had foreseen it in her exchange with Theseus before her departure from Crete when she cited the dangers of divine love for 'mortal maidens' ('o tom, chto smertnykh dev liubili bozhestva, vedaesh'?').[53] The elevation of Theseus to tragic status also illustrates Tsvetaeva's idealization of the male protagonist, who despite his despicable conduct was still portrayed as a hero torn between passion and fate. She perhaps perceived Rodzevich in the same idealized light at least at first and most certainly was reluctant to blame Pasternak for departing without seeing her.

Theseus, standing at the centre of Tsvetaeva's exploration of female characters in the trilogy, lost his 'soul' (Ariadne) as he came of age in pursuit of his heroic fate. Maria Stadter Fox observed that 'Theseus is interesting as a tragic subject for Tsvetaeva, because by focusing on his desire, she can explore a whole range of female characters ...'.[54] The binary opposition between male and female was decided in the first play of the trilogy in favour of the male protagonist: he was enabled to make the choice, while she played the silent or rather enabling role. In that role Ariadne was deprived of the full range of character typical of tragic Greek heroines. She was a far cry from Clytemnestra, Helen, Phaedra, Medea or Antigone, whose male antagonists yielded and were sacrificed to the intensity of the women's desires or hatred. Although Ariadne was Aphrodite's favourite, she was undone by her desire for an ordinary woman's fate: a husband and children. When she was given the voice to articulate her feelings (as late in the play as the third tableau), she argued powerfully that she could not follow Theseus because that would lead to unhappiness for both of them. But her strong argumentation was interrupted by the chorus of Athenian youths and maidens saved by Theseus from the Minotaur; one stanza countered all of Ariadne's good reasoning and explained her fatal choice and her later muteness in the play:

Stav' vetrila,
Kormchii! K iugu!
Grekh iskuplen!
Kamen' sniat!
Budu miloi
I suprugoi
I baiukat' budu chad![55]

Put up the sails,
Helmsman! Southward!
The sin is expiated!
The stone is removed!
I will be beloved
And a wife
And I will rock my children to sleep.

Ariadne's resistance to Theseus vanished as she contemplated that ordinary happiness and decided against her best judgment to follow Theseus. Her voice to regret that decision later in the play was taken away because the reader had seen Ariadne no longer as a powerful princess but a girl of marriageable age longing for progeny. Ariadne's successor in Theseus' affections, Phaedra, would receive that completed dimension of a tragic heroine able to voice her passion and her sorrow in her own right.

Phaedra: *speaking up*

Tsvetaeva's *Phaedra* (*Fedra*), the second play of the trilogy, must be considered a continuation of the lyrical cycle written in March of 1923 and also entitled *Phaedra*. Tsvetaeva's passionate feelings for Boris Pasternak and her inability to see him in Berlin must again have contributed to the main theme of first the lyric cycle and then the tragedy: the emotions of unresolved passion and longing.[56] The first poem of the cycle entitled 'Zhaloba' ('Complaint') opened with a play on Hippolytus' name, which rhymes in Russian text with the word 'bolit' ('it hurts'): 'Ippolit! Ippolit! Bolit!'[57] The whole poem was a description of the physical pain inflicted on Phaedra by her passion for her stepson. Here the description of Phaedra's love had familiar Euripidean overtones of *eros-nosos* ('love-sickness') complete with fever and outright physical pain. Phaedra addressed Hippolytus as 'son and stepson' emphasizing his youth and her dominant role in the passion and the poem. In this poem (unlike the tragedy of the same name) Phaedra's love was seen not as a choice of the beloved but almost as a natural force (compared to the destruction of Herculaneum), a fate inflicted by vengeful gods. The second poem of the cycle, 'Poslanie' ('A Letter'), written in the form of letter from Phaedra to Hippolytus, continued the theme of unrequited passion and can be interpreted as a send-off of her fellow poet, Boris Pasternak. The connection between physical desire and the longing of the soul was especially striking in this poem:

Utoli moiu dushu! (Nel'zia, ne kosnuvshis' ust,
Utolit' nashu dushu!) nel'zia, pripadia k ustam,
Ne pripast' i k Psikhee, porkhaiushchei gost'e ust ...
Utoli moiu dushu: itak, utoli usta.[58]

Quench my soul! (it's impossible without touching the lips
To quench our soul!) it's impossible, pressing against the lips,
Not to touch the Psyche, the fluttering guest of lips ...
Quench my soul: thus, quench my lips.

The spiritual consummation of love became intertwined with physical consummation. The poem was permeated by the sexuality of longing. Hippolytus, however, was again described as the beloved not the lover, a passive recipient of Phaedra's devouring emotions ('voracious Phaedra' – 'nenasytnaia Fedra' – she called herself in the last line of the poem). In the first stanza he was described as 'capricious boy, whose beauty, ... flees Phaedra' ('prikhotlivomu mal'chiku, ch'ia krasota ... ot Fedry bezhit'). In the fourth stanza he was called 'virgin, youth, rider, and hater of pleasures' ('devstvennik! otrok! naezdnik! neg/nenavistnik'), while Phaedra was at pains to find a definition for herself. She called herself first a Mother, then Phaedra, and then the Queen. That stark contrast between the appellations of Hippolytus and Phaedra drew attention to the inequality of their feeling: he was the youthful *eromenos* ('beloved'), she the mature dominating *erastês* ('lover'). She finally identified herself also as a rider ('ia naezdnitsa tozhe').[59] That detail, in my opinion, shows that Tsvetaeva was a careful reader of Euripides. In Euripides' *Hippolytus*, the love-sick Phaedra searched for the space where her union with Hippolytus would be natural:

Phaedra:
Bring me to the mountains! I will go to the mountains!
Among the pine trees where the huntsmen's pack
trails spotted stags and hangs upon their heels.
God, how I long to set the hounds on, shouting!
And poise the Thessalian javelin drawing it back –
here where my fair hair hangs above the ear –
I would hold in my hand a spear with a steel point. [60]

Tsvetaeva's Phaedra, like Euripides' heroine, wanted to become an Amazon, the only type of woman Hippolytus, named after his mother the Amazon Hippolyta (also known as Antiope), did not despise.[61] All these themes of the lyric cycle *Phaedra* were to resonate through the second play of the 'Theseus' trilogy.

Tsvetaeva's tragedy *Phaedra* consisted of four scenes and had far fewer characters than *Ariadne*: Phaedra, Hippolytus, Theseus, the Nurse and the Servant. The action of the play was set in Troezen where Theseus had brought his young wife Phaedra to visit his adult son Hippolytus (Ippolit).[62] The play opened with a long chorus of Hippolytus' huntsmen friends who praised their patron Artemis, rejected marriage as a pitiable lot, and described Hippolytus as an outstanding hunter and marksman who shunned all female company. The chorus of huntsmen echoed both Hippolytus' first entrance in Euripides' *Hippolytus* and his misogynistic monologue later in the play.[63] In his first appearance, Hippolytus emphasized his vow of chastity as he sang his hymn to Artemis; in the second he condemned 'woman's wickedness' and declared in a somewhat exaggerated manner his hatred for the whole female sex.[64] The monologue of Tsvetaeva's Hippolytus, which immediately followed the chorus, was, however, far from the self-assured and slightly arrogant Euripidean version. He described his dream of ill omen in which his dead mother appeared to him wounded. Hippolytus was troubled by the dream and his friends tried to offer him consolation. His loyal Servant, however, became apprehensive, warning Hippolytus that 'a mother does not rise from her grave in vain' ('mat' iz groba ne vstanet darom').[65] At that point Phaedra appeared and the two of them revealed their identities, he as a worshipper of Artemis, she as a servant of Aphrodite. The divine juxtaposition familiar from Euripides was thus established here also.

The second scene found Phaedra sick with love, while her maidservants questioned the nature of her sickness: 'this unknown foreign illness' ('khvor' nevemaia. – Zamorskaia').[66] Here the importance of the character of the Nurse in the play became manifest. The Nurse, recognizing Phaedra's symptoms as love-sickness, began to slander Theseus, emphasizing his old age and inability to give Phaedra a child. Loyal to her duty at first, Phaedra was horrified by the Nurse's practical and somewhat cynical revelations. Eventually she admitted her love for Hippolytus. The Nurse, unlike Phaedra, was thrilled rather than shocked by this confession. She, living vicariously through Phaedra's passion, insisted that it must be consummated. The physical imagery in the speech of the unlovable old Nurse is striking in its stark description of sexual desire.[67] To prove her point that love should be more powerful than any other loyalty, she even somewhat illogically invoked the fate of all of Phaedra's ill-fated female relatives:

Izdali, izdavna povedu:
Gor'kie zhenshchiny v vashem rodu, –
Tak i slava vam budet v budushchem!
Pasifaia liubila chudishche:
razonravilsia tsar', mil zver'.
Dshcher' ty ei ili ne dshcher'?
Materinskaia zla krovinochka!
Ariadnu suprug tvoi nyneshnii
Bogu prodal vo vremia sna.
Ariadne – sestra
Dvazhdy: lonom i lozhem svadebnym ...[68]

From afar, from the past I start my story:
Wretched are the women in your race, –
Such in the future will be your fame!
Pasiphae loved a monster:
The king ceased to please, the beast becomes dear.
Are you her daughter or not?
Maternal evil blood-drop!
Your present husband sold Ariadne
To a god as she slept.
To Ariadne – a sister
twice: by womb and by marriage bed ...

The same recounting of Phaedra's female relatives' ill-fated love appeared in Euripides' play in the form of a dialogue between Phaedra and the Nurse:

Phaedra:
Unhappy Mother, what a love was yours!
Nurse:
It is her love for the bull you mean, dear child?
Phaedra:
Unhappy Sister, bride of Dionysus!
Nurse:
Why these ill-boding words about your kin?
Phaedra:
And the unlucky third, see how I end!

108

Nurse:
Your words are wounds. Where will your tale conclude?
Phaedra:
Mine is an inherited curse. It is not new. [69]

Schwab's rendition of the story (although based largely on Euripides' play)
omitted any reference to Pasiphae and her unconventional progeny since
his versions were intended for educating young people. Euripides used the
reference to Phaedra's mother to imply hereditary necessity in choosing
forbidden objects of passion. For Euripides (and later for Seneca), Phaedra's love for Hippolytus was as much a perverison as her mother's mating
with the bull. Tsvetaeva's Nurse, however, used the reference to *advance*
her argument as she prepared to approach the misogynistic Hippolytus.
Tsvetaeva completely excised the idea of 'unnatural' and incestuous passion (of which Phaedra was not really guilty, strictly speaking); her love
was depicted as the longing of a young woman for a young man who could
also fulfil her yearning for offspring.

The third scene, 'Priznanie' ('The Confession'), was set in Hippolytus'
lair and began with the Servant's story of Hippolyta's (Antiope's) battles
and death. In the Servant's retelling, Hippolyta's death was a direct result
of her love for her son (a theme crucial, it seems, for Tsvetaeva's interest
in the legend). It was important for Tsvetaeva that Hippolyta died defend-
ing Athens from an attack by her own Amazons:[70]

Sluga:
Za syna,
Za ptentsa dralas', nasedka,
Za synovnee nasledstvo.
Za synka legla, krasotka,
Za synovnee gospodstvo.
Protiv roda – radi syna
Za synovnie Afiny
Pala – materinstva zhertva
Chistaia.[71]

Servant:
For her son.
For her chick she fought, broody hen,
For her son's inheritance.
For her son she fell, the beauty,
For her son's dominion.
Against her people – for her son's sake
For her son's Athens
She fell – her maternal sacrifice
Pure.

It is clear from Tsvetaeva's notes to the play that she was initially
indecisive about whether to make Hippolytus' Amazon mother a happy

wife to Theseus or his enemy. She settled on the latter and intended to use the fate of Hippolyta (Antiope) as the means to justify Hippolytus' own behaviour in the play: 'The image of Hippolyta as a woman who did not love her husband and who fought for her son is more valuable. Hippolyta, to the end, was entirely within the female kingdom. Theseus, to the end, was an enemy for her. Hippolyta did not love anyone except her son. Just the same ([concerning] relations with women) is Hippolytus.'[72]

While one must avoid the temptation to identify life and art too closely, in Tsvetaeva's case several biographical events help clarify certain themes of the play.[73] Although Tsvetaeva wrote her first notes to the play in 1923, she only completed the two first scenes in 1926 and the whole play in December 1927.[74] Her son Georgii Efron (Mur) was born on 1 February 1925 and became the centre of Tsvetaeva's own emotional life, which directed and eventually decided the tragic turn of her life.[75] Her sympathy for Hippolyta's plight as a single-mindedly devoted mother can be explained through her exponentially growing attachment to her third but only male child. Also noteworthy is Tsvetaeva's uneasy relationship with her mother, who had always wanted a son and to that end even preferred her stepson Andrei (from Ivan Tsvetaev's first marriage with V.D. Ilovaiskaia) to her own two daughters.[76] Biographical influences notwithstanding, the figure of the Amazon, so central to Tsvetaeva's poetic mythology in general, acquired an additional dimension in the play.[77] Hippolyta in the Servant's recollection was caught in the conflict between her identity as a warrior and her duty as a mother, both roles emphasized by differences between her breasts – one severed ('skudomiasaia') and the other nourishing her child.[78]

Furthermore, the Servant's reminiscences of Hippolytus' mother's selfless maternal love and sacrifice prompted Hippolytus to reflect sadly on his own childless state (doubts that were unknown to his Greek predecessor although Euripides' Hippolytus entertained the idea of procreating without women): 'I will die childless, it is not the first time I lament that' ('Umru bezdetnym,/Ne vpervye o tom skorbliu').[79] However, his wish for progeny did not neutralize his expressions of hatred for all womankind and was akin to his ancient counterpart's diatribe against women in which he chastized them for being too talkative and oversexed. Just as Hippolytus was expounding on his hatred of women, the Nurse entered carrying a secret letter from Phaedra. Hippolytus threw away the tablet on which the letter was written, insulted by its clandestine nature. Thereupon Phaedra entered Hippolytus' lair herself. In his shock and confusion, he believed at first that he was feverish and hallucinating. She interrupted him and in a disjointed confession admitted her passion for him, asking him to accept her love not as a momentary whim but as an eternal devotion. She even hinted at the possibility of committing suicide together and finding union in death, thus eerily anticipating the end of the play. As he, stunned but silent, listened to her shocking plea, she finished it with: 'Just a word! Just one word!' ('Slovo! Slovo odno lish'!') to which he replies: 'Vermin!'('Gadina!').[80]

It remains an open question whether Tsvetaeva was aware of the first version of Euripides' *Hippolytus* in which Phaedra made her proposal of love directly to her stepson and which Euripides had to revise, because the play outraged the audience by 'the shamelessness of its Phaedra who openly declared her guilty passion to Hippolytus, and when rebuffed, just as brazenly confronted her husband face to face and herself accused Hippolytus of sexual assault'.[81] If Tsvetaeva was aware of Euripides' early version of the play, she was clearly interested only in the first manifestation of Phaedra's unruly nature: her confession of love to Hippolytus. Tsvetaeva would hardly have found the brazen slander of Hippolytus by Phaedra attractive or advantageous to her own poetic agenda since she was developing her Phaedra as a tragic victim of unrequited love, not as a duplicitous female character in the image of Aeschylus' Clytemnestra. Tsvetaeva's decision to give her Phaedra the power of voice, which she had denied to her Ariadne, was central to Tsvetaeva's interest in Phaedra's own articulation of love. It has been pointed out that one of Tsvetaeva's main interests in both plays was the problem of feminine voice and speech.[82] Nancy Rabinowitz in her analysis of Euripides' play argued that '*Hippolytus* empowers men and reaffirms their authority; ... the female emerges as carnal, her language and activity curtailed'.[83] We have seen that Tsvetaeva's Ariadne, mostly because of her gender, was also deprived altogether of the most decisive speech in the tragedy that bore her name and was allowed to express only doubt. While Tsvetaeva allowed her Phaedra to speak, she at the same time seemed to suggest 'that despite its truth, feminine speech and writing were rejected or fatally misunderstood'.[84] Hippolytus never read the letter from Phaedra brought by the Nurse, and it was only in the end that the letter was read and understood by Theseus the way Phaedra intended it to be understood by Hippolytus. While Phaedra's letter in Euripides' *Hippolytus* was a weapon of deception and slander, in Tsvetaeva's play it was a baring of the loving heart, a disarming. Phaedra's death did not entail vengeance by her. She took Hippolytus' rejection and curse to her grave stoically and, like Ariadne, without a word of reprimand. It is evident from the letter to Anna Tesková cited above that, while Tsvetaeva saw Ariadne as an embodiment of soul, she saw Phaedra as an embodiment of passion who thus must be given a full voice to express it. Hippolytus' underwhelming and self-righteous response in the play must be interpreted therefore not as a sign of loyalty to his father or as an exercise in self-restraint, but as an inability to match Phaedra's strength in her recklessness to sacrifice everything for love.

At the beginning of the fourth and last scene, the Nurse lamented over the body of Phaedra and swore to avenge her mistress's death, holding Hippolytus responsible for it. When Theseus returned from his travels and inquired about Phaedra, the Nurse blamed Hippolytus' inappropriate conduct for her mistress's suicide. Theseus, invoking his father Poseidon, cursed Hippolytus. An interesting choral interlude followed in which the chorus of Phaedra's female friends lamented her death and Hippolytus' sense of loyalty by re-enacting their roles in the tragic affair:

– Strast' moe pravo!
– Chest' moi dospekh!
Machekhe – slava,
Pasynku – smekh.[85]

'Passion is my right!'
'Loyalty is my armour!'
Glory to the stepmother,
To her stepson – ridicule!

It is clear from this choral ode that the chorus sided with Phaedra and blamed Hippolytus for her death. When the herald entered, bearing the account of Hippolytus' death, Theseus was unperturbed by the sad news until the Servant handed him the remains of the tablet containing Phaedra's letter. This revelation forced the Nurse to confess her role in the tragic events. Unlike the letter in the Euripidean play, this one saved Hippolytus' reputation rather than destroying it. Theseus, however, did not blame the Nurse but rather the necessity of fate and Aphrodite's old hatred for him on account of his abandonment of Ariadne. Tsvetaeva thus reduced Phaedra's traditional guilt in Hippolytus' demise. In an unexpected final twist Theseus ordered Hippolytus and Phaedra to be buried together under a myrtle tree in the unity of final unearthly love:

Tezei:
Tam, gde mirt shumit, eia stonom poln,
Vozvedite im dvuedinyi kholm.
Pust' khot' tam obov'et – mir bednym im! –
Ippolitovu kost' – kost' Fedrina.[86]

Theseus:
There, where the myrtle rustles, with her groan replete,
Raise for them a single doubled mound.
So at least there let – peace to the wretched ones! –
Phaedra's bones entwine Hippolytus' bones.

This posthumous consummation of love is another revealing feature in Tsvetaeva's treatment of the myth. The semi-happy conclusion itself was borrowed from Schwab's version, aiming to provide some brightness in the generally hopeless situation. Tsvetaeva, however, turned Schwab's naïve and contrived optimism into an eternal and natural union after death. One noteworthy detail of the final line is that 'Phaedra's bones' ('kost' Fedrina') are the subject of the sentence whereas 'Hippolytus' bones' ('Ippolitovu kost' ') are the direct object. Thus even beyond the grave Phaedra remains the active agent of love and Hippolytus the recipient of her passion. Furthermore, Tsvetaeva was also much more attentive to the details of Phaedra's death than Schwab; she selected the myrtle tree, sacred to Aphrodite, as Phaedra's chosen tool of suicide. Tsvetaeva herself explained that choice: 'I would like to depict Phaedra as an incarnate myrtle, to twine her all around a myrtle sapling'.[87] By choosing Aphrodite's tree, Phaedra insisted on her right to passion and confirmed it even in her final act.

The plot of *Phaedra* was more limited and one-dimensional than that of *Ariadne*. It is also evident, as demonstrated above, that Tsvetaeva's dependence on Schwab's version of the story is rather doubtful, and that Euripides played a significant if not decisive role as her source for the structure of the plot, together probably with Seneca's *Phaedra* and Racine's *Phèdre*. The latter is more likely to have been on Tsvetaeva's mind since Tsvetaeva idolized Sarah Bernhardt all her life and could not possibly have remained ignorant of her most celebrated role.[88] It has been noted, however, that Racine's play had made no use of a chorus and Tsvetaeva's *Phaedra* reveals no traces of the academic style characteristic of French Classicists.[89] Seneca's *Phaedra* appears to have been a less influential source, although, as Thomson noted, it is the only play to begin (like Tsvetaeva's) with a series of extended choral hymns in praise of the hunt, followed by Phaedra's ill-conceived intrusion into the male world.[90]

The figure of the Nurse is especially remarkable in Tsvetaeva's divergence from her sources. Tsvetaeva's preliminary notes to the play show that she attached great importance to the role of the Nurse and defined it clearly:[91]

The role of the Nurse? She is *not* a seductress, she only persuades Phaedra in her *luck*, gives her the last confidence. The role of the nurse is *very* important.

Thus Tsvetaeva viewed the Nurse as instrumental in Phaedra's demise only because the old woman wanted to ensure the latter's happiness while fulfilling her own vicarious wishes. Euripides' Nurse was at first shocked by Phaedra's confession whereas Tsvetaeva's seized that confession as a long-awaited outlet for her dominating but repressed personality. She enabled the articulation and vocalization of Phaedra's sexuality and also made it possible for Phaedra to replace Hippolytus as the tragic focus of the play. The connection between sexuality and its articulation set Tsvetaeva's Phaedra apart from her predecessors; Phaedra became 'a woman-poet in a world traditionally dominated by men'.[92] Phaedra's ability to voice her passion and pain was translated by Tsvetaeva into misunderstood and unfulfilled artistic potential.[93] Through Phaedra Tsvetaeva attacked the world of mere appearance and lamented a wilful, unrestrained, and at times excessively emotional heroine's preclusion from creative productivity. Phaedra's failed love for Hippolytus translated into her failure in any self-expression, whether her own impossible motherhood or her misread and misheard words.

Despite Tsvetaeva's self-proclaimed ignorance of the classics, this 'modernized' version of Euripides' play is in some aspects more 'classical' than any of its Russian predecessors. In her choice of Phaedra's method of death Tsvetaeva remained faithful to the ancient sources and turned away from Racine's suicide through poison back to Euripides' hanging, the exclusively feminine means of suicide in classical antiquity.[94] The play is also remarkable in following Aristotelian concepts of tragedy closely: the observation of the unity of time; the emphasis on the tragic flaw of the heroine brought down by necessity that was beyond her control; the feelings of pity and fear – the two required conditions of the tragic *katharsis*. However, the most important aspect of Tsvetaeva's modifications of the traditional myth reflected her own position as a woman in juxtaposition to her male predecessors.[95] Antonina Gove rightly observed that a recurrent strain in the development of Tsvetaeva's lyric verse was 'a rejection by the poet of the conventional roles imposed on the individual by society, particularly certain characteristics of the feminine role'.[96] It is therefore relevant to consider briefly Tsvetaeva's own view of herself as a female poet. In her *Tale of Sonechka* Tsvetaeva referred to the title 'poetessa' ('poetess') as a 'disgusting thing to say' about her.[97] Svetlana Boym explained the strength of this reaction on Tsveteava's part: 'The poetess is ahistorical, extremely subjective and incapable of stepping out of her little emotional home into the disinterested objectivity of language ... The poetess becomes an unconscious parody of a poet'.[98] Even in some of her very early poetry Tsvetaeva always referred to herself as a 'poet' without the damning feminine suffix, the signifier of what Osip Mandelshtam saw as excessive emotional exaltation and lack of taste in the use of poetic metaphor.[99] There is no doubt that Marina Tsvetaeva's poetry in general and her classical plays in particular are emotionally charged and contentious writings, qualities that have been regarded by some of her readers in a negative light. However, Tsvetaeva's gender alone cannot explain why her classical heroines, especially Phaedra, are the speaking subjects of passion, rather than the victims of it. On the other hand, Tsvetaeva's persistent choices of poetic and life paths deemed too radical, inappropriate, and sometimes perhaps even shocking according to the expectations of the public contribute greatly to the interpretation of her poetics. The outrageous element in the eyes of the Greek audience that forced Euripides to change the original plot of his *Hippolytus* became for Tsvetaeva the forbidden but inevitably chosen fruit: the emotional intensity of the female protagonist. Tsvetaeva, if anything, wanted to escape the ghosts of predictable female discourse and resisted her enforced literary identity as a 'woman-poet' while embracing the femininity of her tragic heroines.[100] In that respect Tsvetaeva remained true to her unchanging stance of siding with the underdog and writing against the grain.

4. Marina Tsvetaeva's Tragic Heroines

The real issue for Tsvetaeva, unlike for Euripides, Seneca or even Racine, was not Hippolytus' *hybris* in imagining that he, as a servant of the virgin goddess Artemis, could place himself above the powers of Aphrodite, the embodiment of sexual desire and femininity. Neither were any considerations of incest or inappropriate behaviour on the part of Phaedra the moral focus of Tsvetaeva's drama. For Tsvetaeva the main concern in *Phaedra* was one of female sexuality and the right to articulate it.[101] In Euripides' play Phaedra's love was not only an inherited curse but also an *eros-nosos* ('love-sickness', and eventually a cause of dishonourable behaviour), as one of the choral odes explicitly stated:

Love distils desire upon the eyes,
love brings bewitching grace into the heart
of those he would destroy.
I pray that love may never come to me
with murderous intent,
in rhythms measureless and wild.[102]

Although Tsvetaeva's Phaedra was still a victim of mortal and uncontrollable disease, she was at the same time a sympathetic character whose love lacked the treachery and deceit of her ancient counterpart. Phaedra's only guilt was succumbing to and voicing her passion in a way that was socially inappropriate for a woman. Ariadne's silence in the first drama of the trilogy followed the expectations of the social norm: men wooed or disparaged and rejected her and decided her fate. Phaedra was granted the self-affirmation denied to her sister, and because of that she found in the play virtually no equal in range and power. Although in *Ariadne* Theseus was as much the focus of the play as the title character, in *Phaedra* he was marginalized, while the female heroine was brought to the forefront. Tsvetaeva was indeed much more interested in the fate of Theseus' women than she was in the hero of her planned trilogy 'Theseus'. However, it would trivialize Tsvetaeva's place in the Russian poetic landscape to see her merely as a woman-poet describing female emotions in her poetry. Joseph Brodsky, when asked if 'women's poetry ('zhenskaia poeziia') is something specific', aptly answered that 'you can't apply adjectives to poetry'.[103] It is hard not to agree with Anya Kroth who described Tsvetaeva's poetic vision as 'dichotomous', infused with the notion of androgyny, 'sexlessness of the soul', a desire that must transcend cultural sexual stereotypes.[104]

Furthermore, an interpretation of Tsvetaeva's poetry must, as has been demonstrated, move carefully between literature and biography. It is possible to assume that the circumstances of writing the classical plays (Tsvetaeva's expatriation and the loss of her native literary milieu) found reflection in Tsvetaeva's exploration of both the feminine voice and words in tragedy and the heroines' alienation from and rejection by their male counterparts. Although Tsvetaeva in her classical tragedies did not write explicitly about exile, the experience of it marked all the poetry she wrote abroad.[105] In *Phaedra* exile is metaphorically explored in Phaedra's sense of loneliness, isolation and confusion.

In this context, it is necessary also to make a few remarks about the diction of both poems. While *Ariadne* is stylistically uniform and easier to read, *Phaedra* appears more innovative in its use of Russian folk songs, neologisms and archaisms, as if the play were clinging to the core and fabric of the lost mother tongue. In that respect both plays stand in a contradictory relation to at least one of Tsvetaeva's Russian predecessors in neoclassical tragedy; Tsvetaeva's diction is far removed from Ivanov's high-flown and at times difficult language and allusions, which require intricate knowledge of Greek mythology and literature. Tsvetaeva's plays, where the conventional language is pushed to its limits, are still far more touching pieces of poetry and are replete with emotions familiar to a reader of Tsvetaeva's lyric poetry. In these plays Tsvetaeva shines with full force as an innovator of Russian poetic language: she omits verbs, uses difficult phrases allowed only by the inflected language, and clothes dramatic action in an equally intensely dramatic rhythm of verse. A feeling of despair haunts her experimentation with the language of this play, despair familiar to a poet physically removed from the space that resounds with her native tongue, the space she tries to recreate in her poetry.

It is perhaps because of the difficult diction of both plays, but especially of *Phaedra*, that they did not win Tsvetaeva any acclaim. Tsvetaeva's classical plays have not been treated kindly by either contemporary or later critics of her poetry.[106] Tomas Venclova went so far as to call *Phaedra* a 'chaotic and anarchic work'.[107] There is no doubt that even for a native speaker of Russian these plays present a difficult reading challenge with their tangle of language, unusual metre, and often inexplicable choice of words. I tend, however, to agree with Maria Stadter Fox in her analysis of *Phaedra*:

> The text of the play, viewed as a labyrinth, produces a certain community of readers: readers willing to engage with and become entangled in the text and learn paths or ways through and amid it, readers willing to 'produce' the play from words and syllables that can only be understood through a blend of reading graphically and aurally, readers willing to define and work with and against boundaries and constraints of genre, tradition, and language ... Her work attempts to push those constraints and categories to the limits.[108]

Furthermore, the impossibility of staging Tsvetaeva's plays becomes especially apparent in her choice of diction for them. Tsvetaeva remained unwavering in her rejection of theatre as a medium for her dramas. In this respect her neoclassical attempts were akin (perhaps unintentionally so) to those of Ivanov and Annenskii. The plays need to be read, not performed, because they represent for Tsvetaeva first and foremost a form of literature that must remain static for the reader and faithful to its literary sources and thus resists the interpretation inherent in any staged performance. The supreme importance of the word, both spoken and written, penetrates the plot as well as the meaning of the play. Unlike Annenskii's tragedies, the plays do not provide stage directions or descriptions of the appearances of the characters.[109] All the specifics are left to the imagination of the reader. *Phaedra* as well as *Ariadne* should be seen as a continuation of Tsvetaeva's lyric voice and even to some degree, as demonstrated above, a reflection of her emotional life. In penning the end of Phaedra, Tsvetaeva gave herself an 'archetypal' script that she could carry out more than a decade later in the despair of her life in Elabuga.

Helen, the last play of the intended trilogy, was never written for reasons that remain unknown. It is possible that for Tsvetaeva *Phaedra* represented the pinnacle of experimentation with classical drama and thus, after writing it, she abandoned the form altogether.[110] It is also possible that the lack of support and critical acclaim for her tragedies led Tsvetaeva, motivated by more practical considerations, to take a new direction in her poetry that would enable her to fare better with the critics and publishing venues.

In one of her earliest poems written in 1913. 'Moim stikham napisannym tak rano ...'[111] ('To my poems written so early...'), Tsvetaeva expressed doubt about her poetic legacy and hoped that time would prove their quality. The poem ends with an optimistic exclamation:

> Moim stikham, kak dragotsennym vinam,
> Nastanet svoi chered.

> For my poems, as for precious wines
> Their turn will come ...

It seems that Tsvetaeva's classical plays have finally entered that stage of increasing and much deserved interest. What were perceived at first as their shortcomings (unusual diction, entangled verbal texture, idiosyncratic use of well-known myths) can now be seen as yet another proof of Tsvetaeva's innovative and progressive poetic vision, which left an indelible impression on Russian poetic language.

Osip Mandelshtam: 'Yearning for World Culture'[1]

Vse bylo vstar', vse povtoritsia snova,
I sladok nam lish' uznavan'ia mig.[2]

What happened once, will be repeated anew
And only the moment of recognition is sweet to us.

Osip Mandelshtam, 'Tristia'

Traditionally discussed in the context of the Acmeist school of poetry, Osip Mandelshtam outgrew its main principles by the sheer breadth of his cultural interests and concerns. In 1910 the Symbolist movement underwent an ideological crisis. When Acmeism was born within the Symbolist movement, it accepted the main precepts of Symbolism but renounced all the mysticism associated with it.[3] The title of the movement was perhaps jokingly suggested by none other than the great maestro of Symbolism, Viacheslav Ivanov, who derived the word from the Greek word 'acmê' ('summit') to humour the group of young poets who were breaking away.[4] Described as a neorealist or neo-Parnassian movement, Acmeism owed its foundation to Nikolai Gumilev, the first husband of Anna Akhmatova, shot by the Bolsheviks in 1921 when he was thirty-five years old. In 1911 Gumilev and Sergei Gorodetskii formed the *Guild of Poets*, whose title stressed the notion of poetry as a craft over the Symbolists' conception of it as a priestly or mystical endeavour. In Gumilev's 1912 manifesto 'Acmeism and the Heritage of Symbolism' he called for an end to abstract German ideas and promoted a new emphasis on the preoccupation of French poetry with exact and faultless verbal workmanship.[5] Gumilev rejected Symbolism both as a literary phenomenon and as a world view, although his formulation of the new creed was not clearly defined: 'To take Symbolism's place there comes now a new movement, whatever its name might be, either Acmeism (from the word *acmê*, signifying the supreme degree which a thing may attain, its peak or bloom), or Adamism (a firm and manly vision of life) – but which at any rate demands a greater balance of powers and a more precise notion of the tie between subject and object than was the case with Symbolism ...'.[6] The models Gumilev named for Acmeist poetry were Rabelais, Théophile Gautier, François Villon and the French Parnassians, who advocated Gautier's doctrine of art for art's sake. The essence of the new movement was that at the centre of the new poetics 'there stands man, not prostrated by pseudo-Symbolist horrors, but the master of his own house'.[7]

Among the Symbolists the Acmeists allied themselves most with Innokentii Annenskii who, as has been noted, also considered Symbolist mysticism alien to his poetics and who, not unlike his idol Euripides, saw men, not gods, as the measure of all things.[8] Acmeism adopted as a part of its credo what Mandelshtam defined before his final arrest in 1938 as a 'yearning for world culture' ('toska po mirovoi kul'ture').

Mandelshtam's poetic output did not entirely conform to all the aims outlined by Acmeist manifestos. Mandelshtam's poetry was typical of Acmeism only in 'its assumption that the reader, knowledgeable in the classics of Western literature, will recognize explicit and implicit quotations from extraneous texts'[9] because Acmeism first and foremost stressed precision of language, to which the use of quotation from classical sources contributed. Mandelshtam's lyrical impulses, however, were stronger than the doctrinal statements of the Acmeist school.

Mandelshtam's early experiences account for much of his cosmopolitanism and his capacity to make connections across national boundaries. The poet was born in Warsaw on 15 January 1891 to the family of a merchant who was descended from Spanish Jews and was fascinated by European culture. The family moved to St Petersburg, where in 1900 Mandelshtam entered the Tenishev School; it was one of the best institutions in pre-Revolutionary Russia (attended a few years later also by Vladimir Nabokov), where education included the study of foreign languages, classical and European history, art and the sciences. By its untraditional encouragement of creative thinking, the Tenishev School unquestionably helped the future poet conceive of culture in universal terms – as a unified entity not divided by the borders of geography, customs or language. Moreover, after graduation, Mandelshtam spent some time abroad, especially in France and Italy, and in 1909-10 he studied philosophy and philology at Heidelberg University, then a major centre of classical philology. His passionate interest in the ancient world, which developed there, led to and further intensified with his participation in the 'Tower' ('Bashnia') of Viacheslav Ivanov, whose erudition undoubtedly impressed Mandelshtam.[10] As a result of his own brief educational stint in Heidelberg, the young poet craved a well-rounded and deep understanding of the Western cultural heritage. Mikhail Gasparov succinctly observed that Mandelshtam, being a somewhat provincial, middle-class Jew, did not feel entitled to either Russian or European culture. The choice of culture was for him, as for his hero Chaadaev, 'an act of personal will' ('akt lichnoi voli') and the way to overcome his life-long isolation, especially after 1917.[11]

The changes in the orientation of Russian poetry coincided with dramatic political changes that culminated in the October Revolution of 1917. While many elected to emigrate in the aftermath of the Revolution, Mandelshtam – whose poems focused not on the contemporary but on the timeless, and endeavoured to tie Russian culture to the West – stayed. The time and place into which Mandelshtam was born account for much of his desire to embrace all culture and to disregard geographical and linguistic boundaries. As Russia was engendering (in Bradbury and McFarlane's words) 'an apocalypse of cultural community', Mandelshtam, like Viacheslav Ivanov, preferred to live in 'bol'shoe vremia', a sense of time unperturbed by political and economic turmoil.[12]

Mandelshtam's life and poetry demonstrate that he never adjusted to the new Soviet reality, although he did write a few great political poems between 1913 and 1923.[13] In general, however, as his lyrical 'I' defiantly declared in one poem of 1924:

Net, nikogda, nichei ia ne byl sovremennik,
Mne ne s ruki pochet takoi.[14]

I was never anyone's contemporary, no,
That kind of honour does not suit me.

Mandelshtam considered himself a contemporary of the world's culture from its beginning to the present time, but he had a special affinity with the Western and classical heritage. In post-revolutionary Russia a certain opposition developed between 'Pastists' and Futurists, and the very notions of 'past' and 'future', 'tradition' and 'innovation' became closely intertwined with the poet's self-positioning in the Russian literary landscape. While the Futurists, most notable among them Vladimir Maiakovskii, called for casting off the 'past' from the 'Steamship of Modernity', poets who proclaimed their allegiance to the poetic *acmê* sought to demonstrate that the ' "Steamship of Modernity" was the "ship of eternity" ',[15] and that embracing the past did not mean alienating oneself from the future. In 'The Word and Culture' Mandelshtam articulated his challenge to the Futurists: 'One often hears: that is good but belongs to yesterday. But I say yesterday has not yet been born ... I want Ovid, Pushkin and Catullus to live once more, and I am not satisfied with the historical Ovid, Pushkin and Catullus'.[16] That statement had its roots in the beliefs of Symbolism and would have been characteristic of Ivanov: 'the past has not passed', 'what has been, has passed – is a barbarian's wisdom' whereas 'the wisdom of culture is: what once was, still is'.[17] This stance by Mandelshtam therefore did not mean that his longing to re-live the past prevented him from feeling an affinity with the events transpiring in Russia. He simply preferred to view them against the larger picture of the history of the world. This 'uncommon visage' – to invoke Baratynskii's words – made him something of a pariah in his own society, but it also made him an influential, eloquent mouthpiece for the feelings of loss and nostalgia unleashed by the 1917 October Revolution among the intelligentsia.[18] During his lifetime, however, this indifference toward the Revolution and its new ideology did not win him popularity with the new government. Along with many intellectuals Mandelshtam was arrested for the second time in 1938 and disappeared into the abyss of the GULAG.[19] He died of hunger and unbearable conditions in December of the same year somewhere in the concentration camps near Vladivostok.

Greek dreams

Despite Mandelshtam's fascination with ancient Greece, repeatedly expressed in his poetry and prose, I find it hard to assert that all his 'Greek' poetry can be analyzed within a unified system characteristic of his poetics as a whole.[20] In this respect Mandelshtam differed significantly from the representatives of Russian classicism, from the poet-scholars Ivanov and Annenskii, or even from his own contemporary, Marina Tsvetaeva. There was a wide thematic range in Mandelshtam's 'Hellenistic poems' in which an idyllic picture of Hellas coupled with the contemplation of the Hellenic heritage can be detected.[21] The main focus of Mandelshtam's 'Hellenistic' poetics was explained in his essay 'O Prirode Slova" ('On the Nature of the Word'):

> Hellenism is the conscious surrounding of man with utensils, instead of indifferent objects; it is the changing of these objects into utensils; it means to humanize the world around us, to impart on it the subtle warmth of a teleology. Hellenism is any stove, with a man warming himself at it and valuing its warmth as kindred to his own, inner warmth .... Hellenism is a system in the Bergsonian sense of that word, a system that man spreads out around himself, like a fan of phenomena freed of temporal dependence, but coordinated by the inner bond of the human 'I'.

In this 'Hellenistic' system Mandelshtam included his vision of the word ('slovo'), which for him had the meaning of *logos* rather than a mere 'utterance' or means of communication: 'the word, in a Hellenistic conception, is active flesh, ready to give birth to the event'.[22]

Several poems in Mandelshtam's oeuvre reflected his preoccupation with poetic *logos*. One was *'Silentium'* (1910) in which Mandelshtam contemplated that 'active flesh' of the *logos*:

Ona eshche ne rodilas',
Ona – i muzyka i slovo,
I potomu vsego zhivogo
Nenarushaemaia sviaz'.

Spokoino dyshat moria grudi,
No, kak bezumnyi, svetel den',
I peny blednaia siren'
V cherno-lazurevom sosude.

Da obretut moi usta
Pervonachal'nuiu nemótu,
kak kristallicheskuiu notu,
Chto ot rozhdeniia chista!

Ostan'sia penoi, Afrodita,
I, slovo, v muzyku vernis',
I, serdtse, serdtsa ustydis',
S pervoosnovoi zhizni slito![23]

She's still unborn
she's music and she's word,
and thus she's the unbreakable link
of all the living things.

The sea's breasts breathe calmly,
but the day is madly bright,
and the pale lilac of the foam
is in the black-azure vessel.

O let my lips acquire then
the primordial muteness,
Like a crystal note
pure from birth.

Remain foam, oh Aphrodite,
and, word, return to music again,
And, heart, you be ashamed of heart,
Merged with the protoplast of life.

The Greek myth about Aphrodite's birth from sea-foam has been used brilliantly in this poem. Aphrodite was equated with the *logos*, the physical manifestation of the unspoken, and was engendered by the foam, the primordial muteness containing the true, fleshless utterance that combines music and word. Victor Terras suggested that this juxtaposition 'of the *logos* to a primeval *silentium* could have been developed from Heraclitus, but was more likely to have been from Paul Verlaine's "Art Poétique" ' ('De la musique avant toute chose ...').[24] It seems to me that the *Quellenforschung* for this poem is inconsequential; the image used here by Mandelshtam was a manifestation of his uncanny poetic intuition and imagination. The most important element in this poem (which would find a more precise reflection in Mandelshtam's Roman poems) was the connection that he established between natural phenomena disguised in mythological metaphors and the artistic medium of the poetic word. The exploration of that connection was repeated again in yet another poem written in 1914:

Est' ivolgi v lesakh, i glasnykh dolgota –
V tonicheskikh stikhakh edinstvennaia mera.

5. Osip Mandelshtam: 'Yearning for World Culture'

No tol'ko raz v godu byvaet razlita
V prirode dlitel'nost', kak v metrike Gomera.

Kak by tsezuroiu ziiaet etot den':
Uzhe s utra pokoi i trudnye dlinnoty;
Voly na pastbishche, i zolotaia len'
Iz trostnika izvlech' bogatstvo tseloi noty.[25]

There are orioles in the woods, and the length of vowels
is the only measure in metrical verse.
But only once a year there is a lengthiness
spread out in Nature too, like in Homer's poetry.

This day is agape as if with a caesura:
Rest and difficult spondees from early morning,
oxen at pasture and golden laziness
oh, to draw the wealth of a whole note from a reed.

The final version of this poem appeared under the title 'Equinox' ('Ravnodenstvie'). The poem also had an interesting prehistory, recorded in the memoirs of K. Mochul'skii, Mandelshtam's teacher of ancient Greek. Mochul'skii related the following reminiscence from 1912, when he was preparing the poet to pass the examination in ancient Greek:

> He always came to the class horribly late, utterly stunned by the newly revealed mysteries of Greek grammar. He would flail his hands, running around the room and reciting in a singsong manner the declensions and the conjugations. The reading of Homer metamorphosed into a fairy-tale event. The adverbs, enclitics, and pronouns pursued him in his dreams and entered into mysterious personal relationships with him. When he found out that the participle from the verb *'paideuô'* ('to educate') is *'pepaideukôs'*, he choked from exultation and could not study any longer that day. He came to the next class with a guilty smile and said: 'I did not prepare anything, but I have written a poem.' And without even taking off his coat he began to sing. I remembered two stanzas:
>
> And the bell of verb endings
> Directs me on my way from afar,
> So that in the cell of a modest philologist
> I rest from my sadness.
>
> I forget my vexations and my sorrows,
> And one question pursues me:
> Is there an augment needed in the aorist
> And what is the voice of 'pepaideukôs'?[26]

While this poem from Mochul'skii's memoir was nothing more than a philological joke understandable only to a student of ancient Greek, the general state of exultation that the poet derived from learning and reciting

123

Greek paradigms and poetry evinced clearly Mandelshtam's overwhelming fascination with the Greek language and with Homeric verse. The poem 'There are orioles ...' was written in alexandrine verse (iambic hexameter) with a caesura after the third foot, thus conveying in form what Mandelshtam tried to explain in the theme of the poem: an impression of a perfect autumn day full of sleepy languor. Homeric verse was equated with the autumnal equinox, the equality of night and day. The measured pace of the days in early fall was likened to the balance of long and short syllables in the dactylic hexameter. Joseph Brodsky observed that the importance of the Greek echo in this poem extended also to its metre, the alexandrine verse, which, he noted, 'is the nearest kin to hexameter [dactylic], if only in terms of using the caesura'.[27] Out of all Greek poets it was Homer who appeared in Mandelshtam's lyrics with the most remarkable consistency because he seems to have represented for the poet that perfect combination between music and *logos*, the primordial sound of poetic perfection.

The myths that Mandelshtam borrowed from Homer, however, did not receive any profound treatment. I do not believe that it will be helpful to suggest a unifying 'scenario' for Mandelshtam's persistent return to Homer. His allusions were dense and intricate, at times exultant and at times full of lamentations. His two most famous 'Homeric' poems 'Bessonitsa, Gomer, tugie parusa' ('Insomnia, Homer, full sails', 1915)[28] and 'Zolotistogo meda struia' ('A golden spurt of honey', also titled 'Vine', 1917) were dreamy evocations of the Homeric epics and considerations of their central themes. In the former the poet compared the Catalogue of Ships from the *Iliad* to a wedge of cranes ('sei dlinnyi vyvodok, sei poezd zhuravlinyi') over Hellas.[29] This poem might have been influenced by Innokentii Annenskii's essay 'What is Poetry?' (1911), published in *Apollon (Apollo)*, a journal respected by the Acmeists; in it Annenskii explained the significance of this catalogue, which even extremely devoted students of ancient Greek often find overwhelmingly tedious: 'And is it so strange that once upon a time even the symbols of names introduced into a poem's music evoked in those who heard the poem a whole range of impressions and recollections, in which echoes of battle forced their way through a hymn to the word, and the brilliance of gold armour and crimson sails mixed with the sound of the shadowy waves of the Aegean Sea?'[30] It is easy to see from this excerpt why Homer's monotonous piling up of names evoked in Mandelshtam the unusual response of insomnia (when a more ordinary reaction in a less zealous reader would be exactly the opposite). Like Annenskii, Mandelshtam again detected even in this lengthy recounting of Greek names the merging of music and word, the primordial musical *logos*. 'Where are you sailing', asked the poet, 'if it weren't for Helen, what is Troy to you, Achaean men?' ('Kuda plyvete vy? Kogda by ne Elena, / Chto Troia vam odna, akheiskie muzhi?'). The evocation of Helen elicited the anticipated response in the last stanza:

5. Osip Mandelshtam: 'Yearning for World Culture'

I more, i Gomer – vse dvizhetsia liubov'iu,
Kogo zhe slushat' mne? I vot Gomer molchit,
I more chernoe, vitiistvuia, shumit
I s tiazhkim grokhotom podkhodit k izgolov'iu.[31]

And the sea, and Homer – all is moved by love.
Whom should I heed? And now Homer is silent,
And the black sea, orating, resounds,
and with a heavy rumbling approaches the head of my bed.

In the last stanza, influenced perhaps by the famous line from Dante's *Paradiso* (33,1.145) 'l'amor che move il sole e l'atre stelle'[32] ('love which moves the sun and the other stars'); the poet envisioned the poetic *logos* of Homer merging with nature again as the catalogue of Achaean warriors in the opening stanza had become the wedge of cranes. The central theme of this poem was the invincible power of love, the embodiment of which, Helen, had set the Greek fleet in motion towards Troy. The 'divine foam on kings' heads' ('na golovakh tsarei bozhestvennaia pena') was the foam from which Aphrodite, the goddess of love, was born, who directed the voyage and was the cause of the Trojan War. The distress engendered by the power of love was not yet uttered, but only implied in the intimidating roar of the sea.

The theme of the Trojan War returned in yet another extremely complicated poem written in 1920, 'Za to chto ia ruki tvoi ne sumel uderzhat' ...' ('Because I was not able to keep your hands ...'):

Za to, chto ia ruki tvoi ne sumel uderzhat',
Za to, chto ia predal solenye nezhnye guby,
Ia dolzhen rassveta v dremuchem akropole zhdat'.
Kak ia nenavizhu pakhuchie drevnie sruby!

Akheiskie muzhi vo t'me snariazhaiut konia,
Zubchatymi pilami v steny vgryzaiutsia krepko,
Nikak ne uliazhetsia krovi sukhaia voznia,
I net dlia tebia ni nazvan'ia, nu zvuka, ni slepka.

Kak mog ia podumat', chto ty vozvratish'sia, kak smel?
Zachem prezhdevremenno ia ot tebia otorvalsia?
Eshche ne rasseialsia mrak i petukh ne propel,
Eshche v drevesinu goriachii topor ne vrezalsia.

Prozrachnoi slezoi na stenakh prostupila smola,
I chuvstvuet gorod svoi dereviannye rebra,
No khlynula k lestnitsam krov' i na pristup poshla,
I trizhdy prisnilsia muzham soblaznitel'nyi obraz.

Gde milaia Troia? Gde tsarskii, gde devichii dom?
On budet razrushen, vysokii Priamov skvoreshnik.

I padaiut strely sukhim dereviannym dozhdem,
I strely drugie rastut na zemle, kak oreshnik ... [33]

Because I was not able to keep your hands,
Because I betrayed your salty, tender lips.
I have to wait for dawn here in the dense acropolis
How I hate ancient weeping log walls!

Achaean men outfit the horse in the dark,
And deeply cut into the walls with toothed saws,
The blood's dry commotion does not subside,
And there is no name for you, nor sound, nor moulded cast.

How could I have believed in your return, how did I dare?
Why did I pull myself away from you prematurely?
The darkness has not yet dissipated, the cock hasn't crowed,
Hot axes haven't cut into wood.

Resin seeps from wooden walls, like clear tears,
The city feels its wooden ribs,
But blood gushed to the ladders and besieged the walls,
And three times the men dreamed of a seductive image.

Where is beloved Troy? Where the royal house of the maidens?
It will be destroyed, Priam's lofty starling house.
And the arrows fall in a dry, wooden rain,
As other arrows grow from the ground like a nut-tree grove ...

As Mikhail Gasparov noted, the poem is very confusing if analyzed from a strictly mythological perspective.[34] The only clear allusion was the 'seductive image', which must allude to *Odyssey* 4.271-89. This described Telemachus' visit to Sparta during which Menelaus told Odysseus' son how the wooden horse had been brought inside the Trojan citadel and how Helen in a failed attempt to unravel the Greek plot had circled it three times calling on the heroes hidden inside in imitation of their wives' voices. There, however, any precision of mythological reference ended. The main difficulty lay with the narrator of the poem: who was he? a Trojan? a Greek? Who was waiting for dawn in the 'dense acropolis'? The lines of the fifth stanza pointed to a Trojan narrator, who predicted the fall of the beloved city and Priam's royal house. But then the theme of love became confusing. No Trojan in the ancient mythology of the Trojan War lamented the loss of his beloved while waiting for Troy to be toppled. If, however, the speaker were assumed to be a Greek, then Menelaus must be speaking: he lost Helen and waged war for ten years, but in this poem, just before the imminent victory, he understood that all of this bloodshed had been in vain; Helen would never love him again.[35] This would of course be an extremely psychologized and romanticized notion of antiquity.

There is also, as Gasparov suggested, another possible interpretation,

126

which would be accessible, however, only to a real connoisseur of classical myth.[36] The speaker could be none other than Paris, longing not for Helen but for Oenone. The myth of Paris and Oenone achieved some popularity in Russia thanks to the translation of Ovid's *Heroides* by Zelinskii, published in 1912-13. According to the myth, Oenone had been Paris' lover during his shepherding years. After he regained his position as a Trojan prince, he abandoned her and pursued Helen. Wounded by the poisoned arrow of Philoctetes, he called for her to come back and heal him. She refused and then repented too late. It is possible perhaps to imagine the narrator of this poem to be Paris, who upon his deathbed hoped for Oenone, whom he had once betrayed, to return and heal him. By the time the wooden horse was constructed, however, Paris had long been dead, which is an insurmountable difficulty for this interpretation. It is clear then that the poem was not intended as an easily identifiable mythological allusion. Rather the Greek myth served an auxiliary purpose to the narrative of love and loss. Several critics pointed out that the poem was addressed to an actress, Ol'ga Arbenina, with whom Mandelshtam was in love in the last months of 1920.[37] The 'Trojan' theme, then, was a signifier of unrequited love, the loss of the beloved and suffering associated with it. Mandelshtam used mythological metaphor as an auxiliary in several of his other poems.

In the poem 'A golden spurt of honey', the *Odyssey* was on Mandelshtam's mind while he was in 'rocky Tauride' – the Crimea – a region, which, as is explored in greater detail later, Mandelshtam identified closely with Greco-Roman culture.[38] The last stanza of the poem deserves particular attention:

> Zolotoe runo, gde zhe ty, zolotoe runo?
> Vsiu dorogu shumeli morskie tiazhelye volny,
> I, pokinuv korabl', natrudivshii v moriakh polotno,
> Odissei vozvratilsia, prostranstvom i vremenem polnyi.[39]

> Golden Fleece, where are you, o Golden Fleece?
> The heavy sea-waves roared the whole journey,
> And abandoning his ship, with the sail worn out at sea,
> Odysseus returned sated by space and time.

The Greek mythology of these lines is blatantly incorrect. I would like to ponder here why Odysseus has become part of the Argonaut myth in this poem; it would be rather implausible to assume that Mandelshtam wrongly thought that Odysseus was one of the heroes who retrieved the Golden Fleece. That adventure belonged to the first generation of heroes, one that had come before the Trojan cycle which was Odysseus' rightful place. It seems to me that an answer to this question can be derived at least partially from the previous stanza, which ended with the following lines:

Pomnish', v grecheskom dome: liubimaia vsemi zhena,-
ne Elena, drugaia – kak dolgo ona vyshivala?

Do you remember, in the Greek house: the wife loved by everyone,
Not Helen, but the other one – how long was she weaving?

Penelope was not mentioned by name, as if the poet had forgotten it; he seems to have wanted to elicit the answer from his readers, warning them that his memory was blurred and imprecise, and that he was only interested in the feeling, not the factual details. He simply juxtaposed her to Helen, the antithesis of a loyal wife. Odysseus in the poem stood not as a familiar mythological figure connected with a precise mythological journey but as a metaphor for a poet-traveller for whom return would be possible only when satiation 'with space and time' had been achieved. Such a vague and even loose use of the ancient material reappeared later in another poem on the 'Trojan' theme 'I'll tell you with final frankness' ('Ia skazhu tebe s poslednei priamotoi', 1931):

Ia skazhu tebe s poslednei
Priamotoi:
Vse lish' bredni, sherri-brendi,
Angel moi.

Tam, gde ellinu siiala
Krasota,
Mne iz chernykh dyr ziiala
Sramota.

Greki sbondili Elenu
Po volnam,
Nu a mne – solenoi penoi
Po gubam ...[40]

I'll tell you with final
frankness:
it is all nonsense, sherry-brandy,
my angel!

Where beauty shone
for the Greeks,
for me out of black holes
shame yawns.

The Greeks filched Helen
Across the waves,
But only salt foam
washed across my lips ...

The third stanza of the poem contained a gaping blunder: it was not the Greeks, but the Trojan Paris who stole Helen.[41] The vulgarism 'sbondili' ('filched') would especially attract attention to the line, although the reader, taken by surprise by the unexpected use of a rare vulgarism, may miss the meaning of the word completely and barely notice the mythological blunder.[42] This poem was not about the Greeks or the Trojans; it evoked the end of a beautiful heroic epoch: who stole Helen mattered little at that point; in the place of beauty the poet saw nothing but shame staring at him from descending darkness.

It would be an exaggeration to say that Mandelshtam's 'Hellenistic' poetry always reflected a preoccupation with preciseness of poetic *logos*, a fusion of nature and culture, or a deep interpretation of a mythological metaphor. It was rather a set of fragments of ancient Greece, bearing an almost dreamlike quality in which traces of Mandelshtam's 'Hellenism', better formulated as a philosophical system in his prose, can occasionally be detected. Mandelshtam was not a 'Hellenist' or an antiquarian in Ivanov's sense, or a mythographer in Annenskii's image, nor was he preoccupied throughout his poetry with any binary juxtapositions like Tsvetaeva. Greek mythology offered the poet a set of permanent thematic signifiers of war, nostalgia, love and death as he struggled to make sense of his own world that had been torn apart, especially in his post-revolutionary poetry. It was mostly in his 'Roman' poems (as I demonstrate later) that the impulse to connect the past and present became especially apparent, but there is one 'Greek' poem that also manifested this search for the lost world and its meaning. That poem was 'Nashedshii Podkovu' ('The Horseshoe Finder'), written in 1923 when the havoc of the Revolution and civil war had made it clear that the past had been lost irrevocably.

This long and complicated poem appeared for the first time in the publication *Krasnaia Nov'* (*Red Virgin Soil*) in the spring of 1923 with the subtitle 'A Pindaric Fragment', which disappeared in the following editions. Mandelshtam began the poem with a reverie about the forest, which in his 'Hellenistic' vision had a practical use in shipbuilding. The central question of the poem that follows this initial reverie is about the practical use of poetry. In this light the subtitle 'Pindaric fragment' becomes clear. In one of the stanzas Mandelstam himself explained it:

Trizhdy blazhen, kto vvedet v pesn' imia.
Ukrashennaia nazvan'em pesn'
Dol'she zhivet sredi drugikh, –
Ona otmechena sredi podrug poviazkoi na lbu,
Istseliaiushchei ot bespamiatstva ...[43]

Thrice blessed is the man who will introduce a name into his song,
The song adorned with a name
Lives longer among the others, –

129

She is singled out among her friends by a fillet on her forehead,
Which heals from oblivion …

Clare Cavanagh demonstrated convincingly and thoroughly the numerous parallels between the Pindaric odes and this poem and offered, I believe, a persuasive explanation of Mandelshtam's subtitle, showing at the same time that Mandelshtam's reception of the legacy of ancient Greece was sometimes firmly rooted in the reality that surrounded him.[44] Pindar, observed Cavanagh, was 'one of history's great poetic stories' who was recognized and acclaimed as a poet during his life-time and 'remained until his death in high demand among the ruling families of ancient Greece for the victory odes he wrote to commemorate their triumphs in the various athletic competitions and games staged throughout the different city-states'.[45] Mandelshtam in this stanza interpreted Pindar as the greatest example of the possibility for mutually beneficial relations between poetry and the State, a possibility on which pre- and especially post-revolutionary Russia cast great doubt. Mandelshtam expressed his yearning for a poet's practical use, since the name of an understanding and great patron would give a poet a meaningful existence, one that Pindar enjoyed from celebrating Hieron, ruler of Syracuse from 478 to 466 BCE, in his poems.[46] Richmond Lattimore noted that Pindar's poetry was 'formidably studded with proper names' and sometimes presented a puzzle even for an expert classicist to decipher.[47] These names, drawn from genealogies, ancient myths and Pindar's own contemporaries, showed the poet's connection with both the past and the present as he moved easily between the two. Furthermore, such a song composed under a benevolent patron who is the subject of the song can live forever and is safe from the danger of being forgotten. Through the evocation of Pindar, Mandelshtam contemplated his own standing as a poet in relation to the new State and that State's need for a new poetic voice that would look towards the future not the past. At the end of the poem, however, he predicted his fate pessimistically in the figure of the horseshoe finder, for whom the only vestige of the great Pindaric tradition was the horseshoe signifying the end of the chariot races about which Pindar had sung:

Tak
Nashedshii podkovu
Sduvaet s nee pyl'
I rastiraet ee sherst'iu, poka ona ne zablestit;
Togda
On veshaet ee na poroge,
Chtoby ona otdokhnula,
I bol'she uzh ei ne pridetsia vysekat' iskry iz kremnia.[48]

Thus
The horseshoe finder
Blows the dust from it,
And rubs it with wool until it shines,

Then,
He hangs it above the threshold,
So that it rests.
It does not need any longer to strike sparks from flint.

The 'horseshoe finder' of these lines was left with only the material memory of the great but bygone age. However, in Russian folk tradition, a horseshoe hanging over a threshold is supposed to bring luck, new hope, and that is how Mandelshtam, despite the overall pessimistic message of these lines, tried to remain wistful and hopeful despite his nostalgia for the days past. By the end of the poem that wistfulness also dissipates. Although the first stanzas of Mandelshtam's poem contained the pronoun 'we', which in the Pindaric image cast the poet as the mouthpiece of his community, by the end of the poem the poet reduced it to 'I', and even that in the last lines was not sufficient:

Vremia srezaet menia, kak monetu,
I mne uzhe ne khvataet menia samogo.[49]

Time cuts me out like a coin
And for me there is no longer enough of me.

Mandelshtam's Pindaric aspirations were shattered as he found himself unable to establish a connection between the new age and poetry. Like an old even if attractive coin, his poetry lost its currency with the arrival of the new brutalizing age. The 'gnawing' beastly age reoccurred in Mandelshtam's poetry again in 1931, this time with better defined and prophetic features:

Mne na plechi kidaetsia vek-volkodav,
No ne volk ia po krovi svoei,
Zapikhai menia luchshe, kak shapku, v rukav
Zharkoi shuby sibirskikh stepei.[50]

The century, that wolfhound, pounces on my shoulders,
But I am not a wolf in my blood,
Better cram me in like a hat into a sleeve
Of a hot fur coat of the Siberian steppes.

In these proleptic lines all hope was gone; the poet did not have a place in an age that killed even the savage wolves not to mention gentle poets. That stranded and confused state was reflected most tragically and eloquently in Mandelshtam's Roman poems, which in the following pages I use as a key to understanding the development of the most tragic protagonist of Mandelshtam's poetry: the city of St Petersburg.

'I was born in Rome and Rome returned to me'

Osip Mandelshtam wrote brilliantly and compellingly of Western culture and his main influences were Western classics, especially before he went to Moscow in 1916. There he met Marina Tsvetaeva, who gave him the gift of a firmer pride in the Russian past and cultural heritage, and whom, according to some testimonies, he loved.[51] As a cosmopolitan Jewish poet, Mandelshtam, as the analysis of his 'Greek' poems has illustrated, understandably felt more affinity with the classical heritage than with the Russian one. After the meeting of the two poets, however, Mandelshtam's Russian sensibility became closely intertwined with his stance as a poet who embraced the whole world's culture. His newly acquired facility and indebtedness to Tsvetaeva were manifested in his next collection of verse. The collection contained a long poem, 'Tristia', in homage to Ovid and three poems addressed to Tsvetaeva that were a new departure in his poetics.[52] In the poem 'V Raznogolositse' ('In Discordant Polyphony') Tsvetaeva, disguised as the goddess Aurora, entered to show that Mandelshtam had achieved the poetic symbiosis of Russian and Western traditions in his poetry. The fusion of Western and Russian poetics reached its most compelling *acmê*, however, in Mandelshtam's perception of St Petersburg.

St Petersburg as Rome

An Italian architect who helped to shape the imperial appearance of St Petersburg, Carlo Rossi, viewed the city as another Rome and drew his chief inspiration from the grandeur and opulence associated with the ancient Empire. In 1802 the 26-year-old Rossi, son of an Italian ballerina who had retired to the suburbs of St Petersburg, studied in Rome under the tutelage of the famous architect and designer Vincenzo Brenna, whose work was greatly influenced by Roman palatial interiors. Rossi returned to the Russian capital intending to create a new architectural style that would 'surpass that which the Romans [had] considered sufficient for their monuments'.[53] He fulfilled his dream by creating numerous buildings, among them the Mikhailovskii Palace, which blended the ancient style with Rossi's own vision.

Subsequent Russian artists and intellectuals likened St Petersburg to Rome, often admiringly, sometimes pejoratively, while an energetic debate continued over which of Russia's two capitals, Moscow or St Petersburg, should be considered the true heir to the classical tradition that connected Russia to the West. This debate went all the way back to Filofei's Third Rome doctrine, discussed in the first chapter of this book, which claimed for Moscow the honourable position of the centre of Christendom.[54]

The city built by Peter the Great changed that perception in the minds of Russian intellectuals. As the Russian court gradually migrated from

Moscow to St Petersburg, the city became the centre of everything sophisticated, refined and fashionable. Moscow suddenly seemed a merchants'
capital, unlike the magnificent city on the Neva River to which Western
aristocrats, architects and fashion-conscious courtiers flocked, mesmerized by its sprawling grandeur and limitless wealth. The new city, as I
have demonstrated in the first chapter, introduced the meaning of the
Greco-Roman cultural legacy (especially Roman) into Russian society and
realized the nation's desire to be part of the Western heritage.[55] As Dmitrii
Likhachev observed, 'Petersburg is not between the East and the West, it
is the East and the West simultaneously'.[56]

While Slavophiles saw the city as an alien, Westernized locus that
drained the country's lifeblood and created unprecedented slums ridden by
poverty and disease, for the majority St Petersburg became not only the
'window onto Europe', but also the only Russian city culturally connected
to Greco-Roman antiquity and the Western heritage.[57] For many, Falconet's equestrian statue of Peter the Great erected on Senate Square
evoked the statue of Marcus Aurelius on the Capitoline Hill in Rome.
Indeed, according to Przybylski, 'all the great architects of Russian Classicism – Rastrelli, Quarenghi and Zakharov – attempted to make the city
on the Neva look like the Eternal City on the Tiber'.[58] Russian poets
likewise identified St Petersburg with Rome, through a loaded metaphor
that enabled them to present their city as a victory over fate, time and
space.[59]

Mandelshtam and Rome

The many manifestations of Mandelshtam's Hellenism in his poetry did
not include frequent, explicit reference to any cities or provinces of ancient
Greece, while in contrast a significant number of his poems were devoted
to the city of Rome.[60] Mandelshtam's approach to ancient Rome was
remarkably consistent. The eternal city was not material for Mandelshtam; it existed as an idealized entity, an unbroken focal point of
human existence, a timeless symbol rather than a network of streets and
buildings. Furthermore Mandelshtam limited his idealized perception of
Rome only to the ancient city. Medieval or contemporary Rome and Italy
did not emerge in his poetry in the same haze of unreality as the city of the
Caesars, which in his verses acquired a mythical dimension. The poet's
understanding of Rome as a symbol was best expressed in a poem written
in 1917:

Pust' imena tsvetushchikh gorodov
Laskaiut slukh znachitel'nost'iu brennoi.
Ne gorod Rim zhivet sredi vekov,
A mesto cheloveka vo vselennoi.

Im ovladet' pytaiutsia tsari,
Sviashchenniki opravdyvaiut voiny,
I bez nego prezreniia dostoiny,
Kak zhalkii sor, doma i altari.[61]

Let the names of blossoming cities
Caress the ear with their ephemeral importance.
It's not the city of Rome that lasts forever,
But man's place in the universe.

Kings try to overtake it,
Priests use it to justify wars,
and without it houses and altars,
are wretched rubble worthy of disdain.

This poem glorified the human ability to conquer nature and create culture. Though it was a place of houses and altars – the places of life and worship – what made these constructions important was the human creator. The mighty of the world – kings and priests – were opposed to the creative force of man. Thus according to Mandelshtam's conception of 'Hellenism', pagan Rome was a unified and natural body, absorbing even the civilization created by brutality, greed and conquest.[62]

Mandelshtam made this symbolic view of Rome explicit in another poem composed in 1917, 'Priroda tot zhe Rim' ('Nature is the same as Rome'):[63]

Priroda - tot zhe Rim i otrazilas' v nem.
My vidim obrazy ego grazhdanskoi moshchi
V prozrachnom vozdukhe, kak v tsirke golubom,
Na forume polei i v kolonnade roshchi.

Priroda – tot zhe Rim, i, kazhetsia, opiat'
Nam nezachem bogov naprasno bespokoit' –
Est' vnutrennosti zhertv, chtob o voine gadat',
Raby, chtoby molchat', i kamni, chtoby stroit'.[64]

Nature is the same as Rome, and is mirrored by it.
We see its images of civic grandeur
In the transparent air as in a blue circus,
In the forum of the fields and in the colonnades of groves.

Nature is the same as Rome, and again it seems
Pointless to needlessly trouble the gods,
There are entrails of sacrifices to fathom war,
Slaves to be silent and stones to build.

Here Mandelshtam expressed an idea that persisted throughout his poetry: there was always a possibility of a conflict produced by culture when man attempted to impose his order and artifice on the spontaneity of nature. In Mandelshtam's vision of ancient Rome, however, there was no urban defilement of nature's serenity. Instead, Mandelshtam linked three representative elements of Roman urban culture: the circus, forum and colonnade, with three aspects of nature: blue sky, fields and groves. This harmony of nature and culture, this 'natural city' created a harmonious locale for the man who felt like a citizen of the world.

The dichotomy between nature and culture was resolved in this poem through the simple solution of identifying Rome as the city where everything had its proper place and purpose. The controversy that troubled the human spirit for centuries – man's guilt over destroying nature while creating culture – was defused by Mandelshtam in the idea of a perfect symbiosis between the two, epitomized by ancient Rome. Viacheslav Ivanov's philosophical views (and also his poetry) reflected the perception that ancient civilization was a synthesis of nature and culture and a remedy against the barbarism that threatened cultural continuity, as previously discussed. In the same spirit, the Rome of Mandelshtam derived its power not from the brutality of man but from imitation of the perfect model: nature. The circus was created in the image of the sky, the forum 'copied' wide-open fields, and the colonnades 'mirrored' sacred groves.

Mandelshtam did not allow into his construction of 'natural' Rome the laws inherent in nature that favour the stronger and destroy the weak. He was also not concerned with Rome's foundation myths, which rested on conquests and brutal force far removed from ethical considerations. His 'natural' Rome was a city that deemed itself beyond ethics and morality. In one of his essays, Mandelshtam revealed his approach to antiquity:

> Poetry as a whole is always directed toward a more or less remote, unknown addressee, whose existence a poet cannot doubt unless he doubts himself. [65]

Ancient Rome for Mandelshtam was precisely that kind of addressee, idealized and remote, a universal idea rather than a historical reality. In his Roman themes he was a romantic very much in the manner of Vasilii Zhukovskii, who also perceived antiquity as a life-affirming, bright world, now lost forever. That nostalgic vision of Rome as a powerful locus of ruined glory, the grave of sublimity, also reflected the sense of irrevocable loss that some Russians felt after the dramatic changes of 1917. For Mandelshtam, at least in this poem, Rome was the metaphor for power that was not oppressive but natural, hence the equation between Rome and nature. Whatever the ruthlessness of nature, Mandelshtam viewed human laws as much more ruthless. It was through this dichotomy – Rome as *physis* (nature) and St Petersburg as *nomos* (man-made law) – that the poet's relationship with his own city and his sense of its irrevocable loss must be considered.

While Mandelshtam mentioned no Greek cities in his poetry, Rome challenged St Petersburg as the poet's most frequent addressee. The Rome of the Caesars conceived as the Arcadia of a poet's imagination was opposed yet kindred to the physical reality of St Petersburg, his own 'paradise lost'. The feeling of loss was especially pronounced in the theme of separation that marked many of the poems about Rome and St Petersburg. Mandelshtam's Rome poems addressing the theme of exile can easily be mapped onto his attempt to hold onto the 'old' Petersburg, reflecting his longing and pain for the 'dying' city as it becomes Petrograd, the alien and foreign entity bred by the First World War and Revolution. The theme of separation from Rome was thoroughly explored in the poems that evoked, following Pushkin, Ovid's exile by Octavian Augustus. The last stanza of Mandelshtam's poem 'O vremenakh prostykh i grubykh' ('About Simple and Crude Times', 1914) referred specifically to Ovid's banishment from Rome as a possible analogy for his own yearning:

Kogda s driakhleiushchei liubov'iu,
Meshaia v pesniakh Rim i sneg,
Ovidii pel arbu volov'iu
V pokhode varvarskikh teleg.[66]

When Ovid, his love turning
feeble, blending Rome and snow in his songs,
was singing ox carts
in the march of barbarians' wagons.

The poem offered the traditional image of Ovid as a man oppressed by misery, mourning the loss of the only city suitable for living. It echoed to some degree Pushkin's evocation of Ovid, in which Pushkin, as we saw in the second chapter of this book, had recalled the Roman poet's plight only to 're-write' both the landscape hated by Ovid and the exilic *tristia*; although Pushkin had opened the poem with Ovid's sadness about his banishment, he had replaced the Roman poet's treatment of the country of the Getae with a much warmer depiction. He also had not offered Ovid unconditional empathy but had rather adopted a didactic tone aimed at persuading the poet that his poetic immortality must somehow mitigate his sadness caused by exile. Mandelshtam also adopted a lamenting tone in his 1918 poem titled 'Tristia' ('Ia izuchil nauku rasstavan'ia'/ 'I have mastered the great craft of separation'), which evoked Tibullus as well as Ovid, and combined the theme of exile with amatory themes.[67] This poem, written by Mandelshtam in 1918 during his stay in the Crimea, which he linked directly with Roman culture, alluded unambiguously to the lines in Ovid's *Tristia* 1.3.1-4 where Ovid's departure from Rome was described:

Cum subit illius tristissima noctis imago,
    qua mihi supremum tempus in urbe fuit,
cum repeto noctem, qua tot mihi cara reliqui,
    labitur ex oculis nunc quoque gutta meis.

When the most sorrowful image of that night comes back, on which it was my last hour in Rome; when I recall the night on which I left behind so many things dear to me, even now a tear rolls out of my eyes.

The first strophe of Mandelshatm's 'Tristia' reads as follows:

Ia izuchil nauku rasstavan'ia
V prostovolosykh zhalobakh nochnykh.
Zhuiut voly, i dlitsia ozhidan'e,
Poslednii chas vigilii gorodskikh;
I chtu obriad toi petushinoi nochi,
Kogda, podniav dorozhnoi skorbi gruz,
Gliadeli vdal' zaplakannye ochi
I zhenskii plach meshalsia s pen'em muz.[68]

I have mastered the great craft of separation
amidst the bare unbraided pleas of night,
those lingerings while oxen chew their ration,
the watchful town's last eyelid's shutting tight.
And I revere that midnight rooster's descant
when shouldering the wayfarer's sack of wrong
eyes stained with tears were peering at the distance
and women's wailings were the Muses' song.[69]

There are several levels of Ovidian allusion in this poem. Theodore Ziolkowski observed that this strophe offered almost a 'pastiche' of Ovidian lines from *Tristia* where he 'describes the weeping of his wife, household, and friends as he delays his departure to the last minute in the early morning hours, until Caesar's command finally forces him to depart'.[70] There is also a hint in the first line at one of the reasons for Ovid's exile: Mandelshtam's play on Ovid's infamous *Art of Love* (*Ars Amatoria*) in the phrase 'craft of separation'. It was Ovid's expertise in the 'craft of love' that allegedly caused the poet his unhappy knowledge of the 'craft of separation'.[71] As the weeping of women in his household ensued, so did the new song of his Muse: the song of nostalgia. Thus 'Tristia', not unlike Puskin's 'To Ovid', attached to Ovid's exile a positive dimension of renewed poetic creativity: he took his Muses with him, and they would continue to inspire his new although sad songs.

This positive spin was explored further in another poem written in 1915 (not surprisingly in the Crimea) that explicitly and curiously alluded to Ovid and surpassed even Pushkin's reconfiguration of Ovid's exile, rendering it as an entirely joyous state:

S veselym rzhaniem pasutsia tabuny,
I rimskoi rzhavchinoi okrasilas' dolina;
Sukhoe zoloto klassicheskoi vesny
Unosit vremeni prozrachnaia stremnina.

Topcha po oseni dubovye listy,
Chto gusto steliutsia pustynnoiu tropinkoi.
Ia vspomniu Tsezaria prekrasnye cherty –
Sei profil' zhenstvennyi s kovarnoiu gorbinkoi.

Zdes', Kapitoliia i Foruma vdali,
Sred' uviadaniia spokoinogo prirody,
Ia slyshu Avgusta i na kraiu zemli
Derzhavnym iablokom katiashchiesia gody.

Da budet v starosti pechal' moia svetla:
Ia v Rime rodilsia, i on ko mne vernulsia;
Mne osen' dobraia volchitseiu byla,
I – mesiats tsezarei – mne avgust ulybnulsia.[72]

Herds of horses graze, neighing happily,
And the valley is covered with Roman rust;
Time's transparent rapids carry away
The dry gold of classical spring.

This autumn, trampling oak leaves
That densely cover a deserted path –
I'll think of Caesar's fine features,
That feminine face, that nose with a treacherous bump!

Here, far from Capitol and Forum,
Amid nature's calm withering
I hear Augustus and, on the world's edge,
I hear years rolling like a sovereign apple.

Let my sorrow be lucid in old age:
I was born in Rome, and Rome returned to me;
The autumn was my kind she-wolf
And Caesar's month, August, smiled at me.

Despite the obvious absence of Ovid from this poem, and its first-person-singular authorial persona, the allusion to Ovid's exile can hardly be missed. Here Mandelshtam used the same 'ventriloquist' technique earlier employed by Pushkin. The poem functioned as Ovid's farewell letter to Rome and did away with nostalgia. Old age had come to the poet who was banished from the city of his youth, but the resultant 'sorrow' became 'lucid' and the autumn of his life was transformed into a nourishing she-wolf.[73] However, the poem can be also viewed as Mandelshtam's own perception of Rome as the city that follows her offspring wherever they go.

Ovid, of course, was born not in Rome but in Sulmo, and Mandelshtam himself was born in Warsaw, not St Petersburg, which in many poems was his Rome, as will be demonstrated subsequently. The reference to the month of August in the last line of the poem is puzzling and can have two possible interpretations. One is the word play in Russian: the month of August and Augustus are rendered in Russian by the same word, 'avgust'. Thus Caesar himself as well as the month in his honour smiled benevolently at the exiled poet. The second interpretation is more complex. In his poetry Ovid never expressed any particular fondness for the month of August or for the autumn. Thus 'mesiats tsezarei' ('the month of Caesars') did not make much sense in an Ovidian context, but it was appropriate in the context of another exile, Peter Chaadaev, with whom Mandelshtam was preoccupied during this period. Chaadaev, 'the discoverer of the nomadic Russian spirit', was declared insane upon his return from abroad and became essentially an exile, due to his isolation in Russia, a condition that Mandelshtam understood all too well.[74] In his article on Chaadaev, Mandelshtam wrote:

> And so in August of 1825, in a little seaside village near Brighton, a foreigner appeared whose bearing combined the solemnity of a bishop with the correctness of a worldly mannequin.[75]

As Victor Terras noted, this is the only mention of the month in the whole article and 'it refers to an event of import and "*ulybnulsia*" ['smiled' in the poem of 1915] does not seem out of place to describe it'.[76] In Russian literature Chaadaev remained a person contextualized within the Russian relationship with the Western world. The textual fusion of the two famous exiles in the poem, the Roman to the East and the Russian to the West, served as a perfect device for Mandelshtam to link together the 'tales' of Rome and St Petersburg. However, Mandelshtam's choice of Ovid for the poem, particularly Ovid in exile, reveals an attempt on Mandelshtam's part not only to re-centre and reinterpret the present through the past, but to do so through a past that was itself radically decentred and self-alienated.[77]

In Ovid's poetry of exile, the country of the Getae, the land of his banishment, was a barren terrain deprived of trees and of the joy of bountiful nature. But Mandelshtam, in Pushkin's wake, portrayed a very picturesque landscape, with Ovid wandering amid fallen oak leaves while horses graze peacefully in pastures. Mandelshtam transformed the landscape and Ovid's sorrow to render his Ovid inseparable from Rome. The second stanza also echoed Ovid's *Epistolae ex Ponto* 2.8.1-5, which described the portraits of the imperial family that he had recently received from Rome, more precisely the portraits of Augustus, Tiberius, and Livia:

> Redditus est nobis Caesar cum Caesare nuper,
>   quos mihi misisti, Maxime Cotta, deos;
> utque tuum munus numerum, quem debet, haberet,
>   est ibi Caesaribus Livia iuncta suis.

I have recently received a Caesar together with a Caesar – the gods whom you sent me, Cotta Maximus; and so that your gift might be complete, Livia appeared there joined with her Caesars.

The tone of Ovid's poem was fawning and appeared insincere and exaggerated in its exultant praise, which quickly changed into a lament about his plight as an exile. In Mandelshtam's poem, however, the poet, although banished from his city by the implacable Augustus to the outskirts of the Empire, remained sincerely unwavering in his loyalty to the *princeps*. The only line that suggested animosity was the reference to Augustus' 'feminine face' and his nose with 'treacherous bump', which nonetheless were called 'prekrasnye cherty' ('fine features'). Another remarkable aspect of this poem is that the poet did not return to his beloved city; it was the city that returned to him. Rome was perceived as a *retour éternel*, a cyclical motion of life rather than a geographic location. The poet ultimately triumphed over his fate, inasmuch as a sovereign cannot truly banish the poet from the city that defines him. This poem about Ovid's plight as an exile was dauntingly optimistic and must be interpreted in connection with Mandelshtam's relationship to his own Rome – St Petersburg. Indeed, Mandelshtam returned to the theme of exile and nostalgia in many of his poems on St Petersburg. His 'rewriting' of Ovid's historical and physical exile shed some light on Mandelshtam's perception of his own 'internal' exile from post-revolutionary St Petersburg and the metamorphosis his beloved city suffered from a locus of imperial grandeur to a place of death.

Mandelshtam's St Petersburg

One of the many Russian poets to become infatuated with St Petersburg, Pushkin immortalized its image in his *Bronze Horseman* by showing the most magnificent as well as the deeply devastating aspects of the mighty polis. In Russian poetry of the twentieth century, St Petersburg emerged as a 'Third Rome', not in a Muscovite, Christian sense but rather as a seat of a new, vigorous and (more importantly) secular empire. Mandelshtam, whose poetry was imbued with images of Greco-Roman antiquity, wanted to see his own city of St Petersburg as another Rome of the Caesars. Yet for him Peter's city, unlike Rome, was not an immaterial, idealized entity. Anna Akhmatova observed that he 'managed to be the last writer about Petersburg mores – precise, vivid, dispassionate, and unique. In his writing, the half-forgotten and many times vilified streets reappear in all their freshness.'[78]

Whereas Rome for Mandelshtam, as discussed above, was an eternal ideal of harmony with nature, his own city changed its relationship to his poetic text as the imperial St Petersburg transformed into the city of loss and nostalgia. The city, forever changing, experienced numerous transformations in his poetry, particularly after 1917. This fluctuating image of

Osip Mandelshtam.
Moscow, 1934.

the city illustrates Mandelshtam's contribution to the 'Petersburg mythos',
which emerged in the art of the early twentieth century. The St Petersburg
'syndrome', as Helena Goscilo argued, was perpetuated in paintings by
Mikhail Dobuzhinskii and Alexander Benois, poems by Aleksandr Blok,
and Andrei Belyi's novel, all of which, in their own ways, recreated the
myth of St Petersburg.[79] In contrast to the gloomy St Petersburg of Blok
('Night, street, street light, pharmacy' – 'Noch'. Ulitsa. Fonar'. Apteka')
and the tragic visions of Dobuzhinskii, Mandelshtam's 'Petersburg Strophes' created a St Petersburg of power and splendour:[80]

Nad zheltiznoi pravitel'stvennykh zdanii
Kruzhilas' dolgo mutnaia metel'.
I pravoved opiat' saditsia v sani,
Shirokim zhestom zapakhnuv shinel'.

Zimuiut parokhody. Na pripeke
Zazhglos' kaiuty tolstoe steklo.
Chudovishchna, – kak bronenosets v doke, –
Rossiia otdykhaet tiazhelo …

Tiazhka obuza severnogo snoba
Onegina starinnaia toska;
Na ploshchadi Senata – val sugroba,
Dymok kostra i kholodok shtyka …

141

Cherpali vodu ialiki, i chaiki
Morskie poseshchali sklad pen'ki,
Gde, prodavaia sbiten' ili saiki,
Lish' opernye brodiat muzhiki.

Letit v tuman motorov verenitsa,
Samoliubivyi, skromnyi peshekhod,
Chudak Evgenii, bednosti styditsia,
Benzin vdykhaet i sud'bu klianet.[81]

Over the yellow tint of government buildings
The blurry snowstorm whirled for a long time
and the lawyer climbs again into the sleigh,
with a broad sweep pulling his coat closed.

Ships are hibernating. In direct sun
thick cabin-glass lights up.
Monstrous, like a docked battleship,
Russia rests, heavily...

Heavy is the discomfort of a northern snob,
Onegin's ancient boredom;
out on Senate Square – a snowdrift,
bonfire smoke, and a chill of a bayonet ...

Skiffs ladle water, sea gulls
visit the hemp warehouse
where only muzhiks of the opera stage
wander, selling hot honey teas and rolls.

A flock of cars flies into the fog;
a self-content, modest pedestrian –
like eccentric Evgenii – is ashamed of poverty,
breathes gasoline and curses at his fate!

The calm diction of Mandelshtam's 'Petersburg Strophes' seems to be born out of the city's imperial, classical architecture. In the slowly flowing lines of the poem Mandelshtam captured the width of the Neva and the magnificence of the imperial buildings. Yet the language of the poem was very modern and full of descriptive details that emphasized the classical tone of the work. St Petersburg in this poem closely resembled Mandelshtam's Rome: the city was unpalatable, unembraceable and intimidating, but at the same time idealized. The landscape captured in this poem and others was authentic (Senate Square, the riverbanks near the Winter Palace), but it was not merely a sketch of what the poet beheld, for the whole picture was permeated with history, including cultural history, through the references to Pushkin's *Bronze Horseman* and *Eugene Onegin*. Connecting the past (Peter the Great's ships, the bayonets evoking the Decembrist uprising) with the present (cars, gasoline), the poem reflected the end of an epoch.

The atmosphere of tranquillity in 'Petersburg Strophes', however, was unstable, for 'Senate Square' and the 'docked battleship' not only alluded to the past, but also foreshadowed social change and war. Though short, the work was replete with meaning and metaphor, evoking the historical role of the city as 'a window onto Europe', albeit with delayed industrial development: the sleds and the *muzhiks* trading their goods. The dreamy quiet of government buildings in the falling snow also contrasted starkly with the only feature of industrial progress, cars. Allusions from a proud literary tradition in this poem intermingled with important historical events: the Decembrist uprising on Senate Square, connected here some-what obliquely with Onegin's famous boredom, and the tragedy of the small man, Evgenii, from *The Bronze Horseman*. This detailed scene was built around the Bronze Horseman as a metaphor for a decisive moment in Russia's history – a metaphor materialized in the famous statue that was conspicuously unnamed but clearly present.

In the same year (1913) Mandelshtam composed 'Admiralty', another poem about St Petersburg that contains a stanza crucial for his under-standing of the place of humankind in the metropolis:

Lad'ia vozdushnaia i machta-nedotroga,
Sluzha lineikoiu preemnikam Petra,
On uchit: krasota – ne prikhot' poluboga,
A khishchnyi glazomer prostogo stoliara.[82]

Boat made of air, a mast of touch-me-not
Serving as a yardstick to Peter's heirs
It teaches: beauty is not the whim of a demigod,
But the simple carpenter's predatory eye.

Jane Harris has argued that this poem 'is another fine example of Mandelshtam's Acmeist principles, applied in this instance to his be-loved St Petersburg, emphasizing its place in the cosmos'.[83] In this poem, not only was the image of the city idealized, but so was the work of the builders who made the city's magnificence possible. Peter the Great's Admiralty was depicted as a complex and vital structure tower-ing majestically over the Neva River and beckoning the open sea. Symbolized by the Admiralty, the city emerged as the Horatian ship of state (*Odes* 1.14) that originated not in semi-divine inspiration, but in a carpenter's hands. Mandelshtam here paid tribute to human creativ-ity in terms that were specific and concrete, but also acknowledged the historical import of Empire, for the elongated, needlelike spire of the Admiralty tower appeared in the poem as a ship's untouchable mast, a metaphor that conveyed the poet's perception of the city as the Empire's pre-eminent port. At the same time, according to Clarence Brown's analysis, the Admiralty building 'incarnates the original ideology of Petersburg and its dual, synthetic and paradoxical nature: the "northern capital" that is touched by the "medusas", "demigods", and "acropolis" of the Mediterranean world'.[84]

In these early poems Mandelshtam glorified St Petersburg in the same way he idyllically penned imperial Rome, with its bold streets and its haughty buildings. For the poet, Petersburg was an unforgettable city of dreams not yet destroyed by revolution. However, unlike his treatment of ancient Rome as *caput mundi* and the perfect symbiosis of nature and culture, Mandelshtam idealized his own city only until the reality of the streets and common buildings entered the verse. In other words, his poetic view was not limited to magnificent imperial edifices, but took into account the gray fog and sorrow-ridden quarters whose inhabitants experienced life's trials. Written four years before the October Revolution of 1917, 'Admiralty' was full of melancholy foreboding, a harbinger of the 'unsaintly' theme in later depictions of St Petersburg as a locus that killed rather than engendered life:

V Petropole prozrachnom my umrem,
Gde vlastvuet nad nami Prozerpina.
My v kazhdom vzdokhe smertnyi vozdukh p'em,
I kazhdyi chas nam smertnaia godina.[85]

We shall die in transparent Petropolis
Where Proserpina rules over us.
With each breath we drink the air of death,
And each hour is our year of death.

This poem of 1916 identified the city, the 'cradle of revolution' as a place of mutiny, discord and death. Proserpina, the Roman name of Persephone, brought to the city the rule of Hades. The language is monotonous and repetitive, which gives the poem the ring of a 'death knell'.[86] The repetition of the sound 'z' in 'prozrachnom' ('transparent'), 'vzdokhe' ('breath') 'vozdukh' ('air') is linked with the Russian 'z' in Prozerpina, who defeated the goddess Athena with her stone helmet, by extension also defeating the stony solidity and endurance of Petersburg.[87] Here the loss of the celebratory and classical image of St Petersburg is clearly presented. The imperial city had ceased to be, but Mandelshtam refused to accept its metamorphosis into the seat of yet another empire. As the suffocating stench of death permeated the air, rule over the devastated city was entrusted to the queen of the Underworld. Volkov observed that 'to suffer together with Petersburg became a ritual' for Russian poets.[88]

Another Mandelshtam poem, written in 1918 immediately following the Revolution, reinforced the theme of suffering and inevitable despair expressed in the last line of the first stanza, which becomes the poem's refrain:

144

5. Osip Mandelshtam: 'Yearning for World Culture'

Na strashnoi vysote bluzhdaiushchii ogon',
No razve tak zvezda mertsaet?
Prozrachnaia zvezda, bluzhdaiushchii ogon',
Tvoi brat, Petropol', umiraet.[89]

On a terrible height a wandering light,
But does a star twinkle so?
Oh transparent star, wandering light,
Your brother, Petropolis, is dying.

In the last stanza Mandelshtam offered a variation on the refrain with the emphatic repetition of 'your' first with the 'city' and then with the 'brother' to draw attention to his personal, familial attachment to the city destined for demise:

O, esli ty zvezda, – Petropol', gorod tvoi,
Tvoi brat, Petropol', umiraet.

But if you are a star, Petropolis,
Your city, your brother, Petropolis, is dying.

Unsurprisingly, this and many other poems that Mandelshtam wrote after the Revolution dwelt on death and stripped St Petersburg of its status as the New (Third) Rome. Peter's dreamy, imperial city became a devastated, ravaged environment that was almost a stranger to the poet, eliciting fear, anxiety and a premonition of his own destruction. His love for St Petersburg became equivocal when Mandeshtam positioned himself as an exile within his own city. Although it is possible to interpret these lines not as the death of the beloved city but as its metamorphosis, for Mandelshtam the changes were harder to bear than destruction. Therefore he transformed his city into a dream, a myth of his own memory.[90]

This poetic reality of St Petersburg struck close to Mandelshtam's perception of Rome. The city existed only in his poetic imagination. The world beyond the window was the city-vampire, its metamorphosis occurring in the poet's imagination. Mandelshtam's imaginary city remained Petersburg, and Roman in its idealization, whereas the city of Petrograd and Leningrad was a physical entity and was associated with destruction and death. The 'death of Petersburg' caused by the war and Revolution led Mandelshtam to evoke in his poetry the elements of the 'old' city. That nostalgia for the past (a nostalgia that clings to the city even today) found expression in his poem written in 1931, at the start of Stalin's terror:

S mirom derzhavnym ia byl lish' rebiacheski sviazan,
Ustrits boialsia i na gvardeitsev gliadel ispodlob'ia
I ni krupitsei dushi ia emu ne obiazan,
Kak ia ni muchal sebia po chuzhomu podob'iu.

S vazhnost'iu glupoi, nasupivshis' v mitre bobrovoi,
Ia ne stoial pod egipetskim portikom banka,
I nad limonnoi Nevoiu pod khrust storublevyi
Mne nikogda, nikogda ne pliasala tsyganka.

Chuia griadushchie kazni, ot reva sobytii miatezhnykh,
Ia ubezhal k nereidam na Chernoe more,
I ot krasavits togdashnikh, ot tekh evropeianok nezhnykh,
Skol'ko ia prinial smushchen'ia, nadsady i goria!

Tak otchego zh do sikh por etot gorod dovleet
Mysliam i chuvstvam moim po starinnomu pravu?
On ot pozharov eshche i morozov nagleet,
Samoliubivyi, prokliatyi, pustoi, molozhavyi.

Ne potomu l', chto ia videl na detskoi kartinke
Ledi Godivu s raspushchennoi ryzheiu grivoi,
Ia povtoriaiu eshche pro sebia, pod surdinku:
'Ledi Godiva, proshchai! Ia ne pomniu, Godiva ...'[91]

To the sovereign world I was tied only childishly,
Afraid of oysters, sullen with policemen,
And I do not owe it a grain of my soul,
Though I tormented myself in somebody else's image.

In a beaver mitre, frowning with stupid importance
I never stood under a bank's Egyptian portico,
And never a gypsy danced for me over
The lemon Neva, never, to the crackle of hundred-ruble notes.

Sensing future executions, from the roar of mutiny
I ran to the Nereids on the Black Sea –
And how much embarrassment, torment, and grief I took
From those tender European women, from the beauties of those times.

So why does this city hold these ancient rights
Over my thoughts, my feelings?
It becomes more insolent after fires and frosts,
Touchy, damned, empty, and youthful!

Maybe it's because, on a child's picture, I saw
Lady Godiva with her ginger mane let down,
Maybe that's why I still say to myself all the time
'Lady Godiva, goodbye! I don't remember, Godiva ...'

The poem presented two different views of the city: on the one hand, the mythic St Petersburg of the glamorous past (the 'sovereign world' of pre-revolutionary St Petersburg), of which Mandelshtam had been unable to partake because he had experienced it while still a child; on the other hand, the all too real Leningrad (the 'cradle of the revolution'), plundered,

146

rebellious and violated, yet a city from which he could not separate himself. The poem conveyed a mood of despair and irrevocable loss by the exasperated repetition of the word 'never'. Mandelshtam's nostalgia for the city that was lost to him differed starkly from Ovid's, for the Roman poet had enjoyed all the luxurious and decadent aspects of Rome without ever witnessing the decline of the city. Mandelshtam's flight from the city to the Black Sea (also the locus of Ovid's exile) was full of 'torment and grief', and, as the last lines indicated, his city – not what it used to be, though still 'youthful' and 'touchy' – continued to hold sway over him. The idealization, however, was gone, for the city was also 'damned' and 'empty'. The image of Lady Godiva, which brought the reader back to the poet's childhood memories, was eloquent: like Godiva, vulnerable in her nakedness, partly hidden by her luxurious mane of hair, Mandelshtam's beloved city was impressive only on the outside, but 'naked' and vulnerable under its deceptive glamour.

Yet Mandelshtam's relationship with the city that simultaneously inspired and devastated him resembled Ovid's relationship with Rome in the nostalgia both experienced. Mandelshtam's exile, unlike Ovid's, was not physical, but internal; his loss was not geographical, but spiritual. Faced now with the reality of the metamorphosis undergone by St Petersburg, he felt alienated from it, exiled to the outskirts of his own memory, which yearned to preserve his earlier apperception of the city, a place where he had friends, loved, and suffered. One of his most famous poems, written in the winter of 1920-1, began with lines that inscribed his painful familiarity with the city:

V Peterburge my soidemsia snova,
Slovno solntse my pokhoronili v nem,
I blazhennoe, bessmyslennoe slovo
V pervyi raz proiznesem.[92]

We shall meet again in Petersburg
As if we had buried the sun there
And shall pronounce for the first time
That blessed senseless word.

While evoking nostalgia for that city that was lost forever, Mandelshtam introduced the image, extraordinary to anyone familiar with St Petersburg's far from sunny climate, of Petersburg as a city where the sun 'is buried'. That theme of the buried sun had been used also in another poem 'Kogda v teploi nochi zamiraet ...' ('When in the warm night dies away ... ', 1918):

Eto solntse nochnoe khoronit
Vozbuzhdennaia igrami chern',
Vozvrashchaias' s polnochnogo pira
Pod glukhie udary kopyt.[93]

The nocturnal sun is now buried
By the mob excited by their games.
Returning at midnight from feasting
To the muffled thudding of hooves.

That startling image was explicated in his essay 'Pushkin and Scriabin':

Pushkin and Scriabin, two transformations of the same sun ... served as an
example of a collective Russian death .... Pushkin was buried at night ...
secretly .... The sun was placed in the coffin at night, and the sled runners
scraped the frozen January ground as they bore the poet's remains away for
the funeral.[94]

The buried sun, in short, is a metaphor for the source and the summit of
the Russian poetic tradition – Pushkin. With the death of the supreme
poet, the power of the poetic word as prophesy perished.

The theme of Petersburg in Russian poetry is closely connected with
Pushkin, who exerted an incalculable influence on Mandelshtam. As a
Russian poet and especially as a poet of Petersburg, Mandelshtam could
not escape the powerful aura of Pushkin's poetry. He also nurtured a
certain reverence for Pushkin's name, which appeared only twice in all his
poetry. That reverence – bordering on worship – also has a biographical
basis: Mandelshtam's childhood was spent in Kolomna, where Pushkin
had his first apartment, and the Tenishev School, with its preference for
the humanities, unusual teachers, and poetry evenings, was for young
Mandelshtam essentially what the Lyceum in Tsarskoe Selo had been for
Pushkin. In his formation as a poet Mandelshtam felt a close affinity to
Pushkin, and his contemporaries even observed similarities in the two
poets' physical appearance.[95] Given the intertwining of Petersburg and
Pushkin in Mandelshtam's poetic imagination, the metaphor of the 'buried
sun' constituted Mandelshtam's homage to The Poet whose fate and fame
were inseparable from Mandelshtam's beloved city.

The reference to the 'blessed, meaningless word', echoed another poem by
Mandelshtam that had opened with the phrase, 'Ia slovo pozabyl, chto ia
khotel skazat'' ('I have forgotten the word that I wanted to say', 1920), posing
a riddle. In both works the poet tried to remember some mystical, unspeak-
able word, connected to a mysterious, elusive world. This word most likely
was the all-embracing Greek *logos*, a word that for the Acmeists represented the ultimate 'reality' capable of changing the course of events in the
world.[96] Jane Harris interpreted this cryptic line as a reference to Hades:
'Another remarkable aspect of "I have forgotten the word" is its vivid,
almost tangible portrayal of the netherworld'.[97] The shadows inhabiting
the realm of Proserpina do not speak, and, more importantly, Pushkin, the
embodiment of the poetic voice, is dead and silenced, imposing his muteness on other poets. The word uttered by a poetic genius became lost as the
city that once brimmed with vitality, emotion, and passion became devas-

tated and ruined. The only way to regain all these elements would be to return to that city and reunite with friends, so that the word would be reanimated.

Whatever gloomy predictions had been prompted for him by the Revolution, Mandelshtam suffered acutely from the loss of his beloved Petersburg. A poem from 1930 eloquently captured his ambivalence upon his return from Caucasus:

Ia vernulsia v moi gorod, znakomyi do slez,
Do prozhilok, do detskikh pripukhlykh zhelez.
Ty vernulsia siuda, tak glotai zhe skorei
Rybii zhir leningradskikh rechnykh fonarei.[98]

I returned to my city familiar to tears
Like my veins, like children's half-swollen glands.
You've returned here – then swallow at once
The cod liver-oil of Leningrad's river lamps.

Nothing idealized or grand marked his depiction of the city, which was a far cry from Rome, with its imperial fora and the perfect symbiosis between the human race and nature. 'Children's half-swollen glands' resulted from the city's perpetual humidity; the cod liver-oil of the street lamps represented the city whose everyday life was too familiar to the poet, unlike the life of Rome, which remained in his imagination clad in marble and void of human flesh.

In his article on Mandelshtam, A.I. Nemirovskii observed that he could never decide whether Mandelshtam had really visited Rome or whether all his poems about the Eternal City simply sprang from his imagination.[99] For Mandelshtam such a question was irrelevant, for his poetry did not need a concrete, modern Rome, but a city equal to the task of symbolizing a grand idea. Not so with St Petersburg, however: its idealized image was circumscribed by the poet's everyday interaction with the city. Nostalgia for it was not sweet, but painful, and therefore devoid of Ovidian elements. The city was 'familiar to tears', shed not on account of a long anticipated reunion, but, as the rest of the poem made clear, in expectation of imminent arrests and suffering:

Peterburg, ia eshche ne khochu umirat':
U tebia telefonov moikh nomera.

Peterburg, u menia eshche est' adresa,
Po kotorym naidu mertvetsov golosa.

Ia na lestnitse chernoi zhivu, i v visok
Udariaet mne vyrvannyi s miasom zvonok.

I vsiu noch' naprolet zhdu gostei dorogikh,
Shevelia kandalami tsepochek dvernykh.

Petersburg! I am not ready to die yet,
You've still got all my telephone numbers.

Petersburg! I still have the addresses
For finding the voices of the dead.

I live on a back staircase, and the bell yanked
Out with flesh hits me in the temple.

And all night long I wait for my dear guests,
Rattling like shackles the chains of my door.

Though the poet returned to the city without which his life was unthinkable, the reunion was not a happy one – a stance familiar to anyone who lived through the horrors of Stalin's persecutions. Nocturnal arrests as people sat in the darkness of their apartments listening for steps on the staircase and hoping that the terror would bypass their doors were all too familiar to Mandelshtam, whose 'voices of the dead' referred to those friends and acquaintances who fell victim during this chilling epoch.

The sorrow of Ovid's nostalgia, as conceived in Mandelshtam's imagination, was lucid and bright, even joyous. Mandelshtam's return to his city, however, could not ignore brutal reality, as the city that had once served as a symbol – as the embodiment of a historical idea – now proved lethal, with himself as the next victim. St Petersburg as a city of death infused yet another of his poems, written in 1931:

Pomogi, Gospod', etu noch' prozhit':
Ia za zhizn' boius'– za Tvoiu rabu –
V Peterburge zhit'– slovno spat' v grobu.[100]

Lord, help me live through this night,
I fear for my life – your humble slave –
Living in Petersburg is like sleeping in a coffin.

The earlier poems about St Petersburg exhibited some philosophical and psychological ambivalence toward the city and the drastic historical changes it was undergoing. By 1931 Mandelshtam's city had metamorphosed into a threat, a hostile force familiar from the pages of works by Dostoevskii. Poems written in anticipation of Mandelshtam's arrest and exile were utterly devoid of idealization and nostalgia, for the New Rome had become as tortured and sorrowful as its inhabitants.

For many poets cities are the most important protagonists of their poetry. For Sophocles, Athens was a tragic hero; for Ovid in exile, Rome became the cruel object of his no longer requited love; for Mandelshtam, St Petersburg was both of the above. These cities entered the Western poetic imagination endowed with the power to mesmerize, intimidate and devastate the poets who 'sang' of them.

5. Osip Mandelshtam: 'Yearning for World Culture'

Cities, and especially ancient ones, are easy to idealize. Mandelshtam sometimes depicted his poetic Petersburg in the same way as he characterized Rome – as a detached soaring ideal that simultaneously attracted and intimidated. The ancient Rome of his verses was the realm of Caesars, military triumphs and perfect harmony between nature and humanity. While Rome's past might elicit reverence and awe as a great civilization, it nonetheless raised qualms when the human cost of such national glory was considered. As a former Acmeist, Mandelshtam perceived Rome as the embodied 'acmē' of human creativity and as a ceaseless inspiration for posterity. His poetic *Roma aeterna* had little to do with the rise and fall of ancient Rome as a historical city, verging, instead, on the mystical. His representation of it united the visual image of the city with its cultural legacy, while the act of material observation reflected his changing emotional and poetic experience.

In his early poems dedicated to St Petersburg Mandelshtam viewed his beloved city as historical yet eternal, paying homage to cultural continuity, in which he perceived St Petersburg as another Rome. Later, however, the myth of St Petersburg was constructed through the juxtaposition of 'the cold, dark, northern capital and the world of sunlight' associated for Mandelshtam with the entire Mediterranean world but specifically with Rome, the Crimea, and the Black Sea.[101]

The sources of that juxtaposition clearly lay in Mandelshtam's myth of Rome as the perfect symbiosis between art and life. The Crimea and Black Sea, however, are of course precisely the region Ovid had portrayed as a bare northern wasteland in which the barbarians drove their chariots across a frozen river. There was thus at play in Mandelshtam at least a double displacement; Mandelshtam's Rome was in exile from itself, and Ovid's exile was depicted as if it had been played out in Mandelshtam's Rome, when in fact it was located on the very coast of the Black Sea that for the Russian poet stood as a synecdoche for a myth of Mediterranean sunshine, culture, and civilization, a lost Golden Age of the seamless marriage of nature and art.[102]

In the same vein the early celebratory image of St Petersburg, a city of dazzling magnificence and classical heritage, became 'mythologized' while in stark opposition to that ideal St Petersburg emerged yet another Petropolis, neither Roman nor bathed in sunshine. In that new city glamour was transformed into intimidation, the monotonous, regal flow of the Neva River became a threat, and harmony and calmness yielded to anxiety, loss and death. That side of the Petersburg myth reflected Mandelshtam's concern over Russia's cultural heritage, the continuity of civilization as a never-ceasing process of human creativity. Ambivalent and yearning, Mandelshtam envisioned St Petersburg as created in the seductive image of the Italian classical model, which was irresistible to the poet. Yet with the years it became harder to idealize the city that had turned hostile as the storms of history swept it off its classical foundations.

The poet confronted the challenge of St Petersburg's metamorphosis with a desire to soar over the abyss of time and history that he could never actualize. In his poetic vision ancient Rome met that ideal of unchanging civilization, but St Petersburg did not. Mandelshtam's passionate attachment to St Petersburg resulted in his depiction of the city's death as the death of a tragic protagonist – tortured, yet triumphant in its suffering. The city-hero succumbed to the all-devouring power of time and historical change, but remained invincible because of the power of the poetic Word it inspired.

Joseph Brodsky: 'The Uncommon Visage'

In general, one should have his left hand on Homer, the Bible, Dante, and the Loeb series, before grabbing the pen with the right.

Joseph Brodsky[1]

The anxiety of influence

'While antiquity exists for us, we, for antiquity, do not. We never did, and we never will. This rather peculiar state of affairs makes our take on antiquity somewhat invalid. Chronologically and, I am afraid, genetically speaking, the distance between us is too immense to imply any causality: we look at antiquity as if out of nowhere'.[2] So began Joseph Brodsky's essay 'Homage to Marcus Aurelius', whose statue on the Capitoline Hill reminded Brodsky acutely of the famous bronze horseman in his own beloved city, which he never saw again after 1972. Antiquity had a persistent and vivid presence in Brodsky's poetics, providing a lens through which most of his main themes came into sharper focus. His acculturation and reception of the classical tradition on Russian ground was, however, certainly more complex and perhaps more irreverent than that of his predecessors because it was presented not in terms of homage but as a dialogue with the void, an attempt to converse, like Odysseus, with the shadows of the Underworld. In his 'Letter to Horace', Brodsky defined his audience precisely:

> Because when one writes verse, one's most immediate audience is not one's own contemporaries, let alone posterity, but one's predecessors. Those who gave one a language, those who gave one forms. Frankly, you know that far better than I. Who wrote those asclepiadics, Sapphics, hexameters, and Alcaics, and what were their addressees? Caesar? Maecenas? Rufus? Varus? Lydias and Glycerias? Fat lot they knew about or cared for trochees and dactyls! And you were not aiming at me, either. No, you were appealing to Asclepiades, to Alcaeus and Sappho, to Homer himself. You wanted to be appreciated by them, first of all. For where is Caesar? Obviously in his palace or smiting the Scythians. And Maecenas is in his villa. Ditto Rufus and Varus. And Lydia is with a client and Glyceria is out of town. Whereas your beloved Greeks are right here, in your head, or should I say in your heart, for you no doubt knew them by heart. They were your best audience, since you could summon them at any moment. It's they you were trying to impress most of all. Never mind the foreign language. In fact it is easier to impress them in Latin: in Greek you wouldn't have the mother tongue's latitude. So if you could do this to them, why can't I do that to you?[3]

There are several keys in this passage important for understanding Brodsky's classicism and Brodsky's anxiety of influence in relation to his predecessors, both Western and Russian. First of all, as David Bethea pithily observed, Brodsky did not seek 'solidarity with any group or "interpretive community" other than his own private "dead poets' society" ', which included everyone from Homer, Martial, Vergil and Ovid to Auden, Frost, Tsvetaeva and Mandelshtam.[4] In that respect Brodsky's anxiety of influence ran contrary to the idea of poetic succession as emulous.[5] Second, Brodsky was not 'anxious' at all about duly impressing them, although 'their shades disturb [him] constantly', Brodsky, even as he paid homage to his predecessors, did not think of himself as an aftermath of their greatness, but as 'their sum total, though invariably inferior to any of them individually'.[6] Third, at the time the *Letter to Horace* was written in 1995, one year before the poet's death, Brodsky was already an American poet laureate and a Nobel prize winner whose primary audience was in another language and another culture. Both the West and Russia had been duly impressed.

Much united Brodsky with his Russian predecessors: like Pushkin he was a reformer of Russian poetic language;[7] like Ivanov he tried to maintain and sustain cultural continuity when poetry was losing its currency; like Tsvetaeva he wrote verse that was at times uncomfortable in its passion and grief about the betrayal of love and passage of time; like Osip Mandelshtam, he knew and understood the lot of exile both political and existential, deep love of one city, and was interested in establishing the social duties of the poet whose main preoccupation was the poetic Word. There was also a palpable link between Brodsky's 'classicism' and the classical tradition in Russian poetry. That interplay between foreign and native, modern and ancient sources, which David Bethea termed Brodsky's 'triangular vision', became a form of a poetic signature in Brodsky's reception of the classics.[8]

Brodsky bridged Russian and Western cultures effortlessly and harmoniously, decisively dispelling the myth 'that a Russian writer cannot live without his motherland' and that emigration inevitably resulted in linguistic death.[9] Like Viacheslav Ivanov, Brodsky never cultivated the image of the writer in exile, considering his move to the West nothing more than a 'continuation of space'.[10] Like Pushkin, as I discuss later, he even found a certain creative inspiration in it. Furthermore, with Brodsky the Russian inferiority complex towards European culture disappeared. Mandelshtam's 'yearning for the world's culture' was sated in Brodsky's poetry. Brodsky's self-positioning within poetic traditions, both Western and Russian, was remarkable for its complete inversion of the familiar poetic idiom, since in his tributes to tradition the reader detects a noticeable absence of Bloomian anxiety coupled with irony directed towards himself and the world.

A person who was born and grew up in St Petersburg perceives antiq-

6. Joseph Brodsky: 'The Uncommon Visage'

Joseph Brodsky. Photo
by Boris Shvartsman,
1962.

uity, as Mandelshtam's poetry has demonstrated, differently from a native of any other city in Russia. In his essay 'A Guide to a Renamed City', Brodsky wrote about this most classical of Russian cities that cultivated the love of Greece and Rome in every poet who lived and created there: 'For two and a half centuries this school from Lomonosov and Derzhavin to Puskin and his *pleiad* (Baratynskii, Viazemskii, Del'vig) to the Acmeists, Akhmatova and Mandelshtam in this century – had existed under the very sign under which it was conceived: the sign of classicism'.[11] The image of Brodsky's beloved city was connected with many ancient motifs that dealt with exile, the price of victory, and certainly with the theme of Empire.

The role and meaning of ancient motifs in Brodsky's poetry changed with the evolution of the poet and his migration from one culture to another, but Brodsky's natural incorporation of 'classics' into his poetry remained unchanged, unusually for a poet of the second half of the twentieth century. That 'naturalness' was even more striking because Brodsky never received any formal education and was almost entirely self-taught.[12] In his early poetry his antiquity might have been 'second-hand', received from Pushkin, Baratynskii, Mandelshtam, Tsvetaeva or even from Nikolai Kun's *Legends and Myths of Ancient Greece*, familiar to every post-war child of the Russian intelligentsia, the Russian equivalent of Schwab's German bowdlerized version of ancient mythology or Edith Hamilton's English one. Brodsky's poetry from the mid-sixties, however, displayed not only an impressive knowledge of Horace and Ovid, but even

155

of some authors who were not routinely included in the traditional school anthologies (at least not in Soviet Russia) such as Propertius, Simonides, Martial and Hesiod. In his later essays 'Letter to Horace' and 'Homage to Marcus Aurelius', Brodsky showed an even more profound and uncanny understanding of the classics. Antiquity in Brodsky's poetic genesis repeatedly served as a point of reference against which he constantly measured modernity and his own position within it.

In the middle of the 1960s Brodsky himself acknowledged his debt to classicism by admitting in one of his poems 'I am infected by routine classicism' ('ia zarazhen normal'nym klassitsizmom').[13] What he meant by 'routine' can be a subject of debate. Alexei Losev (Lev Loseff) observed that 'one thing to which he [Brodsky] bears no resemblance is classicism, in the ranks of which the author numbers himself'.[14] It is certainly true in the sense that his poetry hardly followed in the steps of classicism in so far as reception of antiquity was concerned. His prosody is diverse and untraditional, his use of language at times shocking. However, Brodsky saw himself as a poetic heir to a tradition that encompassed all poets starting with classical times. Despite the revolution accomplished by Brodsky in Russian poetic language, despite his tendency for self-effacement and the power of understatement that has sometimes been mistaken for coldness, Brodsky, as Valentina Polukhina noted, was 'the most traditional of contemporary poets'.[15] In one of his interviews Brodsky explained his relationship with antiquity in the following words: 'Upon closer examination one finds that there is a staggering similarity between what we call antiquity and what is titled as modernity: the observer begins to feel that he is faced with some gigantic tautology ... Modern literature at its best is a commentary to ancient literature, the notes on the margins of Lucretius and Ovid. The more or less attentive reader can't help but feel that we are they with only one difference – they are more interesting than we, and the older someone gets, the more inescapable is the identification with the ancients.'[16] Brodsky's whole poetic journey from his early poems 'published' at first in *samizdat* to his later essays written after his emigration was peppered with this 'identification with the ancients'. Especially significant in this respect was Brodsky's reception of classical myth.

Mythological inversions[17]

Brodsky's mythological metaphors did not 'speak for themselves', but, as David Bethea noted, they 'have coalesced into a kind of "system", one whose verbal layering and retrieval, whose archaeology if you will, is consistently non-rational, paradoxicalist, fragmentary (both in image and method), and defiant of any explanation from origin'.[18] Brodsky sensed keenly the untrodden paths in the reception of classical myth and those were the paths he was most eager to take. At times the classical paraphernalia in his poetry had a merely 'decorative effect helping to establish a particular neo-classical quality'.[19] But more often the mythical mask became an essential aspect of the poetic structure inseparable from the presentation of the theme. In his recent biography of Brodsky, Lev Loseff observed that the writers of his generation made extensive use of what came to be termed 'Aesopian language'. This allegorical language was created in anticipation of the censor who would read the work before it could reach the reader and hence had to be tricked into believing that he was reading something innocuous. While it is tempting to interpret Brodsky's use of classical metaphor in that light, I tend to agree with Loseff that Brodsky was a staunch supporter of artistic autonomy and for him that sort of 'literary play' held no attraction.[20] Brodsky's use of classical idiom unquestionably contained elements of allegory and circumlocution, but these were used without any consideration of the 'third party' or a mediator between the poet and the reader.

Although it is impossible to discuss in the following pages all Brodsky's mythological references and his 'making contemporary of myth',[21] in the words of Michael Kreps, there were several themes in Brodsky's classical poetics whose exploration may facilitate a better understanding of the unity of many of Brodsky's works. One of the themes permeating most of Brodsky's 'mythological poems' was the contemplation of heroic endeavour wrought with sorrow for the hero. There are four poems that I would like to examine in this respect that, although written in the early period of Brodsky's poetry before his emigration to the West in 1972, resonate also in his later poems. The first poem, 'Sonet' ('Sonnet'), was written in 1962 when Brodsky was only 22 years old:

Velikii Gektor strelami ubit.
Egu dusha plyvet po temnym vodam,
shurshat kusty i gasnut oblaka,
vdali nevniatno plachet Andromakha.

Teper' pechal'nym vecherom Aiaks
bredet v ruch'e prozrachnom po koleno,
a zhizn' bezhit iz glaz ego raskrytykh
za Gektorom, a teplaia voda
uzhe po grud', no mrak perepolniaet
bezdonnyi vzgliad skvoz' volny i kustarnik,
potom voda opiat' emu po poias,
tiazhelyi mech, podkhvachennyi potokom,
plyvet vpered
i uvlekaet za soboi Aiaksa.[22]

Great Hektor is slain by arrows,
His soul sails through the dark waters,
the bushes rustle and the clouds dim,
and somewhere far Andromache is crying.

One sad evening now Ajax
struggles along up to his knee in a stream,
and life flees out from his open eyes
in pursuit of Hektor, but the warm water
now reached his chest, and darkness overfills
his senseless gaze through waves and shrubs,
and then he is waist-deep in water,
the heavy sword, swept by the flow of water,
sails ahead
and carries Ajax along.

This poem was, as Dan Ungurianu noted, 'a beautiful vignette, an animated picture from a Greek vase', which reflected Brodsky's enchantment
with antiquity.[23] This concise version of the myth was perhaps not that
different from a traditional interpretation of Sophocles' *Ajax* in which the
distinction between victory and defeat was blurred and the boundary that
separated enemies from friends changed in the course of time.[24] More
importantly, however, the poem introduced the main theme of Brodsky's
mythological poetics: the price of heroic accomplishment entailed dire
consequences and the victor followed the vanquished.

That theme of the price of heroic achievement was explored especially
in a brilliant and striking poem, 'Odissei Telemaku' ('Odysseus to Telemachus'):

Moi Telemak,
            Troianskaia voina
okonchena. Kto pobedil – ne pomniu.
Dolzhno byt', greki: stol'ko mertvetsov
vne doma brosit' mogut tol'ko greki ...
I vse-taki vedushchaia domoi
doroga okazalas' slishkom dlinnoi,
kak budto Poseidon, poka my tam
teriali vremia, rastianul prostranstvo.
Mne neizvestno, gde ia nakhozhus',
chto predo mnoi. Kakoi-to griaznyi ostrov,
kusty, postroiki, khriukan'e svinei,
zarosshii sad, kakaia-to tsaritsa,
trava da kamni ... Milyi Telemak,
vse ostrova pokhozhi drug na druga,
kogda tak dolgo stranstvuesh'; i mozg
uzhe sbivaetsia, schitaia volny,
glaz, zasorennyi gorizontom, plachet,
i vodianoe miaso zastit slukh.
ne pomniu ia, chem konchilas' voina,
i skol'ko let tebe seichas, ne pomniu.

Rasti bol'shoi, moi Telemak, rasti.
Lish' bogi znaiut, svidimsia li snova.
Ty i seichas uzhe ne tot mladenets,

pered kotorym ia sderzhal bykov.
Kogda b ne Palamed, my zhili vmeste.
No mozhet byt' i prav on: bez menia
ty ot strastei Edipovykh izbavlen,
i sny tvoi, moi Telemakh, bezgreshny.[25]

My Telemachus,
         the Trojan War is over.
Who was the victor? I do not recall.
It might have been the Greeks: only the Greeks
could have forsaken so many corpses so far from home ...
But still the way leading home
turned out to be too long.
as if Poseidon had stretched the space
while we were wasting time.
I don't know where I am,
what I behold in front of me. Some squalid island,
bushes, little buildings, pigs snorting,
an overgrown garden, some queen,
grass and stones ... My darling Telemachus,
all islands look just the same,
when you have been wandering so long, and your mind
trips by counting the waves,
your eye soiled by sea horizon, weeps,
and water's flesh stuffs your ears.
I don't recall how the war ended.
And how old you are I don't recall.

Grow strong, my Telemachus, grow up,
Only the gods know if we'll see each other again.
Still now you are no longer a baby
in front of whom I restrained the bullocks.
If it were not for Palamedes, we would have been together,
But perhaps, he was right: without me
you are safe from Oedipus' passions,
and your dreams, my Telemachus, are sinless.

The poem, written in the form of a letter from Odysseus to Telemachus, presented Odysseus in an almost anti-Homeric fashion. The Russian predecessor of this poetic hero, discussed previously, the Odysseus of Mandelshtam, 'leaving his ship, its sails worn out at seas', had returned 'sated by time and space' thus fulfilling his Homeric destiny. The Odysseus of Brodsky's poem was significantly different from his Homeric counterpart obsessed with his *nostos* (homecoming) – and perpetually conniving and plotting against people and gods who tried to detain him or offered a false *nostos*.

By contrast, Brodsky's Odysseus was a weary traveller and an indifferent man who surprisingly referred to the proud point of Greek military achievement without remembering who had won the war and more importantly what part he himself had played in the outcome of that war. The poem dealt with the subject that was central to Brodsky's poetics in general: 'What interests me most of all, has always interested me, on this earth ... is time and the effect that it has on man, how it changes him, grinds away at him ...'.[26] Homer's poem was certainly concerned with the same idea, but the Homeric treatment of the hero's journey depicted a driven, not fatigued, Odysseus. In Homer's poem the twenty years that passed between Odysseus' departure from Ithaca and his voyage home hardly altered his ardent yearning for homecoming. The time away from his kingdom only intensified his desire to return and reclaim his legacy as a king, husband and father. Brodsky's Odysseus had succumbed to the Sirens' song or tasted the sweet flowers of Lotus. He stated thrice his loss of memory, indicating his confusion in both space and time. The most poignant moment of this disorientation was Odysseus' inability to remember the age of his own son. The idea of time had lost its relevance for Odysseus in this poem. The indifference to the passage of time was played out in the poem on several levels. The phrase 'waste time' in the first part of the poem has a double meaning in Russian: not only to lose time but also to lose the awareness of it.[27]

Another interesting detail is that Brodsky used the word 'rastianut" ('to stretch') in relation to space although in Russian it is normally used in relation to time. However, in Odysseus' wanderings the space became as stretched out as the time, and the characteristics of time were applied to space in the unusual sense of the metaphor. The dizzying effect of this metaphor was the disorientation of Odysseus in whose mind time and space had become one just as the sea and the horizon had become inseparable. The expression 'rastianut' vremia' is also used in Russian with the meaning of 'wasting time', and here the transferred metaphor is again effectively employed. Not only time but also space was wasted since Odysseus in his wanderings strayed from the homeward path and encountered places and people opposed to his homecoming. Odysseus' Homeric predecessor maintained a firm grasp of memory even during his prolonged dalliances (on Calypso's island for example) and even upon the promises of immortality.

In this inversion of the Homeric hero there was more a deflation of the literary Odysseus than an aggrandizement of Brodsky's own.[28] Any hint of the heroic was deliberately eliminated from the poem. It would be hard in analysis of the poem not to notice subtle political overtones, although political implications appeared more overtly in Brodsky's 'Roman' poems. The poet obliquely recalled the devastation of World War II ('only the Greeks could have forsaken so many corpses so far from home') when the Soviet state machine sacrificed twenty million of its own citizens to ensure victory. This almost cynical statement was akin to the words with which Homer's Odysseus addressed his nurse after slaughtering the suitors in his house. He refused to gloat over the slain men, for there must be no glory in any kind of war (*Od.* 22.412): 'It is not proper to rejoice over the slain men'. Similarly, Brodsky's Odysseus refused to recall his heroic halcyon days with any wistful longing. Many critics have viewed the *Odyssey* as a response to the heroic code in the *Iliad*. The idea of glory (*kleos*) experienced a transformation from the lofty ideals of military excellence to mundane notions of simple human happiness, for the hero's only concern was to return home to his wife. However, the Odysseus of Brodsky was denied even that fundamental desire. In fact, he was utterly devoid of any kind of strong emotion of the sort that was so central to the Homeric character. Brodsky's 'all islands resemble each other' evoked the failure of Odysseus to recognize his final and most desired destination after the Phaiakians had delivered him, sleeping, to Ithaca in Book 17. Unlike Homer's Odysseus, he was not in a state of despair, panic or even fear, but accepted this disorientation and confusion as the inevitable consequence of separation and time 'grinding at him'.

This apathy, with which Brodsky endowed his Odysseus, surfaced in two other poems from Brodsky's early period. One was the fourth poem in the lyric cycle 'Iiul'skoe intermezzo' ('July Intermezzo') written in 1961. The third stanza of the poem which started with the words 'Vorotish'sia na rodinu. Nu chto zh.' – 'You will return home. So what' reads):

Kak khorosho, chto nekogo vinit',
kak khorosho, chto ty nikem ne sviazan,
kak khorosho, chto do smerti liubit'
tebia nikto na svete ne obiazan ...[29]

How nice that there is nobody to blame
How nice that you have no ties to anyone
How nice that nobody is bound to love you
Until death ...

Another is his 1962 poem 'Ot okrainy k tsentru' ('From Outskirts to the Centre'):

Slava Bogu, chuzhoi.
Nikogo ia zdes' ne obviniaiu.
Nichego ne uznat'.
ia idu, toroplius', obgoniaiu.
kak legko mne teper',
ottogo chto ni s kem ne rasstalsia.
Slava Bogu, chto ia na zemle bez otchizny ostalsia.[30]

Just a stranger, thank God.
I don't blame anybody.
Everything is unrecognizable.
I walk, I hurry, I pass.
How easy I feel now
Since I haven't parted with anyone.
Thank God I have been left on this earth without my fatherland.

In both poems the bitterness of separation was mixed with relief that there were no unbreakable attachments, and the fatherland ('otchizna') was viewed as a burdensome liability, not a coveted destination. The loss of memory, the unrecognizable landscape, the feeling of not belonging were embraced. The final line of the last poem, moreover, was especially poignant: a man without his fatherland must feel truly liberated.

The letter of Odysseus to his son should be viewed also from a perspective that reveals the nature of Brodsky's recurrent interest in the figure of Odysseus: the problematic effects of the passage of time following the end of a lengthy war. The hero was subjected to the adverse forces of time and violence, the reflection of which can be found in Brodsky's 'A New Life' (1988): 'Imagine the war is over, that peace reigns ... And if anybody should ask a question, "Who are you?" answer, "Who – I? I am nobody." As Odysseus replied to Polyphemus'.[31] In his response to Polyphemus, the withholding of his identity by Odysseus was an act of self-preservation. In his letter to Telemachus, Odysseus wanted to diminish himself to the state of 'nobody' because the war was over and he had lost his heroic identity. The twenty years that had passed while away from his family had reduced him to the status of a 'nobody' both as a hero and as a man. The evolution of the loss of his self-identity was complete only when there was no such identity left. However, Odysseus still felt an emotional connection to his son, as evidenced by his opening words 'my Telemachus', both possessive and a term of endearment. That is why the ending of the letter, which was supposed to be the final legacy of the father to the son, seems abrupt. If the self-alleged Nobody used the possessive pronoun charged with emotional connotation, then the self-identity was still present. The final lines, however, explain why this last attempt at self-identification was not pursued any further.

The closing lines of the poem presented two mythological names that were equally important in the message Odysseus was trying to convey to his son. One was Palamedes, the hero who had exposed Odysseus' deception when the latter had feigned madness to avoid participation in the Trojan War.[32] In revenge, Odysseus had forged a letter from Priam to Palamedes, planted gold in his tent, and exposed him as a traitor of the Greek army. As a result, Palamedes had been put to death by his own peers.[33] In a strange inversion of traditional logic, Odysseus in Brodsky's poem admitted that Palamedes had been right all along in forcing Odysseus to join the Trojan campaign and depriving his son of a relationship with his father. The explanation for this sudden reversal became clear in the allusion to Oedipus; in Svetlana Boym's apt observation, 'Brodsky brings together two myths of family romance that are opposed to each other'.[34] Brodsky's Odysseus has found probably the most important redeeming feature of his absence from the life of his son: the lack of Oedipal rivalry. This perspective was never an explicit part of the Homeric poem, although in the lost poem *Telegonia* Odysseus was killed by his son with

Circe, Telegon.[35] The *Odyssey*, however, began with the 'Telemachy' during which the son came of age by going on a journey to become more like his father so that he could be ready to meet him and fulfil his expectations. In Homer, the continuity of the male offspring was the single most important legacy that a man could leave behind. In Brodsky's poem that continuity could only become a source of discord; ironically, sons were better off without their fathers. At the risk of invoking 'a crude biographism which Brodsky himself rejects', the poem undoubtedly dealt with Brodsky's conflicted feelings towards his son Andrei.[36] 'Odysseus to Telemachus', written in 1972, the year of Brodsky's forced departure to the West, was a moving farewell to his son, a small boy not unlike Telemachus when Brodsky emigrated leaving Andrei in Leningrad. This letter thus can be interpreted as a muted quest to justify this abandonment as the best choice for the future of his son. The forsaking of his son was interpreted in the poem not in terms of neglect but as a liberation of his son from a painful legacy. To be a son of a dissident poet was a sure way to be trampled by the state machine; to be a son of Nobody would be a far better choice. The reference to Oedipus, however, was only partially ironic and rather more disturbing. Brodsky chose to evoke Oedipus not in a Sophoclean but rather a Freudian rendition; the patricide and the incest became a conscious choice rather than crimes committed in ignorance. The overall meaning of the reference led to the same conclusion as the reference to Palamedes: sons are better off without their fathers. In the poem 'Laguna' ('The Lagoon') written in 1973 shortly after the emigration the same theme also emerged:

> I voskhodit v svoi nomer na bort po trapu
> postoialets, nesushchii v karmane grappu,
> sovershennyi nikto, chelovek v plashche,
> poteriavshii pamiat', otchiznu, syna ...[37]

> And the lodger checks into his room boarding a ship,
> Carrying in his pocket grappa,
> An utter nobody, a man in a raincoat,
> having lost his memory, fatherland, son ...

Odysseus' return to Ithaca was one of the most persistent themes in Brodsky's poetry. In 1993, some twenty years after 'Odysseus to Telemachus' and 'The Lagoon' Brodsky wrote 'Ithaca', a poem that served as an epilogue to his earlier poems:

> Vorotit'sia siuda cherez dvadtsat' let,
> otyskat' v peske bosikom svoi sled.
> I podnimet barbos lai na ves' prichal
> ne priznat'sia chto rad, a chto odichal.

Khochesh', skin' s sebia propotevshii khlam;
no prisluga mertva opoznat' tvoi shram.
A odnu, chto tebia, govoriat zhdala,
ne naiti nigde, ibo vsem dala.

Tvoi patsan podros; on i sam matros,
i gliadit na tebia tochno ty – otbros.
I iazyk, na kotorom vokrug orut,
razbirat', pokhozhe, naprasnyi trud.

To li ostrov ne tot, to li vpriam', zaliv
sinevoi zrachok, stal tvoi glaz brezgliv:
ot kuska zemli gorizont volna
ne zabudet, vidat', nabegaia na.[38]

To return here after twenty years,
to find barefoot in the sand your own foot prints
and the mongrel dog's barking fills the entire wharf
not because he is happy but because he has gone wild.

If you wish to, throw off those rags soaked in sweat
but the servant who can recognize your scar is dead,
and the one, they say, who waited for you
is nowhere to be found for she put out for everybody.

Your son has grown tall: he is a sailor himself
and he looks at you as if you were scum.
And the language they all shout in
is a futile labour, it seems, to decipher.

Whether it's not that island or it is indeed
because you drowned your pupil in blueness, your eye became fastidious:
from the patch of earth, it seems, the waves will
not forget the horizon, dashing on.

The parallels between this poem and the earlier ones are apparent, but the style and the language have changed. Furthermore, this poem might have yet another intertextual tier connected not with the Homeric Ithaca but with that of one of Brodsky's favourite poets, the Greek poet Constantine Cavafy (1863-1933). In the poem of 1894 Cavafy recreated Odysseus' 'homeland as a symbol for the journey that is itself the goal, not a destination'.[39] After colourful descriptions of Odysseus' many adventurous stops Cavafy concluded:

Always keep Ithaca in your mind.
You are destined to arrive there.
But don't hurry your journey at all.
far better if it takes many years,
and if you are old when you anchor at the island,
rich with all you have gained on the way,

164

not expecting that Ithaca will give you wealth.
Ithaca has given you a beautiful journey.
Without her you would never have set out.
She has no more left to give you.
And if you find her poor, Ithaca has not mocked you.
As wise as you have become, so filled with experience,
you will have understood what these Ithacas signify.[40]

The end of Cavafy's poem was left open; he did not spell out for the reader what, in fact, 'these Ithacas signify'. Brodsky, however, did. The earlier poems that invoked Odysseus' plight were filled with a sense of irrevocable loss and sadness. Brodsky's 'Ithaca' was a reflection of an Odysseus whose spirit had degenerated into blind cynicism. Homer's nostalgia was transformed into a radical denial of it. The great 'destroyer of the cities' had gone to seed; restless longing devolved into rejection of any attachment. The key recognition scenes of the *Odyssey* became in Brodsky's rendition the opposites of themselves; the moving welcome of the master of the house, husband, and father could never take place because he had been forgotten by everyone. Homeric text became 'palimpsestic' in 'Ithaca' and Brodsky wrote the new inverted text over it.[41] Penelope became a whore, Eurycleia was dead, Argus had gone wild, and Telemachus, although grown tall and a traveller like his father, spoke another language and viewed his father with disdain. The Oedipal worry of the earlier poem/letter had been realized. The beginning of the last stanza 'whether it is not that island' echoed 'all islands resemble one another'. The final loss of vision, the blindness caused by continuous travel over the blue of the sea towards the blue of the sky, recalled the earlier phrase 'the eye soiled by the sea horizon'. The extension of mythological allusion was taken to its extreme: Odysseus, the sacker of the cities, the man of intense and obsessive curiosity (emphasized both by Homer and Cavafy), the devoted husband and protective father, the proud king of Ithaca, now had become a pariah, an unwelcome stranger. The disguise, which Odysseus had employed in Homer to accomplish his transition from a war hero to the reinstated king of his realm, became the essence of Brodsky's Odysseus. Not only Homer but Cavafy as well was inverted in Brodsky's rendition: he was *not destined* to go back, in fact, it would be much better if he did not. The classical allusion thus received a distinct local colour characteristic of Russian exile poetry in general: the journey back was not only impossible, it was ultimately undesirable.[42] The diction of the poem also reflected the cynicism of its message. The choice of phrases and words like 'vsem dala' ('put out for everybody') in relation to Penelope or 'otbros' ('scum') reflect the depth of alienation from the once dear past. Especially significant in that respect is the finale of the poem, 'nabegaia na' ('dashing on') which in English translation loses its play on the Russian curse 'idi na ...' (the English equivalent of 'go to hell' but with an implication of a curse word), perhaps the only instance of a dangling preposition in Russian, and thus an easily identifiable word-play.[43]

The notion of exile was also closely intertwined with another idea pivotal to Brodsky's 'mythological' poetics. In all of the poems alluding to heroic myth Brodsky contemplated the brutalizing price of heroic endeavour. Odysseus' disorientation in time and space and the loss of his relationship with his son marginally touched upon this theme, which was explored in much more elaborate detail in two other poems by Brodsky. In the poem, 'Didona i Enei' ('Dido and Aeneas') Brodsky offered an unusual take on Book 4 of Vergil's *Aeneid*:

Velikii chelovek smotrel v okno,
a dlia nee ves' mir konchalsia kraem
ego shirokoi, grecheskoi tuniki,
obil'em skladok pokhodivshei na
ostanovivsheesia more.
          On zhe
smotrel v okno, i vzor ego seichas
byl tak dalek ot etikh mest, chto guby
zastyli, tochno rakovina, gde
tailsia gul, i gorizont v bokale
byl nepodvizhen.
          A ee liubov'
byla lish' ryboi – mozhet i sposobnoi
pustit'sia v more vsled za korablem
i, rassekaia volny gibkim telom,
vozmozhno obognat' ego ... no on –
on myslenno uzhe stupil na sushu.
I more obernulos' morem slez.
No, kak izvestno, imenno v minutu
otchaian'ia i nachinaet dut'
poputnyi veter. I velikii muzh
pokinul Karfagen.
          Ona stoiala
Pered kostrom, kotoryi razozhgli
pod gorodskoi stenoi ee soldaty,
i videla, kak v mareve ego,
drozhavshem mezhdu plamenem i dymom,
bezzvuchno rassypalsia Karfagen

zadolgo do prorochestva Katona.[44]

The great man stared through the window
but her entire world ended with the border
of his broad Greek tunic, whose abundant folds
resembled the sea on hold.
          But he
stared out through the window, and now his gaze
was so far away from here, that his lips were immobile
like a seashell where the roar is hidden, and the horizon
in his goblet was still.
          But her love

was just a fish – which might perhaps
plunge into the sea in the pursuit of the ship,
and knifing the waves with the supple body,
perhaps yet pass it – but he,
he in his thoughts already strode upon the land.
And the sea became a sea of tears.
But, as one knows, precisely at the moment
of despair, the auspicious wind begins to blow.
And the great man left Carthage.
          She stood,
before the bonfire which her soldiers
had kindled by the city walls,
and she envisioned looking at the flame and smoke
how Carthage silently crumbled

ages before Cato's prophecy.

David Ross observed that Vergil's Dido was a composite of several Greek mythological heroines: Nausicaa of *Odyssey* Book 6, Apollonius' Medea, and Catullus' Ariadne, betrayed and abandoned by the hero.[45] The last two allusions evoke the inevitability of heroic betrayal and the 'fatal attraction of heroism'.[46] However, despite her vulnerability as a woman and notwithstanding her shortcomings as a queen, Vergil's Dido was never a shadow of Aeneas' greatness;[47] on the contrary, she was his rescuer, his only chance to recover from the devastating effects of the fall of Troy and to continue his search for a new one. Initially, he was only a suppliant at her mercy, nothing but a *hospes* (guest) later elevated to the status of consort. She was the queen, one who had the power of choice, which she lived to regret: to succumb to Aeneas' charm and heroic past. She was also at the core of the love affair, whether she was confiding her feelings to Anna, confronting Aeneas, or ascending the funeral pyre she built to make her final regal statement. In the fourth book of the *Aeneid*, for the first time Aeneas' claim to heroic greatness was called into question when juxtaposed with the character of Dido. Dido's only weakness was her love for Aeneas, which drove her to neglect her primary responsibility as a Carthaginian queen: the building of her city, her greatest aspiration and accomplishment ('*non coeptae adsurgunt turres*' – 'the towers having been started no longer rise', *Aen.* 4.86). Even at the time of her suicide, she remained a powerful figure whom Vergil compared with the famous male tragic protagonists Pentheus and Orestes. Her suicide was not depicted as a final failure but as the harbinger of Carthage's future threats to Rome in the figure of Dido's most famous historical avenger, Hannibal. It is also worth noting what concerned Vergil and what he deemed unimportant or suppressed in this very dramatic book of his epic; Dido's erotic madness and suicide moved the reader beyond words and elicited unconditional sympathy, but Aeneas' human emotions were entirely, or almost entirely, glossed over. That was, as David Ross argued, 'Virgil's whole point – that the anguish felt by Dido's lover has to be suppressed and cannot be uttered to her or even admitted to himself'.[48] But in the final analysis this love story was about two people separated by divine destiny and led into madness, suicide and heroic isolation.

In Brodsky's poem the focus was primarily on Aeneas; Dido was only a shadow on his destiny, almost an annoying obstacle to his divinely inspired designs. Here Brodsky's classical metaphor evoked two radically different views of love: 'his' and 'hers'. The two contrasting perspectives were described in terms of 'movement' and 'immobility'.[49] The recurrent imagery of the sea only intensified Aeneas' temporary immobility: his tunic was like a sea that had stopped its motion, his lips resembled a seashell, the horizon reflected in his goblet was a sea horizon and he himself was a ship which Dido (the fish) was ready to follow.[50] In contrast to this picture of his immobility stood the description of Dido's emotional state. Her love was full of motion, speed and impulsiveness. But as his plans were about to be set into motion, her mobility would freeze. The phrase 'whole world ends with the border of his ... tunic' acquired both temporal and spatial meaning. The folds of his tunic on which her adoring eyes lingered reflected his temporary halt in time and space contrary to his predestined duty and predicted Dido's limitations and future inability to follow Aeneas on his journey. The Vergilian Dido, *dux femina facti*, who had confronted Aeneas after his attempt to leave her secretly, was replaced by Brodsky's Dido, who only gazed as speechlessly as a fish.[51] Brodsky juxtaposed 'he already strode upon the land' with the comparison of Dido to a fish. Fish do not live on land; Aeneas belonged to a realm where Dido had no natural place. The sea upon which he was about to embark turned out to be a sea of Dido's tears.

The poem was explicitly concerned with Aeneas' destiny and duty. While Dido was referred to only as 'she', Aeneas was twice described as a 'great man'. The Vergilian hero's constant epithet was '*pius*', for his dedication to destiny and the divine will enabled him to endure both the loss of his homeland and of everyone he held dear.[52] Aeneas' duty-bound fate left little if any room for individual choice. Brooks Otis observed that 'there could have been no Rome, as Vergil conceived it, without men like Aeneas, men of supreme *pietas*'.[53] His human side was manifested only in a few instances during the course of the *Aeneid* and every time it was dominated by his sense of duty that surpassed his vulnerability to love or pain.[54] This aspect of Aeneas in Vergil was his most attractive yet most ambivalent characteristic. However, strength of character was attributed by Vergil, at least in Book 4, not to Aeneas but to Dido.[55] At the end of the book, embittered and suicidal, she was nonetheless given the power of voicing her anguish and her desire for an avenger of her trampled pride (*Aen.* 4.621-9). In her darkest hour Vergil's Dido foresaw an everlasting rivalry and hostility between Carthage and the future city of Rome as she struggled to regain her dignity as a Carthaginian queen. Dido, and subsequently Carthage, were defeated by destiny, and the failed love between Aeneas and Dido was only a casualty in the process. When measured against the intensity of Dido's character, Aeneas of Book 4 emerged as less of a hero despite his unwavering sense of duty.[56] It was Dido with whom the reader identified and who showed moral superiority and conscious (not divinely ordained) understanding of her legacy.[57]

Brodsky's Dido acquired a different dimension. The Vergilian bonfire upon which she threw herself in her final hour of despair becomes a conflagration that would eventually consume Carthage, her proud legacy. In the departure of Aeneas she did not predict Hannibal's attack on Italy during the Punic Wars, she foresaw even further the undoing of her own Carthage, reduced to ashes at the end of those wars. Her vision foreshadowing Cato's *'Carthago delenda est'* was consistent with the Dido of the whole poem. Without Aeneas there was no Dido, and without Dido there was no Carthage. Furthermore, as Brodsky himself stated in one of his interviews, it was not a love poem, but 'a poem about destruction – the destruction of Carthage which happened before it happened in the flesh'.[58] The dramatic destruction of the woman anticipated the historical catastrophe of the city. The theme of revenge was notably absent. In this brief poem Dido became the passive victim of the 'great man's' decisions. On a purely lyrical level a common theme of poetry is the instability of human relationships, which are too often defined by betrayal, abandonment, loss and suffering. The Vergilian grandiosity of epic design had no place in Brodsky's lyric, which was intended to show the final separation between a man and a woman. Aeneas paid a private price for national greatness, one of personal loss and forsaken love. Aeneas' choice, however, was never questioned, conveying the inescapability of Brodsky's own choice of saving his art while forsaking his human connections.

The theme of Aeneas betraying his saviour Dido was closely connected with his mission as a founder of Rome. It was because of that mission that Brodsky's Dido foresaw Carthage crumbling in the fire that was her own funeral pyre. The achievement of the supreme goal was possible only through the ultimate sacrifice. Furthermore, this sacrifice also entailed the ideal that the hero (or the poet) would act alone. The rewards for what the Russians call 'podvizhnichestvo' (martyrdom achieved through a heroic feat that is expressed in Russian with a word of the same root as the word for a heroic feat itself – 'podvig') preclude any personal happiness. Brodsky identified with Aeneas through the act of 'podvizhnichestvo', but there was an undisguised feeling of uneasiness and self-contempt connected with the abandonment of the hero's human ties.

The same idea of 'podvizhnichestvo' overlapping with the presence of an anti-heroic sense of shame found another more articulated reflection in the 1967 poem 'Po doroge na Skiros' ('On the Way to Scyros') which invoked the myth of Theseus:

Ia pokidaiu gorod, kak Tezei –
svoi Labirint, ostaviv Minotavra
smerdet', a Ariadnu – vorkovat'
v ob"iat'iakh Vakkha.
          Vot ona, pobeda!
Apofeoz podvizhnichestva! Bog
kak raz togda podstraivaet vstrechu,
kogda my, v tsentre zavershiv dela,
uzhe bredem po pustyriu s dobychei,
naveki ukhodia iz etikh mest,
chtob bol'she nikogda ne vozvrashchat'sia.

V kontse kontsov, ubiistvo est' ubiistvo.
Dolg smertnykh opolchat'sia na chudovishch.
No kto skazal, chto chudishcha bessmertny?
I – daby ne mogli my vozomnit'
sebia otlichnymi ot pobezhdennykh –
Bog otnimaet vsiakuiu nagradu
(taikom ot glaz likuiushchei tolpy)
in nam velit molchat'. I my ukhodim.

teper' uzhe i vpravdu – navsegda.
ved' esli mozhet chelovek vernut'sia
na mesto prestuplen'ia, to tuda,
gde byl unizhen, on priiti ne smozhet.
I v etom punkte plany Bozhestva
i nashe oshchushchen'e unizhen'ia
nastol'ko absoliutno sovpadaiut,
chto za spinoiu ostaiutsia: noch',
smerdiashchii zver', likuiushchie tolpy,
doma, ogni. I Vakkh na pustyre
miluetsia v potemkakh s Ariadnoi.

Kogda-nibud' pridetsia vozvrashchat'sia.
Nazad. Domoi. K rodnomu ochagu.
I liazhet put' moi cherez etot gorod.
Dai Bog togda, chtob ne bylo so mnoi
dvuostrogo mecha, poskol'ku gorod
obychno nachinaetsia dlia tekh,
kto v nem zhivet, s tsentral'nykh ploshchadei
i bashen.
         A dlia strannika – s okrain.[59]

I abandon this city, as once Theseus abandoned
the Labyrinth, leaving the Minotaur
to rot, and Ariadne to murmur words of love
in Bacchus' embrace.
         This is my victory!
An apotheosis of moral virtue ('podvizhnichestvo').
God has devised our meeting
at just that moment when in the middle of it all,

170

with our endeavour accomplished,
we now stroll through the vacant lot,
with booty in our hands leaving forever
these places, with no intention of ever coming back.

At the end of the day, a murder
is a murder. The duty of mortals
is to take up arms against all monsters.
But who has claimed that monsters are immortal?
For secretly God – lest we arrogantly assume
ourselves to be different from the vanquished –
takes away any reward secretly from the exultant mob
And bids us to be silent. And we walk away.

This time, certainly, we do leave for good. Men can
return to where they committed a crime,
but men do not return to the place of their humiliation.
On this point God's design and our feeling of abasement
coincide so completely that behind our back remain
the night, the rotting beast, the exultant mob, our homes,
our hearth fires. And Bacchus in a vacant lot
with Ariadne in the dark makes out.

But one day the return is inevitable. Back home.
Back to the native hearth. And my own journey
will pass through this very city. So God grant that I
shall not carry with me then the double-edged sword –
since cities start, for those who inhabit them,
with central squares and towers –
  but for the traveller – with their outskirts.

The use of mythology is striking in this poem. The king of Scyros, Lycomedes, is an obscure mythological figure, famous mostly in connection
with the story that Thetis, in order to hide her son Achilles, put him among
the daughters of Lycomedes disguised in girl's dress.[60] However, a more
obscure mythological tradition related by Plutarch asserted that after a
rebellion in his native Athens, Theseus was banished and went to Scyros
and was murdered there by king Lycomedes, who violated the laws of
hospitality by throwing Theseus off a high cliff into the sea.[61] Brodsky's
choice of the title 'On the Way to Scyros' indicated Theseus' hastening
towards death. The later title of the poem, in fact, was 'To Lycomedes on
Scyros', which made the connotation of the final journey even more explicit.[62] The geographic 'itinerary' of the myth, however, was also somewhat askew in this poem. Theseus killed the Minotaur on Crete and
abandoned Ariadne on the island of Naxos on his way back to his native
Athens. In this poem the hero was about to embark on some journey,
allegedly to Scyros, and was planning to return home some time in the
indefinite future. The ethical conflict of the myth was also shifted even in

171

comparison with Brodsky's Russian predecessor in the treatment of the Theseus myth. Although Marina Tsvetaeva was aware of the ancient sources (Catullus 64, Diodorus Siculus, and perhaps Ovid's *Heroides* 10 and *Metamorphoses* 8.175ff.), in her rendition of the myth, discussed in the previous chapter, she contemplated with great care the reason for Theseus' abandonment of Ariadne and decided to endow Theseus with the aura of self-sacrifice: he abandoned her not because he was a coward but because he wished her to become immortal. But in Brodsky's poem *all* accounts were intentionally amiss. Brodsky's Ariadne here was a willing participant in Theseus' abandonment and she caused his eagerness to meet his death at the hands of Lycomedes. As he left her behind, she welcomed and enjoyed Bacchus' embrace. It was she who was forgetful while he was burdened with a sorrowful memory. The word 'vorkovat" (rendered in English by 'murmur') has an erotic connotation in Russian. Ariadne was whispering 'sweet nothings' in Bacchus' arms, overwhelmed by her new lover.

In Brodsky's exploration of the famous myth a paradoxical ethical law emerged, according to which heroic accomplishments were followed by the humiliation of the hero, rather than a reward. The fulfilment of destiny was again based on an ultimate sacrifice. For Aeneas this was the loss of Dido, for Theseus – of Ariadne. But in the fulfilment of the heroic act lay also the undoing of the hero as an individual. Thus the title of the poem became especially poignant; Theseus left the Labyrinth foreseeing his imminent defeat and the triumph was replaced with resignation. He was ready to meet his final Minotaur, Lycomedes, and his darkest hour. The idea of 'podvizhnichestvo', as in the case of Aeneas and Dido, again became intertwined with the heroic achievement that must expect not reward but humiliation.

The myth of Theseus who, after killing the Minotaur, lost his beloved Ariadne to Bacchus, served as a mask 'for the real situation of the lyric "I" '.[63] In the first two lines the protagonist presented his destiny as similar to that of Theseus. However, later in the poem the similarity was not mentioned again. The protagonist faded into anonymity and the classical metaphor told the story that the poet wanted to convey about himself; the poet became the hero. Michael Kreps observed that a mythological hero and his situation attract a poet because they offer a ready formula for a conflict charged with psychological turmoil.[64] The name of the hero is transformed into a sign conveying the subtext of trials and emotions perceived by a poet as his own.

The pivotal point of this confession disguised under a classical mask began in the last phrase of the first stanza 'with no intention of ever coming back'. The poem was written in 1967, a year that signified a moment in the poet's life for summing up both his youthful poetic activity and the difficulty of his position within a society that treated him as a hostile element. For the three preceding years Brodsky had been subjected to severe government persecution and he had been forced to flee from city to city hiding from the police. Despite the rarity of political motifs in Brodsky's early work and the intensely intimate lyrical nature of this poem, it is possible to read the allusion to the Minotaur as 'Aesopian language'.[65] The Minotaur was seen by some Russian readers not only as a cannibalistic monster from the remote island of Crete, but as a beast of the man-devouring state. This feeling was especially intensified with the phrase 'we mortals have a duty to take up arms against all monsters', and then with the hopeful phrase 'who has claimed that monsters are immortal?'. The word choice of these lines deserves explication. Initially the word 'monster' appeared in Russian as 'chudovishche', which is a neutral word that can be applied equally either to a scary creature or to a dominating police state. However, in the latter usage, also translated into English as 'monsters', Brodsky chose the syncopated version of the same word 'chudishcha' which usually is applied ironically to a cartoonish version of a real monster, a sort of a bogey-man. The monster that brings death was reduced to an awkward almost funny creature, which should not be feared but ridiculed.

The late sixties in Russia was a time that still wistfully remembered the 'ottepel' ' ('thaw') of the Khrushchev years (1956-62), which had followed the freezing, terrifying years of Stalin's rule. The monster, however, even if weakened and already ridiculous, was only half dead and the 'reward' for even the suspicion of dissidence was either a 'journey' to prison in the North or, for the fortunate ones, exile to the West. Brodsky would experience both in his lifetime, but the poem was prophetic of his final exile from Russia in 1972. 'This time, certainly, we do leave for good', echoed the last phrase of the first stanza 'with no intention of ever coming back'. The reason for such a drastic cutting of all ties was rather simple: one could not return to the place of humiliation – a notion applicable to both a hero and a poet. The home left behind was lost amid the 'rotting beast' and the 'exultant mob'. The first phrase once again reiterated the idea of a half-dead beast (the decaying Soviet machine). The second phrase, on the other hand, emphasized the gap between the aspirations of the intelligentsia and those who eagerly and sincerely hailed the leaders of the Communist party on the steps of Lenin's mausoleum while parading past them on national holidays.

Strangely enough, however, the very last stanza brought back the Odyssean motif: 'But one day the return is inevitable. Back home. Back to the native hearth', which also echoed the lines in one of the most famous of Brodsky's early poems written in 1962: 'I will return to Vasil'evskii island to die'.[66] These lines were marked by the disappearance of anger, by irony and even resignation. The reason for such a sudden change of heart was not stated but was self-evident, as in Odysseus' case: the poet's self-identity was connected with the land from which he came. The humiliation once endured could not be given priority. The lines 'so God grant that I/ shall not carry with me then the double-edged sword' expressed the only remnants of anger and frustration, but even these articulated clearly the melancholy of the hero's (poet's) 'new' status as an outsider. Brodsky's Theseus had very little in common with any Theseus in the classical or even Russian literary renditions: he was neither a treacherous man, nor a coward running away from divine wrath. Neither did he experience any sudden loss of memory or, like Tsvetaeva's hero, surge of a noble impulse to sacrifice his love for the immortality of his beloved. Theseus emerged as a different type of a tragic hero, one that stood for the figure of the poet himself: bitter, exiled and contemplative.

In another poem '1972 god' ('The Year 1972') Brodsky returned to the theme of Theseus one more time:[67]

Tochno Tezei iz peshchery Minosa,
vyidia na vozdukh i shkuru vynesia,
ne gorizont vizhu ia – znak minusa
k prozhitoi zhizni. Ostrei, chem mech ego,
lezvie eto, i im otrezana
luchshaia chast'. Tak vino ot trezvogo
proch' ubiraiut, i sol' ot presnogo.
Khochetsia plakat'. No plakat' nechego.[68]

Just like Theseus out from the lair in the Minos ring,
coming up for air with the pelt of that menacing
beast, it's not a horizon I see but a minus sign
on my previous life. This line is clearly
keener than a hero's sword, and shorn off by its cutting blade
the dearest part. Thus they take away a costly blend
from the sober man, and salt from what's bland.
I feel like crying. But it's pointless, really.[69]

There was no mention of Ariadne this time. The emergence of Theseus from the cave represented for Brodsky exile into the West and 'the minus sign' was the only mention of the losses and betrayals of his prior life. This clinging to the myth of Theseus allowed Brodsky to convey the painful experience of separation from his loved ones and to express through the images of sword and blade the idea of impotence, most likely linguistic, since exile from Russia was associated for him with the loss of his most powerful weapon, his language, which for a poet can sometimes signify a 'linguistic death sentence'.[70] Thus the mythological metaphor became intertwined with yet another of the central themes in Brodsky's poetics, the theme of Empire.

Wrestling with Empire

'Imperiia – strana dlia durakov'.

'Empire is the land for fools'.

Joseph Brodsky, 'Post Aetatem Nostram'[71]

In the early seventies Brodsky's Roman poems started supplanting the Greek ones. This change was similar to Mandelshtam's progression in what Brodsky himself described as 'the poet's growing identification with the archetypal predicament of "a poet versus an empire" '.[72] Empire was Brodsky's largest 'mythologeme' and entered his poetics decisively some time during the late sixties and early seventies. During that period the main signifiers of the Empire theme were also the signifiers of the Roman Empire, as, for example, in the poem 'Post Aetatem Nostram' (1970): emperors, prefects, cohorts, legions, money-lenders, gladiators, the Roman fora, the Colosseum.[73] Brodsky's Empire, however, was, as Lev Loseff noted, a universal realm with no distinct geographical or historical boundaries in opposition to the freedom-seeking individual.[74] While at different times it could signify either the Roman, the Soviet, or even the British Empire, it was first and foremost closely connected with Brodsky's self-perception as an exile from Empire, the contemplation of that Empire's power and sway over his thoughts and feelings, and his eventual liberation. That Empire included two sets of motives and emotional responses on which discussion in the following pages focuses. First, I will analyze how Brodsky's treatment of the Ovidian theme of exile and nostalgia within the context of Empire evoked that of his predecessors' but differed from them significantly. Secondly, I will look at those poems of Brodsky's that constituted his contemplation of poetic legacy through the classical metaphor as he penned several of his 'monument' poems in imitation and also in defiance of the preceding tradition.

Brodsky's Roman Empire started 'from the outskirts': the first poem on the theme '*Ex Oriente*' written in 1963 described the death of a nameless hero (perhaps a legionary?) in the sands of some Eastern province. In the first stanza Titus Livy appeared in Brodsky's favourite form of paradigmatic comparison:

> Da, tochno tak zhe, kak Tit Livii, on
> sidel v svoem shatre, no byl nezrimo
> shirokimi peskami okruzhen
> i mial v rukakh pis'mo iz Rima.[75]

> Yes, exactly in the same way as Titus Livy, he
> was sitting in his tent, but was invisibly
> surrounded by vast sands
> and crumpled in his hands a letter from Rome.

The theme of exile from the beloved city was palpable in these lines, and 'letter from Rome' led directly to Ovid, the most famous writer of letters *to Rome*, with whom Brodsky was frequently compared during his own exile in the North.[76] Ovid occupied an important place in Brodsky's poetic imagination throughout the whole evolution of his poetry; Brodsky, a pariah of the Soviet state, following in the steps of Pushkin and Mandelshtam, found in Ovid his ancient double not only in biographical terms but also in terms of poetics. 'If you want to learn a pattern of metaphoric thinking', he stated in one of his interviews, 'reading Ovid is crucial, to see how this guy animates mythology.'[77] While Ovid's *Metamorphoses* unquestionably enthralled Brodsky in his later poetry, it was his plight as an exile that entered Brodsky's early poems.[78] During his own exile in the tiny village of Norenskaia[79] in the Archangel region of Northern Russia (March 1964 to November 1965), Brodsky wrote two poems connected with the Ovidian theme – 'Otryvok' ('A Fragment') and 'Ex Ponto' with a subtitle 'Poslednee pis'mo Ovidiia v Rim' ('The Last Letter of Ovid to Rome'). The first connected Brodsky directly with the Ovidian theme of his Russian predecessor Osip Mandelshtam:

> Nazo k smerti ne gotov.
> Ottogo ugrium.
> Ot sarmatskikh kholodov
> v bersporiadke um.
> Blizhe Rima ty, zvezda.
> Blizhe Rima smert'.
> Preimushchestvo: tuda
> mozhno posmotret'.
>
> Nazo k smerti ne gotov.
> Blizhe (cherez Pont,
> opustevshii ot sudov)
> Rima – gorizont.
> Blizhe Rima – Orion
> mezhdu tuch skvozit.
> Rimom zvat' ego? A on?
> On li vozrazit.
>
> Tochno tak svecha vo t'mu
> daleko vidna.
> ne gotov? A chto k nemu
> blizhe, chem ona?
> Rimom zvat' ee? Liubit'?
> Izredka vzyvat'?
> Potomu chto v smerti byt',
> v Rime ne byvat'.
>
> Nazo, Rima ne trevozh'.
> Uzh ne pomnish' sam
> tekh, komu ty pis'ma shlesh'.
> Mozhet, mertvetsam.
> Po privychke. Utochni
> (zdes' ne do obid)
> adres. Rim ty zacherkni
> i postav': Aid.[80]
>
> Naso's not ready to die.
> That is why he's grim.
> His mind's in disarray

176

From the Sarmatian freeze.
Star, you're closer than Rome
Death's closer than Rome.
The only advantage is: one can see the star.

Naso's not ready to die.
The horizon across the Pontus
void of the ships
is closer than Rome.
Orion closer than Rome
glimpses through the clouds.
Should I call it Rome? So what?
Will it contradict?

That's the way a candle is
seen in darkness far.
Not ready? But who is closer
to him than death?
Should he call it Rome? Fall in love with it?
For in death he will be, yes,
But in Rome, alas!

Naso, don't disturb Rome
You yourself forgot
To whom you're sending letters.
Maybe to the dead.
Just a habit. Check again
(don't take it as offence)
the address and then
cross out Rome please
and insert: Hades.

The intertwining of two of Mandelshtam's most prominent themes was unmistakable in this poem: one was Ovidian, but the other was of the dying Petropolis ('Petersburg! I still have the addresses for finding the voices of the dead').[81] The importance of this connection was manifested in another poem, undated but probably written in the sixties, which contained the following lines:

Ved' krai zemli eshche ne krainost' zhizni?
sam materik podderzhivaet to, chto
ne v silakh sdelat' severnaia pochta.
I eta zviaz' dopodlinno tverda,
pokuda ehshe mozhno na konverte
postavit' 'Leningrad' zamesto smerti.[82]

For the end of the earth does not mean the end of life?
The continent itself supports the very thing
that northern post is powerless to support.
And that connection still remains quite sturdy,

until one is able on the envelope
to put 'Leningrad' instead of death.

These intertextual links reveal clearly that, as for Mandelshtam, so also for Brodsky the theme of Rome was inextricably connected with the theme of his own city as an unattainable beloved and to his fate in it and away from it. The other poem, 'Ex Ponto', continued the Ovidian theme in Russian poetry transmitted by Pushkin and Mandelshtam. However, while both Pushkin and Mandelshtam 'edited' Ovid's sadness and nostalgia, Brodsky stayed remarkably close to the plight of the original *Ex Ponto*:

Tebe, ch'i milovidnye cherty,
dolzhno byt', ne strashatsia uviadan'ia,
v moi Rim, ne izmenivshiisia kak ty,
so vremeni poslednego svidan'ia,
pishu ia s moria. S moria. Korabli
siuda stremiatsia posle nepogody,
chtob podtverdit', cho eto krai zemli.
I v triumakh ikh ne otyskat' svobody.[83]

To you, whose pretty features
perhaps do not fear fading,
into my Rome, which, like you, has not changed,
since our last meeting,
I am writing from sea. From sea. The ships
Strive to these shores after a storm
in order to prove that this is the edge of the earth
and in their holds there is no freedom.

In this short poem Brodsky established concisely what he had in common with the ancient poet: his abandoned beloved whose features haunted him, the city as a metaphor for that beloved, the proximity of the sea, and his feelings about being on 'the edge of the earth' ('krai zemli'). The last line in the poem was especially striking; it stood independently and in juxta-position to the whole poem revealing Brodsky's conviction about the futility of any kind of journey in pursuit of happiness or freedom, a thought that Brodsky had expressed before in Odysseus' 'all the islands resemble each other'. The theme of exile from Rome reappeared several times in the poetry of this period, most notably in four poems: 'Anno Domini' (1968),[84] 'Neokonchennoe' ('Unfinished', 1970),[85] 'Vtoroe Rozhdestvo na beregu nezamerzaiushchego Ponta ...' ('Second Christmas on the shores of never freezing Pontus ...', 1971),[86] and 'Pis'ma rimskomu drugu' ('Letters to a Roman Friend', 1972) with the subtitle 'Iz Martsiala' ('From Martial').[87] In the last poem, written on the eve of Brodsky's permanent departure for the West, the theme of Empire was particularly emphatic. There were also several intertextual 'Roman' levels in the poem. The poem belonged to the 'genre' of letters to Rome, which immediately contextualized it as an Ovidian allusion. The subtitle, however, 'From Martial' could be misleading since the poem was neither the imitation nor an adaptation from Martial.[88] Rather, it introduced the context of invective poetry, irony, and satire. Despite numerous Roman *realia* in the poem – Caesar, a legionary, war in Libya – there was no historical Rome, only a contemplation of life within the Empire:

> Pust' i vpravdu, Postum, kuritsa ne ptitsa,
>   No s kurinymi mozgami khvatish goria.
> Esli vypalo v Imperii rodit'sia,
>   luchshe zhit' v glukhoi provintsii, u moria.
>
> I ot Tsezaria daleko, i ot v'iugi.
>   Lebezit' ne nuzhno, trusit', toropit'sia.
> Govorish', chto vse namestniki – voriugi?
>   No voriuga mne milei, chem krovopiitsa.[89]
>
> Perhaps, indeed, Postumus, chickens are not really birds
>   But there is danger in having chicken-brains.
> If one's fated to be born in an Empire
>   Let him live in a remote province, by the sea.
>
> It is far from Caesar and the blizzard,
>   One does not need to fawn, be cowardly, or hurry.
> There, you say, the governors are thieves?
>   But thieves are dearer to me than bloodsuckers.

In this poem the 'joy' of exile characteristic of Pushkin's and Mandelshtam's Ovidian theme has reappeared. The distance from Rome was seen again as a liberating experience, an opportunity for creative contemplation and heroic endeavour, a theme, as explored above, that was especially poignant for Brodsky's poetics in his rendition of the Odysseus and to some degree the Theseus myth. In that respect Brodsky's approach to the fate of the exile differed drastically from Ovid's. For Ovid Rome represented the Golden Age of civilization and the banishment from the city equalled cultural death which can be avoided only by return. For Brodsky exile was yet another self-ironizing moment replete with the conviction that return was not an option. The name of the addressee of the poem, Postumus, was also significant. He was also the addressee of Horace's *Ode* 2.14, which contemplated the irrevocability of time (*'Eheu, fugaces, Postume, Postume, labuntur anni'*). Furthermore, Postumus in Latin, in reference to children, can mean 'last, latest born'. Brodsky (and perhaps also Horace) thus might address his young descendant who would read the letter after his death. That thought was clarified in the last two stanzas of the poem:

Zelen' lavra, dokhodiashchaia do drozhi.
  Dver' raspakhnutaia, pyl'noe okontse.
Stul pokinutyi, ostavlennoe lozhe.
  Tkan', vpitavshaia poludennoe solntse.

Pont shumit za chernoi izgorod'iu pinii.
  Ch'e-to sudno s vetrom boretsia u mysa.
Na rassokhsheisia skameike – Starshii Plinii
  Drozd shchebechet v sheveliure kiparisa.[90]

Green laurel reaching the point of trembling.
  Door ajar, the dusty little window.
Chair forsaken, abandoned couch,
  Linen soaked in the midday sun.

Pontus roars behind a black fence of pine trees.
  Someone's boat wrestles with the wind near the promontory.
On the cracked bench a book of Pliny the Elder,
  Thrush is chirping in the hairdo of the cypress.

These last stanzas depicted the conspicuous absence of a human figure to whom the chair, the couch, the linen, and the book might belong. But the classical allusions filled the void with 'posthumous' significance. The trembling laurel tree alluded explicitly to Daphne, Apollo's unrequited love, and after her metamorphosis, a tree consecrated to him and crowning his head. This, then, was a place of poetic inspiration, but the poet was gone, leaving behind only the everyday 'utensils' of his craft and the nature that conspired with him. In this locale what reading could be more appropriate than Pliny's *Natural History* with its inquiry into nature's mysteries, a book carelessly left on an old bench, or maybe abandoned when its reader (the poet?) faded away? The life-affirming laurel in the beginning of these stanzas was balanced at the end by the cypress tree, for the Romans a symbol of death and mourning. The poem, however, did not end on a sombre note; the chirping of the thrush animated the tree of sorrow, and life continued without skipping a beat.

The poem, which started as a letter from an exile from the beloved city, ended on a very intimate but also joyous note of life overcoming death. The sad and contemplative mood of the poem resulted not from the feeling of exile and imminent death but from the loss of personal ties mentioned in the poem only once: 'ni podrugi, ni prislugi, ni znakomykh' ('no girlfriend, servants, or acquaintances'). This theme of separation from the loved ones is accentuated in Brodsky's 'Roman' poems by the use of another Roman poet, Sextus Propertius, a rather rare source of allusion in Russian poetry.[91]

The poem 'Anno Domini' (whose title is a direct reference to Anna Akhmatova), describing the miserable life of a Roman prefect in the province, alluded to the name of Propertius' mistress Cynthia:

Ego ne khochet videt' Imperator,
menia – moi syn i Tsintiia.

The Emperor does not want to see him
Cynthia and my son refuse to see me.

and further:

Otechestvo ... chuzhie gospoda
u Tsintii v gostiakh nad kolybel'iu
skloniaiutsia, kak novye volkhvy.[92]

Fatherland ... Some foreign gentlemen
At Cynthia's house lean over the crib
Like the new Magi.

This poem, dedicated to Brodsky's great love and the mother of his son,
Marina Basmanova, contained not only a classical allusion but a Christian
one as well.[93] That overlap of cultural layers so typical of Brodsky's poetics
manifested itself throughout most of his works. Brodsky in almost all of
his 'classical' poems moved freely and sometimes unexpectedly between
ancient and modern, melancholy and irony. An illustrative example of this
abrupt change of tone was the poem 'Biust Tiberiia' ('The Bust of
Tiberius'). The beginning of the poem set up a situation of clichéd homage:
a poet addressing the statue of a famous historical figure. Consequently
the poem started with an appropriate *Ave, Caesar*: 'All hail to you, two
thousand years too late' ('Privetstvuiu tebia dve tyshchi let spustia').[94] The
following lines, however, completely reset the whole homage-giving, contemplative situation of the poem:

... Ty tozhe byl zhenat na bliadi.
U nas nemalo obshchego. K tomu zh
Vokrug – tvoi gorod. Gvalt, abtomobili,
shpana so shpritsami v syrykh pod"ezdakh,
razvaliny. Ia, zauriadnyi strannik,
privetsvuiu tvoi pyl'nyi biust
v bezliudnoi galeree. Akh, Tiberii,
tebe zdes' net i tridtsati. V litse
uverennost' skorei v poslushnykh myshtsakh,
chem v budushchem ikh summy. Golova,
otrublennaia skul'ptorom pri zhizni,
est', v sushchnosti, prorochestvo o vlasti.
Vse to, chto nizhe podborodka, – Rim: ...[95]

I, too, once took a whore in marriage.
We have some things in common. Plus,
all around, your city. Bustle, shrieking traffic.
Damp alleyways with hypodermic youths.

Also, the ruins. I, a standard stranger,
salute your grimy bust in some
dank chamber storing echoes. Ah, Tiberius!
Here you're not thirty yet. The face displays
a greater confidence in trusted sinews
than in the future of their sum. A head
the sculptor severs in one's lifetime surely
sounds like a prophecy of power. All
that lies below the massive jawbone – Rome: ...[96]

What started as an homage to antiquity turned into its opposite. The word
'bliad'' ('whore') brings any reader of Russian down to earth. It is hard to
imagine a word more inappropriate for any kind of elegiac musings about
the past. Brodsky, whose use and understanding of the power of language
was uncanny, sensed unerringly what would stop his readers in their
tracks. Furthermore, why would the Russian poet in exile identify himself
with one of the cruellest emperors in Roman history (apart from the
'whore' reference)? The introduction of a scene from modern Rome made
that clear; there were only two people in the gallery: the poet and the bust
of the emperor, both worn out by time and the weight of the past. Outside
was the noise of the modern city. What remained of the *urbs aeterna* was
the ruins, an extremely charged motif in Brodsky's poetry that was reiterated at the end of the poem:[97]

ia tozhe opromet'iu bezhal vsego
so mnoi sluchivshegosia i prevratilsia v ostrov
s razvalinami ...[98]

I, too, have often made that headlong dash
from rank reality. I, too, became, an island
replete with ruins ...

The modern and the ancient were intertwined closely in this poem, but the
modern triumphed. Hence Brodsky sighed elegiacally 'Ah, Tiberius', as he
began to 'revive' ancient Rome in the poem. Nevertheless, the Mandelshtamian 'yearning for the world's culture' was satisfied by this symbiosis of ancient and modern, by the paradoxical parallel between a Roman
tyrant and an exiled Russian poet. Brodsky in Rome construed himself as
a relic from classical times, a 'bust, a torso, a living statue', like Tiberius
in the gallery.[99] In his 'Roman Elegies XII' (1981), indeed, he welcomed that
state of being nothing more than a fragment of something once greater as
a path to immortality and a release from the fear of death:

Ia byl v Rime. Byl zalit svetom. Tak,
kak tol'ko mozhet mechtat' oblomok!
Na setchatke moei zolotoi piatak.
Khvatit na vsiu dlinu potemok.[100]

I was in Rome. I was flooded by light. The way
a splinter can only dream about.
Golden coins on the retina are to stay –
enough to last one through the whole blackout.[101]

Rome in these lines emerged almost in the Mandelshtamian sense of a
perfect city that left its mark on anyone who had ever been there and
prepared him for eternity.[102] In that sense the presentation of the city of
Rome must be viewed in the larger picture of Brodsky's relationship with
his own city, his love for Italy, and the broader context of the specific
magnetic attraction that Italy always exercised on Russian artists and
intellectuals.[103] In his interview with Evgenii Rein, Brodsky explained why
he always felt more at home in Italy than anywhere else: 'I did not know
the language, but nonetheless I felt at home there (it was in the winter)
much more than in London or in the States, although in these places I at
least to a certain level knew the language. I was somewhat disturbed by
that feeling until I realized that I felt that way because of all the facades,
statues, mouldings, and so on. All of that in fact was the language.'[104] That
lingua franca was, of course, the architectural language of his native city
of St Petersburg. In this interview Brodsky articulated the feeling of inner
affinity bordering on longing, and the perception that Italy was almost a
surrogate homeland (especially during the winter); this perception has
already been observed in Ivanov's *Roman Sonnets*, but acquired in Brodsky's poetry a new strength and meaning. Brodsky standing in the empty
gallery in Italy looking at Tiberius' bust might have been thinking of
himself, much younger, in the half-empty ancient halls of the Hermitage.
A poem addressed to one of the most ruthless Roman emperors emerged
within the context of Brodsky's 'sculptural nostalgia', a longing for the city
of his youth replete with classical statues, busts and columns.

In 1976, four years after his exile, Brodsky wrote a poem that might be
interpreted as nostalgic but with a peculiar twist. The poem called 'Razvi-
vaia Platona' ('Developing Plato')[105] described Brodsky's own ideal city
where he would love to live:

Ia khotel by zhit', Fortunatus, v gorode, gde reka
vysovyvalas' by iz-pod mosta, kak iz rukava – ruka,
   i chtob ona vpadala v zaliv, rastopyriv pal'tsy,
kak Shopen, nikomu ne pokazyvavshii kulaka ...

I would like to live, Fortunatus, in a city where
a river would thrust out from under a bridge like a hand from a sleeve.
   and would flow into the gulf, spreading its fingers
like Chopin, who never in his life threatened anyone with a fist ...

The addressee of this poem was of Brodsky's own design without any
ancient counterparts. Fortunatus, 'the happy man', was given a descrip-

tion of a vague city with a river in its middle: it could be St Petersburg, or Rome, or even Venice, which Brodsky also loved and which was to be the place of his final rest – until, that is, the familiar 'imperial' features are introduced:

> Chtob tam byla Opera, i chtob v nei veteran-
> tenor ispravno pel ariiu Mario po vecheram;
>   chtob Tiran emu aplodiroval v lozhe, a ia v partere
> bormotal by, szhav zuby ot nenavisti: 'baran'.

> There would be an Opera House, in which an old
> tenor would duly sing in the evenings Mario's[106] aria,
>   and the Tyrant will applaud him from his loge, but I from the pit
> would mumble my teeth clenched in hatred: 'Mutton-head'.

The poem ended as it moved from the abstract portrayal of the Empire to the concrete features of a familiar one, and nostalgia again acquired its sculpted features:

> I tam byli by pamiatniki. Ia by znal imena
> ne tol'ko bronzovykh vsadnikov, vsunuvshikh v stremena
>   istorii svoiu nogu, no i ikhnikh chetveronogikh.
> uchityvaia otpechatok, ostavlennyi imi na

> naselenii goroda. I, s prisokhshei k gube
> sigaretoiu, sil'no za polnoch' vozvrashchaias' peshkom k sebe,
>   kak tsygan po ladoni, po treshchinam na asfal'te
> ia gadal by, ikaia, vslukh o ego sud'be.

> I kogda by menia skhvatili v itoge za shpionazh,
> podryvnuiu aktivnost', brodiazhnichestvo, menazh-
>   a trua, a tolpa by, besnuias' vokrug krichala,
> tycha v menia natuzhennymi ukazatel'nymi:
>   'Ne nash!', –

> ia by vtaine byl schastliv, shepcha pro sebia: 'Smotri,
> eto tvoi shans uznat', kak vygliadit iznutri
>   to, na chto ty tak dolgo gliadel snaruzhi;
> zapominai zhe podrobnosti, vosklitsaia: "Vive la Patrie!" '

> And there would be monuments there. I would know by name
> Not only the bronze horsemen who have thrust their feet
>   into History's stirrups – but also the names of their steeds
> considering the trace the latter left

> on the city's population. And with a cigarette glued
> to my lip, walking home well past midnight, I would guess aloud
>   like some gypsy tracing an open palm, between hiccups,
> reading the cracks in the asphalt – what fate awaits the city.

And when they would finally arrest me for espionage,
for subversive activity, vagrancy, *ménage-
a-trois*, and the crowd, raving around me, would shout,
poking at me with their work-roughened forefingers:
    'Not one of us!'

Then I would feel secret happiness, whispering to myself: 'See,
this is your chance to learn how it looks from the inside,
    that thing which for so long you beheld from the outside;
so remember all the details as you exclaim: "Vive la Patrie!" '

The closing stanzas of the poem, containing a mention of 'bronze horsemen' (an allusion to Pushkin's 'sculptural myth') and direct biographical associations with Brodsky's own arrest at night on the street while walking to a friend's house, left little doubt what city he meant here. Was this, however, a nostalgic poem? The allusion to Plato in the title is especially important here. In his utopian construction of an ideal city Plato considered what kind of a citizen should be allowed to live in it. Poets were not welcome in Plato's ideal city since they would interfere with the appropriate upbringing of a strong citizenry by introducing them to 'inappropriate' passions. At the same time the classical parallel went deeper; Brodsky had been put on trial in his beloved city for 'social parasitism' ('tuneiadstvo'), as Socrates had been accused in Athens for his 'corruption of youth'. But while Socrates had refused Crito's offer to rescue him and met his end at the hands of his accusers in a state of near-elation, Brodsky had fled the city of his youth. It is clearly perceptible in this poem that Brodsky 'envied' Socrates' choice: to insist on belonging to a place even if it rejected him as an alien body ('Ne nash!').[107] Furthermore, as the title *'Developing Plato'* suggests, this poem offered a sense of *Brodsky's* ideal archetypal city – even of his ideal archetypal persecution – elucidating Brodsky's complicated relationship with his fate of exile. Brodsky never associated his exile with grief: 'Displacement and misplacement are this century's commonplace', he once stated.[108] Much has been made of Brodsky's failure or lack of desire to return to his beloved city of St Petersburg. Even Brodsky himself could not quite explain it, sometimes dodging the question with a joke that one should not return either to the place of his crime or to the place of his past love.[109] Brodsky, like Mandelshtam, was one of the most cosmopolitan poets in the history of Russian poetry. For him, then, Russia and the West constituted two sides of one coin. In his essay on Mandelshtam, 'The Child of Civilization', he identified Russian cultural inferiority toward the West as one of the defining features of the Russian cultural identity. 'Out of this inferiority,' he further noted, 'grew the ideal of a certain cultural unity "out there" and a subsequent intellectual victory toward anything coming from that direction. This is, in a way, a Russian version of Hellenicism, and Mandelshtam's remark about Pushkin's "Hellenistic paleness" was not an idle one.'[110]

In this quotation the whole tradition of Russian classical metaphor has come full circle, to be realized completely in Brodsky's two unusual takes on *Exegi monumentum*. One of them contemplated the poet's legacy, in Dante's words, 'nel mezzo del cammin di nostra vita' ('in the middle of the path of our life'); the other, written sixteen years later, was an acknowledgment of the approaching end and presented a culmination of both Brodsky's poetics of self and his use of classical metaphor.

Epilogue to *Exegi monumentum*

'May 24, 1980'

Ia vkhodil vmesto dikogo zveria v kletku,
vyzhigal svoi srok i klikukhu gvozdem v barake,
zhil u moria, igral v ruletku,
obedal chert znaet s kem vo frake.
S vysoty lednika ia oziral polmira,
trizhdy tonul, dvazhdy byval rasporot.
Brosil stranu, chto menia vskormila.
Iz zabyvshykh menia mozhno sostavit' gorod.
Ia slonialsia v stepiakh, pomniashchikh vopli gunna,
nadeval na sebia chto syznova vkhodit v modu,
seial rozh', pokryval chernoi tol'iu gumna
i ne pil tol'ko sukhuiu vodu.
Ia vpustil v svoi sny voronenyi zrachok konvoia,
zhral khleb izgnan'ia, ne ostavliaia korok.
Pozvolial svoim sviazkam vse zvuki, pomimo voia;
pereshel na shepot. Teper' mne sorok.
Chto skazat' o zhizni? Chto okazalas' dlinnoi.
Tol'ko s gorem ia chuvstvuiu solidarnost'.
No poka mne rot ne zabili glinoi,
iz nego razdavat'sia budet lish' blagodarnost'.[111]

I have braved, for want of wild beasts, steel cages,
carved my term and nickname on bunks and rafters,
lived by the sea, flashed aces in an oasis,
dined with the devil-knows-whom, in tails, on truffles.
From the height of a glacier I beheld half the world, the earthly
width. Twice have drowned, thrice let knives rake my nitty-gritty.
Quit the country that bore and nursed me.
Those who forgot me would make a city.
I have waded the steppes that saw yelling Huns in saddles,
worn the clothes nowadays back in fashion in every quarter,
planted rye, tarred the roofs of pigsties and stables,
guzzled everything save dry water.
I've admitted the sentries' third eye into my wet and foul
dreams. Munched the bread of exile: it's stale and warty.
Granted my lungs all sounds except the howl;
switched to a whisper. Now I am forty.

What should I say about life? That it's long and abhors transparence.
Broken eggs make me grieve; the omelette, though, makes me vomit.
yet until brown clay has been crammed down my larynx,
only gratitude will be gushing from it.[112]

This poem was written on 24 May 1980, the day Brodsky turned 40. It is extremely powerful in Russian, but loses some of its force in English even though the translation is Brodsky's own. It followed the tradition of Horace, Derzhavin and Pushkin as a poem-testament by assuming the first person singular persona and recounting past achievements. However, it was not a summing-up of the poet's contribution to the national literary legacy, nor was it a prophecy of future glory that would shine into eternity. It was simply a summing-up of a personal biography devoid of any 'message for posterity'. In comparison with other examples of the genre of 'Monuments', this one is rather understated and in tune with Brodsky's dismissive 'I am a bard of junk ...' ('Ia pevets drebedeni ...') in his 'Roman Elegies'.[113] The humility of Brodsky's own contemplation of his poetic legacy might have been influenced by his beloved Evgenii Baratynskii, whom he considered the greatest poet of Pushkin's *pleiad* (preferring him even to Pushkin himself). In one arresting poem Baratynskii described his Muse in the same humble strokes ('The Muse', 1829):

I am not bedazzled by my Muse:
No one will call her a beauty,
And youths seeing her will not
pursue her in adoring crowd.
She doesn't have desire or a talent
to seduce with her elegant attire
or with flirting of her eyes,
or her witty conversation;
But sometimes for a little while the world
is affected by the uncommon visage of her face,
by the simplicity of her speeches;
and instead of vicious criticism it
bestows on her some fleeting praise.

Brodsky referred to this poem in his Nobel Lecture, citing 'the uncommon visage' of the Muse's face ('litsa neobshchim vyrazhen'em') in the poem. He then added: 'It's in acquiring this "uncommon visage" that the meaning of human existence seems to lie, since for this uncommonness we are, as it were, prepared genetically. Regardless of whether one is a writer or a reader, one's task consists first of all in mastering a life that is one's own, not imposed or prescribed from without, no matter how noble its appearance may be.'[114]

It is clear from Brodsky's version of the 'Monument' that he wanted to describe in the poem that individual experience, the life that could have been lived only by him, the 'uncommon visage' of his own Muse. That was where he saw his own poetic legacy and instead of tritely (by now) measuring it against the Pyramids or the Alexandrian Column he recounted his own points of reference consistent with his stance as a poet. These points of reference were far less grandiose: prison, travels to remote regions, passing acquaintances, hard manual labour, exile. In his English translation of the poem he replaced one line in Russian; Brodsky's English line reads 'broken eggs make me grieve; the omelette, though, makes me vomit' while the Russian version had a more explicit line 'I feel solidarity only with sorrow'. It seems that in his translation of the Russian version the poet decided to avoid any overtly dramatic or, even worse, melodramatic gesture, any explicit expression of sadness, and end in the English version fully on the note of overwhelming gratitude. There was nothing, however, in either version about poetry or literary achievement. Brodsky himself understood well the discrepancy between his 'Monument' and those of his precursors. In his 'Rimskie elegii' ('Roman Elegies'),[115] a series of snapshots of Rome in August, he explicitly evoked Horace's *Exegi monumentum* in order to juxtapose to it his own:

... i v goriachei
polosti gorla kholodnym perlom
perekatyvaetsia Goratsii.
Ia ne vozdvig ukhodiashchei k tucham
kamennoi veshchi dlia ikh ostrastki.
O svoem – i o liubom – griadushchem
ia uznal u bukvy, u chernoi kraski.[116]

... and a sultry, porous
cavity of a mouth scatters around
cold pearls of Horace.
I've never built that cloud-thrusting stony
object that could explain clouds' pallor.
I have learned about my own, and any
fate, from a letter, from its black colour.[117]

This poem echoed the lines of a much earlier poem, which also gave a title to the whole cycle of poems 'Chast' Rechi' ('Part of Speech'), written in 1975-6:

Ot vsego cheloveka vam ostaetsia chast'
rechi. Chast' rechi voobshche. Chast' rechi.[118]

... What gets left of a man amounts
to a part. To his spoken part. To a part of speech.[119]

Thus it was the power of Word, in the best Mandelshtamian sense, that came before the poet. A part of speech is not a monumental legacy of an individual; rather, it is a communal future cast in ink. It was also a

188

reconfiguration of Horace's *'multaque pars mei'* ('the great part of me'), which Brodsky reduces to an act of utterance and to a precise grammatical term.

In both of these poems the lack of aggrandizement of any achievement or hope for legacy was even more explicit than in the 1980 testament-poem. Brodsky was only forty when he wrote the latter, by Western standards not exactly a man who would have to face his final hour any time soon. But for a Russian poet of the twentieth century, indeed, his life had turned out to be longer than he could have possibly expected while in his Northern exile. Brodsky would go on living sixteen more years, reaching the age of 55 before he died.

The unusual diction in this poem written on the occasion of his fortieth birthday is notable, illustrating the revolution that Brodsky brought to the Russian poetic language.[120] Words and phrases like 'klikukha' ('nickname'), 'chert znaet s kem' ('with devil-knows-whom'), 'slonialsia' ('waded'), 'zhral' ('munched') do not only belong to the realm of *unpoetische Wörter*, they belong outright to the street vernacular, akin to the word 'bliad" in 'The Bust of Tiberius'. Brodsky did what, in my opinion, very few poets if any have done in the Russian language so systematically, unabashedly and skillfuly; he introduced the language of the street, almost a *lumpen* jargon, into the *sancta sanctorum* of the language, its poetry.[121] The ability to mix two semantic levels that had rarely been combined previously stood out in a milestone poem like this one; the content (a combination of the base and the sublime) suggested a form (a combination of high and low semantic levels). The result was dizzying in its effect. It was a poem of great sorrow and nostalgia; it was also a poem of great joy that his life in fact had turned out to be longer than the poet had anticipated. At the same time this poem was an epilogue to all poetic 'Monuments' (in Russian at least) because it spoke for itself about the human and poetic achievement; to elaborate on either would be an exercise in the tautology so abhorred by Brodsky.

The theme of exile also addressed in this poem brought back the Ovidian allusion (even if unintentionally), specifically his exilic poetry. There is little doubt, as the *Letter to Horace* testified, that Brodsky admired Ovid perhaps even more than any other Roman poet, so he surely read him (in translation) carefully. While Ovid's *Tristia* were full of laments and bitterness about the poet's fate, Brodsky construed his poem in stark juxtaposition to Ovid's view of his banishment. One indicative passage in Ovid (*Tr.* I.V.45-84) offers a convenient point of comparison and deserves special consideration:

> If anyone wishes to know all my misfortunes,
> He seeks for more than the state of affairs allows.
> I have endured as many evils as there are stars that shine in the sky,
> Or as many as there are little specks that dry dust contains ...
> I have suffered many things too great to be believed or earn trust

And yet they did happen ...
If I had an unbreakable voice, lungs stronger than brass,
And many mouths with many tongues,
Not even so I could cover all my woes in words
For the subject matter surpasses my powers.
You, learned poets, write of my evils,
Instead of the Neritian leader.[122]
For I have endured more than the Neritian ...
He had a loyal crew and faithful companions;
My friends abandoned me in my flight.
He in joy and victory was seeking his fatherland ;
I have fled the land of my fathers vanquished and an exile.
My home is not Dulichium or Ithaca or Samos,
absence from which is no great punishment,
but the city that sees the whole world from her seven hills,
Rome, the abode of empire and of the gods.
He had a tough body, able to endure toil;
I have frail and slight powers;
He has always been engaged in savage warfare:
I have been used to gentler pursuits.
A god destroyed me, and nobody eased my misfortunes;
To him the warrior-goddess brought aid ...
Add to it that the largest part of his labours is fictional;
No tale is placed in my sufferings.
At last he reached the lands he sought for so long.
But I must be forever deprived of my fatherland,
unless the wounded god's anger mellows.

In the previous chapters I discussed how Pushkin and Mandelshtam 'edited' Ovid's exile. Brodsky continued the trend, though without specifically alluding to Ovid. However, just as Ovid had juxtaposed his own 'odyssey' to that of Odysseus, Brodsky contrasted his with Ovid's, and in that contrast the 'Stern Slav' of Pushkin emerged again through the shipwreck of exile.[123] For Ovid the separation from Rome had been unbearable because no other place was suitable for living; Brodsky simply stated that he 'quit' his country and that the 'bread of exile' is 'stale and warty'. Ovid had hoped that the friends who had abandoned him in his flight still wished to know about him; Brodsky without a hint of doubt acknowledged: 'those who forgot me would make a city'. Ovid had wallowed in self-pity and admitted that his gentle composition and delicate nature could not handle a trial like this; Brodsky in the best Russian tradition was full of gratitude for having been granted a long life. Ovid's only hope for happiness had depended on Augustus' mercy and permission to return; Brodsky did not even mention the possibility of a homecoming and asked for no forgiveness. Most importantly, Ovid had rendered his exile as poetic death and asked *other* poets to compose the story of his travails; Brodsky did it himself without even the use of *praeteritio*, but almost as a passionless factual account. Essentially this poem returned us to Brodsky's numerous

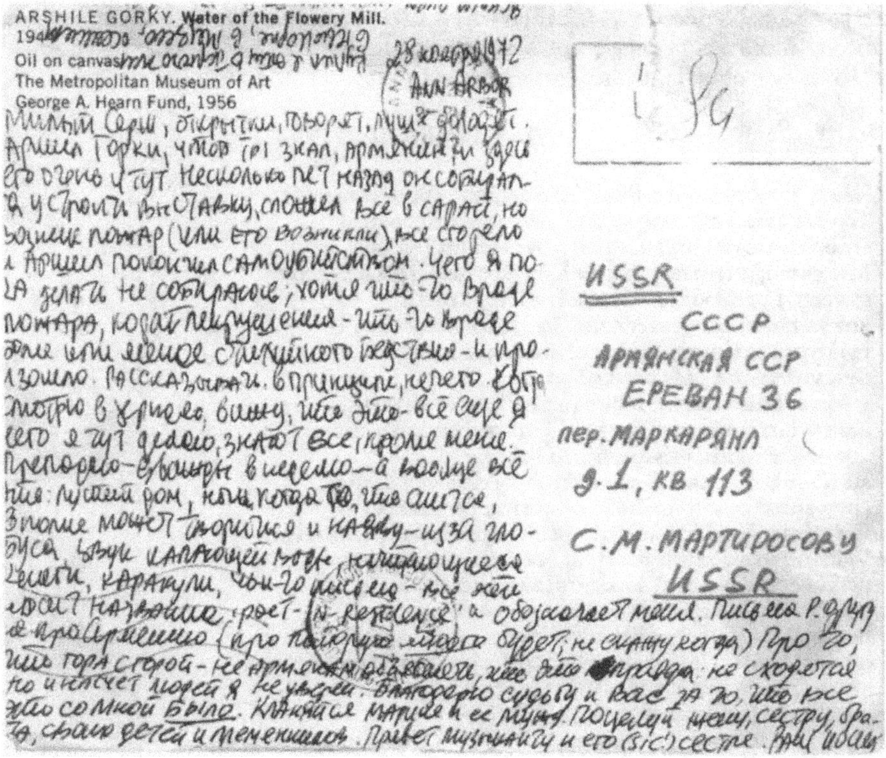
ARSHILE GORKY. Water of the Flowery Mill.
Oil on canvas
The Metropolitan Museum of Art
George A. Hearn Fund, 1956
28 ноября 1972
Ann Arbor
USSR
СССР
АРМЯНСКАЯ ССР
ЕРЕВАН 36
пер. МАРКАРЯНА
д. 1, кв 113
С.М. МАРТИРОСОВУ
USSR

Previously unpublished postcard sent by Joseph Brodsky from Ann Arbor, dated 28 November 1972. On the back he wrote: '… something like a conflagration, a shipwreck, something more or less like a natural disaster – happened to me' ('… chto-to vrode pozhara, korablekrusheniia, chto-to vrode bolee ili menee stikhiinogo bedstviia – proizoshlo'). From the author's family archive.

earlier self-identifications with Odysseus: he was in fact that very Odysseus to whom Ovid had juxtaposed himself: tough, untamed, and to some degree even joyous. In this attitude two themes – exile and contemplation of legacy – fused. There were no regrets; since traditionally for a Russian poet in exile self-pity was unseemly, his legacy must soar above the mundane vicissitudes of an individual fate.

'May 24, 1980' is both Brodsky's *Tristia* and his *Exegi monumentum*, but I believe the true and final testament-poem was written by him many years later in 1993, three years before his death which he probably intensely and soberly sensed approaching.[124] This poem, as Andrew Reynolds observed, revealed 'the ways in which Brodsky participated in his own death and his posthumous reputation'.[125] It also comes as no surprise that he chose a mythological mask to express his final farewell and to close the accounts. This poem has received relatively little attention and yet in many respects it offered a perfect closure to many of the themes in Brodsky's classical and general poetics.[126]

'Dedal v Sitsilii'

Vsiu zhizn' on chto-nibud' stroil, chto-nibud' izobretal.
To dlia kritskoi tsaritsy iskustvennuiu korovu,
chtob nastavit' roga tsariu, to – labirint (uzhe
dlia samogo tsaria), chtoby skryt' ot dosuzhikh vzorov
skvernyi priplod; to – letatel'nyi apparat,
kogda nakonets tsar' doznalsia, kto eto u nego
pri dvore tak sumel obespechit' sebia rabotoi.
Syn vo vremia poleta pogib, upav
v more, kak Faeton, tozhe nekogda prenebregshii
nastavlen'em otsa. Teper' na pribrezhnom kamne
gde-to v Sitsilii, gliadia pered soboi,
sidit glubokii starik, sposobnyi peremeshchat'sia
po vozdukhu, esli nel'zia po moriu i po sushe.
Vsiu zhizn' on chto-nibud's stroil, chto-nibud' izobretal.
Vsiu zhizn' ot etikh postroek, ot etikh izobretenii
prikhodilos' bezhat', kak budto izobreten'ia
i postroiki stremiatsia otdelat'sia ot chertezhei,
po-detski stydias' roditelei. Vidimo, eto – strakh
povtorimosti. Na pesok nabegaiut s zhurchan'em volny,
szadi sineiut zubtsy mestnykh gor – no on
eshche v molodosti izobrel pilu,
ispol'zovav vneshnee skhodstvo statiki i dvizhen'ia.
Starik nagibaetsia i, priviazav k lodyzhke
dlinnuiu nitku, chtoby ne zabludit'sia,
napravliaetsia, kriaknuv, v storonu tsarstva mertvykh.[127]

'Daedalus in Sicily'

All his life he was building something, inventing something
Now for a Cretan queen, an artificial heifer,
so as to cuckold the king. Then a labyrinth, this time for
the king himself, to hide from bewildered glances
an unbearable offspring. Or a flying contraption, when
the king figured out in the end who it was at his court
who was keeping himself so busy with new commissions.
The son on that journey perished falling into the sea.
like Phaeton, who, they say, also spurned his father's
orders. Here, in Sicily, stiff on its scorching sand,
sits a very old man, capable of transporting
himself through the air, if robbed of other means of passage.
All his life he was building something, inventing something.
All his life from those clever constructions, from those inventions
he had to flee. As though inventions
and constructions are anxious to get rid themselves of their blueprints

192

like children ashamed of their parents. Presumably, that's the fear
of replication. Waves are running onto the sand,
behind, shine the tusks of the local mountains.
Yet he had already invented when he was young, the seesaw,
using the strong resemblance between motion and stasis.
The old man bends down, ties to his brittle ankle
(so as not to get lost) a lengthy thread,
straightens up with a grunt, and heads out for Hades.[128]

It is not particularly surprising that the myth of Daedalus captured Brodsky's imagination; Bacchylides and Euripides, Vergil and Ovid, Shakespeare and Marlowe, Goethe and Swinburne: these are only a few predecessors of Brodsky for whom Daedalus had represented the figure of an artist *par excellence* whose genius became closely intertwined with personal tragedy.

Even though the literary background to the myth of Daedalus is vast and deserves a more detailed discussion than it can receive on these pages, the only ancient text to which I intend to compare Brodsky's rendition is Vergil's *ecphrasis* in Book 6 of the *Aeneid*.[129] Although it is clear already from Brodsky's early poem, 'Dido and Aeneas', that Brodsky had read Vergil's *Aeneid*, my argument in no way entails any definitive knowledge that Brodsky had these specific lines of Vergil in mind while writing his poem or that he was even mindful of Vergil's rendition of the Daedalus myth. However, upon closer reading of the poem I came to the conclusion that Brodsky's poem contained such parallels to Vergil's text that they may constitute intertextuality in a broader sense. Indeed Gian Biagio Conte emphasized the role of 'poetic memory' on the part of both author and reader as a possible intertextual discourse that can function independent of subjective intentionality.[130] I would like to replace the somewhat formalistic and narrow term intertextuality with a phrase 'literary filiation' used by Thomas Hubbard in the sense of 'the author's choice of specific precursors or precursor with whose work he stands in a special and significant relation'.[131] This concept, by Hubbard's own admission, owes much to Harold Bloom's emphasis on the importance of the creative subject and his intentionality. That intentionality does not necessarily have to be conscious, since any poet is himself or herself a compilation of the texts previously read. Poets can recall unintentionally a text of their precursors and can even 'creatively "misread"' it as a way of drawing from the 'poetic memory' while appropriating it for their individual poetic expression.[132] It is this, perhaps unintentional, allusion to Vergil's Daedalus that I would like to explore as part of Brodsky's poem-testament.

Book 6 is, briefly stated, the most perplexing book of the *Aeneid*. It contains a major *ecphrasis*, as well as the Golden Bough and the Gates of Sleep – hallmark conundrums of the *Aeneid*. Structurally, it is at once integral and separate, retrospective and proleptic. It is in effect a 'pause'

193

in the middle of the epic intended to contemplate the further meaning of Aeneas' mission. The key to this book and to the *Aeneid* as a whole is the Daedalus *ecphrasis* (*Aen.* 6.14-33), which may be regarded as the book's true core.

I am offering the Latin version of the relevant passage in a footnote since Brodsky did not read Vergil in Latin and it will not play a significant role in my discussion.[133] The following translation of Vergil's passage from the *Aeneid* serves as a point of reference for discussion of Brodsky's poem:

> Daedalus, they say, when fleeing from Minos' kingdom
> dared to entrust himself to the sky on swift wings,
> he floated through the strange journey, up toward the frozen North
> until he gently came to rest on the Chalcidian hill.
> Here he was returned to earth and he dedicated to you, Phoebus,
> his oar-like wings and built a splendid temple.
> Upon the doors he carved Androgeos' death; then the Athenians
> ordered to pay the penalty, alas! each year
> with lives of their seven sons; there stands the urn, the lots are drawn.
> Opposite, rising from the sea, the Cretan land faces this:
> here is the cruel love of the bull, Pasiphae coupled in secret
> and the mongrel offspring, the two-formed progeny,
> Minotaur, a reminder of the unspeakable love;
> here that house of toil, the inextricable maze.
> Daedalus, pitying the princess' great love
> himself unwound the treachery and the duplicitous paths of the palace.
> guiding blind steps with the thread. Icarus, you also
> would have had a large share in such work, had his grief permitted;
> twice the father tried to carve your fall in gold,
> twice the father's hands fell down.

The metapoetry of this passage is obvious. According to Michael Putnam, it is 'the only occasion in ancient literature where an artist is described as constructing his literal, which in this case is also to say his spiritual, or psychic biography'. He further interpreted it 'as a metaphor for the progress of any artist'.[134] The passage was indeed contrived as a *Bildungsroman* of the artist, yet I think that this carefully charted retrospective of self-realization was a very personal voyage. Daedalus is not Every Artist. Furthermore, he was an archetypal persecuted artist bound for exile.

Daedalus' panels within Vergil's *ecphrasis* constituted a triptych reflecting the tripartite divisions echoed throughout the *Aeneid*. Essentially, the first panel rendered crime (Androgeus' death) and punishment (the annual sacrifice of seven Athenian youths); the second, the artist's own tale of artistic complicity (the construction of the artificial bull for Pasiphae) and a subsequent restitution of his product's pernicious consequences (the artist's help to Theseus); the third, emptiness, demarcating the limitations of art's capacities suggested in the previous panel. The conclusion conveyed by the empty frame that the image of his son Icarus would have occupied precluded the success of artistic representation in accomplishing its greatest desideratum. The artistic genius became a source of inconsolable sorrow, the only relief from which would be death.

Brodsky's Daedalus was the old artist in exile. In that respect the title of the poem was significant just like the title of the previously discussed 'On the Way to Scyros'. Daedalus in Sicily, just like Theseus on Scyros, was at the end of his life's journey. According to the mythological tradition, unlike Scyros for Theseus, Sicily for Daedalus, was a safe haven.[135] Protected by the Sicanian king Cocalus and released from Minos' persecution, he continued to create additional wonderful artifacts.[136] Nevertheless, his most important 'creation' had been lost on the way to that safe haven: Icarus had perished during the journey there, and there was Brodsky's focus. Like Vergil, Brodsky listed many great artifacts of Daedalus: the artificial heifer, the Labyrinth, the wings. The 'building' and 'inventing', however, had led not to rewards or glory but to that most devastating loss – Icarus, whose death was mentioned only in passing and was accounted less a casualty of his father's genius than of filial disobedience.[137] The ability, then, to invent and to build in the safe environment in Sicily became for Daedalus not a final reward but a prolonged artistic torment: he paid the highest price for his artistic freedom. It would be trivial, perhaps, to elaborate here on all the obvious parallels with Brodsky's fate.[138] Furthermore, as Andrew Reynolds noted in his analysis of the poem, there was a conspicuous glossing of the story of Icarus through his comparison with Phaeton: 'to give someone else's son pride of place in what appears to be one's own son's narrative seems odd'.[139] Here, however, Vergil's *ecphrasis* was helpful again. Like the Vergilian Daedalus, Brodsky's artist was incapable of facing directly the artistic representation of his ineffable loss. The mythological mask assumed yet another mythological disguise: this time of Phaeton who paralleled Icarus in filial arrogance and his own father's lack of foresight, as well as in the manner of his death, falling from a flight he could not sustain. Brodsky also edited the traditional myth of Daedalus in Sicily by omitting mention of any of his impressive Sicilian inventions: a reservoir for the river Alabon, a steambath at Selinus, a fortress near Agrigentum, and a terrace for the temple of Aphrodite on Mt Eryx.[140] The Daedalus of the ancient tradition thus had not experienced artistic death, but perhaps even an artistic rebirth after the death of Icarus. So had the Vergilian Daedalus, who, despite his inability to depict Icarus, had dedicated his wings to Apollo and built a splendid temple to the god. But Brodsky's Daedalus *ran away from* not *towards* his creations. The artistic rebirth was impossible for two reasons: the loss of Icarus was one, but the other, strangely enough, was the absence of Minos. The artistic decline was precipitated by the severing of the artist's most important human attachment and by the absence of tyranny. Brodsky's Daedalus in that respect was not very different from his Odysseus, Aeneas or Theseus. Artistic as well as heroic success was

Joseph Brodsky in Erevan, Armenia with author's parents, Dr Sergei Martirosov and Samvelina Pogosova. April 1972.

fraught with and depended on the presence of suffering. For a Russian writer, even, in worldly terms, the most successful of them, this remained a constant in the early as well as the late poems.[141]

Brodsky brilliantly inverted one classical metaphor in this poem; he transformed the thread that Vergil's Daedalus, sympathetic to Ariadne's love, had once given to her into a tool for the artist's own survival. Daedalus now was in need of the magic thread that he tied to his ankle as he headed towards his own Labyrinth, Hades. 'So as not to get lost'? What was the meaning of that line? Did it mean that Daedalus was destined for immortality and that he would find his way back to the living by the sheer power of his art? Or maybe like the Icarus panel in Vergil, the image of the thread tied to Daedalus' ankle denoted the limitations of even the greatest artist to find his way around (not to mention back from) Hades. The artist by divine grace was on a par with the lowliest of the mortals when faced with artistic death. The poem's end is puzzling. One thing is certain; the reader's expectations for a last grandiose act by the great craftsman were disappointed.[142] The long Russian journey from Pushkin's poet as *vates* concluded with an old man descending into the Underworld burdened by the full knowledge of his mortality and perhaps insignificance. There would be, in Brodsky's typically irreverent manner, no words of universal import handed down to posterity. In the poet's own words, 'after the last line of a poem nothing follows except literary criticism'.[143]

Post Aetatem Nostram
A Brief Postscript and a Very Short
Introduction

Is poetry in Russia dead? Of course, not; it is thriving. In that country, where for several centuries the poetic word was the most influential of all forms of artistic expression, poetry will always stay alive. As the Russian proverb says, 'sviato mesto pusto ne byvaet' ('a holy place is never empty'). One has only to pick up a few anthologies of modern Russian literature such as *Deviat' izmerenii* (*Nine Dimensions*, 2004), *Nestolichnaia litera-tura* (*Non-Metropolitan Literature*, 2001), and *Osvobozhdennyi Uliss* (*Liberated Ulysses*, 2004), or to go to www.vavilon.ru, to see all the exuberant poetic talent in Russia.[1]

In his introduction to *Nine Dimensions*, an anthology of the newest Russian poetry, Il'ia Kukulin observed that 'in the 1990s Russian poetry had fundamentally changed' and poets had adopted their own approaches to aesthetics in poetry and completely new principles for relating to the previous tradition. Kukulin called the newly emerged generation of poets the 'generation of Babylon' not only because of the famous poetic association under the same name created in 1989 but also because of the unprecedented new mixture of forms and poetic 'languages' in current poetry.[2]

Perhaps this poetry of the new age has lost its crown of poignancy and secular martyrdom and has become, in opinion of some critics, more esoteric and isolated because poetry, thankfully, is no longer a matter of life and death. W.H. Auden's well-known aphorism, that 'poetry makes nothing happen', now rings true for Russia as well. Classical idiom has also become less popular in the poetry of the new generation. It could not have been otherwise. The map of traditional Russian versification, which ad-hered to classical forms for such a long time, is now being completely redrawn. With the opening of the borders it has also become much easier to satisfy the 'yearning for world culture'. However, Russian poetry since the 1990s has not sought to throw the previous poets 'off the ship of modernity', although it seems that the traditional cultural idioms, and the classical among them, have exhausted themselves for the time being. That is not to say that one does not occasionally encounter familiar and pre-viously oft-used classical allusions. For example, the poet Andrei Poliakov called his first collection of poems *Epistolae ex Ponto*, in which he examined his feelings of internal exile in response to Mandelstam's poetry about St Petersburg.[3] In these poems, however, Poliakov does not view a city as forever lost, but rather Russian literature, which acquires the status of his unattainable motherland preserved in his fragmented and tortured memory. In the same vein Ol'ga Grebennikova's poetry employs allusions and symbols connected with classical antiquity, as her lyrical hero tries to isolate herself from mundane modernity and enter the realm of culture that does not belong to any particular time or place.[4] The poetry of Dem'ian Kudriavtsev is also full of classical metaphors and he does not shun even the previously exhausted ones, such as in his poem 'Odysseus'.[5] Konstantin Uvarov returns in his poem 'The Monologue of the Trojan Horse' to the theme of Helen and Troy.[6] Polina Barskova's lyrics contain beautiful vignettes and musings on classical themes.[7] The sustained validity of the classical idiom for Russian poetry is also confirmed in the title of an anthology of Russian poets living outside Russia, *Liberated Ulysses*. In this anthology I would like especially to single out Grigorii Starikovskii whose poetics are informed by his training as a classical scholar. These are only a few examples of the continuing significance of the classical tradition among the current generation of Russian poets.

I have tried to show in the preceding pages the short but eventful path travelled by the classics in Russia from the classicism of the eighteenth century into the poetry of the twentieth century. Historical and cultural events contributed to many versions of classical idiom in Russian poetry. It seems to me that another new wave of classical reception may be rising in Russian poetry, invigorated by innovative twists and unexpected dimensions – and that new wave will someday require a study of its own.

Notes

Introduction

1. Brodsky (1986) 38.
2. Bethea (1998) 3.
3. Cited in Bethea (1998) 3.
4. See Serman (1992) 45.
5. For more detailed discussion on dangers of being a poet in Russia see Donald Loewen's recent book (2008), especially the introduction.
6. Hollander (1997) 62.
7. Loseff (1984) ix.
8. Lincoln (2000) 3.
9. Pumpianskii (1982) 303; translated by Kahn (1993) 747.
10. Cited in Russian in Esalnek (2002) 231.

1. 'Russian Antiquity'

1. Translated in Davidson (1989) 11.
2. Cited in Vitale (1999) 94.
3. See Hardwick (2003) 2.
4. Of course, as Budelmann and Haubold (2008) recently pointed out, it is hard to draw a decisive distinction between 'tradition' and 'reception' as they often tend to overlap. Although there are general points to be made about the difference between the two, the terms are most effective 'when they are tailored from case to case' (14).
5. Even in the recent *Blackwell Companion to Classical Receptions* (see Hardwick and Stray (2008)) Russia was not mentioned at all, not even in the concluding article by James I. Porter (469-81), who explored possible future prospects of reception studies. While he acknowledged that in reception studies connected with intellectual history 'German and Anglo-American perspectives have tended to predominate at the expense of other European and non-European perspectives', he suggested expanding the study of reception into Israel, China, South Africa, Latin and South America and India. Russia, however, would also fit nicely into this list since reception studies there offer a combination of European and non-European influences.
6. Okenfuss (1995).
7. Axer and Tomaszuk (2007) 154.
8. Axer and Tomaszuk (2007) 132.
9. Asoian and Malafeev (2000) 246: 'utverzhdenie kul'tury pri bespiamiatstve o ee smysle'.
10. Axer and Tomaszuk (2007) 132.
11. Martindale (2006) 11.
12. Some preliminary differences between the study of classics in Western

Europe and in Russia were outlined by Zelinskii as early as 1909. See Zelinskii (1909) 14-15.

13. Theoretically Greek could have been an option because of the Russian connection to the Byzantines. For the Byzantine influence on the Kievan Rus' and medieval Russian culture see Frolov (1999) 9-29.

14. Terras (1966) 254.

15. See Hardwick (2003) 9-10 for a detailed explanation of these terms as they are currently used in reception studies.

16. Hardwick (2003) 11.

17. It has to be pointed out that the practitioners of Russian classicism never used that term. It came into use at the beginning of the nineteenth century 'to fence off the new romantic movement from the influences of the previous century'. See Jones (1976) 100.

18. Letter (in French) to Chaadaev dated 19 October 1836 in Pushkin (1906-11) 3: 388. Translated in Figes (2002) 368.

19. Raeff (1999) 162, 164.

20. Rzhevsky (1998) 5.

21. Raeff (1999) 165.

22. See Riha (1969) 2: 307-8.

23. Riha (1969) 2: 313.

24. Riha (1969) 2: 313-14.

25. Shils (1982) 93-109; see also Kalb (2008) 9. I am thankful to Judith Kalb for forwarding to me an advance copy of her book.

26. Kalb (2008) 9.

27. Boym (2001) 17.

28. Bethea (2002) 169.

29. See Wes (1992).

30. Kloszowski (2004).

31. Axer and Tomaszuk (2007) 139.

32. Bethea (2002) 171.

33. Worth (1998) 20.

34. See Davidson (2007) 2, who observed that in the Russian cultural tradition antiquity was always perceived through the religious tradition connected with the Byzantine legacy in Russia.

35. In the eighteenth century the poet Sumarokov shifted the focus to St Petersburg by naming it 'the Rome of the North' so that St Petersburg, not Moscow, would be seen as the *new* Rome. See Baehr (1991) 160. On the connection between the Third Rome doctrine and the ideology of Russian absolute monarchy, see Wolf (1960).

36. Cited in Zernov (1978) 49. For a further analysis of the 'Third Rome' doctrine and its subsequent imperial subtext see Kalb (2008) 15-18.

37. Frolov (1999) 9-29.

38. Knabe (2000) 23-48, 52; Likhachev (1973a) 173-4.

39. Kalb (2008) 16.

40. Milner-Gulland (1997) 140.

41. Uspensky (1984) 376.

42. For the lineage and story of Prus see Wortman (1995) 1: 26. It was only later during the rule of tsar Alexander that panhellenism would function in Russian political thought and imperial propaganda. See Axer and Tomaszuk (2007) 150.

43. Wortman (1995) vol. 1: 26; see also Kalb (2008) 11.

44. See Knabe (2000) 103.

45. Okenfuss (1995) 59. See also Knabe (2000) 103.

46. Hughes (1998) 300.

47. Hughes (1998) 307.

48. Hughes (1998) 299, aptly pointed out that Peter viewed education as a part of the preparation for state service, which Peter saw as the highest calling for a citizen.

49. For more on the origins of publishing and printing in Russia see Marker (1985).

50. Sivkov (1917) 56; see also Hughes (1998) 326.

51. Students of Russian classicism owe a debt to the bibliographies of P.N. Cherniaev (1904-5) and V. Lebedev (1878). For a more modern bibliography see Sviiasov (1988).

52. Hardwick (2000) 10.

53. See Okenfuss (1995) 89.

54. Ibid. 92.

55. Ibid. 93.

56. This critical group of five ancient authors who contributed to 'modern paganism' was emphasized by Peter Gay (1966-9) in the first volume of his influential *Enlightenment*. In 1761 a translation of Cicero's *De Officiis* was published by the Academy of Sciences.

57. As Okenfuss (1995) 113 pointed out, this is an important distinction. See also a detailed account of Feofan Prokopovich's activity in Wes (1992) 27-31.

58. During the years of my study at Moscow University (1985-90) the *Life of Atticus* still remained one of the main texts for Latin instruction.

59. Kantemir will be discussed in more detail in the following chapter.

60. See Okenfuss (1995) 151. The first translation of Homer was undertaken earlier by K.A. Kondratovich (1703-1788), but he translated both the *Iliad* and the *Odyssey* from a Latin version. His translations did not have any influence on the subsequent ones. See Frolov (1999) 102-3.

61. For further discussion of translators' activities during Catherine's time and beyond see Frolov (1999) 119-24.

62. Kalb (2008) 11.

63. Baehr (1991) 50.

64. For the history of Greek colonization of the Black Sea see Tsetkhladze (1994, repr. 2004) 111-36. Tsekhladze also offered an extensive bibliography on excavations in the Black Sea region: 127. The area is still used as the fieldwork training ground for the students at MGU (Moscow State University). I was sent there during the course of my study of classical philology in 1988 for an archaeological expedition. At that time the site was prohibited to tourism and access required special governmental permission because of its proximity to the naval military base of Sevastopol'. Since then many significant archaeological discoveries have been made in the region. See also Samaritaki (2004).

65. In Petersburg, the extravagant Tauride Palace – backed by the vast Tauride gardens – was built for Potemkin at the staggering cost of 400,000 gold rubles. For a chronological overview of the exploration of the newly acquired territories see Frolov (1999) 126-37.

66. For Armenia's connections with the classical literary heritage see Christesen, Martirosova-Torlone (2007).

67. For a more detailed discussion of the translations that appeared during the religious revival see Okenfuss (1995) 216-23.

68. Okenfuss (1995) 233.

69. For more discussion of Petrov's translation see Frolov (1999) 104-5 who mentioned an acerbic statement by a poet V.I. Maikov that Petrov made Vergil 'stutter'. See also Kahn (1993) 752-5, who emphasized Petrov's focus on empress-worship reflected in the translation. There are two more accepted translations of the *Aeneid*: one by a poet, Afanasii Fet (1820-1892), and another by a Russian Symbolist poet, Valerii Briusov (1873-1924), in collaboration with Sergei Solov'ev (the nephew of the famous philosopher Vladimir Solov'ev). The seven books of the latter were published only nine years after Briusov's death and provoked much discussion about its merits and 'literalism'. See Gasparov (1971). Poet and translator Sergei Shervinskii (1892-1991) translated the *Eclogues* and the *Georgics*. For further discussion of Russian translations of the *Aeneid* see Petrovskii (1966).

70. Mechanical memorization and drilling of Greek and Latin paradigms remained a staple of classical education as late as the 1990s when I was undergoing my classical training at MGU (Moscow State University). It produced classicists completely versed in the intricacies of the morphology and syntax of classical languages but often unable to explain the chronology of ancient literature or the significance of certain historical events. On the emphasis on the ancient languages in the curriculum of Moscow University, see Pozdeeva (1962).

71. Pushkin (1949) 13.

72. Hart (2002) 88.

73. Wes (1992) 41.

74. Knabe (2000) 109.

2. From Russian Classicism to Alexander Pushkin

1. Cited and translated by Wachtel (1998) 182.

2. Wachtel (1998) 181.

3. According to Stokmar (1952) 45 the term 'syllabo-tonic' was invented by a Russian critic N. Nadezhdin in the nineteenth century. Other scholars have used different terms such as 'metro-tonic' or 'syllabo-accentual' system. See Silbajoris (1968) 137n.1; B. Gasparov (1994) 249-51.

4. See Knabe (2000) 19-20. See also Savel'eva (1980) 5 and Voitekhovich (2007) 12.

5. See Likhachev (1973b).

6. Hart (2002) 87.

7. The term 'classicism' came into use only later, during the war of the Romantics against eighteenth-century literary traditions. See Serman (1992) 63.

8. For a general chronological survey of Russian systems of versification see Gasparov (1997) 40-53.

9. See Redston (1976) 7-19.

10. Kantemir, being aware of Russian readers' unfamiliarity with these authors, supplied ample philological and historical commentary for his translations, especially Horace's. See Frolov (1999) 79.

11. The name Khariton Makentin is an anagram of Antiokh Kantemir.

12. The text of the whole 'Letter of Khariton Makentin' is cited and translated in Silbajoris (1968) 81-2.

13. The text of the whole poem can be found in Trediakovskii, Lomonosov, Sumarokov (1935) 109-252. A lengthy history of the Russian hexameter can be found in Burgi (1954). See also B. Gasparov (1994) 254-5 and Wachtel (1998) 172, who noted that the specific preoccupation of Russian poets with the hexameter out of all the ancient metres has two explanations: 'the Russian hexameter, in keeping

with its Greek origins, was reserved for epic verse and other large poetic forms. The second point concerns the specifically Russian realization of the hexameter, which is significant insofar as the hexameter line provided the first half of the elegiac distich.' In that Russian prosody seems to have followed the metre of Latin elegy.

14. Burgi (1954) 40-60; see also Frolov (1999) 89.

15. Silbajoris (1968) 40.

16. On a detailed discussion of Trediakovskii's teachings on Russian metre see Gasparov (2000) 35-6.

17. Silbajoris (1968) 40.

18. Wes (1992) 33.

19. See Gasparov (2000) 38.

20. On the examples of Lomonosov's experimentation with Russian versification see Gasparov (2000) 37-8.

21. See Silbajoris (1968) 165n.2.

22. Frolov (1999) 94-6 discussed the translations from Anacreon and Horace as eloquent examples of Lomonosov's poetic talent.

23. See Billington (1970) 189.

24. Kelly (2001) 36.

25. See Morozov's introduction to Lomonosov (1957) iii.

26. For detailed discussion see Borovskii (1960) vol. 4: 212.

27. Lomonosov (1957) 3-4.

28. Lomonosov (1957) 5-6.

29. Lomonosov (1957) 7.

30. Lomonosov (1957) 17.

31. Lomonosov (1957) 22.

32. See *The Oxford Classical Dictionary* (1970) [henceforth *OCD*] s.v. Curtius, 303.

33. Lomonosov (1957) 201-10.

34. Lomonosov (1957) 206, l. 213.

35. Lomonosov (1957) 206, ll. 225-30.

36. Lomonosov (1957) 206, ll. 245-54.

37. Lomonosov (1959) 665.

38. See Knabe (2000) 100.

39. Kahn (1993) 748.

40. B. Gasparov (1994) argued that post-Petrine Russia viewed itself as a direct heir and successor of Greece. This view was among other things founded on a perception of Church Slavonic as a Greek language 'transplanted' to Slavic soil. Gasparov suggested that this idea played an important role in Lomonosov's reform of the Russian stylistic system and prosody since he tried to implement Greek heroic diction in Russian poetry. However, Lomonosov's own experimentation with this diction in his *Peter the Great* suggests to me more indebtedness to Vergil than to Homer.

41. Kahn (1993) 750.

42. Kahn (1993) 751.

43. Lomonosov, however, did write a satire on Trediakovskii with whom he had several disagreements. On polemics between the poets of Russian classicism see Berkov's introduction to Trediakovskii, Lomonosov, Sumarokov (1935).

44. On the differentiation of 'poetic style' in Lomonosov see Berkov in Trediakovskii, Lomonosov, Sumarokov (1935) 40-2.

45. Trediakovksii, Lomonosov, Sumarokov (1935) 45.

46. Serman (1992) 62.
47. See Berkov (1953) 24.
48. See Serman (1992) 64.
49. See Mirsky (1958): 47, 53.
50. See 'Anacreontic Ode to E.V. Kheras'kova' in Trediakovskii, Lomonosov, Sumarokov (1935) 199, ll. 11-12.
51. For a detailed analysis of the *Epistle* in the context of French and Russian classicism see Lang (1948).
52. Trediakovskii, Lomonosov, Sumarokov (1935) 200.
53. Gukovskii (1935) 48.
54. Gukovskii (1935) 43.
55. Serman (1992) 87.
56. Derzhavin (1958) 321.
57. See especially 'Anakreonovo udovol'stvie' ('Anacreon's Pleasure') and the playful 'Anakreon u pechi' ('Anacreon Near the Stove') in Derzhavin (1958) 405 and 331 respectively. For imitations of Sappho's poem 31 (*'Phainetai moi kênos isos theoisin ...'* – 'This man seems to me similar to the gods ...') see Derzhavin's poems 'Safo' ('Sappho') 348 and 'Nevesta' ('Bride') 309.
58. Derzhavin (1958) 263.
59. Derzhavin's 'Pamiatnik' is discussed in more detail below as a precursor of Pushkin's famous poem known by the same title.
60. Averintsev (1996) 128.
61. Pushkin expressed two opinions about Derzhavin: deeply respectful and rather scathing. However, even in the latter he acknowledged Derzhavin's genius. See Pushkin's letter to Anton Del'vig dated June 1825 published by Annenkov in 1855: 'After you left I reread all of Derzhavin, and here is my final opinion. This crank knew neither Russian grammar nor the spirit of the Russian language ... he had no idea about syllables or harmony – or even rules of versification. That is why he has to infuriate any discriminating ear ... So what is it about him? His thoughts, his visions, his movements are truly poetic; while reading him, one is left with an impression that it is a horrible free translation of some wonderful original. I swear, that genius thought in Tartar and did not care to learn Russian grammar.' Cited in Russian in Kucherov's introduction to Derzhavin (1958) liii-liv. For more on Pushkin's relationship to Derzhavin see Bethea (1999b).
62. Pushkin wrote these famous lines on the occasion: 'The old man Derzhavin noticed and blessed us on the way to his grave' ('Starik Derzhavin nas zametil, i v grob skhodia blagoslovil'). Lotman (1981) 29-30 warned the reader not to mythologize that encounter with Derzhavin, admitting, however, that 'for Pushkin himself this was one of the most important events in his life. He felt like a page initiated into knighthood.'
63. Bethea (1999b) 59.
64. Cited and translated in Bethea (1999b) 59 from a letter of October 1986 (Tartu, Estonia).
65. Davie (1964) 7.
66. Cited in Kelly (2001) 39.
67. Dostoevskii in the speech given on 8 June 1880 at the meeting of the Society of Lovers of Russian Letters (Obshchestvo Liubitelei Russkoi Slovesnosti).
68. See Vitale (1999) 154.
69. Bethea (2002) 178.
70. Pushkin (1949) 362.
71. For more on Olenin and his role in Russian interest in the 'classics', see Wes (1992) 128-35.

72. See Frolov (1999) 116.

73. We have seen that Peter Ekimov preceded Gnedich as a translator of the *Iliad* but it was E.I. Kostrov whose translation of the first six books of the *Iliad* in alexandrine verse had more influence on Gnedich's 'high' style and the elegance of his prosody. See Frolov (1999) 103-4.

74. Pushkin (1949) 163, 'To a Translation of the *Iliad*' ('K perevodu Iliady').

75. Translated by Wachtel (1998) 171.

76. I want to thank Michael Wachtel for pointing this out to me.

77. See Pushkin (1949) 83 and 729.

78. Pushkin (1949) 166.

79. Tibullus was also translated into Russian by Dmitriev and De'lvig.

80. Zhukovskii's *Odyssey* is not as precise or as elegant as Gnedich's *Iliad*. Zhukovskii did not know ancient Greek and was translating from the line-by-line German rendition of the Homeric text. See Frolov (1999) 124.

81. Cherniaev (1898) 1-9. One occasion when Pushkin found Latin helpful was after he had written a poem 'On the Convalescence of Lucullus' and tricked the censor by passing the poem off as 'adapted from Latin.' The poem brutally attacked Minister Uvarov's greedy designs on the riches of the mortally ill and spectacularly wealthy Count Sheremetev. Sheremetev's miraculous recovery prompted Pushkin's merciless mockery of Uvarov, which was never forgiven.

82. Cited in Russian in Bukalov (2004) 128; this report was dated 15 March 1812.

83. Nabokov (1981) vol. 2: 23; see also Wes (1992) 157.

84. In 1817 Koshanskii published a textbook entitled *A Manual of Ancient Classical Letters, Containing Archaeology, a Survey of Classical Authors, Mythology and Greek and Roman Antiquities* (*Ruchnaia kniga drevnei klassicheskoi slovesnosti, soderzhashchaia arkheologiiu, obozrenie klassicheskikh avtorov, mifologiiu i drevnosti grecheskie i rimskie*). Before the publication of the book he was already using it for teaching at the Lycée.

85. Batiushkov's influence manifested itself already in such early poems as 'Vospominaniia v Tsarskom Sele' ('Recollections in Tsarskoe Selo', 1815), the form and diction of which he borrowed from Batiushkov's 'Na razvalinakh zamka v Shvetsii' ('On the Ruins of a Castle in Sweden', 1814). See Bethea (1999b) 63. That influence is also apparent in the epicurean tone of poems 'K Iur'evu' ('To Iur'ev', 1818), and 'K Krivtsovu' ('To Krivtsov', 1819). See Pushkin (1949) 79 and 69 respectively.

86. 'Parni Rossiiskii' in the poem 'Batiushkovu' ('To Batiushkov'). Pushkin (1949) 28.

87. Tomashevskii (1990) 183.

88. See Gasparov (1986) 24.

89. Bowersock (1999) 135.

90. I want to thank Glen Bowersock for clarifying his opinion to me through personal correspondence.

91. Pushkin (1949) 171.

92. The same tendency can be seen in his other attempts at translation from Anacreon and Horace. For more details see Frolov (1999) 118.

93. Bukalov (2004) 132 also cited an excerpt from Pushkin's 'Refutation of Criticism' in response to the reviews of *Evgenii Onegin*. There Pushkin stated: '... I have not opened a single Latin book since I left the Lycée and I have completely forgotten Latin. Life is short; there is no time to reread. Wonderful books are crowding me, and in our days nobody writes in Latin'. Faibisovich (1977) in his

analysis of the poem rightly emphasized that, despite the poetic liberties that Pushkin has taken with the Catullan text, the poem was crucial for the 'discovery' of Catullus by the Russian readers.

94. For more examples see Iakubovich (1941) 95.

95. A draft of *Evgenii Onegin*. Cited in Iakubovich (1941) 95.

96. See Wes (1992) 154; see also Liubomudrov (1901) 8-9.

97. Pushkin (1949) 312.

98. Binyon (2002) 34.

99. Another biographical fact might have contributed to Pushkin's deepened interest in antiquity; while visiting his friends in Gurzuf, Pushkin was introduced to a French writer, André Chenier, whom Pushkin in his 'Zametki pri chtenii knig' ('Notes upon reading books', 1825) called a poet 'utterly imbued by antiquity'. See Liubomudrov (1901) 22.

100. The importance of the addressee is obvious since Pushkin recognized Gnedich as an authority on classical antiquity. See B. Gasparov (1985) 130.

101. Pushkin (1949) 83.

102. See Syme (1978) 219-22, who gave several compelling conjectures about Ovid's *'carmen et error'* ('a poem and a mistake') and his possible involvement in Julia's scandalous adultery with Decimus Junius Silenus. See also Conte (1994) 340.

103. Pushkin (1949) 262. For the detailed analysis of sources of the legend about Ovid in the 'Gypsies' see Dvoichenko-Markova (1966).

104. Among all Roman poets Pushkin did try to familiarize himself to an extent with Ovid in Latin. He quoted Ovid in the original several times in his letters to friends. For instance, in another letter to Gnedich, dated 20 April 1822, he accompanied 'The Prisoner of Caucasus' with a quotation from Ovid's *Tristia* 1.1.1-2: *'Parve, nec invideo, sine me liber, ibis in urbem, Heu mihi! quo domino non licet ire tuo'* ('I envy not that you will go, my little book, without me to the city, (alas, me!), where it is not permitted for your master to go').

105. Nemirovskaia (1987) 134-5. See also Dvoichenko-Markova (1966) 322 on the possible contradictory sources of Pushkin's knowledge about Ovid's exile. For more on Ovid's exile see Conte (1994) 340 and Williams (1994).

106. See B. Gasparov (1985) 126.

107. The whole text of the poem can be found in Pushkin (1949) 90.

108. Sandler (1989) 46. Her study contains a detailed analysis of this poem interpreted in the context of Pushkin's exilic poetry as a whole.

109. Sandler (1989) 49.

110. Several scholars have noted that Ovid was rather unfair in his depiction of Tomi, an old and quite cultured Greek colony. See Williams (1994) and Miller (2004) 212-13. As the fifth chapter of this study demonstrates, Osip Mandelshtam repeated Pushkin's description of the Ovidian exilic landscape as a joyous locale.

111. See Pushkin (1947-9) vol. 2, part 1 (1947): 221, different versions cited in vol. 2 (1949), part 2: 720-7, commentary on different variants: 1105.

112. Pushkin's fascination with Ovid went beyond the exilic poetry and manifested itself in poems such as 'Echo', which can be seen as an important re-articulation of the Ovidian story in the *Metamorphoses* long before the interest of the Symbolists in that theme. This poem, like 'To Ovid', was also concerned with the significance of poetic voice and immortality. See Barta (2000) 7.

113. In 1815, at the age of sixteen, Pushkin wrote a poem, 'To Licinius', which has an explicitly political thrust and in which he with youthful passion proclaimed: 'I am a Roman in my heart. Freedom seethes in my breast.' See Pushkin (1949) 27.

114. Pushkin (1949) 135.

115. See Wes (1992) 168 n.62.

116. Pushkin borrowed the geographic boundaries of his poetic fame instead from another of Derzhavin's poems, 'Swan', in which Derzhavin listed Slavs, Huns and Scythians as future recipients of his poetic legacy.

117. Ode 'To Felitsa' ('K Felitse') was Derzhavin's 1782 poem written in praise of the Empress Catherine II.

118. Pushkin (1949) 201.

119. Williams (1968) 368.

120. Jakobson (1975) 29 noted that Pushkin might have parodied here the inscriptional verses of the eighteenth-century poet V.G. Ruban, 'K Pamiatniku Petra Velikogo' ('To the Statue of Peter the Great'). The base of the statue which was made from a rock brought as one piece (*nerukotvornaia gora*) to St Petersburg to support Falconet's famous horseman in the style of the equestrian statue of Marcus Aurelius.

121. Kelly (2001) 12.

122. Jakobson (1975). Among other poems, he also discussed Pushkin's 'sculptural myths' of the destructive statues in *The Bronze Horseman* and *The Stone Guest*. The connections between Pushkin's *Bronze Horseman* and Vergil's *Aeneid* have been convincingly analyzed by Rudich (2002a) and will not be reiterated in this study.

123. 'Alexandriiskii Stolp' can of course signify the Pharos, the lighthouse of Alexandria, as well as Alexander's Column on Palace Square. On the possible meanings see Proskurin (1999) 275-82.

124. Jakobson (1975) 27.

125. Jakobson (1975) 29.

126. The third stanza of Pushkin's poem might be an evocation of another ode of Horace, 2.20.17-20, in which Horace also talks about the vast geography of the Roman Empire and the remote people that will learn his poetry.

127. Pushkin's aversion to crowned heads is also seen in two of his self-portraits. See Alekseev (1967).

128. Pushkin never believed the rumours that his wife was not loyal to him. He was annoyed by the rude and arrogant behaviour of D'Anthès but he knew (correctly, as it turns out, based on the letters discovered by Serena Vitale (1999)) that she was not involved with him. For a detailed account of the whole issue see Binyon (2002) 474-540. See also Feinstein (1998) 232-65.

129. Kelly (2001) 13.

130. Fet's translations of Vergil, Ovid and Juvenal into Russian are read to this day, especially his translation of the *Aeneid*. Tiutchev became important for the poetics of Russian Symbolism discussed in the next chapter. See Gudzii (1930).

131. Freeborne (1989) 248.

3. *Poetae Docti* and their Discontents

1. Mandelshtam (1974) 131.

2. Even before Otsup's essay, two writers used the ancient metallurgical allegory in relation to the history of Russian poetry: Vladimir Piast (1886-1940) and V. Ivanov-Razumnik (1878-1946). See Ronen (2000) 88-96.

3. See Ronen (2000) 37-9.

4. Otsup (1933) 176. Ronen (2000) 86.

5. See Otsup (1933) 175.

6. A detailed discussion of the term 'the "Silver Age" of Russian poetry' remains beyond the scope of this study and can be found in Ronen (2000). He also offered a detailed analysis of Otsup's contradictory and confusing understanding of the term.

7. Erlich (1964) 10.

8. The expression comes from the title of Roman Jakobson's famous essay 'On the Generation that Squandered its Poets' ('O pokolenii ratsrativshem svoikh poetov').

9. Averintsev (2001) 36. Gasparov (1975) 543-8 in his afterword to the fifth volume of Briusov's works (1973-5) analyzed the evolution of Briusov's interest in antiquity from the early works of the 1890s, which lacked historicism, to the works of the 1910s, which showed more attention to historical detail (although there were also some historical inconsistencies in the latter). Briusov's main focus was Rome and he carefully studied the primary sources and scholarship before writing his two historical novels *Altar' Pobedy* (*Altar of Victory*) and *Iupiter Poverzhennyi* (*Jupiter Overthrown*). Briusov himself admitted that his knowledge of Greek is not sufficient to read the authors. He also was more reliant on popular rather than advanced scholarship but, as far as classical antiquity is concerned, he had a great impact on the Russian literary scene (Gasparov 1995, 10). It can be argued that Briusov's lesser erudition and reliance on popular books made his rendition of classical themes more accessible and appealing to a larger audience than those of the poet-scholars. There is a prevalence of Roman themes in Briusov's early work and by his own admission he found Latin the best medium to express his thoughts although 'not his feelings' (see Frajlich 2007, 63). For a detailed discussion of Briusov's 'Roman novels' see Kalb (2008) 76-105. Briusov's work as a translator of Vergil and Ausonius and his 'antiquity', especially Roman, deserve a separate study that is beyond the scope and focus of this chapter.

10. For more details on Zelinskii's activity as a classical scholar see Frolov (1999) 281-8.

11. A good source for the state of classical studies in the first half of the twentieth century can be found in the letters between Olga Freidenberg and Boris Pasternak in Mossman (1982). See also Freidenberg's (1991) memoirs about her university years. For comprehensive account of Freidenberg's classical education see Perlina (2002) 45-88. The most thorough overview of the state and direction of classical studies in Russia before and after 1917 is given in Frolov (1999) 175-425.

12. On the history and nature of classical education at Moscow University see Torlone (2003b).

13. See Kalb's (2008) 25-33 discussion on the subject.

14. Annenskii, as the notes in his diary indicate, was very much astounded and enraptured by Italy and especially Rome during his travels there in 1890. See Setchkarev (1963) 16-23. These emotions were, surprisingly, not reflected in Annenskii's poetry.

15. I discuss Ivanov's tragedies first because his adherence to the Aeschylean model of tragedy provides a point of comparison for interpretation of Annenskii's dramas influenced by Euripides.

16. In his introduction to Annenskii's translations of Euripides, Mikhail Gasparov (Annenskii (2007) 13) observed that for the Symbolists 'he was a belated discoverer of their own discoveries' and that Briusov and Blok in their reviews of Annenskii's first poetic collection condescendingly praised him as a young novice poet not knowing that Annenskii was older than both of them. See also Setchkarev (1963) 31.

17. Punin (1914) 48. Scholars have begun to examine Annenskii's poetic legacy

only in approximately the past four decades. For more on the poet's life and work see Setchkarev (1963), and Fedorov (1984).

18. Fidler (1911) 172.

19. For a recent edition of Annenskii's translations of Euripides with a commentary by Vladimir Gitin see Annenskii (2007). Annenskii's style as a translator has still received very little attention although it changed significantly from his translation of the *Bacchae* (published in 1894) to that of the *Medea* (published in 1903). The last tragedy of Euripides translated by Annenskii was *Iphigenia in Tauris* (*Ifigeniia-zhritsa*), which was not published until 1921. For more on these translations see Gitin's commentary in Annenskii (2007) 359-92.

20. Cited in the introductory article by Fedorov to Annenskii (1990) 13 from Gollerbakh (1927). Annenskii's career and contribution as a teacher of classics have received very little attention. His lectures on the history of the ancient drama have been published only relatively recently. See Annenskii (2003).

21. Gasparov (2001) 373.

22. *De Arte Poetica* 1460b33-4.

23. For example, in Annenskii's translation of *Alcestis* the Greek text has 'you touched my soul and my thoughts', which Annenskii rendered as 'with the bow of anguish you played on my heart and my thoughts'. Gasparov (Annenskii 2007, 11) observed: 'What especially irritated Annenskii's classicist colleagues is not merely the fact that the Greeks did not have violins or bows but that Annenskii was very well aware about it'.

24. See Shelogurova (1988) 107 who noted that in all of Annenskii's lyric poetry there is only one explicit mythological allusion.

25. The title is also a reference to Mikhail Lermontov's 'Angel'.

26. Khodasevich (1922) 123.

27. Pollak (1999) 148.

28. Pollak (1999) 151.

29. The original poems were first collected in 1901 under the sombre title 'From Polyphemus' Cave'. See Gasparov's foreword to Annenskii (2007) 11.

30. Cited in Pollak (1999) 150.

31. Setchkarev (1963) 55.

32. See Gasparov's foreword in Annenskii (2007) 13.

33. In Asoian and Malafeev (2000) 250: 'Zaniatiia klassicheskoi filologiei byli ne prosto obucheniem, no, sverkh togo, sposobom peresozdat' zhizn''. Nikolai Bakhtin studied with Zelinskii along with his brother Mikhail Bakhtin.

34. See Serman (1986) 191-208, esp. 191.

35. Averintsev (2001) 136. For a survey of Solov'ev's works and philosophical views see Connolly (1992) 382-6. Solov'ev himself viewed with scepticism the first generation of Russian Symbolists and even parodied Briusov and his ilk. However, as Wachtel (July 2008) observed in his essay 'Vladimir Solov'ev on Symbolism and Decadence', Solov'ev's views on poetry changed considerably in the years between 1895 and 1899 and he came to re-evaluate Symbolism. While Solov'ev never accepted Briusov's poetry, he did come to accept the Symbolists, especially Ivanov, and he praised the latter's poetry effusively. I would like to thank Michael Wachtel for sharing this essay with me before its publication.

36. Cited in Davidson (1989) 7. For more on Mandelshtam's relationship with Ivanov, see Taranovsky (1976) 83-4 and recently Lekmanov and Glukhova (2006).

37. On 13 August 1909, while travelling abroad, Mandelshtam sent a letter to Ivanov in which he also stated with apparent admiration: 'You are the most incomprehensible, obscure, in the everyday sense of the word, poet of our time ...'

(cited in Russian in Lekmanov and Glukhova 2006, 174). This evaluation of Ivanov's poetry by Mandelshtam certainly cannot be applied to Ivanov's whole poetic corpus. His poetry changed considerably over time as he experimented with many poetic forms and themes. That point has also been demonstrated well in Robert Bird's recent book (2006).

38. I would like to thank Pamela Davidson for pointing this out to me.

39. Wachtel (1994a) 360 has convincingly demonstrated that Otto Hirschfeld was considerably more involved than Mommsen in Ivanov's academic career since Hirschfeld was in charge of the progress of Ivanov's dissertation thesis. Later Ivanov downplayed Hirschfeld's role and exaggerated his own closeness to Mommsen whom he admired immensely.

40. The dissertation was entitled *De societatibus vectigalium publicorum populi Romani (On the Tax-Farming Companies of the Roman People)*. It was published in 1910 in Latin in Moscow and reprinted in 1972. Mikhail Rostovtsev encouraged Ivanov to pursue the publication. An important source for understanding Ivanov's interest in Roman history is his correspondence with the medieval historian I.M. Grevs. See Bongard-Levin, Kotrelev, Liapustina (2006). For more details on Grevs' scholarship see Frolov (1999) 337-49.

41. For more detailed discussion of Ivanov's work in Germany see Rudich (1986) 276-7. Rudich also suggested (277) that the early work of Mikhail Rostovtsev was greatly inspired by Ivanov's research on Roman history. On Mommsen's reaction to Ivanov's thesis see Wachtel (1994a) 358.

42. Davidson (2006) 8.

43. Rudich (1986) 278.

44. See Ivanov (1971-9) 3: 646-9 n.3, 862 and n.2, 395, and 768. For further discussion of Ivanov's 'mystical initiation' see Wachtel (1994b) 151-66.

45. Ivanov (1971-9) 2: 286-7, 711-13. See Frajlich (2007) 119 n.14. Ivanov also corresponded in Latin with Karl Krumbacher, the famous German expert in Byzantine studies. The letters display Ivanov's impressive ease with the language. See Wachtel (1992).

46. See Davidson (2006) 59; for the text of the distichs, see ibid., 82.

47. Ivanov (1971-9) 2: 21 in 'Avtobiograficheskoe pis'mo' ('Autobiographical letter').

48. Rudich (1986) 279. Ivanov's major work on Dionysus is *Dionysus and Predionysanism (Dionis i pradionisiistvo)*. See Ivanov (1923).

49. See Westbroek (2007) 189.

50. These parallels can be seen, for example, in Ivanov's essay 'Ellinskaia religiia stradaiushchego boga' ('Hellenic Religion of the Suffering God') and in his interpretation of Vergil in 'Vergils Historiosophie'. For the publication information of these two works see Davidson's (1996b) *Reference Guide*, xxxi and xxxix respectively. For a detailed philological and philosophical analysis of the first essay see Westbroek (2007). For the insightful analysis of 'Vergils Historiosophie' and its comparison with T.S. Eliot's reception of Vergil see Rudich (2002b).

51. For other works on Ivanov's approach to classical antiquity see Davidson's (1996b) *Reference Guide*, Index, 362.

52. See Averintsev (2001) 18.

53. Davidson (1989) 4.

54. See Ivanov's essay 'Dve stikhii v sovremennom simvolizme' ('Two Elemental Forces in Contemporary Symbolism'). See Ivanov (1971-9) 636-1; also Erlich (1964).

55. Donchin (1958) 73. The question of Annenskii's membership of the Symbol-

ist movement is rather complex and will not be discussed in detail here. It suffices to say that Annenskii, like the first branch of the Symbolist poets, was indebted to the traditions of French Symbolism but remained distanced from the whole Symbolist Russian school because its religious mysticism was foreign to his poetics. See also Setchkarev (1963) 54, who observed that the Symbolist 'label does not fit completely and some of his [Annenskii's] most important characteristics do not correspond to it at all'.

56. Averintsev (2001) 11. This sobriquet was inspired by Lorenzo the Magnificent, the fifteenth-century patron of the arts.

57. Davidson (2006) 9.

58. Davidson (2006) 10, 55. Some of Ivanov's ideas on translation can be found in his late essay 'Mysli o poezii' ('Thoughts on Poetry', 1938-43) and in his Italian essay 'Forma formans e forma formata' (1947). See Ivanov (1971-9) 3: 660-73 and 3: 674-82.

59. Nikolai Bakhtin, a classicist taught by Zelinskii in St Petersburg, observed: 'the evening when Ivanov read us his translation of the *Oresteia* remains the most intense and decisive experience of my life'. See Bakhtin (1963) 41-2. For further information on Ivanov's translations of Aeschylus and the relevant scholarship see Davidson's (1996b) *Reference Guide*, Index: 357. Especially noteworthy are the works of Gasparov (1966) on Ivanov's use of metrics in his translation of the *Oresteia*; of Balashov (1989) on the context and significance of Ivanov's translations as a form of intercultural dialogue; and of Kotrelev (1989) on the history of Ivanov's translations of Aeshylus and of the plans for their publication. The last two essays accompany the text of Ivanov's six translations of Aeschylus in the *Literaturnye Pamiatniki* edition: *The Suppliant Women, The Persians, Seven Against Thebes*, and the *Oresteia* trilogy.

60. Davidson (2006) 11.

61. Averintsev (2001) 53-4. Vladimir Solov'ev's teachings on divine Sophia in his longest poem 'Tri svidaniia' ('Three Meetings') also influenced Ivanov's study of Sophia and to some degree of Dionysiac mysticism. See Davidson (1989) 6 and Masing-Delic (1992) 105-22.

62. Averintsev (2001) 95.

63. Averintsev (2001) passim, but esp. 17 and 167.

64. Rudich (1986) 279.

65. Ivanov (1971-9) 3: 485-645.

66. Cited in Russian by Averintsev (2001) 98.

67. That view was perhaps influenced by Mommsen's frequently expressed 'melancholy presentiment of the coming barbarity'. See Davidson (2006) 8.

68. See Ivanov (1971-9) 3: 69 and 436 respectively. Translated by Rudich (1986) 283.

69. Ivanov did not officially immigrate to Rome but came there, in fact, as a representative of the Soviet state with permission from Lunacharskii and with the assignment of establishing a Russian Academy in Rome. He took this task seriously but nothing came of it. He never renounced his Russian citizenship explicitly although in 1929 he was declared *nevozvrashchenets* ('one who had not returned') and his citizenship lapsed in 1936 (Kalb 2003, 25n.7). It is worth noting here that in the fall of 1995 another Russian poet, Joseph Brodsky, who may or may not have known of Ivanov's efforts, made an appeal to the mayor of Rome that a Russian Academy in Rome be established. See Brodsky Sozzani (2000).

70. 'Po zvezdam: Stat'i i aforizmy' ('By the Stars: Essays and Aphorisms'), cited and translated in Myers (1992) 86.

71. Deschartes mistakenly provided the date of 1894 and several subsequent scholars have followed her. Ivanov (1971-9) 1: 521 described his meetings with Zinov'eva-Annibal in the Coliseum in his poem 'V Kolizee' ('In the Coliseum') with an epigraph from Byron: 'Great is their love, who love in sin and fear'.

72. The *Sonnets* were not published as a cycle until 1936 in *Sovremennye Zapiski*, vol. 62. I am citing the *Sonnets* from Ivanov (1971-9) 3: 578-82.

73. Ivanov returned on several occasions before World War I with his longest stay in 1912-13.

74. Ivanov (1971-9) 1: 636.

75. Frajlich (2007) 100 and 119n.24 citing Toporov's suggestion that in 'Laeta' 'a vivid panoramic description of Rome, synthesized in its various spatial and temporal images, leads to the theme of returning again according to his circuits and faithfulness to Rome ... and further to the theme of homeland'.

76. Ivanov (1971-9) 1: 636.

77. Ivanov (1971-9) 1: 638.

78. Ivanov (1971-9) 1: 639.

79. Kalb (2008) 17. Kalb also points out that Solov'ev himself had acknowledged the fluidity of the term 'East' since it contained 'wide-ranging and at times contradictory associations, from Christian holiness to barbarian mongolism' (18). Some of Solov'ev's poems, such as *'Ex oriente lux'* (1890) and 'Panmongolism' (1894), were especially influential for Ivanov and later Alexander Blok and Valerii Briusov since in these works Solov'ev 'touched upon Russia's national destiny and the future of humanity at large' (Connolly (1992) 384). In the first poem Solov'ev suggested that Russia has a messianic role as the Third Rome and a follower of Christ.

80. Ivanov's vision of Rome was also strongly linked to Solov'ev's advocacy of a unification of the Orthodox and Roman Churches in his most famous theological work *La Russie et L'Eglise universelle (Russia and the Universal Church)*. In this unified church, according to Solov'ev, East and West would be equal partners, but Russia would have a special role to play.

81. See Kalb (2003).

82. In 1920-4 Ivanov was appointed Professor of Classical Philology and Poetics at the newly founded University of Baku.

83. I have adopted Nelson's translation (1986): 135 for the most part. I have however made several changes (noted below) where I do not agree with this otherwise beautiful translation of the poem.

84. Ivanov (1971-9) 3: 578. I have followed the division of the lines in the English translation of the poem according to this edition.

85. Ivanov uses 'tsar' putei' in Russian because 'Rim' ('Rome') in Russian is masculine. Nelson translated it as Latin *regina viarum* because that was the original title of the sonnet. I have chosen to translate it into English since it is in Russian, not Latin, in the original.

86. Here I have changed Nelson's translation of 'ne oslepla' which means 'did not grow blind' rather than 'could not blind the eye', which would have required a different verb form, 'oslepila'.

87. Here Nelson's translation has been changed from 'how strong was Troy in ashes lying cold'.

88. Kalb (2008) 152.

89. Ivanov (1971-9) 1: 574.

90. Rudich (1988) 134.

91. Zelinskii (1916) vol. 3: 103. Zelinskii emphasized Heraclitus as well as Dionysus as a source for Ivanov's interest in rebirth by fire.

92. Klimoff (1986) 131.

93. Rudich (1988) 132.

94. Ivanov's interest in Vergil may have been partially influenced by Solov'ev's interest in him. Solov'ev translated Vergil's *Aeneid* and the Fourth Eclogue, a fact that helped Ivanov in his reading of Vergil. See Davidson (1989) 97. See also Matual (1982) on how Solov'ev's translation of Vergil reflected his overall philosophical and religious views.

95. The numbers indicate the pages in the original publication of the essay. See Ivanov (1931).

96. Kalb (2003) 31. See also Rudich (1988) 139 and (2002b) for further analysis of Ivanov's essay.

97. Ivanov discussed the violence of the founding of Rome elsewhere, specifically in his essay 'O Russkoi Idee' ('On the Russian Idea').

98. Kalb (2003) 32.

99. See Rosenthal (1993), who analyzed the term 'sobornost'' in Ivanov's, Sergei Bulgakov's and Pavel Florenskii's writings.

100. Deschartes (1954) 48; cited and translated in Kalb (2008) 147.

101. See Meerson (Winter 1999) 719. Ivanov (1971-9) 3: 259-60.

102. Kalb (2003) 37.

103. Ivanov (1971-9) 3: 852.

104. Braginskaia (2004) 62 pointed out that the equation of the Russian revolution with foreign attacks on the Roman state was customary at that time among the Russian intellectuals.

105. See Ivanov (1971-9) 3: 326.

106. Ivanov (1971-9) 3: 326: 'ne egoism narodnyi, no providentsial'nuiu voliu i ideiu derzhavnogo Rima, stanoviashchegosia mirom'. In the Russian version the play on the words 'Rim' ('Rome') and 'mir' ('world') gives the lines a special emphasis.

107. Ivanov (1971-9) 3: 558.

108. I use here Pamela Davidson's translation (1996a) 108, which in addition to being literal also takes into consideration the interpretation of certain passages in the Italian version of the poem published by Ivanov in 1934.

109. See *OCD* s.v. Stesichorus, 1012. For a detailed discussion of the story in *Phaedrus*, see Beecroft (2006).

110. Rudich (1986) 288.

111. Deschartes added in relation to 'Palinode' that 'after a short renunciation of humanism he could find it in the spirit of Christianity, as a *docta pietas*'. See Blinov (1986) 466.

112. Davidson (1996a) 102. Deschartes also referred to St Jerome and St Augustine in relation to the 'Palinode' in her introduction to Ivanov's collected works (1971-9) 175-6. She mentioned in addition the teachings of St Justin, which included the reconciliation between paganism and Christianity within a cultural continuum.

113. On Ivanov's conversion to Catholicism see his 'Lettre à Charles Du Bos' in Ivanov (1971-9) 3: 418-19.

114. Ivanov (1971-9) 3: 612.

115. Davidson (1996a) 103.

116. For a sweeping although in places outdated account of the classical tradition see Highet (1976). For a more recent approach see Kallendorf (2007). A detailed bibliography for further reading on the Renaissance approach to antiquity can also be found there (43).

117. See Fox (2001) 33.
118. Two of Kniazhnin's tragedies, *Vladimir and Iaropolk* (1772) and *Rosslav* (1783), addressed, like Sumarokov's plays, the philosophy of heroism but not from a well-defined historical viewpoint – a problem also seen in Sumarokov. Kniazhnin was much more interested in 'an emotional and psychological image of the Russian citizen-patriot' (See Serman (1992) 84).
119. Karlinsky (1986) 181.
120. Nabokov (1981) 82.
121. Mirsky (1949) 68; see also Altshuller (1992) 122. The tragedy was also based on Euripides' *Trojan Women.*
122. Kelly (1989) 236. For a comprehensive history and analysis of the nature of the Slavonic Renaissance see Braginskaia (2004) who attributed the invention of the term to Zelinskii (51).
123. For Zelinskii's views on suitable methods of education and on the study of antiquity in Russia, see Zelinskii (1909).
124. Zelinskii (1934) 245. Cited and translated in Kelly (1989) 238.
125. Kalb (2008) 23. On different phases of Ivanov's and Zelinskii's friendship both in Russia and abroad see Takho-Godi (2002).
126. Ivanov himself invoked the Dionysiac, barbaric tradition in Greece as the principle that gave Hellenism its soul. See Myers (1992) 86. Boris Gasparov (1994) 275 emphasized Ivanov's focus on the Thracian origin of Dionysus in opposition to a pure Hellenistic character of Apollo. According to Ivanov, Dionysus, because of his origin, naturally belonged to the Slavic and Balkan soils and thus was 'our barbarian, our Slavic, god' ('nash varvarskii, nash, slavianskii, bog'). See Ivanov (1971-9) 3: 20 in the 1907 essay 'O veselom remesle i umnom veselii' ('On gay craftsmanship and wise gaiety').
127. Kalb (2008) 24.
128. Cited in Russian in Braginskaia (2004) 59.
129. The 'Union' included Vsevolod Meierkhol'd, Vera Shvarsalon (Ivanov's step-daughter and later his third wife), the Bakhtin brothers, and Adrian Piotrovskii (the son of Zelinskii). It is also noteworthy that Piotrovskii (who was killed by the Soviet authorities in 1938) was extremely dedicated to the translation of classical authors for a broad audience during the periods when ancient languages were mostly eradicated from secondary and even higher education. His translations were sometimes provocatively loose but their main goal was to adapt the classics to modernity.
130. Cited in Russian in Asoian and Malafeev (2000) 250.
131. For Zelinskii's observations on Ivanov as a poet of the 'Slavonic Renaissance' see Zelinskii (1933).
132. Green (1977) 8; Kot (1999) 108.
133. For more on Meierkhol'd and Ivanov see Galanina (2006) 187-205. For Ivanov's contribution to the symbolist theory of the theatre, plans for a Dionysian theatre, and also links with Meierkhol'd, see Lo Gatto (1952) 148-50, 192, 197, 251-2, 289, 317.
134. Kelly (1989) 235. In his essay on Ivanov, Zelinskii (1916) defined 'russkaia narodnost" ('the Russian national spirit) as one of Ivanov's 'guiding stars' along with Dionysus, Heraclitus and Nietzsche.
135. Hetzer (1972). Mureddu (1993).
136. The role of the chorus in Ivanov's and Annenskii's tragedies has been discussed comprehensively by Kelly (1989). My discussion concentrates primarily on the main characters of the play.

137. Kelly (1989) 240. Ivanov expressed his thoughts on the 'revival' of a Dionysian idea of theatre in his 1906 essay 'Predchuvstviia i predvestiia' ('Presentiments and Portents'). Ivanov (1971-9) 2: 86-104.

138. Annenskii (1902) 14; see also Gurevich (1910) 157.

139. Ivanov (1971-9) 2: 85, 102, 99.

140. Al'tman (1968) 321.

141. *Tantalus* was first conceived in 1903, finished in 1904, and published in 1905. See Toporov (1989) 90. *Prometheus* was published in 1919 but had already been completed by the end of 1914. See Mureddu (1993). The first version of *Prometheus* appeared in print in 1915 under the title *Sons of Prometheus (Syny Prometeia)*, but the text differed significantly from the 1919 edition. See Toporov (1989) 96n.76a.

142. See Venclova (1985) 89. For the surviving text of the tragedy (354 lines) with notes, a history of its writing and the text of Ivanov's 'Preface to the Trilogy', see Gerasimov (1984).

143. Losev (1976) 283; see also Gerasimov (1984).

144. See Annenskii (1902) 27.

145. Kelly (1989) 242. Valerii Briusov's models of pagan honour and eroticism in his 1900 poetic collection *Tertia Vigilia* were also indebted to the tradition of the French Parnassians.

146. See Kelly (1989) 236 and Venclova (1985) 90. Ivanov himself offered an 'ideological postscript' to both tragedies in two of his essays 'Simvolika esteticheskikh nachal' ('On the Symbolism of Aesthetic Principles') and 'O deistvii i deistve' ('On Act and Ritual'). See Ivanov (1971-9) 1: 823-30 and 2: 156-70 respectively. The former contains some of Ivanov's main ideas on Dionysus and the nature of a tragic conflict. In the latter he offers an analysis of Prometheus myth in the context of titanism.

147. Pindar, *Olympian* 1. 35-81.

148. See *OCD* s.v. Tantalus, 1037.

149. Apollodorus. *Epit.* 2. 3ff. Venclova (1985) 90.

150. See Mureddu (1993) 142. Bird also (2006) 91 noted that *Prometheus* is reminiscent of Byron's mystery plays *Manfred, Cain,* and *Heaven and Earth*, 'which for Ivanov typified the theomachic attitude of romanticism' (Ivanov (1971-9) 2: 163, 168; (1987) 4: 283, 293).

151. Mureddu (1993) 144.

152. See Mureddu (1993) 148-9.

153. Davidson (1996b) 178.

154. Mureddu (1993) 149.

155. See Bird (2006) 160.

156. Ivanov (1971-9): 2: 158.

157. Ivanov (1971-9) 1: 160.

158. Losev (1976) 282. Losev also offers a survey of the treatment of Prometheus myth from classical antiquity to modern times: 226-92.

159. Bird (2006) 88.

160. Ivanov (1971-9) 2: 167.

161. Toporov (1989) 97.

162. Ivanov (1971-9) 2: 28.

163. Ivanov (1971-9) 2: 128.

164. Ivanov (1971-9) 2: 27.

165. Ivanov (1971-9) 2: 27, 29.

166. Ivanov (1971-9) 2: 31.

167. Ivanov (1971-9) 2: 28. Here the noun *alkanie* ('yearning') from *alkat'* ('to yearn') is repeated again.
168. Kot (1999) 111.
169. Toporov (1989).
170. Ivanov (1971-9) 2: 71.
171. The last tragedy finished in 1906 coincided with the publication of Alexander Blok's *Balaganchik* (*The Puppet Show*), the play with which the concept of Russian lyrical drama has usually become connected. See Khrustaleva (1987) 58.
    172. Ivanov (1971-9) 2: 578.
173. Annenskii (1990) 290.
174. It is noteworthy that Valerii Briusov in his comparison of Ivanov's *Tantalus* and Annenskii's *Laodamia* regarded the former as a superior tragedy in terms of the prosody and lexical devices it uses to resurrect the essence of classical drama. See Briusov (1906).
175. See Fedorov's introduction to Annenskii (1990) 47.
176. Annenksii (1990) 289.
177. See Annenskii's foreword to *Ixion* (1990) 347-9.
178. Annenskii (1990) 290.
179. Annenskii (1979) 126.
180. See Collard, Cropp, Lee (1995).
181. A peculiar feature of this chorus for a work by Annenskii is that it resembles more the first chorus in Aeschylus' *Agamemnon* than any choral ode of Euripides.
182. Khrustaleva (1987) 61.
183. Setchkarev (1963) 169.
184. The inspiration for that interpretation might also have come from *Oedipus Rex* where Oedipus acquired full knowledge of his surroundings only after he lost his physical sight.
185. Annenskii (1990) 349. Here an echo (if unintended) of Nietzsche might be detected.
186. Annenskii (1990) 347-8. Annenskii cited the few fragments left from Euripides.
187. Ivanov (1971-9) 2: 580.
188. Annenskii (1990) 412.
189. See *OCD* s.v. Protesilaus, 890.
190. See Kelly (1985) 76-7.
191. Kelly (1985) 78.
192. Kelly (1985) 84.
193. Kelly (1985) 88 suggested that the play can be read as a metaphor of the struggle between Dionysus and Apollo and by extension between Annenskii's Apollonian mode of neoclassicism and the Dionysiac mode of other Symbolists such as Ivanov.
194. For further discussion of satyrs in *Famira*, see Kelly (1985).
195. Cited in Green (1977) 10.
196. Kot (1999) 119. Kot 115-22 also offered a detailed analysis of the Russian language in *Tantalus*.
197. Pollak (1999) 146.
198. Ivanov's views on tragedy and the mission of theatre were expressed in several of his essays: 'O Sushchestve tragedii' ('On the Essence of Tragedy'), 'Esteticheskaiia norma teatra' ('The Aesthetic Norm of the Theatre'), 'Ekskurs: O krizise teatra' ('Excursus: On the Crisis of Theatre'). See Ivanov (1971-9) 2:

190-201, 205-14, 215-18. In these essays he outlined the shortcomings of the contemporary theatre and defined the relationship between the dramatic creator and his audience.

199. Ivanov (1971-9) 2: 555.

200. Cited in Russian in Asoian and Malafeev (2000) 250: 'Rossia byla iavno na puti k chemu-to sovsem inomu, chem Grecheskoe Vozrozhdenie'. Olga Freidenberg (1991) 154 expressed the same opinion more precisely. When she described her impressions of Zelinskii's last recital (he emigrated in 1921) of the *Bacchae* at St Petersburg (Petrograd) University she wrote: 'The *Bacchae* invoked Dionysus with muffled voices, they had empty stomachs and they were afraid of searches' ('Vakkhanki zvali Dionisa glukho, i v zhivote u nikh bylo pusto, i oni boialis' obyska'). See also Braginskaia (2004) 65.

201. Braginskaia (2004) 66.

202. *Tantalus*, for example, was received extremely enthusiastically by Ivanov's fellow poets Briusov, Blok and Belyi, but the wider reception and the later readership of Ivanov's tragedies were less welcoming. See Toporov (1989) 91.

4. Marina Tsvetaeva's Tragic Heroines

1. Tsvetaeva (1979) 11. The 'Amazon' addressee of the work was the American expatriate, Natalie Barney who was also the addressee of Rémy de Gourmont's widely known collection *Lettres à l'Amazone*. See Perkins and Cook (1993).

2. The archaeological expeditions began in the late eighteenth century once Russia had annexed these territories. See Frolov (1999) 125-37.

3. Tsvetaeva (1971) 23. For a more detailed account of Ivan Tsvetaev's academic career see Frolov (1999) 202-4.

4. Karlinsky (1986) 11. In one of her early poems 'Charodei' ('Wizard') Tsvetaeva recalls the atmosphere in which she grew up:

Tsvet Gretsii i slava Rima, –
Neischislimye toma!
Zdes' skol'ko b solntsa ni vnesli my, –
Vsegda zima.

Poslednim solntsem rozoveiia
Raspakhnutyi lezhit Platon ...
Biust Apollona – plan Muzeia
I vse – kak son.
See Tsvetaeva (1994-95) 3: 13.

Greece's blossom and Rome's glory,
All the countless volumes!
Here – no matter how much sun we bring in –
Winter always rules.

Rosy in the last sun's rays,
Plato lies open ...
Apollo's bust, Museum's plan –
And everything is like a dream.

5. A discussion of other classical motifs in Tsvetaeva's poetry of that period

(Sibyl, Eurydice, Orpheus, Psyche) remains beyond the scope of this study, which is focused entirely on Tsvetaeva's treatment of the myth of Theseus. For comprehensive and detailed discussions of other mythological themes see Hasty (1996) and Ruutu (2006).

6. Tsvetaeva (1988) 342.

7. She dedicated to Holliday the verse cycle *Stikhi Sonechke* (*Poems to Sonechka*) and *Povest' o Sonechke* (*The Tale of Sonechka*). The latter was written in 1937, when Tsvetaeva learnt of Holliday's death. See Schweitzer (1988) 159-60.

8. Tsvetaeva (1988) 360.

9. Venclova (1985) 102.

10. See Venclova (1985) 100 and Karlinsky (1986) 181-2. Tsvetaeva cited Schwab as her source in the letter to Iurii Ivask dated 4 April 1933, although she made a parenthetical note that the real source of her mythology was 'she, herself' ('istochniki-to ia sama, vo mne' – Tsvetaeva (1994-5) 7:381). In the same letter she added: 'I was never under anyone's influence. I began with writing, not with reading poets.' Another source identified by Tsvetaeva herself was Heinrich Stoll's *Die Sagen der klassischen Altertums* (1862). See Tsvetaeva's letter to Rainer Maria Rilke of 22 August 1926 in Tsvetaeva (1994-5) 7: 73.

11. See Ruutu (2006) 14; see also Razumovskaia (1983) 67.

12. Hasty (1996) 12.

13. Tsvetaeva (1994-95) 4: 545. Tsvetaeva's adherence to German literature also stemmed from her mother's heritage. Her mother Maria Alexandrovna Mein (1868-1906) was the half-Polish daughter of a wealthy Baltic German businessman and publisher, A.D. Mein (Karlinsky (1986) 3).

14. See Ruutu (2006) 14.

15. Makin (1993) 268. Voitekhovich (2007) 21, however, pointed out that Tsvetaeva's approach to antiquity vacillated between two binary oppositions so common for Tsvetaeva's poetics: her 'spartanism' on one hand and 'homerism' on the other. The former was characterized by laconism of expression, the latter, by hyperbole. Voitekhovich further suggested that overall antiquity remained for Tsvetaeva a 'beautiful stranger' and that is what enabled and inspired her mythological tragedies.

16. See the letter to Iurii Ivask dated 4 April 1933 in Tsvetaeva (1980-90) 5: 469.

17. Bakhrakh (1960-1); (1960) 299-318; (1961) 322, 337.

18. Cited in Venclova (1985) 108, the same letter dated 4 April 1933.

19. See Vitale (1989) 172.

20. Fox (2001) 32.

21. There are no published translations in English of Tsvetaeva's classical dramas. I want to thank Maria Stadter Fox for generously offering me an advance copy of her translation of *Fedra*. This helped me immensely with my own translations for this chapter.

22. Venclova (1985) 89.

23. Boym (1991) 200. Brodsky (1986) 195-267 in 'Footnote to a Poem'.

24. See Sumerkin's commentary in Tsvetaeva (1980-90), vol. 5 (1990) 469. He notes that Tsvetaeva decided to change the title for the trilogy in October 1924.

25. Cited and translated in Karlinsky (1986) 182.

26. See Armstrong (2006) 12.

27. The play was originally called *Theseus* but later renamed *Ariadne* to avoid confusion with the whole trilogy. It was completed in 1924 and published in 1927.

28. Tsvetaeva (1980-90) 5: 227.

29. Tsvetaeva (1980-90) 5: 231.

30. Lafoy (1981) 112 duly noted that Ariadne has often been considered an embodiment of Aphrodite, which also explains her reliance on and connection to Aphrodite as her mother figure and her protectress in the play.

31. Tsvetaeva (1980-90) 5: 241.

32. The story of Theseus and Ariadne appeared in many ancient sources starting with Homer's *Odyssey* and ending with Ovid's *Heroides* and *Metamorphoses*. For a detailed account of them see Lafoy (1981) and Armstrong (2006).

33. In *Heroides* 10 Ovid transformed Ariadne's indignant speech in Catullus' *ecphrasis* into a letter. Although Ovid's *Heroides* might have been one of the sources for Ariadne's lament by Tsvetaeva, Ovid had also written it with Catullus in mind. See Armstrong (2006) 222.

34. See *OCD* s.v Ariadne, 106.

35. Diodorus Siculus 4.61.5; 5.51.4.

36. Tsvetaeva also intended originally to use fear of the god as the reason for the Theseus' betrayal but then changed her mind, according to Makin (1993) 277, under the influence of the end of her love affair with Konstantin Rodzevich.

37. Tsvetaeva (1997) 265.

38. Tsvetaeva (1997) 299. See Ruutu (2006) 112 for a more detailed discussion of Tsvetaeva's notes to the play.

39. Tsvetaeva's emphasis.

40. Tsvetaeva (1980-90) 5: 252.

41. Tsvetaeva (1980-90) 5: 254.

42. Venclova (1985) 103 suggested the general similarity to the dialogues in the *Bacchae* after Vasilii Rudich brought it to his attention.

43. Euripides (1959) 188.

44. The influence of this particular interpretation by Tsvetaeva on Joseph Brodsky's use of the myth is discussed in Chapter 6.

45. Tsvetaeva (1980-90) 3: 64.

46. Ruutu (2006) 85-6 mentioned Ovid, Schwab and Stoll as Tsvetaeva's sources for the abandonment of Ariadne. As for Tsvetaeva's Russian predecessors in the story of the abandoned maiden, Valerii Briusov treated the theme similarly in his two-poem cycle written in 1918 and also called 'Ariadne' (Briusov (1973-5, 3: 27-9). On the parallels between Tsvetaeva and Brisuov see Ruutu (2006) 87-9.

47. Tsvetaeva (1980-90) 3: 451. This stanza is preserved only in the handwritten draft but not in the published version. Tsvetaeva might have excised the final stanza of the first poem in the *Ariadne* lyric cycle because she later had reconsidered the reason for Theseus' abandonment of Ariadne.

48. Tsvetaeva (1980-90) 3: 64-5.

49. In this line the imagery of sea, which is also pervasive in Catullus' rendition of Ariadne's abandonment, especially stands out (Cat. 64.62-7):

Prospicit et magnis curarum fluctuat undis,
Non flavo retinens subtilem vertice mitram,
Non contecta levi velatum pectus amictu,
Non tereti strophilo lactentis vincta papillas,
Omnia quae toto delapsa e corpore passim
Ipsius ante pedes fluctus salis adludebant.

She [Ariadne] looks on and heaves with great waves of sorrow. She does not hold her fine-woven headband on her fair head, nor does she cover her chest with the light garment, and her milky breasts are not tied up with a smooth band. Everything that slipped randomly from her whole body becomes the sport of the waves underneath her feet.

50. Tsvetaeva and Pasternak (2004) 81; see also Ruutu (2006) 93.
51. See Karlinsky (1986) 136-7, 139, 161, 187, 194.
52. The correspondence started in 1922 in Berlin and continued for many years after that, until 1934. See Karlinsky (1986) 134 and Gove (1977) 251. See also Shevelenko (2002) 239, who cautioned against overstating the influence that the 'non-meeting' (Tsvetaeva called it 'nevstrecha', 'razminovenie') with Pasternak had on Tsvetaeva. For a detailed account of Tsvetaeva's relationship with Pasternak see Ciepiela (2006).
53. Tsvetaeva (1980-90) 5: 241. See Forrester (2000) 367.
54. Fox (2001) 52.
55. Tsvetaeva (1980-90) 5: 243.
56. Tsvetaeva's passion for Pasternak was not unrequited, although, in my opinion, judging from their poetry and correspondence, it was more important to her than it was to him. He was, no doubt, one of very few men who was her equal, not frightened by Tsvetaeva's intensity of feeling. He was, however, considerably more restrained in expressing his own strength of emotion. See Schweitzer (1988) 223-4 and esp. 273-85.
57. Tsvetaeva (1980-90) 3: 54.
58. Tsvetaeva (1980-90) 3: 55.
59. Tsvetaeva's emphasis.
60. Euripides (1955) 172.
61. For the importance of the figure of the Amazon in Tsvetaeva's poetics see Forrester (2000), Gove (1977) 247, Perkins and Cook (1993) 19n.2.
62. See *OCD* s.v. Amazons, 50.
63. Euripides (1955) 165-6, 189-90. There is little doubt that Tsvetaeva was aware of this Euripidean tragedy. Annenskii, Zelinskii and Merezhkovskii had all translated *Hippolytus*. These translations appeared between 1902 and 1920, and several of the editions included commentaries.
64. Euripides (1955) 190.
65. Tsvetaeva (1980-90) 5: 274.
66. Tsvetaeva (1980-90) 5: 275.
67. Tsvetaeva (1980-90) 5: 284-5.
68. Tsvetaeva (1980-90) 5: 279.
69. Euripides (1955) 177.
70. Makin (1993) 285.
71. Tsvetaeva (1980-90) 5: 294.
72. Cited and translated by Makin (1993) 285.
73. I am inclined to agree with Joseph Brodsky's statement that 'Tsvetaeva the poet and Tsvetaeva the person were one and the same ... Tsvetaeva places an equal sign between them'. Cited in Kudrova (2007) 53.
74. See Makin (1993) 285.
75. See Boym (1991) 236, who cited Anastasia Tsvetaeva's observation that 'Marina's suicide, which 'in an uncanny way tied her son and herself together, was a "sacrifice" in order to rescue him'.
76. See Feinstein (1989) 16, Karlinsky (1986) 10.
77. For more on the tensions attending Tsvetaeva's views of gender and sex see Gove (1977), Boym (1991) 192-234.
78. Tsvetaeva (1980-90) 5: 294.

79. Tsvetaeva (1980-90) 5: 294.
80. Tsvetaeva (1980-90) 5: 300.
81. Zeitlin (1985) 52. See also David Grene's introduction to *Hippolytus* in Euripides (1955) 158.
82. Fox (2001) 40.
83. Rabinowitz (1986) 127. See also Gill (1990) on the connection between the 'self-articulation' and *sôphrosynê* ('moderation') in the play.
84. Fox (2001) 40.
85. Tsvetaeva (1980-90) 5: 307.
86. Tsvetaeva (1980-90) 5: 315.
87. Cited in Venclova (1985) 106.
88. See Thomson (1989) 343. Tsvetaeva also would have known two of Osip Mandelshtam's poems: one is the short poem of 1914 on Anna Akhmatova ('Vpolo-borota, o pechal" – 'Half turning around, o sadness') in which she was compared with Racine's *Phèdre* in Rachel's (Élisa Félix's) famous rendition; another is 'Ia ne uvizhu znamenitoi Fedry ...' ('I will not see the famous Phaedra ...') written in 1915, which referred specifically to Racine's play. Another poem by Mandelshtam about Phaedra, which opened the poet's collection *Tristia*, was written in 1916 and drew on *Phèdre* and *Hippolytus* alike. See Freidin (1987) 91-9 and Brown (1973) 207-52.
89. Ruutu (2006) 13 and Lafoy (1981) 193. For a detailed analysis of Tsvetaeva's *Phaedra* in the context of Baroque drama see Osipova (2000).
90. Thomson (1989) 343.
91. Tsvetaeva (2001) 305. All the emphases are Tsvetaeva's.
92. For Tsvetaeva's play on the words 'sounds' ('zvuki') and 'letters' ('bukvy') as the building block of her depiction of Phaedra as a poet, see Thomson (1989) 346-7.
93. See Boym (1991) 234.
94. Cantarella (1986) 57-78.
95. On women in Russian literature and the Russian cultural tradition see Heldt (1987).
96. Gove (1977) 231. For the theoretical basis of the perception of 'female poetry' ('zhenskaia poeziia') in opposition to 'ladies' poetry' ('damskaia poeziia') see Shev-elenko (2002) 64-74 and Perkins and Cook (1993) 1-22, esp. 14-17, who pointed out (2) that the complexities of the lives and poetry of women poets in Russia 'challenge Western feminist criticism'.
97. Boym (1991) 192.
98. Boym (1991) 192-4.
99. See Boym (1991) 327.
100. For more on Tsvetaeva's treatment of gender see Sandler (1990).
101. See Thomson (1989) 343. For a more recent discussion of Tsvetaeva's sympathetic portrayal of a powerful femininity see Dinega (2001).
102. Euripides (1955) 185.
103. Volkov (1998) 42.
104. Kroth (December 1979) 563-82. Tsvetaeva also provided her other tradi-tionally passive heroines, Eurydice and Ophelia, with an active role and authoritative voice. See Hasty (1996) xv.
105. Stock (July 2001) 776. Tsvetaeva wrote some of the most heartbreaking poems of exile and nostalgia such as 'Rassvet na rel'sakh' ('Dawn upon the rails', Tsvetaeva (1980-90) 3: 43) and 'V Parizhe', ('In Paris', ibid.: 1: 52).
106. See Karlinsky (1986) 184.

107. Venclova (1985) 104.

108. Fox (2001) 54.

109. On differences between Annenskii's tragedies and Tsvetaeva's *Ariadne*, see Kahn (1994).

110. Makin (1993) 294. Voitekhovich (2007) 66 questions the validity of the traditional assumption that Tsvetaeva planned *Theseus* as a trilogy. He suggests that Tsvetaeva with first two plays exhausted her interest in the Theseus myth as a story about 'crime and punishment'. Thus her interest in finishing the trilogy with *Helen* faded away (75).

111. Tsvetaeva (1980-90) 1: 140.

Osip Mandelshtam: 'Yearning for World Culture'

1. Parts of this chapter were published in my earlier article Torlone (2008). I would like to thank the editors of the volume *Preserving Petersburg: History, Memory, Nostalgia* in which it appeared, Helena Goscilo and Stephen Norris, for their invaluable criticism and comments on the article.

2. Mandelshtam (1974) 110.

3. The original six 'Acmeists' were N. Gumilev, S. Gorodetskii, A. Akhmatova, O. Mandelshtam, M. Zenkevich, and V. Narbut. See Gasparov and Mets (1997) 11. On the main differences between Symbolism and Acmeism, see Taranovsky (1976) 83 and Gasparov and Mets (1997) 12-14.

4. Freidin (1987) 29.

5. Gumilev (1962-8) vol. 4.

6. Cited and translated in Poggioli (1960) 214.

7. Mandelshtam 'On the Nature of the Word' ('O prirode slova') cited and translated in Myers (1992) 85.

8. For more on connections between Innokentii Annenskii and Acmeist doctrine see Tucker (1986).

9. Ziolkowski (2005) 68. Ziolkowski also pointed out that the same convictions and practices were developed independently during the same years by Ezra Pound and T.S. Eliot. On that subject see also Cavanagh (1995) 52-4.

10. For more on the relationship between Ivanov and Mandelshtam see Lekmanov and Glukhova (2006) 173-9.

11. Gasparov and Mets (1997) 7.

12. Bradbury and McFarlane (1976) 27.

13. One of Mandelshtam's outstanding political poems was 'Proslavim, brat'ia, sumerki svobody' ('Let's hail, brothers, the twilight of freedom'). The poem, written in 1918, conveyed feelings of both excitement and great anxiety about the future, as the poet described (in Horatian manner) 'the ship of the state' in the middle of a sea storm. Political and civic themes in Mandelshtam's poetry have been discussed in great detail by Broyde (1975). On the civic poetry of 1937 see Gasparov (1996).

14. Mandelshtam (1974) 140. I am aware that there are better and more recent editions of Mandelshtam and therefore I would like to explain my choice of this source for citation of the Russian versions of the poems. The copy of this edition in my possession was given to my father by his friend Mikhail Levin, who had received it in turn from Mandelshtam's widow, Nadezhda Mandelshtam. The edition is corrected in blue pen by Nadezhda Mandelshtam herself and contains some unflattering remarks addressed to the editor of the volume, N.I. Khardzhiev. It is not my place in this study to pass judgment about the fairness of her remarks,

but I think that her devotion to the poetic legacy of her husband and her obsessive memorization of his poetry deserves more trust in her correct rendition of the poetic texts than it has received from several critics. I have also consulted, however, two other editions: the edition of Gleb Struve and Boris Filippov and the more recent one by S. Vasilenko; see Mandelshtam (1967) and Mandelshtam (2001) respectively. Except for minor differences in punctuation, the poems under discussion are similar in all three editions.

15. Cavanagh (1995) 6.

16. Mandelshtam (1979) 113.

17. See Al'tman (1995) 88-9.

18. Gasparov and Mets (1997) 21 suggested that his decision not to emigrate was a Chaadaev-like ethical choice, his 'faithfulness in misfortune' ('vernost' v neschast'e').

19. He was arrested for the first time and exiled to Voronezh in 1934 after writing a suicidal poem against Joseph Stalin.

20. Some critics, such as Przybylski (1987) 45-78, have tried to analyze the system of Mandelshtam's Hellenism; the results of these attempts are more convincing when applied to his prose rather than to his poetry.

21. The main differences between Mandelshtam's and Ivanov's 'Hellenism' were outlined in Myers (1992). She contrasted the Dionysiac core element in Ivanov's understanding of Hellenism with Mandeslhtam's, which was more influenced by Christian vision.

22. Cited and translated by Terras (1966) 252.

23. Mandelshtam (1974) 62.

24. Terras (1966) 257. In his commentary on the translations of Mandelshtam's (1973) 317 poems, Sydney Monas detected yet another intertextual layer; the Latin title of the poem was the same as the famous poem by Fedor Tiutchev (1803-73) that contained the idea that every thought verbalized aloud resulted in distortion: 'Mysl' izrechennaia est' lozh''. For a comparison of Tiutchev's and Mandelshtam's poems, see Taranovsky (1976) 122.

25. Mandelshtam (1974) 85-6.

26. Cited in Russian in the commentary of Khardzhiev to Mandelshtam (1974) 264-5. The Russian version of the poem reads:

I glagol'nykh okonchanii kolokol
Mne vdali ukazyvaet put',
Chtoby v kel'e skromnogo filologa
Ot moikh pechalei otdokhnut'.

Zabyvaiu tiagosti i goresti,
I menia presleduet vopros:
Prirashchen'e nuzhno li v aoriste
I kakoi zalog 'pepaidevkos'.

27. Brodsky (1986) 126 in 'Child of Civilization'. Brodsky noted in addition (ibid. 125) that Mandelshtam's interest in Homer also reflected his preoccupation with time and with the ability of letters – vowels especially – to serve as 'almost palpable vessels of time; they allow the moment to continue, to "linger beyond its natural limit" '.

28. Mandelshtam (1974) 92.

29. There are several passages in the *Iliad* that might have inspired this poem.

The two most obvious possibilities are *Il.* 2.459ff., which is the Catalogue of Ships, and *Il.* 3.156ff., the famous scene of Helen on the Trojan wall identifying the Greek commanders. The passage that specifically alluded to the flock of cranes is *Il.* 3.3ff., in which the Trojan squadrons were likened to the cranes descending 'in clamorous lines before the face of heaven'.

30. Cited in Przybylski (1987) 67-8, translated by Madeline G. Levine.

31. Mandelshtam (1974) 92.

32. See Mandelshtam's essay on Blok (1979, 137). See also Gasparov's commentary to the poem in Mandelshtam (2001) 753.

33. Mandelshtam (1974) 121.

34. Gasparov (1995) 66-7.

35. Indeed in the fourth book of the *Odyssey* Homer indicated that Helen's marriage to Menelaus after their return to Sparta was rather loveless; the scene of two of them telling their respective stories about Odysseus to Telemachus visiting their household a decade after the end of the war hints at their difficult relationship.

36. Gasparov (1995) 68-9.

37. Brown (1973) 244-5. Khardzhiev in Mandelshtam (1974) 280.

38. See Taranovsky (1976) 86-7 for a discussion of the imagery of 'poets-bees' and 'poetry-honey' in other poems by Mandelshtam, as well as for the literary sources of this imagery.

39. Mandelshtam (1974) 104.

40. Mandelshtam (1974) 152.

41. This poem would make mythological sense if interpreted in the context of a more obscure episode from Helen's youth when she was kidnapped by the Greek heroes, Theseus and Pirithous. She was intended to become Theseus' wife but was rescued by her brothers, the Dioscuri. Her kidnappers were imprisoned in Hades trying to steal Persephone for Pirithous (Theseus was later freed by Heracles). The reference to the sea, however, suggests that it is the famous kidnapping by Paris that Mandelshtam had in mind here. Some critics suggested that the poem might be alluding to Mandelshtam's unrequited love for Ol'ga Vaksel', who married a Norwegian from Oslo and left Russia. See Gasparov's commentary in Mandelshtam (2001) 773.

42. See Gasparov (1995) 19.

43. Mandelshtam (1974) 133.

44. Cavanagh (1995) 157-92.

45. Cavanagh (1995) 164-5.

46. See, for example, *Olympian I* in which Pindar celebrated the virtues of Hieron (8-17) and *Pythian I* which celebrated the victory of Hieron's chariot in the Pythian Games of 470 BCE.

47. Lattimore (1947) xii; see also Cavanagh (1995) 175.

48. Mandelshtam (1974) 134-5.

49. Mandelshtam (1974) 135.

50. Mandelshtam (1974) 153.

51. Mandelshtam certainly did not *discover* Russian literary heritage through Tsvetaeva. There were definite influences of Pushkin and Tiutchev in the early Mandelshtam as well. The best source for the personal and poetic relationship between Mandelshtam and Tsvetaeva is the second volume of Nadezhda Mandelshtam's (1972) memoirs. See also Vitins (1987).

52. That collection was published later in 1922 under the title *Tristia* as well, supplied not by Mandelstam himself but by his friend Mikhail Kuzmin when he

arranged for its publication in a Russian émigré press in Berlin. See Ziolkowski (2005) 67 and Freidin (1987).

53. Cited in Hamilton (1983) 327; see also Lincoln (2000) 112.

54. See Figes (2002) 300.

55. Knabe (2000) 185.

56. Cited in Knabe (2000) 185.

57. See also Figes (2002) 157, who observed that 'the idea of Moscow as a "Russian" city' developed from the notion of 'St Petersburg as a foreign civilization'.

58. Przybylski (1987) 137.

59. For the relationship between the 'Roman' and 'Petersburg' texts in Russian Symbolist poetics see Frajlich (2007), who concentrated especially on Solov'ev, Merezhkovskii, Briusov, Ivanov, Voloshin, Komarovskii and Kuzmin.

60. Terras (1966) 255. In his essay 'Pushkin and Scriabin' Mandelshtam juxtaposed Greece and Rome and gave preference to Greece which he considered the source of all culture. See B. Gasparov (1994) 279. The theme of Rome, however, received a more complex and thorough treatment in Mandelshtam's poetics.

61. Mandelshtam (1974) 105.

62. There is also another level of interpretation in this poem pointed out by Struve (1962) 606. The symbol of Rome in this poem was closely connected with Mandelshtam's preoccupation at this time with Catholicism and with Chaadaev. In 1915 Mandelshtam published an essay on Chaadaev in *Apollon* (no. 6-7, pp. 57-63), in which he wrote: 'Chaadaev's thought is national in its sources, national even when it flows into Rome. Only a Russian could discover this West, which is far denser and more concrete than the historical West itself' (Mandelshtam (2001), 555). Here Mandelshtam explicitly made the connection between Rome and the Russian tradition although he had the Catholic Rome in mind rather than the ancient city.

63. There seems to be some confusion about the dating of these two poems. In Mandelshtam (1974) 274 they were attributed to 1917 and the date was not corrected by Nadezhda Mandelshtam. However, in the new edition Mandelshtam (2001) 62 they have been dated to 1914. There are also two extant versions of 'Priroda tot zhe Rim ...' (Mandelshtam (2001) 747). Their first stanzas are similar, but the theme emphasized in the first version expressed a dichotomy between ancient Rome and modern times and was more concerned with humankind's place within that dichotomy:

Kogda derzhalsia Rim v soiuze s estestvom,
Nosilis' obrazy ego grazhdanskoi moshchi
V prozrachnom vozdukhe, kak v tsirke golubom,
Na forume polei i v kollonade roshchi.
A nyne chelovek – ne rab, ne vlastelin,
Ne op'ianen soboi, a tol'ko otumanen;
Nevol'no dumaesh': vsemirnyi grazhdanin,
A khochetsia skazat': vsemirnyi gorozhanin.

When Rome maintained her union with nature
The images of her civic might were lofted
In the transparent air as in blue circus,
In the forum of fields and the colonnade of groves.
But now man is neither slave nor master,
Not intoxicated with himself, but only confused;

Involuntarily you think: universal citizen,
But you mean to say: universal city dweller.

In this version, as Gasparov noted (Mandelshtam (2001), 747), the idea of human degeneration was expressed more explicitly: from the Roman universal citizenry to nothing more than a city dweller.

64. Mandelshtam (1974) 105.

65. Mandelshtam (2001) 511, 'O sobesednike' ('On Interlocutor'): '... poeziia kak tseloe vsegda napravliaetsia k bolee ili menee dalekomu, neizvestnomu adresatu, v sushchestvovanii kotorogo poet ne mozhet somnevat'sia, ne usumnivshis' v sebe'.

66. Mandelshtam (1974) 85.

67. Gasparov and Mets (1997) 23 believed that Tibullus (1.3.90-1) in Batiushkov's translation, not Ovid, was the main subtext of the poem, especially the lines 'Tunc mihi qualis eris, longos turbata capillos,/ Obvia nudato, Delia, curre pede ...' ('Then just as you are, with your hair unkempt, run towards me, Delia, on your bare feet'). For numerous layers of poetic allusion in this poem ranging from Ovid and Pushkin to Verlaine and Villon, see Lekmanov (1995) 142-53. See also Osherov (1995) 188-203.

68. Mandelshtam (1974) 110.

69. This translation by Joseph Brodsky (2000b) 499 approximates closely to the rhythm and rhyme of the original.

70. Ziolkowski (2005) 71.

71. On the reasons for Ovid's exile see Chapter 2, n. 102.

72. Mandelshtam (1974) 93.

73. The 'lucid sorrow' was an allusion to Pushkin's poem 'Na kholmakh Gruzii' ('On the hills of Georgia') in which Pushkin used an expression 'pechal' moia svetla' ('my sorrow is lucid').

74. Boym (2001) 17.

75. Translated by Harris and Link in Mandelshtam (1979) 85.

76. Terras (1966) 257.

77. I want to thank Paul Allen Miller, who drew my attention to this in his response to my talk during the panel 'Classical Tradition in Russian Poetry of the Twentieth Century' at the American Association for the Advancement of Slavic Studies Convention (AAASS) in Washington DC, 17 November 2006.

78. See Lincoln (2000) 222.

79. Goscilo (2008). See also Toporov (1984) on the phenomenon of the 'Petersburg Text' in Russian literature.

80. The poem is not cited in full; see Mandelshtam (1974) 76.

81. Mandelshtam (1974) 76-7.

82. Mandelshtam (1974) 79.

83. Harris (1988) 24.

84. Brown (1973) 258.

85. Mandelshtam (1974) 98.

86. The comparison is by John Kopper (2004).

87. The image of the stony solidity of St Petersburg, as Kopper (2004) indicated, was 'a central Acmeist mythologeme of the city – indeed *Stone* was the title of Mandelshtam's first verse collection'.

88. Volkov (1995) 223.

89. Mandelshtam (1974) 108.

90. Przybylski (1987) 144.

91. Mandelshtam (1974) 151-2.

92. Mandelshtam (1974) 117-18.

93. Mandelshtam (1974) 108.
94. Mandelshtam (1979) 90.
95. A. Tsvetaeva (1980) 71.
96. Mandelshtam (1979) 61-2 'On the Nature of the Word': 'Too often we fail to see that the poet raises a phenomenon to its tenth power, and the modest exterior of a work of art often deceives us with regard to the monstrously condensed reality contained within. In poetry this reality is the word as such'.
97. Harris (1988) 46.
98. Mandelshtam (1974) 150-1.
99. Nemirovskii (1995) 138. Struve (1962) 602, asked the same question and likewise did not offer a definitive answer about Mandelshtam's possible visit to Rome during his travels abroad.
100. This poem is missing in the 1974 edition but is included in the recent collection. See Mandleshtam (2001) 134.
101. Harris (1988) 37.
102. Miller also pointed this out in his response to the AAASS panel (see above, n. 77). For a discussion of Mandelshtam's connection between Crimean and Hellenistic themes see Levin (1995) 77-103.

6. Joseph Brodsky: 'The Uncommon Visage'

1. Burch and Chin (2002) 69.
2. Brodsky (1995) 267.
3. Brodsky (1995) 439-40.
4. See Bethea (1994) 6.
5. See MacFadyen (2000) 120.
6. Brodsky (1995) 45, 'The Nobel Lecture'.
7. Loseff (2006) 63 noted that young Brodsky was influenced by Boris Slutskii (1919-86) in his experimentation with classical prosody and poetic language.
8. Bethea (1994) 49; see also Ungurianu (1996) 161.
9. Polukhina (1989) 36. Shortly before his departure to the West Brodsky was a guest at my parents' house in the capital of Armenia, Erevan. He talked at length about his pending emigration. In one of the conversations, according to my father's recollection, he pointed out to Brodsky that he would lose the sense of the language and 'miss the cursing on the tram' ('mata v tramvae budet ne khvatat'). To which Brodsky without a trace of hesitation responded: 'Iazyk vsegda so mnoi' ('The language is always with me'). In his 1988 essay 'The Condition We Call Exile' Brodsky seems to have developed this belief even further: 'For one in our profession the condition we call exile is, first of all, a linguistic event: he is thrust from, he retreats into his mother tongue. From being his, so to speak, sword, it turns into his shield, into his capsule' (Brodsky (1995) 32).
10. Loseff (2006) 195: in Russian 'prodolzhenie prostranstva'.
11. Brodsky (1986) 83-4.
12. Loseff (2006) 29. Brodsky, by his own admission, did not know Latin (and most certainly not Greek) and read most of the classical literature in translation. See Brodsky (1995) 434. Loseff (2006) 30, however, asserted that Brodsky in fact could get through a Latin text with a dictionary.
13. Brodsky (2001) 2: 135.
14. Losev (1980) 30. Also see Polukhina (1989) 59. Ranchin (2001) 179 pointed out Brodsky's reverence towards all the representatives of Russian classicism, but especially Kantemir and Derzhavin.

15. Polukhina (1989) 59.
16. Brodsky (2000a) 238-9.
17. Some parts of this analysis have been published in the form of a short article; see Torlone (2003a).
18. Bethea (1999a) 241.
19. Verheul (1973) 490.
20. Loseff (2006) 129-30.
21. Kreps (1984) 147-8.
22. Brodsky (2001) 1: 206.
23. Ungurianu (1996) 162. Brodsky made one mistake in this poem; Hektor was killed by Achilles' spear, not his arrows. Achilles had ordered the Achaean bowmen not to shoot at Hektor (*Il.* 22.203ff.).
24. Easterling (1989) 50.
25. Brodsky (2001) 3: 27.
26. See Brodsky's interview with John Glad (1990) 285.
27. Kreps (1984) 155.
28. Zubova (1999) 29.
29. Brodsky (2001) 1: 71.
30. Brodsky (2001) 1: 204.
31. Brodsky (2001) 4: 48-9.
32. See e.g. Hyginus, *Fabulae* 95.2.
33. Hyginus, *Fabulae* 105.
34. Boym (2001) 288.
35. See *OCD* s.v. Odysseus, 747.
36. See Bethea (1994) 34 who had asserted earlier in his book (8) that 'Brodsky himself would take bitter issue with any outside attempt to place a causal connection ("because", "as a result of") between the facts of his life and, as he puts it in an English phrase that owes its birth to the Russian (*izgiby stilia*), his "twists of language" '. See also Loseff's recent biography of Brodsky (2006, 11-12); he observed that Brodsky considered 'his poems self-sufficient without any need of critical interpretation' especially if that included the circumstances of his biography. The biographical connection I am pursuing here is not causal but rather complementary to the literary interpretation.
37. Brodsky (2001) 3: 44.
38. Brodsky (2001) 4: 138.
39. Powell (2007) 614.
40. Translated by Barry Powell (2007) 615.
41. See Ranchin (2001) 445. Ranchin also drew parallels between Brodsky's 'Ithaca' and James Joyce's *Ulysses* (449-52).
42. The theme of exile will be addressed in more detail below in connection with the theme of Empire and poetic legacy.
43. Ranchin (2001) 446 construed this euphemism as addressed by this 'new Odysseus' to his once beloved Ithaca.
44. Brodsky (2001) 2: 313.
45. Ross (2007) 32-3.
46. Ross (2007) 32-3.
47. For the history of scholarship on the juxtaposition between Dido's and Aeneas' characters, see Spence (1999) 80-2.
48. Ross (2007) 34.
49. See Verheul (1973) n.3.

50. Loseff (1990) 38 pithily observed that 'water is Brodsky's constant metaphor for freedom'.

51. These lines were also evocative of the Nisus and Scylla episode in Ovid's *Metamorphoses* 8. Brodsky may also be playing on a Russian proverb 'mute as a fish' ('nem kak ryba').

52. See McLeish (1990).

53. Otis (1964) 220.

54. In Book 2 during the storm, Aeneas displayed deep emotional upheaval and fear for his life and the lives of his companions. In Book 6, he also appeared very vulnerable when Dido refused to speak to him. At the end of the poem, he once again showed his emotions when he saw the belt of Pallas on Turnus but in that passage, driven by a sense of revenge and duty, he proceeded to kill his vanquished enemy.

55. See Covi (1964); also Spence (1999) 80-95.

56. See Perkell (1981) 221, who, in an implicit response to Otis, argued that Aeneas, unlike Dido, demonstrated 'incomplete humanity'. See also Monti (1981) 76 who interpreted Aeneas' behaviour in Book 4 as his fall from *pietas*.

57. See Otis (1964) 236, who pointed out that Dido could be understood as Aeneas' alter ego – 'one who has foiled the crime of the past by founding a city of the future, one who likewise has an object of *pietas* (in the dead Sychaeus and in her own mission of empire) – and a tragic figure ...'.

58. Brumm (2002) 15. In the same interview (15) Brodsky discussed two other influences behind the poem: one was Anna Akhmatova's cycle about Dido and Aeneas, which was a sequence of love poems about her separation from her beloved; the second was Henry Purcell's opera, *Dido and Aeneas*.

59. Brodsky (2001) 2: 199-200.

60. See *OCD* s.v. Achilles, 4-5.

61. Plutarch, *Theseus* 35.

62. I want to thank Lev Loseff for clarifying for me through personal correspondence the existence and chronology of two different titles for this poem. In most of Brodsky's collections of poems the title appears as 'On the Way to Scyros'.

63. See Verheul (1973) 127.

64. Kreps (1984) 147.

65. I agree with Vladimir Maramzin (2008) A9, that Brodsky was a 'true individualist – of course, one that reacts strongly to important events and, of course, living within his own time', but he can hardly be called a political poet.

66. Brodsky (2001) 1: 209, 'Ni strany, ni pogosta ne khochu vybirat'' ('I don't want to choose the country or the graveyard').

67. Brodsky (2001) 3: 16-19.

68. Brodsky (2001) 3: 19.

69. This translation, by Alan Myers with Joseph Brodsky, first appeared in *The Kenyon Review* 1: 1, Winter 1979. See Brodsky (2000b) 70, 511.

70. Bethea (1994) 39.

71. Brodsky (2001) 2: 397.

72. Brodsky (1986) 128.

73. Brodsky (2001) 2: 397-405.

74. Loseff (1977) 325.

75. Brodsky (2001) 1: 274. It is not exactly clear to me why Brodsky evoked Titus Livy in this poem; Livy was neither a politician nor a military man. Kovaleva (2001) 194 suggested that Brodsky might have used here the word play in Russian on Livy and Livia (the Russian word for Libya), the ancient appellation of Africa,

but I find that conjecture far-fetched. Lev Loseff offered to me another more plausible explanation, that Brodsky might have confused Titus Livy with Titus Flavius Vespasianus, who prior to becoming emperor of Rome, had gained renown as a military commander serving under his father in Judaea during the first Jewish-Roman war (67-70 CE).

76. Alexander Kushner was the first person to make this connection between Brodsky and Ovid in his poem of 1964 'Zasnesh' s prikushennoi guboi ...' ('You will fall asleep biting your lip ...'). See Ichin (1996) 227. It is clear even in the essay *Letter to Horace* that Brodsky preferred Ovid to all the other Roman poets.

77. Burch and Chin (2002) 70. In the same interview Brodsky stated that if he were younger he would write 'a book of imitations'. That unfulfilled desire was apparent in Brodsky's poem *Vertumnus* (1990), which was influenced by the *Metamorphoses*.

78. The Ovidian theme remained constant in Brodsky and reappeared also in his later play 'Mramor' ('Marble', 1984) devoted exclusively to antiquity. In that play one of the heroes, Tullius (Tullii) quoted Ovid's *Amores*, *Fasti*, and the *Metamorphoses* incessantly. Vertumnus and Pomona also appeared in the play.

79. Kline (1990) 84n.5 offered an alternative spelling of the village 'Norinskaia' based on a photograph of Brodsky and Anatolii Naiman standing beside the sign identifying that town. Brodsky (1980) 8 himself spelled it 'Norenskaia'. See also Loseff (2006) 104, 106.

80. Brodsky (2001) 2: 100.

81. Ichin (1996) 246, n. 14.

82. Brodsky (2001) 2: 350, 'Nu kak tebe v gruzinskikh palestinakh? ('So, how are you in the Georgian palestines?').

83. Brodsky (2001) 2: 124.

84. Brodsky (2001) 2: 213.

85. Brodsky (2001) 2: 378.

86. Brodsky (2001) 2: 416.

87. Brodsky (2001) 3: 10. The poem, however, contained in the third set of stanzas an allusion to the funerary epigram by Simonides of Ceos (556-468 BCE) of a merchant who died in a foreign land while travelling (fr. 156 Edmonds).

88. Kline (1990) 63 noted that 'the principal similarity is one of condition: the poet in exile'. Martial, born in Spain, returned to its provincial obscurity (from 98 CE) after a brilliant literary career in Rome.

89. Brodsky (2001) 3: 11.

90. Brodsky (2001) 3: 12.

91. In the Autumn 1993 issue of the *Wilson Quarterly* Brodsky published an essay on Propertius accompanying a translation of the seventh elegy of Propertius' *Monobiblos* (Brodsky (1993)). The essay was concerned with a 'rehabilitation' of Propertius in the eyes of American readers after the latter was unfairly presented, in Brodsky's harsh opinion, by the 'moronic pastiche of our eternal sophomore, Ezra Pound' (86). The essay showed Brodsky's reason for his deep preoccupation with Propertius' elegy; 'by reading him', he stated, 'we may at least learn what it takes to endure two thousand years without being a messiah'. This statement is especially important in the light of Brodsky's own take on his poetic legacy, discussed below. It is also worth noting that the inscription on Brodsky's grave in Venice is taken from Propertius' fourth book of elegies (IV.7.1): *letum non omnia finit* ('death does not end everything').

92. Brodsky (2001) 2: 214.

93. For a thorough and reliable account of Brodsky's stormy relationship with Basmanova see Loseff (2006) 72-7, 86, 107, 128, 297.
94. See Ungurianu (1996) 176.
95. Brodsky (2001) 3: 274.
96. This translation by Alan Myers with Joseph Brodsky first appeared in the *New York Review of Books*, 25 June 1987. See Brodsky (2000b) 282, 522.
97. See Ungurianu (1996) 169, 176. The motif of ruins was also used by Brodsky in, for example, 'Letters to a Roman Friend': 'My ogliadyvaias' vidim lish' ruiny' ('When looking back, we see only ruins') and in 'Piazza Mattei' (XV) where he explicitly equated himself with a bust (Brodsky (2001) 3: 211):

Moi rot oskalen
ot radosti: emu znakoma
sud'ba razvalin.
Ogryzok tsezaria, atleta,
pevtsa chem pache
est' variant avtoportreta.

My mouth scowls
with joy: it is familiar
with the fate of ruins.
The stub of a Caesar, athlete,
and especially a bard
is a version of self-portrait.

In another poem 'To Cornelius Dolabella' written in 1995, shortly before Brodsky died, he again evoked the image of posthumous glory cast in marble alluding also to his heart condition: 'i mramor suzhaet moiu aortu' ('and the marble narrows my aorta').
98. Brodsky (2001) 3: 276.
99. See Nivat (1990) 91.
100. Brodsky (2001) 3: 232.
101. Brodsky's translation (2000b) 280. The same exhilaration about being at Rome Brodsky expressed in the 'Piazza Mattei' connecting it explicitly to his fascination with antiquity. Brodsky (2001) 3: 209:

... ia schastliv v etoi kolybeli
Muz, Prava, Gratsii,
gde Nazo i Vergilii peli,
veshchal Goratsii.

I am happy in this cradle
Of Muses, Law, Graces,
Where Naso and Vergil sang
And Horace prophesied.

102. The coin ('piatak') refers to Charon, the sombre ferryman who transported the dead over the Styx into the Underworld and who required an obol for his services, usually put in the mouth (not on the eyes) of the deceased. See *OCD* s.v. Charon, 228.
103. For a fascinating study of the relationship between the Russians and Italy

from the seventeenth century to the present day, see Lo Gatto (1971). In his interview with Valentina Polukhina, Tomas Venclova said about Brodsky's 'love affair with Rome': 'At this point it is well worth recalling the palindrome *Rim – mir* (Rome – world). Rome is one with the world and at the same time its opposite ... It is precisely that identity, that mirroring, that Brodsky's Roman poems are about'. See Polukhina (1992) 282. In that respect Brodsky continued the tradition of Ivanov's and Mandelshtam's Rome.

104. Cited in Russian in Brodsky (2000a) 421.

105. Brodsky (2001) 3: 122-4.

106. A reference to Mario Cavaradossi in Puccini's opera *Tosca*.

107. This, as Kline suggested (1990) 78, might be a rare reference to the hostile reaction of the crowd outside the Leningrad courthouse when Brodsky was on trial for 'social parasitism' in February/March 1964. One of the ironic details of Brodsky's Kafkaesque trial was that his persecutors also used classical idiom in the slandering article that appeared on 29 November 1963 in *Vechernii Leningrad* (*Evening Leningrad*). The authors of that article favoured the references to Parnassus so much that it appeared four times in phrases labelling Brodsky 'a pigmy climbing Parnassus', or stating that 'he does not care by what means he climbs Parnassus', that 'he cannot get rid of the thought about Parnassus', and that he wants to 'climb Parnassus in isolation'. Cited in Russian in Loseff (2006) 82.

108. Brodsky (1995) 23.

109. See Brodsky's (2000a) 664 interview with Dmitrii Radyshevskii. See also Loseff (2006) 260. For a detailed discussion of the issue see Reynolds (2005).

110. Brodsky (1986) 130.

111. Brodsky (2001) 3: 191.

112. Brodsky (2000b) 211. This poem first appeared in the *Times Literary Supplement*, 29 May 1987.

113. Brodsky (2001) 3: 228.

114. Brodsky (1995) 47.

115. It is not every clear what Brodsky meant by this title because the poems are not written in elegiac distich and they rhyme. The title might have been also influenced by Brodsky's interest in Propertius and Ovid.

116. Brodsky (2001) 3: 229.

117. Brodsky's own translation (2000b) 276. The same rejection of his predecessors' 'monumental' legacies was reflected in the 1987 poem 'Mysl' o tebe udaliaetsia ...' ('The thought of you departs ...') in the line 'Vidimo, nikomu iz nas ne sdelat'sia pamiatnikom' ('It seems that none of us will become a monument'). See Brodsky (2001) 4: 26.

118. Brodsky (2001) 3: 143.

119. This translation by Daniel Weissbort, first appeared in *Poetry* (March 1978) and was subsequently revised with Brodsky. See Brodsky (2000b) 114, 513.

120. See a detailed discussion of metre and diction in Bethea (1994) 12-15.

121. Vladimir Maiakovskii had also used vernacular, even vulgar, language in his poetry.

122. Odysseus, called thus after Mt Neritus in Ithaca.

123. Brodsky himself compared his exile to a shipwreck in an unpublished postcard, which he sent to my parents from Ann Arbor dated 28 November 1972. See p. 191. In it he wrote: '... something like a conflagration, a shipwreck, something more or less like a natural disaster – happened to me' ('... chto-to vrode pozhara, korablekrusheniia, chto-to vrode bolee ili menee stikhiinogo bedstviia – proizoshlo').

124. Loseff (2006) 275 pointed out that Brodsky wanted his 'valediction' poem

to be a poem written in 1994 'Menia uprekali vo vsem okromia pogody' ('I was blamed for everything save the weather' – Brodsky (2001) 4: 173). In the first stanza of this poem Brodsky envisioned himself becoming a star in the sky after death. The allusion, Loseff suggested, was to *Metamorphoses* Book 15 in which Julius Caesar became a star (276). It could also be an allusion to Vergil's *Eclogues* (especially 9. 47 where the motif of Caesar as a star was mentioned explicitly), which Brodsky loved and had read carefully.

125. Reynolds (2007) 555.

126. Several critics pointed out the importance of the poem. See Smith (2005) 401, Reynolds (2007).

127. Brodsky (2001) 4: 137.

128. Brodsky's own translation (2000b) 404. This translation first appeared in the *New York Review of Books*, 7 October 1993.

129. There was also an obvious allusion in the poem to Ovid's *Metamorphoses* 8.183-235, especially in the lines 'capable of transporting himself through the air, if robbed of other means of passage'. Cf. Ovid's ' "Terras licet" inquit "et undas obstruat: at caelum certe patet, ibimus illac' " (he may [Minos] hinder us on land and on sea: but the sky is surely open, we will go that way').

130. Conte (1986) 32-40.

131. Hubbard (1998) 11. See also Forrester (2004) 2-3 on distinction between the terms 'affiliation' and 'filiation' and their use in scholarship on modernist authors.

132. Hubbard (1998) 11.

133.

Daedalus, ut fama est, fugiens Minoia regna,
praepetibus pinnis ausus se credere caelo,
insuetum per iter gelidas enavit ad Arctos
Chalcidicaque levis tandem super adstitit arce.
redditus his primum terris tibi, Phoebe, sacravit
remigium alarum posuitque immania templa.
in foribus letum Androgeo; tum pendere poenas
Cecropidae iussi, miserum! septena quotannis
corpora natorum; stat ductis sortibus urna.
contra elata mari respondet Gnosia tellus:
his crudelis amor tauri suppostaque furto
Pasiphae mixtumque genus prolesque biformis
Minotaurus inest, veneris monumenta nefandae;
his labor ille domus et inextricabilis error;
magnum reginae sed enim miseratus amorem
Daedalus ipse dolos tecti ambagesque resolvit,
caeca regens filo vestigia. tu quoque magnam
partem opere in tanto, sineret dolor, Icare, haberes;
bis conatus erat casus effingere in auro,
bis patriae cecidere manus.

134. See Putnam (1987) 174.

135. One place where the English translation differed from the Russian original was the reiteration in English of 'here, in Sicily', whereas in Russian that line contained only a word meaning 'now' ('teper").

136. See *OCD* s.v. Daedalus, 309.

137. The idea of mentioning Icarus only in passing recalls also W.H. Auden's

famous 1938 poem 'Musée des Beaux Arts', in which there is the *ecphrasis* of Pieter Breughel's *Fall of Icarus*. For more on the issue of Auden's profound influence on Brodsky, see Loseff (2006) 178-82 and Reynolds (2007). Among other influences on this poem of Brodsky, Reynolds also mentioned Shakespeare's Prospero and Tennyson's 'Ulysses' (576).

138. Gillespie (2004) 37 observed that 'Brodsky's portrait of the ancient inventor in old age is also a trenchant self-portrait'.

139. Reynolds (2007) 560.

140. See *OCD* s.v. Daedalus, 309.

141. Reynolds (2007) 578 had a less pessimistic reading of this poem arguing that 'one, may perhaps consider Daedalus happy'. I agree in the sense that Brodsky's Daedalus, as an old man, was free from the yearnings and pitfalls of his youthful ambitions.

142. It would be futile to look for any kind of lofty message in any of Brodsky's *Monumentum*-like poems, including his explicitly Horatian 'Imitation of Horace' ('Podrazhanie Goratsiiu', Brodsky (2001) 4: 155), written in 1993 in which he, using Horace's famous metaphor of the 'ship of the state', somewhat sarcastically contemplated the collapse of the USSR (see Loseff 2006, 265-6), '*Aere Perennius*' (Brodsky 2001, 4: 202), or even his last poem written in January 1996, 'August' (Brodsky 2001, 4: 204). For a detailed discussion of the last poem see Reynolds (2005).

143. Brodsky (1986) 133.

Post Aetatem Nostram: A Brief Postscript and a Very Short Introduction

1. I am thankful to my colleague Vitaly Chernetsky for sharing with me his expertise in modern Russian poetry.

2. Kukulin (2004) 7.

3. In an additional inversion of Ovid, Poliakov lives in Simpheropol', which is located near the Black Sea; he is therefore not in exile in that region, but at home.

4. Kukulin (2004) 16.

5. See Kudriavtsev on www.vavilon.ru

6. In *Nestolichnaia Literatura* 107-8.

7. Barskova's poems 'Daphnis and Chloe', 'Horace', and 'Delia' can be found online at www.sguez.com/za-granizza/polibars.html.

Bibliography

Alekseev, M.P. (1967) *Stikhotvorenie Pushkina 'Ia pamiatnik sebe vozdvig ...': problemy ego izucheniia'*. Leningrad: Nauka.

Al'tman, M.S. (1968) 'Iz besed s poetom Viacheslavom Ivanovichem Ivanovym', *Uchenye zapiski Tartuskogo gos. univ.* 209: 304-25.

Al'tman, M.S. (1995) *Razgovory s Viacheslavom Ivanovym*. St Petersburg: Inapress: 88-9.

Altshuller, M. (1992) 'The Transition to the Modern Age: Sentimentalism and Preromanticism', in C.A. Moser (ed.) *The Cambridge History of Russian Literature*, Cambridge: Cambridge University Press: 92-135.

Annenskii, I.F. (1902) 'Antichnaia tragediia. Publichnaia lektsiia', *Mir Bozhii*. November: 1-41.

Annenskii, I.F. (1979) *Kniga Otrazhenii*. Moscow: Nauka.

Annenskii, I.F. (1990) *Stikhotvoreniia i tragedii*. Introduction by A.V. Fedorov. Leningrad: Biblioteka Poeta.

Annenskii, I.F. (2003) *Istoriia antichnoi dramy. Kurs lektsii*. St Petersburg: Giperion.

Annenskii, I.F. (2007) *Teatr Evripida*, ed. with commentary by V. Gitin. St Petersburg: Giperion.

Armstrong, R. (2006) *Cretan Women: Pasiphae, Ariadne, and Phaedra in Latin Poetry*. Oxford: Oxford University Press.

Asoian, Iu. Malafeev, A. (2000) *Otkrytie idei kul'tury. Opyt russkoi kul'turologii serediny XIX- nachala XX vekov*. Moscow: OGI.

Averintsev, S.S. (1996) *Poety*. Moscow: Shkola 'Iazyki russkoi kul'tury'.

Averintsev, S.S. (2001) *'Skvoreshnits vol'nykh grazhdanin'; Viacheslav Ivanov, put' poeta mezhdu mirami*. St Petersburg: Aleteiia.

Axer, J., Tomaszuk, K. (2007) 'Central-Eastern Europe', in C.W. Kallendorf (ed.) *A Companion to Classical Tradition*. Oxford: Blackwell: 132-55.

Baehr, S.L. (1991) *The Paradise Myth in Eighteenth-Century Russia: Utopian Patterns in Early Secular Russian Literature and Culture*. Stanford: Stanford University Press.

Bakhrakh, A. (ed.) (1960-1) *Pis'ma Mariny Tsvetaevoi. Mosty* 5 (1960) 299-318. *Mosty* 6 (1961) 319-46.

Bakhtin, N. (1963) 'The Symbolist Movement in Russia', in *Lectures and Essays*. Birmingham: University of Birmingham: 34-44.

Balashov, N.I. (1989) 'Eskhil Viacheslava Ivanova – dvoinoi pamiatnik kul'tury', in N.I. Balashov, D.V. Ivanov, M.L. Gasparov, G.Ch. Guseinov, N.V. Kotrelev (eds) *Tragedii Eskhila*, tr. V. I. Ivanov. Moscow: Nauka: 453-63.

Barta, P.I. (2000) 'Introduction: Russian Literature and the Metamorphic Theme', in P.I. Barta (ed.) *Metamorphoses in Russian Modernism*. New York: Central European University Press: 1-14.

Beecroft, A.J. (2006) ' "This is not a True Story": Stesichorus's *Palinode* and the Revenge of the Epichoric', *Transactions of the American Philological Association* 136, no. 1: 47-70.

Bibliography

Berkov, P.N. (1953) 'A.P. Sumarokov', in *Sumarokov A. P. Stikhotvoreniia.* Leningrad: Sovetskii Pisatel'.

Bethea, D.M. (1994) *Joseph Brodsky and the Creation of Exile.* Princeton: Princeton University Press.

Bethea, D.M. (1998) *Realizing Metaphors: Alexander Pushkin and the Life of the Poet.* Madison: University of Wisconsin Press.

Bethea, D.M. (1999a) 'Joseph Brodsky's "To my daughter" ', in L. Loseff, V. Polukhina (eds) *Joseph Brodsky: The Art of a Poem.* New York: St Martin's Press: 240-57.

Bethea, D.M. (1999b) 'Where to Begin: Pushkin, Derzhavin, and the Poetic Use of Filiation', in Stephanie Sandler (ed.) *Rereading Russian Poetry.* New Haven: Yale University Press: 58-70.

Bethea, D.M. (2002) 'Literature', in N. Rzhevsky (ed.) *The Cambridge Companion to Modern Russian Culture.* Cambridge: Cambridge University Press: 161-206.

Billington, J.H. (1970) *The Icon and the Axe: An Interpretive History of Russian Culture.* New York: Vintage.

Binyon, T.J. (2002) *Pushkin.* London: HarperCollins.

Bird, R. (2006) *The Russian Prospero: The Creative World of Viacheslav Ivanov.* Madison: University of Wisconsin Press.

Blinov, V.N. (1986) 'Chronology of the Life and Works of Vyachelav Ivanov', in *Vyacheslav Ivanov: Poet, Critic and Philosopher.* New Haven: Yale Center for International and Area Studies: 413-74.

Bongard-Levin, G.M., Kotrelev, N.V., Liapustina, E.V. (eds) (2006) *Istoriia i poeziia. Perepiska I.M. Grevsa i Viach. Ivanova.* Moscow: ROSSPEN.

Borovskii, Ia. M. (1960) 'Latinskii iazyk Lomonosova', in *Lomonosov: Sbornik statei i materialov.* Moscow-Leningrad, vol. 4: 212.

Bowersock, G.W. (1999) 'The Roman Emperor as Russian Tsar: Tacitus and Pushkin', *Proceedings of the American Philosophical Society* 143, no. 1. Paper delivered at a Joint Meeting with the Royal Swedish Academy of Sciences, Stockholm, 24-26 May 1998: 130-47.

Boym, S. (1991) *Death in Quotation Marks: Cultural Myths of the Modern Poet.* Cambridge, MA: Harvard University Press.

Boym, S. (2001) *The Future of Nostalgia.* New York: Basic Books.

Bradbury, M., McFarlane, J. (1976) 'The Name and Nature of Modernism', in *Modernism*: 1890-1930. New York: Penguin: 27.

Braginskaia, N. (2004) 'Slavianskoe vozrozhdenie antichnosti', in *Russkaia teoriia 1920-1930-e gody. Materilay 10-kh Lotmanovskikh chtenii*: 49-80.

Briusov, V. (1906) 'Review of "*Sbornik: severnaia rech'*" ', *Vesy* 6 (June): 64. Reprint Nendeln, Leichtenstein: Kraus Reprint Ltd (1968).

Briusov, V. (1973-75) *Sobranie Sochinenii v semi tomakh,* vol. 3 (1974): P.G. Antokol'skii, A.S. Miasnikov, S.S. Narovchatov, I.S. Tikhonov (eds) *Stikhotvoreniia 1918-1924 godov.* Moscow: Khudozhestvennaia Literatura.

Brodsky, J. (1980) *A Part of Speech.* New York: Farrar, Straus and Giroux.

Brodsky, J. (1986) *Less than One: Selected Essays.* New York: Farrar, Straus, and Giroux.

Brodsky, J. (1993) 'Sextus Propertius', *Wilson Quarterly* 17, no. 4: 86-8.

Brodsky, J. (1995) *On Grief and Reason: Essays.* New York: Farrar, Straus and Giroux.

Brodsky, J. (2000a) *Segodnia – eto vchera. Bol'shaia kniga interv'iu,* ed. Valentina Polukhina, 2nd edn. Moscow: Zakharov.

Brodsky, J. (2000b) *Collected Poems in English.* New York: Farrar, Straus and Giroux.

Bibliography

Brodsky, J. (2001) (Brodskii Iosif). *Sochineniia Iosifa Brodskogo* [Collected Works of Joseph Brodsky], 7 vols, ed. Ia.A. Gordin. St Petersburg: Pushkinskii Fond.

Brodsky Sozzani, M. (2000) 'The First Brodsky Fellowships', *New York Review of Books* 47.4. http://www.nybooks.com/articles/183.

Brown, C. (1973) *Mandelshtam.* Cambridge: Cambridge University Press.

Broyde, S. (1975) *Osip Mandelshtam and his Age: A Commentary on the Themes of War and Revolution in the Poetry 1913-1923.* Cambridge, MA: Harvard University Press.

Brumm, A-M. (2002) 'The Muse in Exile: Conversations with the Russian Poet, Joseph Brodsky', in C.L. Haven (ed.) *Joseph Brodsky: Conversations.* Jackson: University Press of Mississippi.

Budelmann, F., Haubold, J. (2008) 'Reception and Tradition', in L. Hardwick, C. Stray (eds) *A Companion to Classical Receptions.* Oxford: Blackwell: 13-25.

Bukalov, A. (2004) *Pushkinskaia Italia.* St. Petersburg: Aleteiia.

Burch, E., Chin, D. (2002) 'Interview with Joseph Brodsky', in C.L. Haven (ed.) *Joseph Brodsky: Conversations.* Jackson: University Press of Mississippi: 55-70.

Burgi, R. (1954) *A History of the Russian Hexameter.* Hamden, CT: Shoe String Press.

Cantarella (1986) 'Dangling Virgins: Myth, Ritual, and the Place of Women in Ancient Greece', in Susan R. Suleiman (ed.) *The Female Body in Western Literature.* Cambridge, MA: Harvard University Press.

Cavanagh, C. (1995) *Osip Mandelshtam and the Modernist Creation of Tradition.* Princeton: Princeton University Press.

Cherniaev, P.N. (1898) 'Vliianie shkoly, obstanovki i epokhi na razvitie v A.S. Pushkine liubvi k antichnomu miru', *Gimnaziia* 11.6: 1-9.

Cherniaev, P.N. (1904-5) 'Sledy znakomstva russkogo obshchestva s drevne-klassicheskoi literaturoi v vek Ekateriny II', *Filologicheskie zapiski* (Voronezh): nos 3-4: 1-64, nos 5-6: 65-128; nos 1-2: 129-60; nos 3-4: 161-232.

Christesen, P., Martirosova-Torlone, Z. (2007) 'Eusebius' Olympic Victor List: Text, Translation, and Commentary', *Traditio* 61: 31-93.

Ciepiela, C. (2006) *The Same Solitude: Boris Pasternak and Marina Tsvetaeva.* Ithaca: Cornell University Press.

Collard, C., Cropp, M.J., Lee, K.H. (eds) (1995) *Euripides: Selected Fragmentary Plays.* Warminster, UK: Aris and Phillips.

Connolly, J. (1992) 'The Nineteenth Century: The Age of Realism', in C.A. Moser (ed.) *The Cambridge History of Russian Literature.* Cambridge: Cambridge University Press: 333-86.

Conte, G.B. (1986) *The Rhetoric of Imitation: Genre and Poetic Memory in Virgil and Other Latin Poets*, tr. C. Segal. Ithaca: Cornell University Press.

Conte, G.B. (1994) *Latin Literature: A History*, tr. J.B. Solodow. Baltimore and London.

Covi, M.C. (1964) 'Dido in Vergil's *Aeneid*', *Classical Journal* 60: 57-60.

Davidson, P. (1989) *The Poetic Imagination of Vyacheslav Ivanov: A Russian Symbolist Perception of Dante.* Cambridge: Cambridge University Press.

Davidson, P. (1996a) 'Hellenism, Culture, and Christianity: The Case of Vyacheslav Ivanov and His "Palinode" of 1927', in P.I. Barta, D.H.J. Larmour, P.A. Miller (eds) *Russian Literature and the Classics: Studies in Russian and European Literature*, vol. 1. Amsterdam: Harwood Academic Publishers: 83-116.

Davidson, P. (1996b) *Viacheslav Ivanov: A Reference Guide.* New York: G.K. Hall & Co.

Davidson, P. (2006) *Vyacheslav Ivanov and C.M. Bowra: A Correspondence from*

Bibliography

Two Corners on Humanism. Birmingham: Centre for Russian and East European Studies, University of Birmingham.

Davidson, P. (2007) 'Afiny i Ierusalim: dve veshchi nesovmestnye? Znachenie idei Ivanova dlia sovremennoi Rossii', *Toronto Slavic Quarterly* 20: 1-7, online at www.utoronto.ca/tsq/20/davidson20.shtml.

Davie, D. (1964) Review of 'The Letters of Alexander Pushkin, tr. by J.T. Shaw', *Guardian* 21: 7.

Derzhavin, G.R. (1958) *Stikhotvoreniia*, ed. with introduction by A.Ia. Kucherov. Moscow: Gosudarstvennoe Izdatel'stvo Khudozhestvennoi Literatury.

Deschartes, O. (1954) 'Viacheslav Ivanov', *Oxford Slavonic Papers*, vol. 5: 48.

Dinega, A. (2001) *A Russian Psyche: The Poetic Mind of Marina Tsvetaeva*. Madison: University of Wisconsin Press.

Donchin, G. (1958) *The Influence of French Symbolism on Russian Poetry*. Leiden: Mouton, Slavistic Printings and Reprintings 19.

Dvoichenko-Markova, E.M. (1966) 'Istochniki legendy ob Ovidii v "Tsyganakh" Pushkina' in *Voprosy antichnoi literatury i klassicheskoi filologii*. Moscow: Nauka: 321-9.

Easterling, P.E. (1989) 'Sophocles', in P.E. Easterling and B.M.W. Knox (eds) *The Cambridge History of Classical Literature*. Cambridge: Cambridge University Press: 43-63.

Erlich, V. (1964) *The Double Image: Concepts of the Poet in Slavic Literatures*. Baltimore: Johns Hopkins University Press.

Esalnek, A.Ia. (2002) 'Tematologiia na rasput'e', in *Literatura, kul'tura i fol'klor slavianskikh narodov. Materialy konferentsii*. Moscow: IMLI RAN: 228-36.

Euripides (1955) *Alcestis, The Medea, The Heracleidai, Hippolytus*. David Grene, Richmond Lattimore (eds), tr. David Grene. Chicago and London: Chicago University Press.

Euripides (1959) *Electra, The Phoenician Women, The Bacchae*. David Grene, Richmond Lattimore (eds), tr. William Arrowsmith. Chicago and London: Chicago University Press.

Faibisovich, V.M. (1977) 'K istochniku perevoda Pushkina "Iz Katulla" ', *Vremennik pushkinskoi komissii*. Leningrad: Nauka, 1980: 69-75.

Fedorov, A.V. (1984) *Innokentii Annenskii: Lichnost' i tvorchestvo*. Leningrad: Khudozhestvennaia Literatura.

Feinstein, E. (1989) *Marina Tsvetaeva*. London: Penguin Books.

Feinstein, E. (1998) *Pushkin: A Biography*. New York: Ecco Press.

Fidler, F.F. (1911) ed. *Pervye literaturnye shagi: Avtobiografii sovremennykh russkikh pisatelei*. Moscow: Tipografiia I.D. Sytina.

Figes, O. (2002) *Natasha's Dance: A Cultural History of Russia*. New York: Metropolitan Books.

Forrester, S. (2000) 'Daphne's Tremor: Tsvetaeva and the Feminine in Classical Myth and Statuary', *Indiana Slavic Studies* 11: 367-80.

Forrester, S. (2004) 'Sons, Lovers and the Laius Complex in Russian Modernist Poetry', *Slavic Review* 63, no. 1: 1-5.

Fox, M.S. (2001) *The Troubling Play of Gender: The Phaedra Dramas of Tsvetaeva, Yourcenar, and H.D.* Selinsgrove: Susquehanna University Press.

Frajlich, A. (2007) *The Legacy of Ancient Rome in the Russian Silver Age*. Amsterdam and New York: *Studies in Slavic Literature and Poetics* 48.

Freeborne, R. (1989) 'The Nineteenth Century: The Age of Realism, 1855-80', in C.A. Moser (ed.) *The Cambridge History of Russian Literature*. Cambridge: Cambridge University Press: 248-332.

Bibliography

Freidenberg, O. (1991) 'Universitetskie gody', *Chelovek* 3: 154.

Freidin, G. (1987) *A Coat of Many Colors: Osip Mandelshtam and His Mythologies of Self-Presentation*. Berkeley: University of California Press.

Frolov, E.D. (1999) *Russkaia nauka ob antichnosti*. St Petersburg: Izd. S.- Peterburgskogo Universiteta.

Galanina, Iu. E. (2006) 'V.E. Meierkhol'd na Bashne Viach. Ivanova', in *Bashnia Viacheslava Ivanova i Kul'tura Serebrianogo Veka*. St Petersburg: Filologicheskii Fakul'tet S.-Peterburgskogo Universiteta: 187-205.

Gasparov, B. (1985) 'Encounter of Two Poets in the Desert: Pushkin's Myth', in A. Kodjak, K. Pomorska, S. Rudy (eds) *Myth in Literature*. Columbus: Slavica Publishers: 124-53.

Gasparov, B. (1994) 'Russkaia Gretsiia, russkii Rim', in R.P. Hughes and I. Paperno (eds) *Russian Culture in Modern Times*, vol. 2: *Christianity and the Eastern Slavs*. California Slavic Studies XVII. Berkeley: University of California Press: 245-86.

Gasparov, M.L. (1966) 'Antichnyi trimetr i russkii iamb', in *Voprosy antichnoi literatury i klassicheskoi filologii*. Moscow: Akademiia Nauk SSSR: 393-410.

Gasparov, M.L. (1971) 'Briusov i bukvalism', in L. Ozerov (ed.) *Masterstvo perevoda*. Moscow: Sovetskii Pisatel'.

Gasparov, M.L. (1975) 'Briusov i antichnost' ', in Briusov, V. (1973-5) *Sobranie Sochinenii v semi tomakh*, (eds) P.G. Antokol'skii, A.S. Miasnikov, S.S. Narovchatov, I.S. Tikhonov. Moscow: Khudozhestvennaia Literatura, vol. 5: 543-56.

Gasparov, M.L. (1986) 'Perevod Pushkina "Iz Ksenophana Kolofonskogo" ', *Vremennik Pushkinskoi komissii* 20: 24-5.

Gasparov, M.L. (1995) *Antichnost' v russkoi poezii nachala XX veka*. Pisa: Istituto di lingua e letteratura russa.

Gasparov, M.L. (1996) *O. Mandelshtam: Grazhdanskaia lirika 1937 goda*. Moscow: RGGU.

Gasparov, M.L. (1997) 'Oppozitsiia "stikh – proza" i stanovlenie russkogo literaturnogo stikha', in M.L. Gasparov, *Izbrannye trudy*, vol. 3: 'O Stikhe'. Moscow: Iazyki Russkoi Kul'tury: 40-53.

Gasparov, M.L., Mets, A.G. (1997) 'Poet i kul'tura. Tri poetiki Osipa Mandel'shtama', in *O. Mandelshtam. Polnoe sobranie stikhotvorenii*. St Petersburg: Gumanitarnoe Agenstvo "Akademicheskii Proekt".

Gasparov, M.L. (2000) *Ocherk istorii russkogo stikha*. Moscow: Fortuna Limited.

Gasparov, M.L. (2001) 'Evripid Innokentiia Annenskogo', in *O Russkoi poezii. Analizy. Interpretatsii. Kharakteristiki*. St Petersburg: Azbuka: 373-88.

Gay, P. (1966-9) *The Enlightenment, an Interpretation*, vols 1-2. New York: Knopf.

Gerasimov, I.K. (1984) 'Neokonchennaia tragediia Viacheslava Ivanova "Niobeia" ', in K.N. Grigorian (ed.) *Ezhegodnik rukopisnogo otdela Pushkinskogo doma na 1980 god*. Leningrad: Nauka.

Gillespie, A.D. (2004) 'Joseph Brodsky (Iosif Aleksandrovich Brodsky)', in M. Balina, M. Lipovetskii (eds) *Russian Writers since 1980. Dictionary of Literary Biography 285*. Detroit, MI: Gale: 17-39.

Gill, C. (1990) 'The Articulation of the Self in Euripides' *Hippolytus*', in A. Powell (ed.) *Euripides, Women, and Sexuality*. London and New York: Routledge: 76-107.

Glad, J. (1990) 'Nastignut' utrachennoe vremia', in *Vremia i my: Al'manakh literatury i obshchestvennykh problem*. Moscow: Iskusstvo. New York: Vremia i My.

Bibliography

Gollerbakh, E.F. (1927) 'Iz zagadok proshlogo (Innokentii Annenskii i Tsarskoe Selo)', *Krasnaia gazeta*, 3 July.

Goscilo, H. (2008) 'Unsaintly St Petersburg? Visions and Visuals', in H. Goscilo, S. Norris (eds) *Preserving Petersburg: History, Memory, Nostalgia*. Bloomington: Indiana University Press: 57-87.

Gove, A.F. (1977) 'The Feminine Stereotype and Beyond: Role Conflict and Resolution in the Poetics of Marina Tsvetaeva', *Slavic Review* 36, no. 2: 231-55.

Green, M. (1977) 'The Russian Symbolist Theater: Some Connections', *Pacific Coast Philology* 12: 5-14.

Gudzii, N. (1930) 'Tiutchev v poeticheskoi kul'ture russkogo simvolizma', in *Izvestiia po russkomu iazyku i slovesnosti*, vol. 3. Leningrad: ANSSR: 465-549.

Gukovskii, G.A. (1935) 'G.P. Derzhavin', in *Derzhavin G. Stikhotvoreniia*. Leningrad: Sovetskii Pisatel': 48.

Gumilev, N. (1962-8) *Sobranie sochineneii*, ed. Gleb Struve, Boris Filippov, vol. 4. Washington, DC: Kamkin.

Gurevich, L. (1910) 'Zametki o sovremennoi literature: mechty i mysli o novoi drame', *Russkaia mysl'*, no. 4 [section 2]: 146-63.

Hamilton, G.H. (1983) *Art and Architecture of Russia*. New Haven: Yale University Press.

Hardwick, L. (2000) *Translating Words, Translating Cultures*. London: Duckworth.

Hardwick, L. (2003) 'Reception Studies', *Greece and Rome. New Surveys in the Classics* 33. Oxford: Oxford University Press.

Hardwick, L., Stray, C. (eds) (2008) *A Companion to Classical Receptions*. Oxford: Blackwell.

Harris, J.G. (1988) *Osip Mandelstam*. Boston: Twayne.

Hart, P.R. (2002) 'The West', in N. Rzhevsky (ed.) *The Cambridge Companion to Modern Russian Culture*. Cambridge: Cambridge University Press: 85-102.

Hasty, O. (1996) *Tsvetaeva's Orphic Journeys in the Worlds of the Word*. Evanston, IL: Northwestern University Press.

Hayward, M. (1974) *Hope Abandoned*. New York: Atheneum.

Heldt, B. (1987) *Terrible Perfection*. Bloomington: Indiana University Press.

Hetzer, A.V. (1972) *Ivanovs Tragödie Tantal*. Munich: Sagner.

Highet, G. (1976) *The Classical Tradition: Greek and Roman Influences on Western Literature*. New York and Oxford: Oxford University Press.

Hollander, J. (1997) *The Work of Poetry*. New York: Columbia University Press.

Hubbard, T. (1998) *The Pipes of Pan*. Ann Arbor: University of Michigan Press.

Hughes, L. (1998) *Russia in the Age of Peter the Great*. New Haven and London: Yale University Press.

Iakubovich, D. P. (1941) 'Antichnost'' v tvorchestve Pushkina', *Vremennik pushkinskoi komissii* 6: 92-159.

Ichin, K. (1996) 'Brodskii i Ovidii', *Novoe literaturnoe obozrenie* 19: 227-49.

Ivanov, V.I. (1923) *Dionis i pradionisiistvo*. Baku: 2-ia Gosudarstvennaia Tipografiia.

Ivanov, V.I. (1931) 'Vergils Historiosophie', *Corona*, Year I, no. 6: 761-74.

Ivanov, V. (1971-9) *Sobranie Sochinenii* [collected works], ed. D.V. Ivanov, O. Deschartes. Brussels: Foyer Oriental Chrétien, vol. 1-1971; vol. 2-1974; vol. 3-1979, online at http://www.rvb.ru/ivanov/.

Jakobson, R. (1975) *Pushkin and His Sculptural Myth*, tr. John Burbank. The Hague: Mouton.

Jones, G.W. (1976) 'A Trojan Horse within the Walls of Classicism: Russian

Bibliography

Classicism and the National Specific', in A.G. Cross (ed.) *Russian Literature in the Age of Catherine the Great*. Oxford: Willem A. Meeuws: 95-120.

Kahn, A. (1993) 'Readings of Imperial Rome from Lomonosov to Pushkin', *Slavic Review* 52, no. 4: 745-68.

Kahn, A. (1994) 'Chorus and Monologue in Marina Tsvetaeva's *Ariadna*: An Analysis of their Structure, Versification and Themes', in *Marina Tsvetaeva: One Hundred Years*. Papers from the Tsvetaeva Centenary Symposium, Amherst College, MA, 1992, Viktoria Schweitzer et al. (eds) *Modern Russian Literature and Culture*, vol. 32. Oakland, CA: Berkeley Slavic Specialities: 162-93.

Kalb, J. (2003) 'Lodestars on the Via Appia: Viacheslav Ivanov's "Roman Sonnets" in Context', *Die Welt der Slaven* XLVIII: 23-52.

Kalb, J. (2008) *Russia's Rome: Imperial Visions, Messianic Dreams (1890-1940)*. Madison: University of Wisconsin Press.

Kallendorf, C.W. (ed.) (2007) *A Companion to Classical Tradition*. Oxford: Blackwell: 132-55.

Karlinsky, S. (1986) *Marina Tsvetaeva: The Woman, Her World, and Her Poetry*. Cambridge: Cambridge University Press.

Kelly, C. (1985) 'Bacchic Revels? Annensky's *Famira-Kifared* and the Satyrs', *Essays in Poetics* 10, no. 2: 76-92.

Kelly, C. (1989) 'Classical Tragedy and the "Slavonic Renaissance": The Plays of Viacheslav Ivanov and Innokentii Annensky Compared', *Slavic and East European Journal* 33, no. 2: 235-54.

Kelly, C. (2001) *Russian Literature. A Very Short Introduction*. Oxford: Oxford University Press.

Khodasevich, V. (1922) 'Ob Annenskom', in *Feniks. Sbornik khudozhestvenno-literaturnyi, nauchnyi, filosofskii*, vol 1: 123.

Khrustaleva, O. (1987) 'Evolutsiia geroia v dramaturgii Innokentiia Annenskogo', in *Russkii teatr i dramaturgiia epokhi revoliutsii 1905-1907 godov: sbornik nauchnykh trudov*. Leningrad: LGITMiK 58-71.

Klimoff, A. (1986) 'The First Sonnet in Viacheslav Ivanov's *Roman Cycle*', in R.L. Jackson and L. Nelson, Jr. (eds) *Viacheslav Ivanov: Poet, Critic and Philosopher*. New Haven: Yale Center for International and Area Studies: 123-33.

Kline, G. (1990) 'Variations on the Theme of Exile', in L. Loseff and V. Polukhina (eds) *Brodsky's Poetics and Aesthetics*. New York: St. Martin's Press: 56-88.

Kloszowski, J. (ed.) (2004) *Histoire de l'Europe du Centre-Est*, 2 vols. Paris: Presses Universitaires de France.

Knabe, G.S. (2000) *Russkaia Antichnost'*. Moscow: Russian State University for the Humanities.

Kopper, J.M. (2004) 'Multiple Sadnesses: Osip Mandelshtam's *Tristia* and the Critic's Dilemma in Approaching a Literature of Disengagement', talk given at the 17th Congress of the International Comparative Literature Association, Hong Kong, 2004. Online at www.ln.edu.hk/eng/staff/eoyang/icla/Dissemination.html.

Kot, J. (1999) *Distance Manipulation: The Russian Modernist Search for a New Drama*. Evanston, IL.: Northwestern University Press.

Kotrelev, N.V. (1989) 'Viacheslav Ivanov v rabote nad perevodom Eskhila', in N.I. Balashov, D.V. Ivanov, M.L. Gasparov, G.Ch. Guseinov, N.V. Kotrelev (eds) *Tragedii Eskhila*, tr. V.I. Ivanov. Moscow: Nauka: Literaturnye Pamiatniki.

Kovaleva, I. (2001) 'Na piru Mnemoziny', in I. Kovaleva (ed.) *Iosif Brodskii. Kentavry. Antichnye Siuzhety*. St Petersburg: Izdatel'stvo Zhurnala 'Zvezda': 5-59.

Bibliography

Kreps, M. (1984) *O poezii Iosifa Brodskogo*. Ann Arbor: Ardis.

Kroth, A. (December 1979) 'Androgyny as an Exemplary Feature in Marina Tsvetaeva's Dichotomous Poetic Vision', *Slavic Review* 38: 563-82.

Kudrova, I. (2007) 'The Poet of Passions', *Russian Life*, Sept/Oct: 52-8.

Kukulin, I. (2004) 'Rozhdenie landshafta: Konturnaiia karta molodoi poezii 1990-kh godov', in *Deviat' Izmerenii*. *Antologiia noveishei russkoi poezii*. Moscow: Novoe Literaturnoe Obozrenie: 7-26.

Lafoy, R. (1981) *Ariane: Tragédie de Marina Cvetaeva traduite et commentée. La resurrection d'un mythe grec dans la poésie dramatique russe au XXe siècle*. Clermont-Ferrand: Faculté des Lettres et Sciences Humaines de l'Université de Clermont-Ferrand.

Lang, D.M. (1948) 'Boileau and Sumarokov: The Manifesto of Russian Classicism', *Modern Language Review* 43.4: 500-6.

Lattimore, R. (1947) 'A Note on Pindar and His Poetry', in R. Lattimore (ed. & tr.) *The Odes of Pindar*. Chicago: University of Chicago Press: v-xii.

Lebedev, V. (1878) *Ukazatel' ko vsem uchenym izdaniiam i perevodam po klassicheskim (grecheskomu i latinksomu) iazykam s nachala knigopechataniia do 1871 goda vkliuchitel'no*. Moscow.

Lekmanov, O.A. (1995) 'To chto verno ob odnom poete, verno obo vsekh. Vokrug antichnykh stikhotvorenii Mandel'shtama', in O.A. Lekmanov (ed.) *Mandel'shtam i antichnost': Sbornik statei*. Moscow: Mandel'shtamovskoe Obshchestvo: 142-53.

Lekmanov, O.A., Glukhova, E.V. (2006) 'Osip Mandelshtam i Viacheslav Ivanov', in *Bashnia Viacheslava Ivanova i kul'tura serebrianogo veka*. St Petersburg: Filologicheskii Fakul'tet S.-Peterburgskogo Universiteta: 173-9.

Levin, Iu. I. (1995) 'Zametki o "krymsko-ellinskikh" stikhakh O. Mandel'shtama', in O.A. Lekmanov (ed.) *Mandel'shtam i antichnost': Sbornik statei*. Moscow: Mandel'shtamovskoe Obshchestvo: 77-103.

Likhachev, D.S. (1973a) 'Byzantium and the Emergence of an Independent Russian Literature', in D. Daiches, A. Thorlby (eds) *Literature and Western Civilization*, vol. 2. London: 173-4.

Likhachev, D.S. (1973b) *Razvitie russkoi literatury X-XVII vekov*. Leningrad: Nauka.

Lincoln, B. (2000) *Sunlight at Midnight: St Petersburg and the Rise of Modern Russia*. New York: Basic Books.

Liubomudrov, S. (1901) *Antichnye motivy v poezii Pushkina*. 2nd edn. St Petersburg: Tipografiia N.N. Klobukova.

Loewen, D. (2008) *The Most Dangerous Art: Poetry, Politics, and Autobiography after the Russian Revolution*. Lanham: Lexington Books.

Lo Gatto, E. (1952) *Storia del teatro russo*, vol. 2. Florence: Sansoni.

Lo Gatto, E. (1971) *Russi in Italia. Dal secolo XVII ad oggi*. Roma: Riuniti.

Lomonosov, M.V. (1957) *Sochineniia*, ed. A.A. Morozov. Moscow: Gosudarstvennoe Izdatel'stvo Khudozhetsvennoi Literatury.

Lomonosov, M.V. (1959) *Polnoe sobranie sochinenii*, vol. 8: *Poeziia, oratorskaiia proza, nadpisi 1732-1764*. Moscow and Leningrad: Izdatel'stvo Akademii Nauk SSSR.

Losev, A.F. (1976) *Problema simvola i realisticheskoe iskusstvo*. Moscow: Iskusstvo.

Loseff, L. (1977) ' "Niotkuda s liubov'iu" ... Zametki o stikhakh Iosifa Brodskogo'. *Kontinent*, no. 14: 325.

Losev, A. (1980) (Lev Loseff) (pseudonym of Aleksei Lifshits) 'Iosif Brodskii: Predislovie', *Ekho* I: 30.

242

Bibliography

Loseff, L. (1984) *On the Beneficence of Censorship*. Munich: Verlag Otto Sagner in Komission.

Loseff, L. (1990) 'Politics/Poetics', in L. Loseff, V. Polukhina (eds) *Brodsky's Poetics and Aesthetics*. New York: St Martin's Press: 34-55.

Loseff, L. (2006) *Iosif Brodsky. Opyt literaturnoi biografii*. Moscow: Molodaia Gvardiia. Seriia: Zhizn' zamechatel'nykh liudei.

Lotman, Iu. (1981) *Aleksandr Sergeevich Pushkin: Biografiia Pisatelia*. Leningrad: Prosveshchenie.

MacFadyen, D. (2000) *Joseph Brodsky and the Soviet Muse*. Montreal: McGill-Queens University Press.

Makin, M. (1993) *Marina Tsvetaeva: Poetics of Appropriation*. Oxford: Clarendon Press.

Mandelshtam, N. (1972) *Vospominaniia. Vtoraia Kniga*. Paris: YMCA-Press.

Mandelshtam, O.E. (1967) *Sobranie sochinenii*, ed. Gleb Struve, Boris Filippov. Washington, DC: Inter-Language Literary Associates.

Mandelshtam, O.E. (1973) *Complete Poetry*, tr. B. Burton, A. Burago. Introduction by S. Monas. Albany: State University of New York.

Mandelshtam, O.E. (1974) *Stikhotvoreniia*, ed. N.I. Khardzhiev. Leningrad: Sovetskii Pisatel'. Seriia: Bol'shaia biblioteka poeta.

Mandelshtam, O.E. (1979) *The Complete Critical Prose and Letters*, ed. J.G. Harris, tr. J.G. Harris and C. Link. Ann Arbor: Ardis.

Mandelshtam, O.E. (2001) *Stikhotvoreniia. Proza*. Tekst S. Vasilenko. Predislovie, kommentarii M. Gasparov. Moscow: Ripol Klassik.

Maramzin, V. (2008) 'Rukopisi ne goriat', *Novoe russkoe slovo*, January 26-27: A8-A9.

Marker, G. (1985) *Publishing, Printing, and the Origins of Intellectual Life in Russia*, 1700-1800. Princeton: Princeton University Press.

Martindale, C. (2006) 'Thinking through Reception', in C. Martindale and R.F. Thomas (eds) *Classics and the Uses of Reception*. Cambridge: Cambridge University Press: 1-13.

Masing-Delic, I. (1992) *Abolishing Death: A Salvation Myth of Russian Twentieth-Century Literature*. Stanford: Stanford University Press.

Matual, D. (1982) 'Solov'ev's Translation of Vergil's Fourth Eclogue: Afterword to the History and Future of Theocracy', *Slavic and East European Journal* 26. 3: 275-86.

McLeish, K. (1990) 'Dido, Aeneas, and the Concept of *Pietas*', in I. McAuslan, P. Walcott (eds) *Virgil*. Oxford: Oxford University Press: 134-41.

Meerson, O. (1999) 'Review of Tomas Venclova's *Sobesedniki na piru: Stat'i o russkoi literature*', *Slavic and East European Journal* 43. 4: 718-19.

Miller, P.A. (2004) *Subjecting Verses: Latin Love Elegy and the Emergence of the Real*. Princeton: Princeton University Press.

Milner-Gulland, R. (1997) *The Russians*. Oxford: Blackwell.

Mirsky, D.S. (1958) *A History of Russian Literature from its Beginnings to 1900*, ed. Francis J. Whitfield. New York: Vintage.

Mirsky, D.S. (1949 [repr. 1969]) *A History of Russian Literature*, ed. and abridged by F.J. Whitfield. New York: Alfred A. Knopf.

Monti, R.C. (1981) 'The Dido Episode and the *Aeneid*: Roman Social and Political Values in the Epic', *Mnemosyne Supplement* 66. Leiden.

Mossman, E. (1982) *The Correspondence of Boris Pasternak and Olga Freidenberg 1910-1954*, tr. E. Mossman, M. Wettlin. New York: Harcourt Brace Jovanovich.

Mureddu, D.G. (1993) 'The Tragedy Prometheus by Vjacheslav Ivanov', in Wilfried

Bibliography

Potthoff (ed.) *Vjacheslav Ivanov: Russischer Dichter – europäischer Kulturphilosoph*. Beiträge des IV. Internationalen Vjacheslav-Ivanov-Symposiums. Heidelberg, 4-10 September 1989. Heidelberg: Universitätsverlag C. Winter: 127-62.

Myers, D. (1992) ' "Hellenism" and "Barbarism" in Mandelshtam', in Arnold McMillin (ed.) *Symbolism and After: Essays on Russian Poetry in Honour of Georgette Donchin*. London: Bristol Classical Press: 85-101.

Nabokov, V. (1981) *Eugene Onegin: A Novel in Verse*: Commentary, 2 vols. Princeton: Princeton University Press.

Nelson, L. (1986) 'The Roman Sonnets of Vyacheslav Ivanov', in *Vyacheslav Ivanov: Poet, Critic and Philosopher*. New Haven: Yale Center for International and Area Studies: 134-46.

Nemirovskaia, Iu. (1987) 'Eshche tvoei molvoi zapolnen sei predel', *Kodry: Literaturno-khudozhestvennyi i obshchestvenno-politicheskii zhurnal Soiuza pisatelei Moldavii*: 134-8.

Nemirovskii, A. I. (1995) 'Pogovorim o Rime', in O.A. Lekmanov (ed.) *Mandel'shtam i antichnost'*: *Sbornik statei*. Moscow: Mandel'shtamovskoe Obshchestvo: 129-40.

Nivat, G. (1990) 'The Ironic Journey into Antiquity', in L. Loseff, V. Polukhina (eds) *Brodsky's Poetics and Aesthetics*. New York: St Martin's Press.

Okenfuss, M.J. (1995) *The Rise and Fall of Latin Humanism in Early-Modern Russia: Pagan Authors, Ukrainians, and the Resiliency of Muscovy*. Leiden: E.J. Brill.

Osherov, S.A. (1995) ' "*Tristia*" Mandel'shtama i antichnaya kul'tura', in O.A. Lekmanov (ed.) *Mandel'shtam i antichnost'*: *Sbornik statei*. Moscow: Mandel'shtamovskoe Obshchestvo: 188-203.

Osipova, N.O. (2000) *Tvorchestvo M. I. Tsvetaevoi v kontekste kul'turnoi mifologii serebrianogo veka*. Kirov: Izdatel'stvo VGPU.

Otis, B. (1964) *Virgil: A Study in Civilized Poetry*. Oxford: Clarendon Press.

Otsup, N. (1933) *Serebrianyi vek. Chisla, Sborniki pod redaktsiei N. Otsupa*. Kn. 7-8. Paris.

Oxford Classical Dictionary (*OCD*) (1970) ed. N.G.L. Hammond and H.H. Scullard. Oxford: Oxford University Press.

Perkell, C. (1981) 'On Dido and Creusa and the Quality of Victory in Vergil's *Aeneid*', *Women Studies* 8: 201-23.

Perkins, P., Cook, A. (1993) *The Burden of Sufferance: Women Poets of Russia*. New York and London: Garland Publishing, Inc.

Perlina, N. (2002) *Olga Freidenberg's Works and Days*. Bloomington: Slavica.

Petrovskii, F.A. (1966) 'Russkie perevody "Eneidy" i zadachi novogo ee perevoda', in *Voprosy antichnoi literatury i klassicheskoi filologii*. Moscow: Nauka: 293-306.

Poggioli, R. (1960) *The Poets of Russia 1890-1930*. Cambridge, MA: Harvard University Press.

Pollak, N. (1999) 'Annensky's Anguished Muse', in Stephanie Sandler (ed.) *Rereading Russian Poetry*. New Haven: Yale University Press: 146-60.

Polukhina, V. (1989) *Joseph Brodsky. A Poet for Our Time*. Cambridge: Cambridge University Press.

Polukhina, V. (1992) *Brodsky through the Eyes of his Contemporaries*. New York: St Martin's Press.

Porter, J. (2008) 'Reception Studies: Future Prospects', in L. Hardwick and C. Stray (eds) *A Companion to Classical Receptions*. Oxford: Blackwell: 469-81.

Powell, B. (2007) *Classical Myth*, 5th edn. Upper Saddle River, NJ: Prentice Hall.

Bibliography

Pozdeeva, I.V. (1962) 'Izuchenie drevnei istorii i drevnikh iazykov v Moskovskom universitete 50-70 gg. XVIII v.', *Vestnik Drevnei Istorii*, no. 3: 3-23.

Proskurin, O. (1999) *Poeziia Pushkina, ili podvizhnyi palimpsest*. Moscow: Novoe Literaturnoe Obozrenie. 275-300.

Przybylski, R. (1987) *An Essay on the Poetry of Osip Mandelstam: God's Grateful Guest*, tr. Madeline G. Levine. Ann Arbor: Ardis.

Pumpianskii, L.V. (1982) 'K istorii russkogo klassitsizma (Poetika Lomonosova)', *Kontekst*: 303.

Punin, N.N. (1914) 'Problema zhizni i poezii I. Annenskogo', *Apollon* 10: 48.

Pushkin, A.S. (1906-11) *Sochineniia*, vol. 3: *Perepiska*, St Petersburg: Izdatel'stvo Imperatorskoi Akademii Nauk.

Pushkin, A.S. (1947-9) *Polnoe sobranie sochinenii*, vol. 2, parts 1 (1947) and 2 (1949): M.A. Tsiavlovskii (ed.) *Stikhotvoreniia 1817-1825*. Izdatel'stvo Akademii Nauk SSSR.

Pushkin, A.S. (1949) *Sochineniia*, ed. M.A. Tsiavlovskii, S.M. Petrov. Moscow: Gosudarestvennoe Izdatel'stvo Khudozhestvennoi Literatury.

Putnam, M.C.J. (1987) 'Daedalus, Vergil, and the End of Art', *American Journal of Philology* 108, no. 2: 173-98.

Rabinowitz, N.S. (1986) 'Female Speech and Female Sexuality: Euripides' *Hippolytus* as Model', in M. Skinner (ed.) *Rescuing Creusa: New Methodological Approaches to Women in Antiquity*. Special Issue of *Helios*: Texas Tech University Press: 127-40.

Raeff, M. (ed.) (1999) *Russian Intellectual History: An Anthology*, Introduction by Isaiah Berlin. Amherst: Humanity Books.

Ranchin, A. (2001) *Na Piru Mnemoziny. Interteksty Brodskogo*. Moscow: Novoe Literaturnoe Obozrenie.

Razumovskaia, M. (1983) *Mif i deistvitel'nost'*. London: Overseas Publications Interchange.

Redston, D. (1976) 'Kantemir's Translation of Horace', *Study Group on Eighteenth-Century Russia (SGECR)* 4: 7-19.

Reynolds, A. (2005) 'Returning the Ticket: Joseph Brodsky's "August" and the End of the Petersburg Text', *Slavic Review* 64, no. 2: 307-32.

Reynolds, A. (2007) 'Feathers and Suns: Joseph Brodsky's "Dedal v Sitsilii" and the "Fear of Replication" ', *Slavic and East European Journal* 51.3: 553-81.

Riha, T. (ed.) (1969) *Readings in Russian Civilization*, 2nd edn, vol. 2. Chicago and London: University of Chicago Press.

Ronen, O. (2000) *Serebrianyi vek kak umysel i vymysel*. Moscow: OGI.

Rosenthal, B.G. (1993) 'Lofty Ideals and Worldly Consequences: Visions of *Sobornost'* in early Twentieth Century Russia', *Russian History* 20, nos 1-4: 179-95.

Ross, D. (2007) *Virgil's Aeneid: A Reader's Guide*. Oxford: Blackwell.

Rudich, V. (1986) 'Vyacheslav Ivanov and Classical Antiquity', in *Vyacheslav Ivanov: Poet, Critic and Philosopher*. New Haven: Yale Center for International and Area Studies: 275-89.

Rudich, V. (1988) 'Viacheslav Ivanov i Antichny Rim', in Fausto Malcovati (ed.) *Cultura e Memoria: atti del terzo simposio internazionale dedicato a Viacheslav Ivanov*, vol. 2. Florence: 131-41.

Rudich, V. (2002a) 'On Pushkin and Vergil', *Arion* 10.1: 35-53.

Rudich, V. (2002b) 'Vergilii v vospriiatii Viach. Ivanova i T.S. Eliota', *Europa Orientalis* XXI.1: 339-51.

Ruutu, H. (2006) *Patterns of Transcendence – Classical Myth in Marina Tsvetaeva's Poetry of the 1920s*. Helsinki: Slavica Helsingiensia 30 (PDF).

Bibliography

Rzhevsky, N. (1998) 'Russian Cultural History: Introduction', in N. Rzhevsky (ed.) *The Cambridge Companion to Modern Russian Culture*. Cambridge: Cambridge University Press: 1-18.

Samaritaki, E. (2004) *Antichnye Pamiatniki Kryma/Ancient Greek Sites in the Crimea*, bilingual edn. Kyiv: Mistetstvo.

Sandler, S. (1989) *Distant Pleasures: Alexander Pushkin and the Writing of Exile*. Stanford: Stanford University Press.

Sandler, S. (1990) 'Embodied Words: Gender in Tsvetaeva's Reading of Pushkin', *Slavic and East European Journal* 34.2: 139-57.

Savel'eva, L.I. (1980) *Antichnost' v russkoi poezii kontsa XVIII-nachala XIX veka*. Kazan': Izdatel'stvo Kazanskogo Universiteta.

Schweitzer, V. (1988) *Tsvetaeva*, tr. R. Chandler, H.T. Willets. Harvill: HarperCollins.

Serman, I. (1986) 'Viacheslav Ivanov and Russian Poetry of the Eighteenth Century', in *Viacheslav Ivanov: Poet, Critic, and Philosopher*. New Haven: Yale Center for International and Area Studies: 190-208.

Serman, I. (1992) 'The Eighteenth Century: Neo-Classicism and the Enlightenment, 1730-90', in C.A. Moser (ed.) *The Cambridge History of Russian Literature*. Cambridge: Cambridge University Press: 45-91.

Setchkarev, V. (1963) *Studies in the Life and Works of Innokentii Annenskii*. The Hague: Mouton.

Shelogurova, G.N. (1988) 'Antichnyi mif v russkoi dramaturgii nachala veka: I. Annenskii. Viach. Ivanov', in A.G. Sokolov, M.V. Mikhailova (eds) *Iz istorii russkoi literatury kontsa XIX-nachala XX veka*. Moscow: Isdatel'stvo Moskovskogo Universiteta: 105-22.

Shevelenko, I.D. (2002) *Literaturnyi Put' Tsvetaevoi: Ideologiia-poetika-identichnost' avtora v kontekste epokhi*. Moskva: Novoe Literaturnoe Obozrenie.

Shils, E. (1982) 'Center and Periphery', in *The Constitution of Society*. Chicago and London: University of Chicago Press: 93-109.

Silbajoris, R. (1968) *The Theories of Trediakovskii, Lomonosov, and Kantemir*. New York and London: Columbia University Press.

Sivkov, K.V. (1917) 'Petr-Pisatel'', in *Tri Veka*, vol. 3. Moscow: 56.

Smith, G.S. (2005) 'Joseph Brodsky: Summing Up', in *Literary Imagination: The Review of the Association of Literary Scholars and Critics* 7.3: 399-410.

Spence, S. (1999) '*Varium et Mutabile*: Voices of Authority in *Aeneid* 4', in Christine Perkell (ed.) *Reading Vergil's Aeneid: An Interpretive Guide*. Norman: University of Oklahoma Press: 80-95.

Stock, U. (July 2001) 'Marina Tsvetaeva: The Concrete and Metaphoric Discourse of Exile', *Modern Language Review* 96: 762-77.

Štokmar, M.P. (1952) *Issledovaniia v oblasti russkogo narodnogo stikhoslozheniia*. Moscow: Izdatel'stvo Akademii Nauk SSSR.

Struve, G. (1962) 'Ital'ianskie obrazy i motivy v poezii Osipa Mandel'shtama', *Studi in onore di Ettore Lo Gatto e Giovanni Maver*. Roma: Sansoni: 601-14.

Sviiasov, E.V. (1988) 'Anctichnaia liricheskaia poeziia v russkikh perevodakh i podrazhaniiakh XVIII-XX vekov: o bibliografii', *Russkaia Literatura* 2: 206-15.

Syme, R. (1978) *History in Ovid*. Oxford: Clarendon Press.

Takho-Godi, E. (2002) 'Piat' pisem F. F. Zelinskogo k Viach. Ivanovu', in *Viacheslav Ivanov. Tvorchsetsvo i sud'ba*. Moscow: Nauka: 227-43.

Taranovsky, K. (1976) *Essays on Mandelshtam*. Cambridge, MA: Harvard University Press.

Terras, V. (1966) 'Classical Motives in the Poetry of Osip Mandelshtam', *Slavic and East European Journal* 10, no. 3: 251-67.

Bibliography

Thomson, R.D.B. (1989) 'Tsvetaeva's Play *Fedra*: An Interpretation', *Slavic and East European Journal*, 6.3: 337-52.

Tomashevskii, B.V. (1990) *Pushkin. Raboty raznykh let*. Moscow: Kniga.

Toporov, V.N. (1984) 'Peterburg i peterburgskii tekst russkoi literatury', in *Semiotika goroda i gorodksoi kul'tury: Peterburg*. Issue of *Trudy po znakovym sistemam* 18.

Toporov, V.N. (1989) 'Mif o Tantale: Ob odnoi pozdnei versii – tragediia Viach. Ivanova', in V.P. Neroznak (ed.) *Paleobalkanistika i antichnost': Sbornik nauchnykh trudov*. Moscow: Nauka: 61-110.

Torlone, Z.M. (2003a) 'Classical Myth in Three Poems of Joseph Brodsky', *Classical and Modern Literature*: 95-114.

Torlone, Z.M. (2003b) 'Classical Philology in Russia: Past, Present, and Future', *Classical Bulletin* 78.2: 195-206.

Torlone, Z.M. (2008) 'A Tale of Two Cities: Ancient Rome and St Petersburg in Osip Mandelshtam's Poetry', in H. Goscilo, S. Norris (eds) *Preserving Petersburg: History, Memory, Nostalgia*. Bloomington: Indiana University Press: 88-114.

Trediakovskii, V., Lomonosov, M., Sumarokov, A. (1935) *Stikhotvoreniia*, ed. P. Berkov, G. Gukovskii. Moscow: Sovetskii Pisatel'.

Tsetkhladze, G.R. (1994, repr. 2004) 'Greek Penetration of the Black Sea', in G.R. Tsekhladze, F. De Angelis (eds) *The Archaeology of Greek Colonization: Essays to Sir John Boardman*. Oxford: Oxford University School of Archaeology: 111-36.

Tsvetaeva, A. (1971) *Vospominaniia*, 1st edn. Moscow: Sovetskii Pisatel'.

Tsvetaeva, A. (1980) '*Osip Mandelstam i ego brat Aleksandr*', *Daugava* 7: 71.

Tsvetaeva, M. (1979) *Mon frère feminin: lettre à l'Amazone*. Paris: Mercure de France.

Tsvetaeva, M. (1980-90) *Stikhotvoreniia i poemy v piati tomakh*. [*Lyric Poetry and Long Poems in Five Volumes*], ed. A. Sumerkin. New York: Russica Publishers, vol. 1 (1980), vol. 3 (1983), vol. 5 (1990).

Tsvetaeva, M. (1988) *Teatr*, ed. A. Efron, A. Saakiants. Moscow: Iskusstvo.

Tsvetaeva, M. (1994-5) *Sobranie sochinenii v semi tomakh*. [*Collected Works in Seven Volumes*], ed. Anna Saakiants, Lev Mnukhin. Moscow: Ellis Lak.

Tsvetaeva, M. (1997) *Neizdannoe: Svodnye tetradi*, ed. E.B. Korkina, I.D. Shevelenko. Moscow: Ellis Lak.

Tsvetaeva, M. (2001) *Neizdannoe: Zapisnye knizhki v dvukh tomakh*, vol. 2: *1919-39*, ed. E.B. Korkina, M.G. Krutikova. Moscow: Ellis Lak.

Tsvetaeva, M., Pasternak, B. (2004) *Dushi nachinaiut videt': Pis'ma 1922-1936 godov*, ed. E.B. Korkina, I.D. Shevelenko. Moscow: Vagrius.

Tucker, J.G. (1986) *Innokentii Annenskii and the Acmeist Doctrine*. Columbus, Ohio: Slavica.

Ungurianu, D. (1996) 'The Wandering Greek: Images of Antiquity in Joseph Brodsky', in P.I. Barta, D.H.J. Larmour, P.A. Miller (eds) *Russian Literature and the Classics*, vol. 1 of *Studies in Russian and European Literature*. Amsterdam: Harwood Academic Publishers: 161-91.

Uspensky B, (1984) 'The Language Situation and Linguistic Consciousness in Muscovite Rus", in H. Birnbaum, M. Flier (eds) *Medieval Russian Culture*. Berkeley: University of California Press.

Venclova, T. (1985) 'On Russian Mythological Tragedy: Viacheslav Ivanov and Marina Tsvetaeva', in A. Kodjak, K. Pomorska, S. Rudy (eds) *Myth in Literature*. Columbus: Slavica Publishers: 89-109.

Bibliography

Verheul, K. (1973) 'Iosif Brodskii's "Aeneas and Dido" ', *Russian Literature Triquarterly* 6, reprinted in Russian translation (1986) in L. Loseff (ed.) *Poetika Brodskogo*: 121-31.

Vitale, S. (ed. & tr.) (1989) *Marina Cvetaeva: Deserti luoghi: Lettere, 1925-1941.* Milan: Adelphi Edizioni.

Vitale, S. (1999) *Pushkin's Button*, tr. Ann Goldstein, Jon Rothschild. New York: Farrar, Straus and Giroux.

Vitins, I. (1987) 'Mandelshtam's Farewell to Marina Tsvetaeva: "Ne veria voskresen'ia chudu" ', *Slavic Review* 46.2: 266-80.

Voitekhovich, R. (2007) *Antichnye motivy v tvorchestve Mariny Tsvetaevoi*. Tartu: Humaniora: Litterae Russicae.

Volkov, S. (1995) *St Petersburg: A Cultural History*. New York: Free Press.

Volkov, S. (1998) 'Marina Tsvetaeva', in *Conversations with Joseph Brodsky: A Poet's Journey through the Twentieth Century*, tr. M. Schwartz. New York: Free Press: 37-56.

Wachtel, M. (1992) 'Die Korrespondenz zwichen Vyaceslav Ivanov und Karl Krumbacher', *Zeitschrift für Slawistik*. 37.3: 330-42.

Wachtel, M. (1994a) 'Viacheslav Ivanov – Student Berlinskogo Universiteta', *Cahiers du monde russe et soviétique* 35: 353-76.

Wachtel, M. (1994b) 'Vyacheslav Ivanov: From Aesthetic Theory to Biographical Practice', in I. Paperno, J. Grossman (eds) *Creating Life: The Aesthetic Utopia of Russian Modernism*. Stanford: Stanford University Press: 151-66.

Wachtel, M. (1998) *The Development of Russian Verse: Meter and its Meanings*. Cambridge: Cambridge University Press.

Wachtel, M. (July 2008) 'Vladimir Solov'ev on Symbolism and Decadence', *Russian Review* 67: 387-94.

Wes, M.A. (1992) *Classics in Russia 1700-1855: Between Two Bronze Horsemen*. Leiden, New York, Köln: Brill's Studies in Intellectual History.

Westbroek, P.L. (2007) *Dionis i Dionisiiskaia tragedia. Viacheslav Ivanov. Filologicheskie i filosofskie idei o Dionisiistve*. Amsterdam: Academisch Proefschrift.

Williams, G.D. (1994) *Banished Voices: Readings in Ovid's Exile Poetry*. Cambridge: Cambridge University Press.

Williams, G.W. (1968) *Tradition and Originality in Roman Poetry*. Oxford: Clarendon Press.

Wolf, R.L. (1960) 'The Three Romes: The Migration of an Ideology and the Making of an Autocrat', in H.A. Murray (ed.) *Myth and Myth Making*. New York: George Braziller: 174-98.

Worth, D.S. (1998) 'Language', in N. Rzhevsky (ed.) *The Cambridge Companion to Modern Russian Culture*. Cambridge: Cambridge University Press: 19-37.

Wortman R.S. (1995) *Scenarios of Power: Myth and Ceremony in Russian Monarchy*, vol. 1. Princeton: Princeton University Press.

Zeitlin, F. (1985) 'The Power of Aphrodite: *Eros* and the Boundaries of the Self in the *Hippolytus*', in P. Burian (ed.) *Directions in Euripidean Criticism: A Collection of Essays*. Durham: Duke University Press: 52-111.

Zelinskii, F.F. (1909) *Our Debt to Antiquity*, tr. H.A. Strong, H. Stewart. London: Routledge.

Zelinksii, F.F. (1916) 'Viacheslav Ivanov' in S.A. Vengerov (ed.) *Russkaia Literatura XX Veka*, vol. 3, book 8. Moscow: Izdanie T-va Mir: 101-13.

Zelinskii, F.F. (1933) 'Poeta Odrodzenia Sowiańskiego: Wiĉcysaw Iwanow', *Pion* 12 (23 December): 9. Warsaw.

Bibliography

Zelinskii, F.F. (1934) 'Introduzione all'opera de Venceslao Ivanov', *Il Convegno* 15: 241-51.

Zernov, N. (1978) *The Russians and Their Church*. Crestwood, NY: St Vladimir's Seminary Press.

Ziolkowski, Th. (2005) *Ovid and the Moderns*. Ithaca and London: Cornell University Press.

Zubova, L (1999) 'Odysseus to Telemachus', in L. Loseff, V. Polukhina (eds) *Joseph Brodsky: The Art of a Poem*. New York: St Martin's Press: 26-43.

Index

Acmeism 118, 119, 222n.3, n.8
Aeschylus 77-80, 82, 86, 95, 111,
    211n.59, 216n.181
Aesop 17, 18, 26, 33, 43
Aesopian language 157, 173
Akhmatova, Anna 2, 4, 118, 140, 155,
    180, 221n.88, 222n.3, 229n.58
Alcaeus 64, 153
Alexander I 18, 19
Anacreon 25, 28, 29, 35, 40, 43,
    203n.22, 204n.50, n.57, 205n.92
Andreev, Leonid 90
Annenskii, Innokentii 4, 10, 55-60, 63,
    74-6, 82-96, 116-17, 119, 121, 124,
    129, 208nn.14-17, 209nn.19-20,
    nn.23-4, n.29, n.32, 210n.55,
    214n.136, 215n.138, n.144,
    216nn.173-5, nn.177-9, n. 181,
    nn.185-6, n.188, n.193, 220n.63,
    222n.109, n.8.
  writings of: *Cypress Chest*
    (*Kiparisovyi Larets*) 60; *Thamyris
    Cytharoede* (*Famira-Kifared*) 82,
    84, 88, 89; *King Ixion* (*Tsar'
    Iksion*) 82, 86; *Melanippa-Filosof*
    (*Melanippe the Philosopher*) 82,
    84-5; *Laodamia* (*Laodamiia*) 82,
    87, 216n.174; *Quiet Songs* (*Tikhie
    pesni*) 59
Athenaeus 40
Auden, W.H. 154, 197, 233n.137,
    234n.137
Bakhrakh, Alexander 95, 218n.17
Bakhtin, Mikhail 4, 65, 209n.33,
    214n.129
Bakhtin, Nikolai 61, 75, 91, 209n.33,
    211n.59, 214n.129
Bal'mont, Konstantin 59, 63
Baratynskii, Evgenii 44, 120, 155, 187
Batiushkov, Konstantin 39, 40,
    205nn.85-6, 226n.67
Bayer, Gottfried Siegfried 25

Belinskii, Vissarion 26, 36
Belyi, Andrei 56-7, 63, 65, 141,
    217n.202
Blok, Alexander 56-7, 61, 63, 65, 90,
    141, 208n.16, 212n.79, 216n.171,
    217n.202, 224n.32
Briusov, Valerii 10, 56-7, 59, 61-3, 76,
    88, 202n.69, 208n.9, n.16,
    209n.35, 212n.79, 215n.145,
    216n.174, 217n.202, 219n.46,
    225n.59
Brodsky, Joseph ix, x, 1, 4, 5, 10, 56,
    96, 115, 124, 153-96, 211n.69,
    218n.23, 219n.44, 220n.73,
    223n.27, 226n.69, 227-34
  writings of: '*Anno Domini*' 178, 180;
    'The Bust of Tiberius' ('Biust
    Tiberiia') 181-3, 189; 'Daedalus in
    Sicily' ('Dedal v Sitsilii') 192-6;
    'Developing Plato' ('Razvivaia
    Platona') 183-5; 'Dido and Aeneas'
    ('Didona i Enei') 166-9, 193; 'Ex
    Ponto' ('The Last Letter of Ovid to
    Rome' – 'Poslednee pis'mo Ovidiia
    v Rim') 176, 178; 'A Fragment' –
    'Naso's not ready to die ...'
    ('Otryvok'– 'Nazo k smerti ne
    gotov ...') 176-7; 'From Outskirts
    to the Centre' ('Ot okrainy k
    tsentru') 161-2; 'A Guide to a
    Renamed City' 155; 'Homage to
    Marcus Aurelius' 153, 156;
    'Imitation of Horace'
    ('Podrazhanie Goratsiiu')
    234n.142; 'I was blamed for
    everything save the weather ...'
    ('Menia uprekali vo vsem,
    okromia pogody ...') 233n.124;
    'Ithaca' 163-5, 228n.41; lyric cycle
    'July Intermezzo' ('Iiul'skoe
    intermetstso (1-10)') 161; 'The
    Lagoon' ('Laguna') 163; 'Letter to

Horace' 153-4, 156, 189, 230n.76; 'Letters to a Roman Friend' ('Pis'ma rimskomu drugu') 178-80, 231n.97; 'Marble' ('Mramor') 230n.78; 'May 24, 1980' – 'I have braved, for want of wild beasts, steel cages ...' ('Ia vkhodil vmesto dikogo zveria v kletku ...') 186-91; 'The Nobel Lecture' 187, 227n.6; 'Odysseus to Telemachus' ('Odissei Telemaku') 158-63; 'On the Way to Scyros' ('Po doroge na Skiros') 169-74, 195, 229n.62; lyric cycle 'Part of Speech' ('Chast' rechi') 188; 'Piazza Mattei' 213n.97, n.101; 'Post Aetatem Nostram' – 'Empire is the land for fools ...' ('Imperiia – strana dlia durakov ...') 174-5; 'Roman Elegies' ('Rimskie elegii') 182, 187-8; 'Second Christmas on the shores of never freezing Pontus ...' ('Vtoroe Rozhdestvo na beregu nezamerzaiushchego Ponta ...') 178; 'Sonnet' – 'Great Hektor is slain by arrows ...' ('Sonet' – 'Velikii Gektor strelami ubit ...') 157-8; 'Unfinished' – 'Friend, being attracted to the hidden forms of flattery ...' ('Neokonchennoe' –'Drug, tiagoteia k skrytym formam lesti ...') 178; 'Vertumnus' ('Vertumn') 230n.77; 'The Year 1972' ('1972 god') 174
Bunin, Ivan 55, 65
Catherine the Great 7, 17-20, 33, 36, 201n.61, 207n.117
Catullus 18, 28, 37, 41, 57, 70, 87, 94, 99, 102-3, 120, 167, 172, 206n.93, 219n.33, n.49
Caucasus 19, 78, 149, 206n.104
Cavafy, Constantine 164-5
Chaadaev, Peter 10, 11, 12, 37, 44, 119, 139, 200n.18, 223n.18, 225n.62
Cicero 11, 12, 17, 27, 201n.56
Claudius Claudianus 19
Cocteau, Jean 96
Corneille, Pierre 18, 74
Crimea 4, 19, 67, 92, 127, 136-7, 151, 227n.102

Dashkova, Ekaterina 19
Decembrists 48
Del'vig, Anton 20, 23, 38, 40, 155, 204n.61
Derzhavin, Gavriil 21-2, 24, 34-6, 38, 49-50, 52, 54, 155, 187, 204n.56, nn.58-9, nn.61-2, 207nn.116-17, 227n.14
  writings of: 'Felitsa' 49, 207n.117; 'To Evgenii. Life at Zvanka' ('Evgeniiu. Zhizn' zvanskaia') 35-6
diglossia 14
Diodorus Siculus 99, 172, 219n.35
Dionysus, in Ivanov 62-4, 70, 77, 79; in Tsvetaeva 100-1, 108; 210n.48, 212n.91, 214n.126, n.134, 215n.146, n.193, 217n.200
Dostoevskii, Fedor 7, 37, 63, 83, 87, 150, 204n.67

Ekimov, Peter 19, 205n.73
Eliot, T.S. 96, 210n.50, 222n.9
eros-nosos 94, 106, 115
Euripides 58-9, 77-8, 83-7, 94, 101, 107-11, 113-15, 119, 193, 208nn.15-16, 209n.19, 214n.121, 216n.181, n.186, 219n.43, 220n.60, nn.63-4, n.69, 221n.81, n.102
exile, treatment of: in Pushkin 43-6; in Tsvetaeva 116; in Mandelshtam 136-40, 145-7, 150-1, 154; in Brodsky 155, 165-6, 173-6, 178-83, 185-6, 188-91, 194-5, 198
Fénelon, François 26
Fet, Afanasii 10, 54, 202n.69, 207n.130
Filofei (Philotheus) 13, 19, 132
Freidenberg, Olga 208n.11, 217n.200
French Parnassians 118, 215n.145
Gautier, Theóphile 118
German Romanticism 79, 94
Gippius, Zinaida 63, 65
Giraudoux, Jean 96
Gnedich, Nikolai 23, 26, 38-9, 43, 46, 205n.73, n.80, 206n.100, n.104
Goethe, Johann Wolfgang von 77, 94, 193
Gorodetskii, Sergei 118, 222n.3
Gumilev, Nikolai 118, 222n.3, n.5
gymnasia (*gimnazii*) 20
Herodotus 48
Hirschfeld, Otto 62, 210n.39

Homer 12, 23, 28-9, 34, 39, 40, 42, 73,
78, 87, 92, 123-5, 153-4, 159-65,
210n.60, 203n.40, 205n.80,
218n.15, 219n.32, 223n.27,
224n.35
Horace 18, 25-6, 35-6, 39, 41, 49-54,
153-6, 179, 187-9, 202n.10,
203n.22, 205n.92, 207n.126,
230n.76, 231n.101, 234n.142, n.7
Ivanov, Viacheslav 4, 5, 10, 55-84, 87,
154, 183, 207-17, 232n.103; and
Mandelshtam 118-21, 129, 135,
222n.10, 223n.21; and Tsvetaeva
90-6, 116; dissertation of 62,
210n.39, n.40;
    writings of: *Dionysus and
    Predionysanism* (*Dionis i
    pradionisiistvo*) 210n.48; 'Hellenic
    Religion of the Suffering God'
    ('Ellinskaia religiia
    stradaiushchego Boga') 210n.50;
    'Laeta' 66-8, 212n.75; 'Legion and
    Communality' ('Legion i
    Sobornost'') 71; *Niobe* (*Nioba*) 77;
    'On Act and Ritual' ('O deistvii i
    deistve') 79, 215n.146; 'On the
    Russian Idea' ('O Russkoi idee')
    71, 213n.97; 'Palinode'
    ('Palinodiia') 72-4, 213n.111,
    n.112; *Pilot Stars* (*Kormchie
    zvezdy*) 59, 64, 66, 69; *Prometheus*
    (*Prometei*) 76-82; 'Roman Sonnets'
    ('Rimskie sonety') 68-72, 183;
    Tantalus (*Tantal*) 76-82; 'Tower'
    ('Bashnia') of 64, 76, 119; 'Vergils
    Historiosophie' 70, 210n.50
Ivask, Iurii 95, 218n.10, n.16
Jauss, Hans Robert 9
Juvenal 25, 42, 70, 207n.130
Kantemir, Antiokh 1, 18, 22, 24-7,
201n.59, 202nn.10-11, 227n.14
'Letter of Khariton Makentin'
    ('Pis'mo Kharitona Makentina')
    25, 202n.11, n.12
Khodasevich, Vladislav 59, 209n.26
Kniazhnin, Iakov 74, 214n.118
Kopievskii, Il'ia 17
Koshanskii, Nikolai 40, 42, 205n.84
Kukhel'beker, V.K. 48, 74
Kushner, Alexander 230n.76
Leconte de Lisle 77

Lomonosov, Mikhailo 21-2, 24-38, 49-
50, 58, 91, 155, 202n.13, 203,
204n.52
    writings of: *A Brief Manual on
    Eloquence – Rhetoric* (*Kratkoe
    rukovodstvo k krasnorechiiu –
    Ritorika*) 27; *Conversations with
    Anacreon* (*Razgovor s
    Anakreontom*) 28; 'Epistle on the
    Usefulness of Glass' ('Pis'mo o
    pol'ze stekla') 30-1; *A Letter On
    the Rules of Russian Versification*
    (*Pis'mo o pravilakh rossiiskogo
    stikhotvorstva*) 27; *The Ode on the
    Siege of Khotin* (*Oda na vziatie
    Khotina*) 27; *Peter the Great* (*Petr
    Velikii*) 32, 203n.40
Lucan 19
Maiakovskii, Vladimir 120, 232n.121
Mandelshtam, Osip ix, 2, 4, 5, 10, 55-
6, 61, 114, 118-52, 154-5, 159,
174-9, 182-3, 185, 188, 190,
206n.110, 207n.1, 209nn.36-7,
221n.88, 222-7, 232n.103
    writings of: 'About Simple and
    Crude Times ...' ('O vremenakh
    prostykh i grubykh ...') 136;
    'Admiralty' ('Admiralteistvo')
    143-4; 'A golden spurt of honey ...'
    ('Zolotistogo meda struia ...') 124,
    127-8; 'Herds of horses graze,
    neighing happily ...' ('S veselym
    rzhaniem pasutsia tabuny ...')
    137-40; 'The Horseshoe Finder'
    ('Nashedshii podkovu') 129-31; 'I
    have forgotten the word that I
    wanted to say ...' ('Ia slovo
    pozabyl, chto ia khotel skazat' ...')
    148; 'I returned to my city
    familiar to tears ...' ('Ia vernulsia
    v moi gorod, znakomyi do slez ...')
    149; 'I'll tell you with final
    frankness ...' ('Ia skazhu tebe s
    poslednei priamotoi ...') 128-9;
    'Insomnia. Homer. Full sails ...'
    ('Bessonitsa. Gomer. Tugie
    parusa ...') 124-5; 'Let the names of
    blossoming cities ...' ('Pust' imena
    tsvetushchikh gorodov ...') 133-4;
    'Nature is the same as Rome ...'
    ('Priroda – tot zhe Rim ...') 134-5;

'On Interlocutor' ('O sobesednike') 226n.65; 'On a terrible height a wandering light ...' ('Na strashnoi vysote bluzhdaiushchii ogon'... ') 145; 'On the Nature of the Word' ('O prirode slova') 121, 222n.7, 227n.96; 'Petersburg Strophes' ('Peterburgskie strofy') 141-3; 'Silentium' 121-2, 'There are orioles in the woods ...' ('Est' ivolgi v lesakh ...') 122-4; 'To the sovereign world I was tied only childishly ...' ('S mirom derzhavnym ia byl lish' rebiacheski sviazan ...') 145-7; 'Tristia' 118, 132, 136-7, 221n.88, 224n.52; 'We shall die in transparent Petropolis ...' ('V Petropole prozrachnom my umrem ...') 144; 'We shall meet again in Petersburg ...' ('V Peterburge my soidemsia snova ...') 147; 'When in the warm night dies away ... ' ('Kogda v teploi nochi zamiraet ...') 147-8

Meierkhol'd, Vsevolod 76, 214n.129, n.133

Merezhkovskii, Dmitrii 65, 220n.63, 225n.59

Mommsen, Theodor 62, 66, 210n.39, n.41, 211n.67

Nabokov, Vladimir 40, 74, 119, 205n.83, 214n.120

Nietzsche, Friedrich 62-3, 79, 82, 95, 214n.134, 216n.185

Nilender, Vladimir 95

nostalgia 4, 44, 120, 129, 131, 137-8, 140, 145, 147, 149-50, 165, 175, 178, 183-4, 189, 221n.105, 222n.1

nostos (homecoming) vii, 159

Olenin, Aleksei 38-9, 74, 204n.71

Ossian 42

Ovid 4, 5, 17-19, 27, 29, 34, 55, 66, 87-8, 206n.102-5, n.110, n.112, 207n.130, 219nn.32-3, n.46, 221n.104, 226n.67, n.71, 226n.51, 230n.76, n.78, 232n.115, 233n.129, 234n.3; treatment of: in Pushkin 43-7; in Ivanov 67; in Mandelshtam 120, 127, 132, 136-

40, 147, 149-51; in Brodsky 154-6, 172, 175-9, 189-91, 193

Ozerov, Vladislav 9,10, 74

Pasternak, Boris 104-6, 208n.11, 220n.50, n.52, n.56

Peter the Great 3, 7, 14, 17, 19, 26, 132-3, 142-3, 207n.120

Petrov, Vasilii 20, 202n.69

Pindar 28-9, 34-5, 40, 61, 64, 78, 129-31

Polonskii, Iakov 54

Pound, Ezra 222n.9, 230n.91

Prokopovich, Feofan 17-18, 25, 27, 201n.57

Propertius 18, 67, 70, 156, 180, 230n.91, 232n.115

Pushkin, Alexander 1, 2, 4, 10-12, 20-2, 36-54, 55, 61, 74, 92, 120, 136-40, 142, 148, 154-5, 175, 178-9, 185, 187, 190, 196, 200n.18, 202n.71, 204n.59, n.61, n.62, n.70, 205-7, 224n.51, 225n.60, 226n.67, n.73

writings of: 'Arion' 47-8; 'Bacchus' Triumph' ('Torzhestvo Vakkha') 40; *Bronze Horseman (Mednyi Vsadnik)* 39, 140, 142-3, 207n.122; *Evgenii Onegin* 38, 41-2, 205n.93, 206n.95; 'From a Letter to Gnedich' – 'In the country where, crowned by Julia ...' ('Iz pis'ma k Gnedichu' – 'V strane, gde Iuliei venchannyi ...') 39, 43-4; 'The Gypsies' ('Tsygane') 44; 'Homer's *Iliad*' ('Iliada Gomerova') 39; 'I have built myself a monument ...' ('Ia pamiatnik sebe vozdvig ...' – ['Pamiatnik']) 49-54; 'On the Convalescence of Lucullus' ('Na vyzdorovlenie Lukulla') 205n.81; 'On the Translation of the *Iliad*' ('Na perevod Iliady') 39; 'To Baratynskii, from Bessarabia' ('Baratynskomu iz Bessarabii') 44; 'To a Boy' – 'From Catullus' ('Mal'chiku' – 'Iz Katulla') 41; 'To Chaadaev' ('Chaadaevu') 44; 'To Licinius' ('Litsiniiu') 206n.113; 'To Ovid' ('K Ovidiiu') 44-7; *The Stone Guest (Kamennyi gost')* 207n.122

Racine, Jean 18, 33, 74, 113-15, 221n.88
Rossi, Carlo 132
Rostovtsev, Mikhail 65, 210nn.40-1
Sappho 35, 64, 153, 204, n.57
Sartre, Jean-Paul 96
Schwab, Gustav 94, 98-9, 101, 109, 112-13, 155, 218n.10, 219n.46
Seneca 17, 26, 70, 94, 109, 113, 115
Silver Age 55-6, 208n.6
Slavonic-Greek-Latin Academy 16, 24-5, 28
Slavonic Renaissance 58, 74-6, 90-1, 214n.122, n.131
Sologub, Fedor 56, 63, 76, 88, 90
Solov'ev, Vladimir 13, 56, 61, 64, 67, 202n.69, 209n.35, 211n.61, 212n.79, n.80, 213n.94, 225n.59
Sophocles 57, 59, 75, 86, 88, 95-6, 150, 158
Sumarokov, Alexander 22, 24, 32-4, 36, 38, 74, 200n.35, 202n.13, 203nn.43-5, 204n.50, n.52, 214n.118
  writings of: 'Ode to E.V. Kheraskova' ('Oda k E. V. Kheraskovoi') 34, 204n.50
Symbolism (movement) 56, 61, 63, 118, 120, 207n.130, 209n.35, 210n.54, 211n.55, 222n.3.
Tacitus 17, 41, 47, 70
Tairov, Alexander 88
Third Rome doctrine and its reflection in literature 13, 19, 67, 71, 132, 200nn.35-6, 212n.79
Terence 19, 26
Tibullus 18, 39, 136, 205n.79, 226n.67
Tiutchev, Fedor 54, 65, 207n.130, 223n.24, 224n.51
Trediakovskii, Vasilii 9, 22, 24-7, 32-3, 36-8, 202n.13, 203n.16, nn.43-4, 204n.50, n.52

  writings of: *New and Brief Method for Composing Russian Verse (Novyi i kratkii sposob k slozheniiu rossiiskikh stikhov)* 26-7
Tsvetaev, Ivan 92, 95, 110, 217n.13
Tsvetaeva, Anastasia 220n.75, 227n.95
Tsvetaeva, Marina 4, 5, 10, 56, 91-117, 121, 129, 132, 154-5, 172, 174, 217-22, 224n.51
  writings of: *Ariadne (Ariadna)* (lyric poetry) 5, 102-4; *Ariadne (Ariadna)* (tragedy) 5, 95, 97-105; *The End of Casanova (Konets Kazanovy)* 93-4; *Helen (Elena)* 96, 117, *Phaedra (Fedra)* (lyric poetry) 5, 106; *Phaedra (Fedra)* (tragedy) 5, 106-17; *Tale of Sonechka (Povest' o Sonechke)* 114, 218n.7; *The Tsar-Maiden (Tsar'-Devitsa)* 94
Ukrainian humanism 15, 17
Uvarov, Sergei 20, 205n. 81
Vergil 17-18, 20, 27, 32, 34, 37, 41, 68, 70-2, 154, 166-9, 193-6, 202n.69, 203n.45, 207n.122, 208n.9, 210n.50, 213n.94, 231n.101, 233n.124
Verlaine, Paul 64, 122, 226n.67
Viazemskii, Peter 7, 43, 155
Villon, François 118, 226n.67
Winckelmann, J.J. 38, 75
Xenophanes of Colophon 40
Yeats, W.B. 96
Zelinskii, Faddei 57, 65, 70, 75-6, 91, 127, 200n.12, 208nn.9-10, 209n.33, 211n.59, 212n.91, 214n.122-5, n.129, n.131, 217n.200, 220n.63
Zhukovskii, Vasilii 26, 39, 40, 43, 135, 205n.80

www.ingramcontent.com/pod-product-compliance
Lightning Source LLC
Chambersburg PA
CBHW071509110726

47908CB00003B/772